Baja
California

a Lonely Planet travel survival kit

**Wayne Bernhardson
Scott Wayne**

D1422104

Baja California

3rd edition
   Published by
   Lonely Planet Publications
   Head Office: PO Box 617, Hawthorn, Vic 3122, Australia
   Branches: 155 Filbert St, Suite 251, Oakland, CA 94607, USA
                   10 Barley Mow Passage, Chiswick, London W4 4PH, UK
                   71 bis rue du Cardinal Lemoine, 75005 Paris, France

Printed by
   Colorcraft, Ltd, Hong Kong

Photographs by
   All photos by Wayne Bernhardson (WB) except:
   Justin Hyland (JH)
   Bernard Nietschmann (BN)
   Robert Raburn (RR)
   Charles Tambiah (CT)

   Front cover: Side road near Bahía de Concepción, Baja, Mexico, Stewart Aitchison (DDB Stock
   Photography)
   Back cover: Road to La Pasión, Toris, Baja California Sur (WB)

First Published
   March 1988

This Edition
   October 1994

**Although the author and publisher have tried to make the information as
accurate as possible, they accept no responsibility for any loss, injury or
inconvenience sustained by any person using this book.**

National Library of Australia Cataloguing in Publication Data

Bernhardson, Wayne
   Baja California – a travel survival kit

   3rd ed.
   Includes index.
   ISBN 0 86442 214 8

   1. Baja California (Mexico) – Guidebooks. I. Wayne, Scott.
   II. Title. (Series : Lonely Planet travel survival kit).
   917.2204834

text & maps © Lonely Planet 1994
photos © photographers as indicated 1994
climate charts compiled from information supplied by Patrick J Tyson, © Patrick J Tyson, 1994

Scott Wayne

Scott Wayne, the original author of this book, is an American who has lived, studied and traveled in the Middle East, Africa and Europe. He graduated from Georgetow University's School of Foreign Service with a degree in International Relations. He also did graduate studies at the Royal Institute of International Affairs in London and the University of Southern California. Scott is also the original author of Lonely Planet's guidebook to *Egypt & the Sudan*, the author of *Egyptian Arabic – a language survival kit* and coauthor of Lonely Planet's guide to *Mexico*.

Wayne Bernhardson

Wayne Bernhardson was born in North Dakota, grew up in Tacoma, Washington, and spent most of the 1980s shuttling between North and South America en route to a PhD in geography from the University of California, Berkeley. He is co-author, with María Massolo, of LP's *Argentina, Uruguay & Paraguay* and author of *Chile & Easter Island*. He also contributed several chapters to the 5th edition of *South America*. Wayne lives in Oakland, California, with María, their daughter Clío and their Alaskan malamute Gardel.

From Wayne Bernhardson

Rey and Marta Ayala of Calexico, California, deserve special mention for their hospitality and for their knowledge of the border area in general and Mexicali in particular. Jorge Lizárraga of Berkeley offered several important insights on the San Quintín area. Dan Arreola of the Department of Geography at Arizona State University also made several useful suggestions.

Serge Dedina and Emily Young of Laguna San Ignacio, Imperial Beach, California, and Austin, Texas, also made notable contributions to the Desierto Central chapter. Justin Hyland of Emeryville, California, and Lucero Gutiérrez of INAH, San Ignacio, hospitably endured countless naive questions on the rock art of the San Ignacio area. Almudena Ortiz of Berkeley,

California, explained the finer points of the bullfight.

James J Parsons of the Department of Geography at the University of California, Berkeley, entrusted me with several useful books which the university library is loath to lend to its patrons. Bob, Pat and Pasha Raburn generously guarded and entertained Gardel in Oakland during my 2½ months of field research in Baja. Phil Niles of San Luis Obispo provided basic instruction in surf-speak.

Francisco Javier Sotelo Leyva of the Cámar Nacional de Comercio (CANACO) in Tijuana provided substantial information on Baja's most important border town. Director General Angel Carlos Covarrubias

R of the Comité Municipal de Turismo y Convenciones de Ensenada was extraordinarily helpful in updating that city and its surroundings. Rigoberto González Peralta of SECTUR made a major contribution to updating the Cape Region in general and La Paz in particular. Dr Aldo Piñeda of INAH in La Paz was also very helpful.

John Spencer of La Rivera, Baja California Sur, and Union City, California, offered useful information and tips on the East Cape. John Laragy of Mobeso's Bakery in Cabo San Lucas, whose expertise on local eateries is unsurpassed, deserves special mention for his patience in reviewing the entire Cabo San Lucas section, even if he's unlikely to agree with my assessment of his adopted hometown.

This Book

Scott Wayne researched and wrote the first two editions of *Baja California*, and Wayne Bernhardson researched this, the third edition. Many of Scott Wayne's observations and suggestions remain in these pages and the depth of detail in this updated edition would not have been possible without such a firm foundation.

From the Publisher

This third edition of *Baja California* is the first book to be produced from Lonely Planet's US office. The following people all made it possible: Kate Hoffman edited the manuscript, Alan Marshall, Hayden Foell, Scott Summers and Hugh D'Andrade redrew and corrected the maps, David Russ and Sue Mitra proofread, indexed, and handled the editorial side of production, and Richard Wilson and Hugh D'Andrade designed the book. Illustrations were done by Hugh and Ann Jeffree. The book cover was designed by Tamsin Wilson. Many thanks to Richard Wilson

and Jeff Stafford who taught us how to use Quark XPress to publish books. Thanks also to Wayne Bernhardson who provided us with a clean manuscript to cut our teeth on.

Thanks

Several independent travelers and others contributed to an improved book with their correspondence. These include:

June Arber (UK), Scott B Berger (USA), Mark Blackie (USA), Marilyn Carien (USA), Virginia & Owen Christie (USA), Tarim Chung (USA), Nathan Cohen (USA), Charles Collins (USA), Rosamariá Colussé (I), Beth Curtis, Jennifer Eberle (USA), Chris Garber (USA), Eliot L Gardner (USA), June Ginge (USA), Jane Harland (UK), Wayne Hibling, Nicole Kaldes (USA), Gillian Key, Gudrun Merkle (D), Dez Pagen (USA), Sandra Perego (I), Elisabettá Pincionå (I), Carlos Ramos (USA), Tony Rousmaniere (USA), Theresa Russell (USA), Claudia Scherrer (CH), Birgitt Stehl (D), Michaeì Walenskù (USA) Vic Warren (USA), Rich Wilkes (USA), and Jenny Zimmerman (USA).

CH - Switzerland, D - Germany, I - Italy, UK - United Kingdom, USA - United States of America.

Warning & Request

Things change – prices rise, schedules fluctuate, good places go bad and bad places go bankrupt. Nothing stays the same, especially in a fast changing place like Baja.

So, if you find things better or worse, recently opened or long-since closed, please write to us to help improve the next edition! All information is greatly appreciated; the best letters will receive a free copy of the next edition or any other Lonely Planet book of your choice. We give away lots of books, but, unfortunately, not every letter/postcard receives one.

Contents

Map Legend

BOUNDARIES

- ·—·—·—·—·—·—·– International Boundary
- –·· —·· —·· —·· —·· – Internal Boundary

ROUTES

Freeway
Highway
Major Road
Unpaved Road or Track
City Road
City Street
Railway
Railway Station
Underground Railway
Ferry Route

AREA FEATURES

Park, National Park
Built-Up Area
Pedestrian Mall
Cemetery
Beach or Desert
Ancient or City Wall

HYDROGRAPHIC FEATURES

Coastline
River, Creek
Intermittent River or Creek
Lake, Intermittent Lake
Swamp
Rapids, Waterfalls

SYMBOLS

✪ NATIONAL CAPITAL	■ Hotel, Pension (Place to Stay)	▭ Swimming Pool
◉ State Capital		🏛 Museum
MAJOR CITY	▼ Restaurant (Place to Eat)	Winery or Vineyard
● City	🍺 Pub, Bar (Place to Drink)	Stately Home
● TOWN		Observatory
● Village		Cave
✚ Hospital	★ Police Station	▲ Mountain or Hill
✈ Airport	✝ Airfield	🗼 Lighthouse
✉ Post Office	☎ Telephone	)(Pass
❶ Tourist Information	ⓢ Bank	Cliff or Escarpment
Transport	🅿 Parking	Fishing
One Way Street	Route Number	✝ Church
Shopping Center	Gas Station	Mosque
RV Park	⚴ Campground	⊥ Buddhist Temple
Golf Course	⛺ Youth Hostel	∴ Archaeological Site or Ruins

Gardens	
🐘 Zoo	
Picnic Site	
Monument	
■ Tomb	
Hut or Chalet	
☀ Lookout	
Shipwreck	
Spring	
⟹ Tunnel	
Dive Site	
Cathedral	
✡ Synagogue	
Hindu Temple	

Note: not all symbols displayed above appear in this book

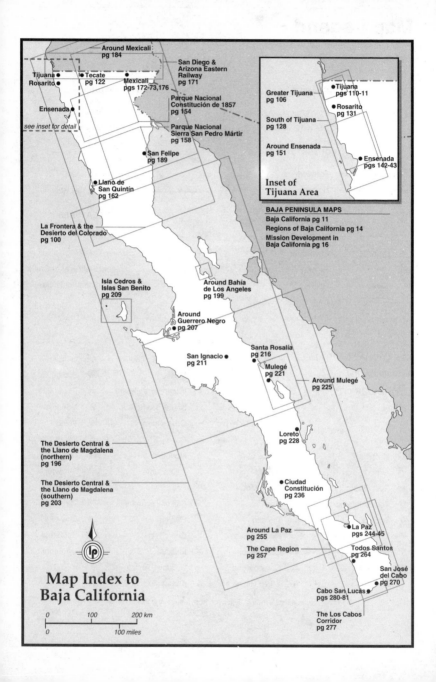

Map Index to
Baja California

0   100   200 km

0   100 miles

Introduction

Ever since the arrival of the first Spanish explorers in the 1530s, Baja has been a land of extremes and, later, a land of escapes and escapades. First thought to be an island, it is still isolated from mainland Mexico, but it now attracts millions of visitors and their dollars to its cities and towns, beaches, mountains and deserts. The Baja Peninsula, however, is much more than a winter off-season amusement park for visitors from north of the border.

Baja California's Cochimí Indians, none of whom survive today, left memorable murals in caves and on canyon walls of the peninsula's central desert. For early European explorers, 'Baja' (its colloquial name among visitors) was both enticing and forbidding, as its coastline of white sandy beaches, tranquil bays and lagoons, and imposing headlands belied its harsh desert interior. Settlement attempts repeatedly failed until the late 17th century, when Jesuit priests established self-sufficient missions, converted local Indians to Catholicism, and taught them to work the fields and build churches, all in the interest of 'civilizing' them. In less than a century, though, these missions began to collapse as the Indians fell prey to European diseases and the Spanish crown expelled the Jesuits from the empire.

In the 19th century, ranchers and fishermen from the Mexican mainland settled parts of the peninsula. Prospectors discovered minerals and dug the first mines. These discoveries prompted foreign companies to establish the first major port facilities and acquire huge tracts of land in

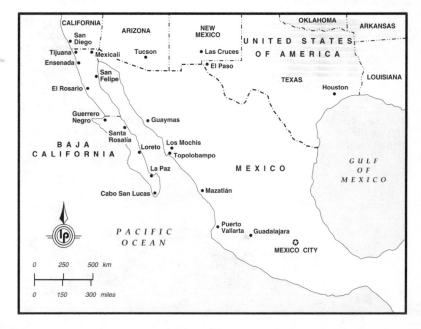

some areas. Encouraged by major mining discoveries, outsiders poured into the peninsula and made small fortunes, but Baja still remained largely undeveloped and unaffected. When most of the mines closed in the early 20th century, many foreigners took the money and ran.

In the 20th century, the Baja peninsula became a land of escape. Some of the first to seek refuge were Magonistas, a splinter group of revolutionaries and mercenaries who briefly 'conquered' northern Baja while fleeing Mexican federal troops. Criminals from mainland Mexico also found remote Baja a good hideout, while during the Prohibition era in the USA, Baja became a popular destination for gamblers, drinkers and other 'sinners' from north of the border. New hotels, restaurants, racetracks, bullrings and casinos lured a new type of escapee – the US tourist.

Today, many of Baja's cities and towns are thriving as, each year, more than 50 million people visit some part of the peninsula. The popular border cities offer short, inexpensive escapes: shopping sprees in duty-free US-style malls and on the streets, sumptuous meals and exotic drinks. The 'escape' continues in bars, discos and nightclubs or at the bullfights, jai alai matches and racetracks. During a fiesta or special event, the pace of celebration becomes frenetic. Visitors exhausted by all this activity can escape to the surrounding mountains, beaches or deserts, where the most popular activity is relaxing in the sun. Outdoor recreation opportunities are nearly limitless: horseback riding in the mountains or on the beach, scuba diving or snorkeling in the Gulf of California (Mar de Cortés), windsurfing, clam-digging, whale-watching, fishing, sailing, kayaking, bicycling, surfing or hiking.

This book describes Baja's most popular attractions, but also offers hints on experiencing this exceptional destination beyond stereotypical tourist activities. Detailed, practical information describes everything from octopus tacos to budget accommodation, while providing essential environmental, cultural and historical background.

A word on terminology: in late Spanish colonial times and under Mexican rule, the general term 'California' meant Baja California (Lower California), while the present US state of California, then a backwater, became known as Alta California (Upper California). Rather than use the latter term, an anachronism except in its historical context, this book will use the more appropriate (if not precisely accurate) term 'mainland California' to refer to areas north of the Mexican border. In many ways, the two form a single California whose political division is misleading – according to one recent analysis, more than 100,000 jobs in mainland California directly depend on exports to Mexico.

Modern Baja California consists of two separate states: Baja California (capital Mexicali) and Baja California Sur (capital La Paz). When necessary for clarity, this book refers to the individual states as Baja California Norte and Baja California Sur.

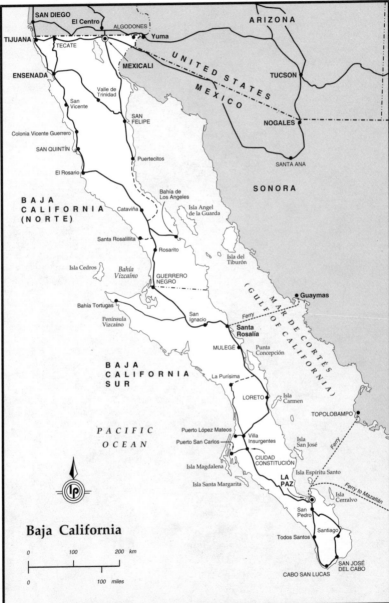

Baja California

SAN DIEGO
El Centro
ALGODONES
TIJUANA
TECATE
Yuma
MEXICALI
ENSENADA
Valle de
Trinidad
San
Vicente
SAN
FELIPE
Colonia Vicente Guerrero
SAN QUINTÍN
Puertecitos
El Rosario

ARIZONA
UNITED STATES
MEXICO
TUCSON
NOGALES
SANTA ANA
SONORA

BAJA
CALIFORNIA
(NORTE)
Cataviña
Santa Rosalillita
Rosarito
Isla Cedros
Bahía
Vizcaíno
GUERRERO
NEGRO
Bahía Tortugas
Península
Vizcaíno
San
Ignacio

Bahía de
Los Angeles
Isla Angel
de la Guarda
Isla del
Tiburón

MAR DE CORTÉS (GULF OF CALIFORNIA)
Guaymas
Ferry
Santa
Rosalía
MULEGÉ
Punta
Concepción

BAJA
CALIFORNIA
SUR
La Purísima
LORETO
Isla
Carmen

PACIFIC
OCEAN

TOPOLOBAMPO

Puerto López Mateos
Puerto San Carlos
Villa
Insurgentes
Isla
San José
Isla Magdalena
CIUDAD
CONSTITUCIÓN
Isla Espíritu Santo
Ferry
Isla Santa Margarita
LA
PAZ
Ferry to Mazatlán
Isla
Cerralvo
San
Pedro
Santiago
Todos Santos
SAN JOSÉ
DEL CABO
CABO SAN LUCAS

0   100   200 km
0   100 miles

Facts about Baja California

HISTORY
Early Peoples

At least 12,000 years ago, perhaps much earlier, one of the most significant human migrations occurred when the accumulated ice of the great polar and continental glaciers of the Pleistocene epoch lowered sea levels around the world, and the ancestors of American Indians crossed from Siberia to Alaska via a land bridge across the Bering Strait. Over millennia, subsequent movements distributed the population southward throughout the Americas.

At least 10,000 years ago, according to radiocarbon dating of artifacts like shell middens, stone tools and arrowheads, descendants of these immigrants reached the Baja peninsula by way of mainland California. Middens at Punta Minitas, in northwestern Baja, indicate that shellfish gathering was a key subsistence activity no later than 8000 years ago, but Baja's first peoples also subsisted by hunting, gathering and, later, rudimentary farming. A recent discovery near San Ignacio, in the Desierto Central of central Baja California, of a fluted point used for hunting megafauna like mammoths dates from about 12,000 years ago.

Perhaps the most spectacular artifacts left by Baja's early inhabitants were their petroglyphs and cave paintings – hundreds or even thousands of rock art sites dot the peninsula from the US border to the tip of Cabo San Lucas. Some of these are abstract designs, while others are representations of humans and animals, reflecting the region's pre-Columbian hunting and gathering economy. The tradition continued even after European contact, as some works include such elements as pack animals and Christian crosses.

The European Exploration of 'California'

On a voyage commissioned by Hernán Cortés, the conqueror of New Spain (Mexico), mutineer Fortún Jiménez became the first Spaniard to set foot on the Baja Peninsula in 1533. Either Jiménez or a later explorer named Francisco de Bolaños applied the name 'California' to the peninsula after a mysterious island mentioned in a romantic narrative called *Las Sergas de Esplandián* (The Exploits of Esplandián), published in Sevilla by Garcí Ordóñez de Montalvo in 1510.

The precise etymology and meaning of the name 'California' have never been convincingly established, but in Montalvo's fiction, a queen named Calafia ruled a race of gold-rich black Amazons; there is now consensus that her name eventually became 'California'. Baja's terrain resembled that of Montalvo's fictional island; even though a later voyage by Francisco de Ulloa in 1539 proved that it was a peninsula, Europeans did not abandon the idea that Baja was an island until Jesuit missionary Eusebio Kino, in several expeditions between 1699 and 1702 from present-day Arizona and Sonora proved that it could be reached by land.

After defeating the Aztecs and occupying most of central Mexico, Cortés despatched several expeditions in search of Calafia's riches. In 1532 Spanish navigator Diego Hurtado de Mendoza sailed north from Acapulco, but his two ships both disappeared shortly after departure. In 1533, the *Concepción* sailed from Tehuantepec in search of Mendoza and Calafia, but soon after leaving Acapulco, the crew mutinied and murdered captain Diego Becerra. Pilot Jiménez took charge, steering the ship into the bay of La Paz, but most of the 22 mutineers died at the hands of Pericú Indians. The survivors, however, returned with a sample of black pearls which stimulated Cortés' own interest in Baja, and in 1535 he himself joined an expedition to the area.

With about 400 Spanish settlers, plus Black slaves and horses, Cortés founded the colony of Santa Cruz at present-day

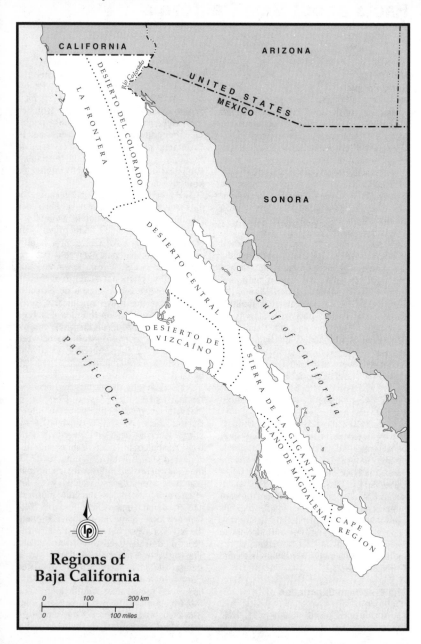

Regions of Baja California

Bahía Pichilingue, an inlet of La Paz bay, and stayed the rest of the year before returning to mainland Mexico. Until late 1536 or early 1537, the rest of the group tried to establish a permanent settlement, but hostile Indians and severe food and water shortages – most of the horses were probably eaten – caused its abandonment. For another century and a half, no Europeans settled in Baja.

In the interim, however, others explored the region. Despite contrary orders from Viceroy Antonio de Mendoza, Cortés sent Ulloa north from Acapulco in 1539. After sailing up the Gulf of California and learning that Baja was a peninsula, Ulloa rounded Cabo San Lucas and sailed up the Pacific Coast as far as Bahía Magdalena, Isla Cedros, and perhaps Punta Baja (near modern El Rosario) before returning south. In 1540 Hernando de Alarcón also reached the mouth of the Colorado River, while in 1542 Portuguese explorer Juan Rodríguez Cabrillo explored the Pacific Coast and became the first European to set foot in mainland California. The Spanish crown granted licenses for pearling expeditions to the Gulf, but there were many unauthorized, clandestine voyages as well.

As Spain consolidated its control of New Spain, it also increased trade with the Philippines (which were under the jurisdiction of the Viceroyalty of New Spain). Laden with Asian luxuries like silk, perfumes and spices, as well as gold and silver, Spanish galleons sailing from Manila to Acapulco attracted bounty-hungry buccaneers like Englishman Thomas Cavendish. After Cavendish captured the prize galleon *Santa Ana* near Cabo San Lucas in November 1587, the Spaniards built a small fortress and occasionally despatched vessels to deter privateers and to explore the coasts.

In 1602 Sebastián Vizcaíno, who had earlier led a pearling expedition to the Gulf, re-explored the Pacific Coast as far as Cape Mendocino in mainland California. A major bay and a large desert in central Baja California still bear his name. In 1633 Francisco de Ortega, attracted by the discovery of black pearls near La Paz, sailed north to the mouth of the Colorado and produced one of the first maritime charts of the Gulf, but permanent European settlement awaited the arrival of Jesuit missionaries.

Baja California at Contact

When Europeans first reached the peninsula, upwards of 48,000 mobile hunter-gatherers lived in an area comprising most of the modern states of Baja California and Baja California Sur; despite the early introduction of European diseases along the Gulf Coast, this population remained fairly stable until the late 17th century. The Río Colorado delta, at the north end of the Gulf, supported a denser population of settled Yuman agriculturalists, perhaps an additional 6000 individuals.

The peoples of Baja belonged to three major linguistic groups, further subdivided into several tribal entities. North of the 31st parallel were Yuman-speaking peoples closely linked to those of southern mainland California; among them were the Dieguino or Diegueño (now commonly known as Tipai), Kamia or Kumiai (also known as Ipai), Paipai, Cocopa (Cucupah), Ñakipa and Kiliwa. To the south, as far as the 26th parallel, the Cochimí were the most numerous of Peninsular Yuman-speaking groups, who also included Cadegomeño, Didiú (Edú), Laymón and Monqui peoples. To their south, non-Yuman speakers included the Guaycura, Cora, Huchití and Pericú.

All these peoples lived in groups which became known as *rancherías*, ranging in size from a few families to upwards of 200 individuals; this term also applied to units linked to Spanish missions but living at a distance from them. Occupying fairly well-defined territories that ranged from the uplands of the central cordillera to the shores of the Gulf and the Pacific, these groups depended on game, wild plant foods (such as pine nuts and the fruit of the pitahaya cactus) and marine resources for their subsistence. In times of stress, they even collected pitahaya seeds from their own excrement and toasted them in what

† San Diego

UNITED STATES

† Descanso
† San Miguel
† Guadalupe

Santo
† Tomás   † Santa
           Catalina
† San
  Vicente

Santo
† Domingo
    † San Pedro
      Mártir

MEXICO

† El Rosario
San
† Fernando
Velicatá   Santa
        † María
          † Calamajué

† San
  Borja

Isla
Cedros

Santa
Gertrudis †

San
† Ignacio

Guadalupe †
  Mulegé †

Pacific Ocean

Gulf of California

La Purísima
† Concepción
San José
de Comondú †   † Nuestra Señora
                 de Loreto
            † San Francisco
              Xavier

Dolores
del Sur †

San Luis
† Gonzaga

† El Pilar
  de la Paz

† Todos
  Santos
        † Santiago

† San José
  del Cabo

0   100   200 km
0   100 miles

**Mission Development
in Baja California**

■ Jesuit 1697-1768

■ Franciscan 1769-1773

■ Dominican 1773-1834

† Missions

Spaniards jokingly called their 'second harvest'.

In Baja's desert environments, Indian peoples usually lived in simple dwellings of local materials near a dependable permanent water source such as a spring or stream. While groups in the north and south enjoyed a fairly dependable subsistence, by most accounts the Cochimí of central Baja, the peninsula's harshest desert, were often destitute. On the entire peninsula, Indians were too few and too dispersed for effective application of the *encomienda*, a system of forced labor and tribute which the Spanish crown instituted in mainland New Spain and other densely populated parts of the empire. Consequently, missionaries directed the colonization of California and, often unwittingly, brought about the demise of its aboriginal peoples.

Only in the northernmost part of the peninsula do Indian peoples still survive, by herding livestock, fishing and building fences. Collecting pine nuts is still an important seasonal activity, and women still produce attractive basketry and pottery.

Misión Nuestra Señora de Loreto

The Missions

In early 1683 Isidro de Atondo y Antillón, governor of Sinaloa in mainland New Spain, crossed the Gulf of California with Jesuit priest Eusebio Kino to establish a settlement at La Paz, which was soon abandoned because of hostile Indian encounters. Some months later Padre Kino founded Misión San Bruno, just north of present-day Loreto, but attempts to catechize local Indians failed and the mission was abandoned within two years.

Twelve years later, in October 1697, Jesuit Padre Juan María Salvatierra arrived with a half dozen soldiers at present-day Loreto on the Gulf coast of Baja, and soon laid the foundation for the Misión Nuestra Señora de Loreto, the first permanent Spanish settlement in the Californias. From Loreto, which became the peninsula's religious and administrative capital, other Jesuits ranged throughout the peninsula to establish similar missions. Over the next 70 years, the Jesuits founded 23 missions and, despite the presence of nominal military authorities, they governed the peninsula.

The Jesuits meant well, but their altruistic intentions backfired. Along with God, grapes and greener pastures, the missionaries also brought an invisible evil – European microbes to which native peoples had had no exposure and lacked immunological resistance. Epidemics of smallpox, plague, typhus, measles and syphilis (the latter probably of New World origin) decimated the Indian population. The concentration of Indians at missions, and regular contact between the missions and between missions and rancherías, spread the contagion; the population plummeted from approximately 48,000 at contact to barely 3000 by 1820. Of these, fewer than 400 remained in southern and central Baja.

Despite the steady decline of the Indian population, which provided the labor for missionary expansion, the Jesuits continued to seek ideal mission sites in Baja. In the mid-18th century, explorers such as Jesuit Fernando Consag brought more sophisticated knowledge of northern Baja, but the Jesuits' expulsion from the Spanish empire in 1767 precluded the founding of missions there and in mainland California.

Franciscan priests, under the authority of Padre Junípero Serra, took over the former Jesuit missions, several of which they closed or consolidated. Serra himself traveled northward to establish a chain of missions in Alta California (mainland California), but the Franciscans accomplished little in Baja because they directed most of their efforts toward the north. In 1773 Dominican priests replaced them in 'La Frontera', the region south of present-day San Diego (USA).

Besides establishing seven new missions in Baja, the Dominicans continued to operate the former Jesuit missions until after the Mexican War of Independence in 1821. Three years later, Baja became a federal territory, headed by a governor; by 1832 a newly appointed governor, with support from Mexico City, put an end to the mission system by converting all missions into secular parish churches. In a sense, however, the missions brought about their own demise: declining Indian populations could no longer support them. After the decline of the missions, a mainland *mestizo* (mixed-race) population filled part of the demographic vacuum left by the disappearance of the Indians; the final blow came in 1857 when President Benito Juárez added to the Mexican constitution a clause that required sale of all church properties.

War & Filibustering

For a year during the Mexican-American War (1846-48), American troops occupied La Paz, which had become the capital of Baja in 1829. By the Treaty of Guadalupe Hidalgo, signed on 2 February 1848, Mexico officially ceded Alta California to the USA but retained sovereignty over Baja.

Many Americans felt that the troops should have stayed after the war and made Baja part of the new State of California,

officially accepted into the Union in 1850. American rabble-rousers like the quixotic William Walker (later infamous for proclaiming himself 'President' of Nicaragua) refused to accept the treaty as official policy.

After backing off a plan to occupy the mineral-rich but heavily defended Mexican state of Sonora, Walker took La Paz in 1853 with a group of mercenaries from San Francisco. Raising the flag of the 'Republic of Lower California', he declared himself president, installed 'cabinet officers' and proclaimed annexation of Sonora. After fleeing La Paz under threat of Mexican retaliation, his forces suffered logistical reverses before their last desperate attempt to take Sonora by marching across Baja and crossing the Colorado River on rafts. They finally surrendered to US authorities.

Foreign Interests & Investment

Establishment of a permanent mestizo population was the key element in consolidating Mexican influence on the peninsula, but by the 1880s, the Mexican government decided to encourage US and European capital investment in Baja and other parts of Mexico. President Porfirio Díaz and his *científicos* (a group of largely Eurocentric, sometimes openly racist advisers), anxious for the Mexican economy to rival those of the USA and Europe, granted major land concessions to foreign investors. The dictatorial Díaz (whose long tenure is known as the *Porfiriato*) and the científicos expected growth in mining, railways, manufacturing and other sectors.

Since the failure of Walker's invasion, various schemes to develop the peninsula had arisen, such as the Lower California Company's concession to collect orchilla, a lichen used as a dye plant, from San Quintín to La Paz. Under Díaz, who took power in 1876, the main investor in Baja was the International Company of Mexico, based in the US state of Connecticut.

Supposedly the International Company made a US$5 million down payment (total charges were US$16 million) for the right to develop an area that now comprises nearly the entire state of Baja California (northern Baja), as well as offshore islands and some areas on the Mexican mainland. Planning to build railroad lines from San Diego to San Quintín, 200 miles (320 km) south of the US border, and to connect to the state of Sonora, the company also constructed port facilities and flour mills at Ensenada and San Quintín.

The International Company also sought to attract settlers and colonists to Baja but, for three years, had little success. Their 1887 pamphlet, *Lower California, the Peninsula, Now Open to Colonists*, glorified Baja's fertile land and resources, excellent climate and great agricultural potential. Testimonials from newspapers and farmers supposedly verified these claims with hyperbole typical of mainland California real estate developers to this day:

In conclusion it must be said that all of this beautiful country with its incalculable wealth, sure and rapid development would still have been left bare to the birds and the sky, had it not been for the courage, capital and enterprise of the International Company.

San Diego Sun, 11 March 1887

The great Peninsula of Lower California has been but little known except as an appendage to the Pacific Coast. . . (it) has been purchased outright from the Mexican Government by the International Company. This purchase covers 18,000,000 acres of land, and in it grass grows and water runs. . . Upon these lands are no settlers nor strange social institutions to be displaced or adopted. They are wild, unsubdued, and offer to American enterprise the last frontier. . . The International Company has perfect title to this enormous grant.

Daily Alta California, 15 July 1886

After too many rainless years, however, the International Company surrendered its 'perfect title' to this 'last frontier' and sold out to an English syndicate for US$7 million.

Bringing in several colonist families, the syndicate finished the mills in San Quintín and Ensenada, built part of a railway and planted wheat, but the rains failed and harvests were nil. Those colonists who did not end up in San Quintín's first cemetery returned to England or moved to other parts of Baja, where Anglo surnames like Jones and Smith are not unusual.

While the International Company and other potential investors were promoting Baja's agricultural development, several important mineral discoveries took place around the peninsula, including gold and silver strikes. One of the largest projects, operated by the French syndicate Compañía del Boleo at Santa Rosalía, produced copper until the 1950s. There were also small nickel, mercury, graphite and sulphur mines, and many foreigners flocked to Baja to find their fortune in the mines.

With thousands of foreign miners, engineers, traders and ranchers living and working in Baja, it was not surprising that rumors began to circulate in mainland California that the USA might annex Baja California. In January 1891, the *Evening Bulletin* of San Francisco carried a story entitled 'Lower California, a Belief that it Will Belong to the United States Soon':

'Sooner or later, and it may come very soon, there is going to be trouble between the United States and Mexico over Lower California,' said General Cadwallader of San Diego to a *Post* man. 'Geographically it is a piece of country that fits into our area much more naturally than as a possession of Mexico. The miners from our side are continually going down there prospecting, and if there should be any big gold discoveries, as is quite probable, seeing that it is very rich in minerals, there would be a rush of people into Lower California who would no more pay respect to the Mexican authority or Mexican laws than they would to the Chinese Empire.

This may not be the origin of the difficulty, but it is only a question of time when trouble will arise, and the best thing to do is to discount such contingency by buying the country from our Mexican friends. . . I don't know what the Mexicans would want for it, or even if they would be willing to sell at all, but they are shrewd people, and doubtless have long ago found out that the strip is of far more value to the United States than to them.

Although the USA never annexed Baja, US investors acquired or controlled huge tracts

The Ejido & Its Future

Historically, from colonial times, the term *ejido* referred to communal grazing lands on the outskirts of rural communities in mainland Mexico. In the mid-19th century, a law intended to divest the church of its extensive landholdings ironically cost Indian communities their ejidos; not until the turn of the century, with the weakening of the Díaz dictatorship, was there agitation for their return. Potential *ejidatarios* were among the most enthusiastic supporters of the Mexican Revolution.

The creation of Mexico's present system of cooperative landholdings in the 1930s, a direct if delayed outcome of the Revolution of 1910, was the achievement of President Lázaro Cárdenas, who oversaw the expropriation of the great haciendas that once controlled nearly half the land in the country. In central and southern Mexico, modern ejidos are largely communities of individual small-scale corn farmers, but in Baja California and other parts of northern Mexico, the institution is rather different. Community members work the land collectively.

In the Mexicali area, for example, most ejidos were formed from lands belonging to the Colorado River Land Company, later to benefit returnees from the US Government's *bracero* program, which had allowed Mexican farm laborers to work north of the border. Like the Company, some collective ejidos could take advantage of economies of scale for production of commodities like cotton, but others entered activities like fishing, forestry, mining and stockraising. In Baja California, they are often involved in tourism – guests in coastal campgrounds are frequently renting their spaces from the ejido and buying their gasoline from ejido-run Pemex stations.

Since the 1930s, the ejido has given a larger segment of the Mexican population a stake in the country's progress. The system's continuing symbolic presence is apparent in the names that ejidos take – names like Revolución, Plan de Ayala, Francisco Villa and Lázaro Cárdenas – which refer back to key elements or personalities in modern Mexican history.

The ejido is under siege, however, from NAFTA. Recent legislation, sponsored by Mexican President Carlos Salinas de Gortari, has made it possible for ejidos to dispose of lands that have been theirs to use but not to sell. The government's explanation is that it wishes to make bank credit more easily available through the use of ejido resources as collateral, so that the ejidos will be more competitive under the new international trade regime.

Many ejidatarios, however, worry that they could lose their lands to the banks as they did to the haciendas over a century ago. The ruling Partido Institucional Revolucionario (PRI) still pays lip service to agrarian reform (it went out of its way to purchase advertising in Baja California dailies on the 47th anniversary of the famous Assault on the Lands (*Asalto a Las Tierras*) in Mexicali in 1937), but there is widespread suspicion of the government's motives. ∎

of land in southern mainland California and northern Baja. Among them were Harrison Gray Otis, publisher of the *Los Angeles Times*, the Spreckels family of San Francisco, who made fortunes in the US sugar industry, and the powerful Southern Pacific railroad.

From the turn of the century, following major agricultural development projects in the Imperial Valley just north of Mexicali, the Mexican government promoted commercial agriculture in the fields between Mexicali, which replaced Ensenada as the territorial capital, and the Colorado River delta. Water development in this region was the motive force behind Baja California's political and economic emergence.

The Revolution & Its Aftermath

The Mexican Revolution of 1910, which lasted a decade, temporarily interrupted development. Warfare had little impact on most of the peninsula, but in 1911 a ragtag army of the Liberal Party, an anarchist force under the influence of exiled Mexican intellectual Ricardo Flores Magón, swept through northern Baja's lightly defended border towns from Mexicali to Tijuana in an attempt to establish a regional power base. Militant labor organizations like the Industrial Workers of the World (IWW or 'Wobblies') from the US side of the border assisted the revolutionaries, many of whom had been imprisoned or exiled in mainland California, with money and weapons.

The Magonistas, as Flores Magon's forces were also known, took Tijuana in a single morning as curious onlookers watched from across the border, but attempts to establish a government failed because many of the Magonistas were foreign mercenaries, soldiers of fortune who were disinterested in government as such. When the Mexican army approached Tijuana, the rebel 'government' crumbled and the Magonistas fled across the border.

After the war Baja continued in isolation, excluded from most of the grandiose political and economic development plans under discussion in Mexico City, but Prohibition in the USA reinvigorated the border economy. After enactment of a US constitutional amendment and passage of legislation outlawing the production, sale and consumption of alcoholic beverages north of the border, mainland Californians flocked to Tijuana, Ensenada and Mexicali for drinking, gambling and sex.

Border towns both prospered and suffered from the ensuing North American invasion, as money flowed in with an assortment of corrupt characters. By the late 1930s, despite the repeal of Prohibition, the situation was so out of control that reformist President Lázaro Cárdenas banned casino gambling, threw the bad guys out of town, instituted various educational and agricultural reforms (such as the *ejido* system of peasant cooperatives) and built the Sonora-Mexicali railway to reduce the territory's economic dependence on the US and its isolation from mainland Mexico. Despite closure of the casinos, gambling and similar diversions still exist on a reduced scale.

One proposal that might have transformed the peninsula was the establishment of a settlement area for Jewish refugees from Nazi Germany, which was briefly but seriously considered by Jewish leaders in the USA, but nothing came of this. In 1952, Baja's political status improved as its northern half became the Mexican state of Baja California; voters chose a governor and state representatives, but most of the peninsula remained isolated from the rest of the country for another two decades.

By 1973 completion of paved México 1, the 1050-mile (1680-km) Carretera Transpeninsular Benito Juárez, linked the northern borderlands to Baja's southern

extremities. Less than a year later, south of the 28th parallel, Baja California Sur became Mexico's 30th state. Countless Americans began to venture across the border and drive the length of the peninsula, and regular ferry services between southern Baja and mainland Mexico also began.

Baja Today

In many ways Baja is still a frontier, as the Transpeninsular did more to reduce the isolation between northern and southern Baja than it did to link the peninsula to the rest of Mexico. The highway's economic benefits have been fewer than anticipated, partly because economic development has been geared to North American visitors and markets, but development has reduced unemployment and generally lifted the standard of living above that of the rest of Mexico.

At the same time, the border towns have grown extraordinarily rapidly as desperate Mexicans and Central Americans have flocked north in hopes of crossing to the USA, for reasons both economic and political. Tijuana is the major destination for immigrants who cross the border, few with official documentation, in search of work or asylum in mainland California. Another attraction is the boom in manufacturing associated with *maquiladoras*, border town industrial plants that take advantage of cheap Mexican labor to assemble US-made components for re-exportation to the north.

Relatively few visitors appreciate that the fast growing cities of Tijuana and Mexicali have become major educational centers, preparing highly qualified professionals in the health sciences and other occupations, and encouraging intellectual exchange both within Baja California and across the border. The Universidad Autónoma, with campuses in both Tijuana and Mexicali, El Colegio del Norte, and the Universidad Iberoamericana are all important research and teaching institutions which have also patronized literature and the arts.

GEOGRAPHY

Between the Pacific Ocean to the west and the Gulf of California (popularly known as the Sea of Cortés) to the east, Baja California is a desolate but scenic peninsula of mountains, plains, headlands and beaches stretching from the mainland California state border, between 32°N and 33°N, to Cabo San Lucas 800 miles (1300 km) south. It also shares short borders with the US state of Arizona and the Mexican state of Sonora, both across the Río Colorado delta at the northeastern corner of the peninsula. Its width ranges from 30 to 145 miles (50 to 230 km), and its total land mass of about 55,000 sq miles (153,000 sq km) is about the size of the US state of Illinois, or of England and Wales combined.

Tectonic activity during late Miocene times, about 12 million years ago, separated the peninsula from mainland Mexico along the famous San Andreas fault. Pacific Ocean water invaded the elongated structural trough which now comprises the Gulf of California, whose extensive coastline, along with Baja's Pacific shores, offers some of world's finest and most isolated beaches. Influenced by the south-flowing California Current, the waters of the Pacific tend to be cooler than those of the Gulf, which enjoy the warmth of the North Equatorial Current for much of the year but also exhibit great spatial and seasonal variation because of the Gulf's great depth and its latitudinal extent. In the Cape Region, cool temperate and warm equatorial waters mix, but in the north, the Gulf waters are very shallow because of sedimentation from the Río Colorado and their temperatures vary with the weather.

North of El Rosario on the Pacific, most beaches are within walking distance of the Transpeninsular or are accessible by ordinary passenger car, but in the Desierto Central (Central Desert) south of El Rosario to the border with Baja California Sur, a tough 4WD vehicle may be necessary to reach isolated coves, beaches and fishing camps. The plains near Guerrero Negro merge into the Desierto de Vizcaíno, which extends to San Ignacio and westward into Península Vizcaíno. Travelers in this area should be cautious in wandering off main thoroughfares without appropriate off-road equipment and supplies. Daytime is often murderously hot, but nights can be frigid.

South of the state border, the Transpeninsular jogs inland beyond Guerrero Negro and eastward to San Ignacio, where an underground spring, utilized by Jesuits in the 18th century to plant thousands of palms and establish a mission, nurtures one of Baja's few substantial oases. Beyond San Ignacio, the highway passes Las Tres Virgenes (Three Virgins), a Quaternary cluster of volcanic peaks and massive lava flows, the towns of Santa Rosalía and Mulegé and several popular Gulf beach areas. It then cuts back west to the Llanos de Magdalena (Magdalena Plain) and other beaches farther south, especially near the town of Todos Santos.

The mountainous Cape Region beyond La Paz, with its rocky headlands, coves and sandy beaches, is an increasingly popular tourist destination. Dotting the shores are numerous islands which are undersea extensions of peninsular mountain ranges; isolated since the creation of the Gulf, they support unique plant associations and large breeding colonies of seabirds. The largest island, Isla Angel de la Guarda, is 42 miles (70 km) long, 10 miles (16 km) wide, and reaches an altitude of 4324 feet (1318 meters).

Several mountain ranges together form the backbone of the entire peninsula. The most northerly major range is the granitic Sierra de Juárez, a southern extension of mainland California ranges; its alpine meadows in Parque Nacional Constitución de 1857 are a surprising highlight. East of the mountains, around Mexicali, the Río Hardy meets the Colorado in the extensively irrigated and intensively cultivated delta.

Farther south, in another national park, the Sierra San Pedro Mártir range features Baja's highest peak – 10,126-foot (3096-meter) Picacho del Diablo (Devil's Peak), often capped with snow. This range resembles mainland California's Sierra Nevada, with low foothills gradually leading up into pine forests and steep mountain peaks, but the Desierto del Colorado on its eastern slope is a brutally hot and arid desert reaching nearly to the 30th parallel, where the Sierra La Asamblea marks its approximate southern limit. The mountains of central Baja are mostly Tertiary marine sediments, but volcanic peaks and recent lava flows often conceal their bedrock.

Beyond Loreto, the Sierra de la Giganta is southern Baja's most prominent range, stretching nearly to La Paz. Farther south the granitic peaks of the forested Sierra de la Laguna, reaching up to 7000 feet (2130 meters), divide the Cape Region in half. The tropic of Cancer runs almost precisely through the town of Todos Santos, about midway between La Paz and Cabo San Lucas.

CLIMATE

Thanks to the cool California Current, which branches off the Subarctic Current at about 45°N latitude, Baja California's Pacific coast is relatively mild throughout the year; average temperatures range from 60°F to 75°F (16°C to 24°C). Summer temperatures often reach 85°F (30°C), but sea breezes and convective fogs like those in mainland California provide a natural air-conditioning. Like mainland California, northern Baja experiences a winter rainy season, with perhaps 90% of total precipitation falling from December to March. At higher elevations, especially in the Sierra Juárez and the Sierra de San Pedro Mártir, precipitation takes the form of snow, which may last well into spring. On winter nights, even at sea level, frosts are not unknown.

Inland from the Pacific, summer temperatures soar upwards of 110°F (43°C), humidity is almost nil and rain is rare, especially across the eastern slopes of the sierras in the Río Colorado delta; summers in the area from Mexicali to San Felipe are murderously hot. The Desierto Central between El Rosario and San Ignacio is blistering and, between El Rosario and Cataviña, strong winds sometimes make driving dangerous. The Gulf coast also suffers strong winds and high summer temperatures.

Temperatures in the Cape Region from La Paz to Cabo San Lucas are also very high, but in summer this area often experiences storms and even violent hurricanes called *chubascos*, because of tropical low pressure areas in the Pacific. Winter is generally warm and sunny.

Climate Charts

The accompanying charts offer a sample of Baja California's climatic conditions. Tijuana represents most of the Pacific coast of northern Baja, while Bahía Magdalena is more typical of the southern coast almost to Guerrero Negro. Figures for San José del Cabo illustrate conditions in the Cape Region, while those for Santa Rosalía more closely resemble those along the Gulf of California (the Colorado desert region at the north end of the Gulf, however, is much cooler in winter, especially at night).

Travelers should remember that temperatures can vary dramatically, especially with

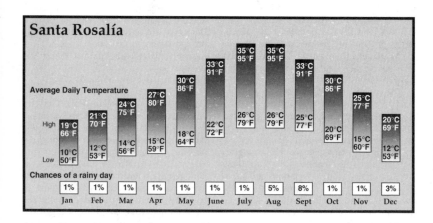

Santa Rosalía

Average Daily Temperature

	High												Low

High: Jan 19°C/66°F, Feb 21°C/70°F, Mar 24°C/75°F, Apr 27°C/80°F, May 30°C/86°F, June 33°C/91°F, July 35°C/95°F, Aug 35°C/95°F, Sept 33°C/91°F, Oct 30°C/86°F, Nov 25°C/77°F, Dec 20°C/69°F

Low: Jan 10°C/50°F, Feb 12°C/53°F, Mar 14°C/56°F, Apr 15°C/59°F, May 18°C/64°F, June 22°C/72°F, July 26°C/79°F, Aug 26°C/79°F, Sept 25°C/77°F, Oct 20°C/69°F, Nov 15°C/60°F, Dec 12°C/53°F

Chances of a rainy day

Jan	Feb	Mar	Apr	May	June	July	Aug	Sept	Oct	Nov	Dec
1%	1%	1%	1%	1%	1%	1%	5%	8%	1%	1%	3%

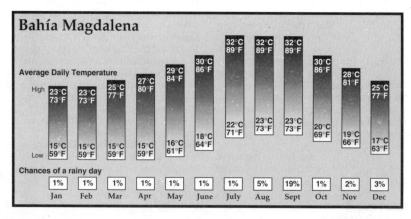

Bahía Magdalena

Average Daily Temperature

High: Jan 23°C/73°F, Feb 23°C/73°F, Mar 25°C/77°F, Apr 27°C/80°F, May 29°C/84°F, June 30°C/86°F, July 32°C/89°F, Aug 32°C/89°F, Sept 32°C/89°F, Oct 30°C/86°F, Nov 28°C/81°F, Dec 25°C/77°F

Low: Jan 15°C/59°F, Feb 15°C/59°F, Mar 15°C/59°F, Apr 15°C/59°F, May 16°C/61°F, June 18°C/64°F, July 22°C/71°F, Aug 23°C/73°F, Sept 23°C/73°F, Oct 20°C/69°F, Nov 19°C/66°F, Dec 17°C/63°F

Chances of a rainy day

Jan	Feb	Mar	Apr	May	June	July	Aug	Sept	Oct	Nov	Dec
1%	1%	1%	1%	1%	1%	1%	5%	19%	1%	2%	3%

altitude, and that low average rainfall figures can disguise infrequent but truly dangerous weather events like hurricanes.

FLORA & FAUNA

For visitors interested in natural history, Baja California offers a wealth of botanical and zoological attractions. A relatively small number are unique to the peninsula, but some, like the migrating gray whales of Scammon's Lagoon, are reason enough to plan a trip to the peninsula.

Plants & Plant Communities

Responding to accusations that Jesuit missionaries engaged in clandestine commerce with the English, Padre Jakob Baegert wrote that 'there is nothing in California except wacke and other worthless rocks, and it produces nothing but thorns'. If, he added, the English would have accepted these in exchange for wood and water, there could have been a flourishing commerce because 'nothing is so common in California as rocks and thorns, nothing so rare as moisture, wood and cool shade'.

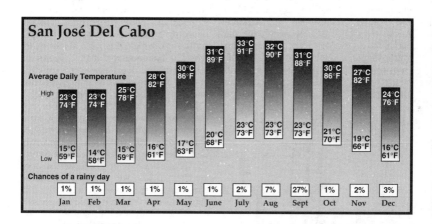

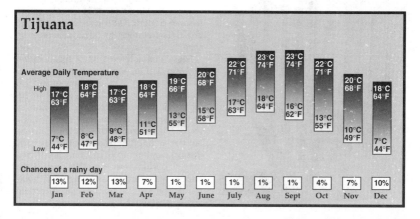

Most of Baja California is conspicuously desert, but there is a greater variety of habitats and species than Padre Baegert knew in his incomplete experience of the peninsula. The following pages present some of Baja's most prominent and interesting plants, identifying them by Spanish and English common names, as well as their biological nomenclature. When more than one species of a genus is present, the abbreviation 'spp' denotes this fact.

In botanical terms, the northern coast and foothills, from the US border to El Rosario, are a continuation of mainland California, covered with oaks and chaparral vegetation like manzanita, ceanothus (California lilac) and chamise *(Adenostoma fasciculatum)*. Above the chaparral belt, paralleling the ocean, the Sierras de Juárez and San Pedro Mártir support a longitudinal strip of coniferous forest that also resembles areas north of the border. The dominant species are piñon pine *(Pinus quadrifolia)*, whose

edible nuts were a key part of the indigenous diet, and Jeffrey pine *(Pinus jeffreyi)*, but other pines, as well as spruce, cypress and fir, are present in smaller numbers.

Below about 3300 feet (1000 meters), east of the sierras and far to the south, the Sonoran Desert region comprises several distinct subregions. From the US border as far as Bahía de Los Angeles, it consists of small-leaved shrubs like ocotillo *(Fouquieria splendens)* and the closely related palo adán *(F burragei* and *F diguetti)*, which bloom only at rare times of heavy rainfall, and cacti like *nopal* (prickly pear, *Opuntia* spp). South of Bahía de Los Angeles almost to La Paz, a narrow coastal strip on the Gulf of California features imposing cacti like the *cardón (Pachycereus* spp), which reaches a height of 65 feet (20 meters), and many species of *biznaga* (barrel cactus, *Ferocactus* spp). All of these cacti produce edible fruit or seeds, most notably the *tuna*, fruit of the nopal.

Nearly unique to Baja is the *cirio* tree *(Idria columnaris)*, popularly known as a 'boojum' because of its supposed resemblance to the tall, twisted creature in Lewis Carroll's poem *The Hunting of the Snark*. Closely related to ocotillo but the only member of a separate genus, the slow growing cirio reaches 65 feet (20 meters) in height; its distribution is limited to an area from the southwestern foothills of the Sierra San Pedro Mártir almost to San Ignacio, to Isla Angel de la Guarda, and to parts of Sonora. Until it branches, it most closely resembles an inverted carrot in shape.

More characteristic than the boojum, however, are the various species of *Agave* ('century plant', a genus which includes *A tequilana*, the source of tequila) and *Yucca*, which dot the Desierto de Vizcaíno of central Baja. The abundant agave was a major food source of the Cochimí Indians, but consuming the plant's nutritious heart involved uprooting it and cooking it in a long, laborious process. The root of the yucca, also known as *guacamote*, was roasted on the fire until edible. In certain areas substantial concentrations of fruit-bearing palms *(Washingtonia robusta* and *Erythea armata)* flourished, but the Cochimí used them more as timber.

Farther south, on the Pacific slope, the Desierto de Vizcaíno and the Llano de Magdalena (Magdalena Plain) support different species of *Agave*, plus cacti like the cardón and the *pitahaya agria (Machaerocereus gummosus)*, whose slightly acid fruit was consumed by native peoples; its stems also made a useful fish poison. The *datilillo (Yucca valida*, a tree-like form of yucca) bears a fruit resembling a date, while the wild figs of the *zalate (Ficus palmeri)* were more palatable to Indians than missionaries.

The Sierra de la Giganta, running from Bahía de la Concepción nearly to La Paz, is home to many common trees and shrubs like acacia and mesquite *(Prosopis* spp), a handful of native palms like *Erythea brandegeei*, and many cacti, including nopal and the pitahaya dulce. As far north as San Borja the *pitahaya dulce (Lemaireocereus thurberi)*, known to English speakers as the organ pipe cactus, yields a sweet fruit that was the Cochimí equivalent of candy (sweets). The pitahaya dulce was a key food source for native peoples who camped near local concentrations of the plant for the late summer and early autumn harvest, which was a major social and religious occasion.

After gorging themselves on the fruit, they would defecate in a particular spot and, later, collect the dry feces to winnow the undigested seeds, which they milled and ate during winter food shortages. German Jesuit Padre Jakob Baegert, who observed the Guaicura Indians at San Luis Gonzaga, wrote that 'It was difficult for me, indeed, to give credit to such a report until I had repeatedly witnessed this procedure' which, he added, was accompanied by 'much joking'.

South of the Sierra de la Giganta, most of the Cape Region is an arid tropical zone of acacia and other leguminous trees and shrubs, sumac *(Cyrtocarpa edulis*, whose fruit is edible) and fan palm *(Erythea brandegeei)*. Pines and oaks, however, appear side-by-side with palms and cacti at higher elevations in the well-watered Sierra de la Laguna; the piñon pine produces edible seeds.

In addition to these major zones, other plant associations appear sporadically in much more restricted geographical ranges, but are botanically significant and comprise critical wildlife habitat, especially for birds. These areas include coastal dunes, coastal salt marshes, freshwater marshes, mangrove swamps and vernal pools.

Many desert plants, including numerous species of cacti, are on Appendix I or II of the CITES (Convention on International Trade in Endangered Species) List. Travelers should not purchase or otherwise obtain living plants, or products made from these plants, for import into the USA. There are restrictions and prohibitions under international law.

Birds

Baja California's bird habitats are strongly correlated with its plant communities, but vary with climate, elevation and latitude. The major geographical divisions of the northern Pacific coast, the mountainous Sierra San Pedro Mártir, the Colorado Desert, the Vizcaíno Desert, and the Cape each have characteristic assemblages, though the desert species are widespread outside those areas.

The many Gulf islands, in addition, have large colonies of nesting seabirds despite their lack of endemics. Among the most noteworthy are the black storm-petrel *(Oceanodroma melania)* and the least storm-petrel *(O microsoma)*, the brown pelican *(Pelecanus occidentalis)*, the cormorants *(Phalacrocorax auritus* and *P penicillatus)*, the frigate bird *(Fregata magnificens)*, the boobies *(Sula nebouxi* and *S leucogaster)*, Craveri's murrelet *(Synthliporamphus craveri)*, Heermann's gull *(Larus heermanni)*, the yellow-footed gull *(L livens)*, and the elegant tern *(Sterna elegans)*, and the brown noddy *(Anous stolidus)*.

Seabirds prosper from the Midriff Islands of the central Gulf south toward

Endangered Species

The Convention on International Trade in Endangered Species of Wild Fauna and Flora (CITES) is a diplomatic agreement regulating trade in biotic resources, including plants and animals, which are either in immediate danger of extinction, or else threatened or declining so rapidly that they may soon be in danger of extinction. Regulations are complex, but in general, such species are either protected from commercial or noncommercial exploitation or subject to severe restrictions. In many instances, all commerce is prohibited in a given species; in most others, the export of plants and animals from a given country is prohibited without express authorization from that country's government.

Under CITES, most species are assigned either to Appendix I (endangered, under immediate threat of extinction without remedial action) or Appendix II (threatened, perhaps regionally endangered); some recovering species have been reassigned from Appendix I to Appendix II. Appendix III listings cover species which require close monitoring to determine their degree of vulnerability to extinction.

Travelers should take special care not to hunt, purchase or collect the following species of plants and animals found in Baja California, nor should they purchase products made from these plants and animals without explicit authority from authorities in Mexico City; otherwise such products may be confiscated by US Customs. The list below is partial, and travelers should also consult with US Customs before attempting to import any such products.

Appendix I

Flora
Salt marsh bird's beak, *Cordylanthus maritimus*

Fauna
Cochito (Gulf harbor porpoise), *Phocoena sinus*. All cetaceans (whales and porpoises) not on Appendix I are on Appendix II, but not all are listed individually here.
Baja pronghorn antelope, *Antilocapra americana peninsularis*
Guadalupe fur seal, *Arctocephalus townsendi*
Cedros mule deer, *Odocoileus hemionus cedrosensis*
Leatherback sea turtle, *Dermochelys coriacea*
Caguama (green sea turtle), *Chelonia mydas agasizii*
Hawksbill sea turtle, *Eretmochelys imbricata*

Loggerhead sea turtle, *Caretta caretta*
Olive ridley sea turtle, *Lepidochelys coriacea*
California least tern, *Sterna antillarum*
Totoava (seatrout or weakfish), *Cynoscion macdonaldi*

Appendix II

Flora
Cacti. All cacti not on Appendix I are on Appendix II, but these are too numerous to be listed individually here.
Cirio (Boojum) *Idria columnaris*

Fauna
Southern sea otter, *Enhydra lutris nereis*
Bighorn sheep, *Ovis canadensis*
California gray whale, *Eschrichtius robustus glaucus*
Coral, *Coelenterata*. Corals of all orders are on Appendix II, but are too numerous to list here. ■

Cabo San Lucas because upwelling of nutrients from deep submarine canyons feeds abundant fish and plankton near the surface. In pre-Columbian times, aboriginal peoples collected eggs and captured birds which had established breeding colonies on the islands and on the mainland. Unfortunately, ever since European settlement, practices like egg collecting, degradation of habitat through agricultural development and the unwise introduction of ecologically exotic species like cats and goats have led to indirect (coincidental) extinctions, while uncontrolled shooting has even brought direct (intentional) extinctions. On the Pacific island of Guadalupe, for example, domestic goats so reduced the vegetative cover that endemic races of flickers, wrens and towhees died out, while cats may have eliminated the Guadalupe storm petrel, and shooters destroyed the crested caracara. Massive agricultural development on the Río Colorado has also eliminated native vegetation and reduced bird habitat.

Sanford Wilbur's *Birds of Baja California* (University of California Press, Berkeley, 1987) is a comprehensive listing of species found on the peninsula and surrounding islands, but its lack of illustrations makes it unsuitable for field use. Field-oriented birders might acquire R T Peterson's & E L Chalif's *A Field Guide to Mexican Birds* (Houghton Mifflin, Boston, 1973), which covers the mainland, the peninsula and offshore islands. *The Audubon Society Field Guide to North American Birds, Western Region* (Knopf, New York, 1977), by Miklos Udvardy, focuses on birds of the USA and Canada, but there is considerable overlap with Baja California and the Mexican mainland.

Land Mammals
Baja is home to a variety of unique mammals, including the black jackrabbit *(Lepus insularis)* of Isla Espíritu Santo and the fish-eating bat *(Pizonyx vivesi)* of the Gulf. More characteristic, however, are animals like the mule deer *(Odocoileus hemionus)*, peninsular pronghorn antelope *(Antilocapra americana peninsularis)*, and endangered desert bighorn sheep *(Ovis canadensis)*. The Cedros Island mule deer *(O hemionus cedrosensis)* is an endangered subspecies.

A Starker Leopold's *Wildlife of Mexico* (University of California Press, Berkeley, 1959) is a good source of information on Mexican mammals (and some birds), though oriented primarily toward game management. Only a handful of Leopold's game animals are found on the Baja peninsula.

Marine Mammals
From January to March, visitors flock to the lagoons of central Baja to view the migration and mating of the California gray whale *(Eschrichtius robustus* or *E gibbosus)*, but other species of whales and dolphins also frequent the waters of the Pacific and the Gulf. Among them are the finback whale *(Balaenoptera physalus)* and the humpback whale *(Megaptera novaeangliae)*.

The following readily available books are good sources of information on whales: *The Book of Whales* by Richard Ellis (Knopf, New York, 1980); *The Sierra Club Handbook of Whales and Dolphins* by Steven Leatherwood (Sierra Club Books, San Francisco, 1983); and *The World's Whales* by Stanley Minasian (Norton, New York, 1984).

For information on whale-watching, see the Tours section in the Getting There & Away chapter, and the Guerrero Negro, Laguna San Ignacio and Bahía Magdalena sections in the Desierto Central chapter.

Other marine mammals include the endangered Gulf of California harbor porpoise *(Phocoena sinus)*, the recovering but still threatened southern sea otter *(Enhydra lutris)*, the threatened Guadalupe fur seal *(Arctocephalus townsendii)*, and the more common sea lion *(Zalophus californianus)*, northern elephant seal *(Mirounga angustirostris)* and harbor seal *(Phoca vitulina)*. Sea lions and elephant seals can be seen at several offshore Pacific islands, most notably Isla Cedros and the Islas San Benito, about midway down the peninsula.

Fish & Marine Life
The waters of the Pacific support a cool temperate flora and fauna resembling that off the coast of mainland California, with kelp (like *Macrocystis*) and mollusks, sea urchins and barnacles, but shallow areas like Laguna San Ignacio and Bahía Magdalena support more tropical life forms.

Because of the range of temperatures in the Gulf of California, its flora and fauna are relatively limited in numbers of species, especially in the northern half of the Gulf. Total biomass is fairly large, however, because of algal blooms – the term 'Vermillion Sea', often applied to the Gulf, derives from this phenomenon. In some shallow lagoons, especially toward the south of the peninsula, mangrove swamps are incubators for Gulf fauna, such as oysters. Crustaceans like spiny lobster and rock crabs were common fare in aboriginal Baja. The poisonous yellow-bellied sea snake *(Pelamus platyrus)* frequents inshore waters of southern Baja.

Most of today's important marine life, especially that of interest to the tourist, is pelagic (native to open seas) rather than inshore. Over 800 species of fish, many of them excellent eating, inhabit the Gulf; many of these attract sport fishing enthusiasts who increasingly have adopted a catch-and-release policy so as not to endanger the abundance of popular game species like the marlin. The totoaba *(Cynoscion macdonaldii)*, known commonly as sea trout or weakfish, is endangered in the Gulf of California.

Souvenir hunters should be aware that all species of black coral, of the order *Antipatharia*, are on Appendix II of the CITES Endangered Species List; exports of black coral products, such as jewelry, require an export permit from Mexico City in order to be allowed into the USA. Black coral is mined with dredge hooks, and substantial reef areas are destroyed in the process of obtaining material for relatively insignificant amounts of these products.

Reptiles

Desert environments support many reptiles, including snakes, lizards and turtles. Baja has an abundant and varied snake population, with rattlesnakes *(Crotalus* spp) a serious concern in the bush. More than half the reptiles on oceanic islands in the Gulf of California are endemic species or subspecies.

Isla Santa Catalina, southeast of Loreto, is home to the so-called rattleless rattlesnake; the endemic *Crotalus catalinensis* has only a single rattle segment which, by itself, is incapable of making any sound. *C ruber lorenzoensis*, a similar species on San Lorenzo Sur, may have either single rattle segments or full rattles.

Sea turtles, all of which are endangered species, inhabit the Gulf of California and nest on some of its beaches. Travelers should avoid consuming any turtle products or acquiring souvenirs made from turtle shells, which may not be imported into the USA. The Pacific green turtle *(Chelonia mydas,* colloquially known as the *caguama negra* or *tortuga prieta)* is the most important, but other species include the leatherback *(Dermochyles coriacea* or *tortuga laud)*, the western ridley *(Lepidochelys olivacea)*, the loggerhead *(Caretta caretta)* and hawksbill *(Eretmochelys imbricata* or *tortuga carey)*. The diminutive hawksbill amputates curious fingers with ease. Mexicans most commonly apply the word *caguama* to the green, but the term can mean any species of turtle.

Turtle-oriented travelers will find a great deal of entertaining and informative literature on the subject, including Archie Carr's *So Excellent a Fishe* (Natural History Press, Garden City, New York, 1967), James J Parsons' *The Green Turtle and Man* (University of Florida, 1962) and Jack Rudloe's *Time of the Turtle* (Penguin, 1980). At Bahía de Los Angeles, the Secretaría de Pesca has a modest turtle conservation project where it's possible to see leatherbacks, hawksbills and greens; see the Bahía de Los Angeles section in the Desierto Central chapter for details.

National Parks

Mexico has established two major *parques nacionales* (national parks) on the Baja peninsula and several *parques naturales* (natural parks). In addition, several of the key islands in the Midriff region of the Gulf are nature preserves, although direct protective activities are limited.

Parque Nacional Constitución de 1857

On the plateau and eastern slope of the Sierra de Juárez, this 12,000-acre (5000-hectare) park, barely an hour's drive from Ensenada, is a good place for camping and rock climbing. Shallow, sprawling Laguna Hanson, surrounded by shady pine forests, is a major stopover for migratory birds on the Pacific flyway.

Parque Nacional Sierra San Pedro Mártir

Reaching altitudes above 10,000 feet (3000 meters) in the Sierra San Pedro

Tracking the Turtle

The great whales get all the press. Few travelers know as much about the sea turtles that, historically, have been as important to the peoples of the tropics as whales have to the peoples of the Arctic. Called 'the world's most valuable reptile' by geographer James Parsons, the green turtle *(Chelonia mydas)* is endangered throughout the world, and its conservation should be a major priority in Baja California and Mexico.

The green turtle *(caguama negra* or *tortuga prieta* in Baja California) is a grazing reptile that feeds on marine grasses of tropical and subtropical seas, though wandering individuals have been found as far north as England and as far south as Argentina and Chile. Individuals weigh as much as 800 lbs (360 kg), though most weigh 300 lbs (135 kg) or less. Males rarely leave the sea, but females migrate long distances to haul up on sandy beaches in isolated tropical islands to lay their eggs.

For millennia, the green turtle has provided protein to human populations in the tropics, both from its meat and eggs, but the exploration of the globe by Europeans marked the beginning of the decline of the species. Northern European sailors netted the abundant turtles of the Caribbean, for example, and kept them aboard ship as a source of fresh meat on their trips around the Horn – feeding them bananas and bathing them in salt water to keep them alive. By the 18th century, fresh turtle meat and turtle soup were luxuries in London, but by the 19th century they had reached the British capital in tins.

Outside the tropics, where protein was otherwise scarce, turtle always remained a delicacy, but commercial pressures resulted in overhunting in such important areas as the Caribbean coasts of Nicaragua and Costa Rica (where nesting beaches at Tortuguero were frequently raided of eggs as well). The result was a transfer of scarce protein from the poor countries of the tropics to the rich countries of the mid latitudes.

Baja California's turtles shared this unfortunate history. At Bahía Tortugas, on Península Vizcaíno, one 19th-century ship netted almost 200 turtles in a single pass offshore. Many were canned or shipped north to San Francisco or San Diego for sale or further processing. As recently as the 1960s, the Ruffo family's Empacadora Baja California was canning as much as 100 tons of turtle soup in a season in Ensenada.

In the 1970s, increasing concern over the green's declining numbers resulted in its placement (and that of all other sea turtles) on Appendix I of the Convention on International Trade in Endangered Species (CITES). Still, it is not unusual to find surreptitious trade in turtle products (a casual inquiry at a taco stand once led to my being told where to find caguama for sale). Perhaps, some time in the future, the species will recover enough to permit it to resume the role it once played in the human ecology of the tropics, but environmental opponents of NAFTA argued, with some credibility, that the Mexican government has done a poor job of enforcing international agreements on turtle conservation.

Baja visitors are unlikely to come across nesting sites, which are usually at remote spots like Isla Socorro in the Revillagigedo group, some 280 miles (450 km) south of Cabo San Lucas, but greens and other turtle species are not unusual in Baja waters. In Baja California (Norte), the green has been recorded at Gulf island sites like Angel de la Guarda, Rasa, Salsipuedes, San Luis and San Lorenzo, as well as Bahía de los Angeles, Bahía San Luis Gonzaga, Puertecitos, San Felipe and even the mouth of the Río Colorado. On the Pacific side, records include Isla Cedros, Bahía San Quintín, and Ensenada.

The warmer waters of Baja California Sur are better turtle habitat, in many of the same areas frequented by calving gray whales: Laguna Ojo de Liebre (Scammon's Lagoon), Laguna San Ignacio, and Bahía Magdalena. The juvenile turtle populations of the Gulf appear to feed more on algae than on sea grasses. ■

Mártir, this roughly 151,000-acre (63,000-hectare) reserve contains some of the peninsula's most varied terrain and vegetation, and is an excellent choice for backcountry camping and backpacking in the spring, well before areas north of the border are free of snow. It can be approached either from Colonet/San Telmo on the Pacific side of the peninsula, or from San Felipe on the Gulf side, where the 10,154-foot (3095-meter) spire of Picacho del Diablo, also known as Cerro Providencia, is most impressive.

GOVERNMENT

The peninsula of Baja California consists of two separate states, Baja California (capital Mexicali) and Baja California Sur (capital La Paz). Each state is further subdivided into *municipios*, roughly equivalent to US counties, each of which is administered by a *cabecera* (county seat). Each municipio in turn consists of several *delegaciones*.

Baja California consists of the municipios of Tijuana, Tecate, Mexicali and Ensenada; Baja California Sur consists of the municipios of Mulegé, Comondú, La Paz and Los Cabos. The size of municipios can be very disproportionate – the municipio of Tijuana, containing the bulk of Baja California's population, is only 576 sq miles (1600 sq km, about 2.2% of the state's area), while that of Ensenada is 18,900 sq miles (52,500 sq km, over 73% of the state's area).

As elsewhere in Mexico, the official Partido Institucional Revolucionario (PRI) has dominated politics for most of this century, but the Partido de Acción Nacional (PAN) is strong here and elsewhere along Mexico's northern frontier. Many observers have labeled PAN 'conservative' because of its assertive free-market orientation, but its appeal derives at least as much from widely felt regional antagonism against Mexico City's centralized, bureaucratic authority. The present governor of Baja California is Ensenada-born Ernesto Ruffo Appel, a businessman with experience in the fisheries sector, while the governor of

Baja California Sur is Guillermo Mercado Romero.

ECONOMY

Agriculture and fishing are major industries, but tourism is the motor that drives the economy. Over the past decade, every major town and city has seen a construction boom in hotels and related infrastructure. Fonatur, Mexico's federal tourism development agency, has promoted major resort complexes at Loreto and Los Cabos (San José del Cabo and Cabo San Lucas) with foreign and Mexican capital, with the intention of transforming these places into luxury resorts similar to Cancún in the Yucatán.

Baja's popularity as a tourist destination is undeniable. Tijuana claims to be the world's busiest border city – in 1991 over 14 million cars, 380,000 trucks and 12 million pedestrians crossed the border from San Ysidro; another 3.6 million cars, 180,000 trucks and 4.5 million pedestrians entered via the Mesa de Otay crossing near Tijuana's international airport. Both Mexicali and Tijuana have recently built new cultural centers to attract more visitors and, each year, more motorists explore the Transpeninsular and its side roads or jet into resorts in Loreto, La Paz or Los Cabos.

Some locals find this interest in Baja ironic because, as more North Americans head south for inexpensive holidays or retirement in Baja, countless Mexicans and Central Americans flock to Tijuana and Mexicali to arrange surreptitious border crossings with smugglers known as *coyotes* or *polleros* for up to US$500 per person. Passage of a tough immigration law in 1986 made it illegal for US businesses to hire undocumented foreigners, but this has not deterred thousands of unauthorized workers from trying to cross the border by any means possible – on foot or hidden in railway boxcars, car trunks or truck trailers. Many have died of thirst or heat exhaustion in the attempt.

Mexicans of all socio-economic categories bitterly resent the high metal fences and stadium lighting which the US govern-

Mural, Escuela General Melitón Albañez, Todos Santos

Mural, Galeria de la Ciudad, Tijuana

Mural, Tierra y Libertad by Juan Zuñiga Padilla, Parque Municipal Abelardo L Rodríguez, Rosarito

Model of Guanajuato, Mexitlán, Tijuana

El Triunfo, Cape Region

Village of Cedros, Isla Cedros

Palacio Frontón Jai Alai, Tijuana

ment has erected along the border in the past several years. These impediments have barely slowed border crossers; instead they have merely rerouted them to other areas. Texas newspaper columnist Molly Ivins recalls that when, in the mid-1980s, a US government official proposed a massive barrier along the Texas border, sponsors of a chili cook-off held a fence-climbing contest for a case of Lone Star beer. The winning time was seven seconds.

Maquiladoras

One alternative to this massive daily exodus to the USA is the promotion of long-term foreign investment to create jobs in Mexico. Presently foreign investment has taken the form of *maquiladoras*, which are twin assembly-plant operations owned and run by foreign companies, usually American or Japanese.

Most Mexican towns along the US-Mexico border, including Tijuana, enjoy duty-free status, allowing foreign companies to import parts and raw materials from the USA to their maquiladoras without paying duty. Mexican workers, whose hourly wage is a fraction of their counterparts across the border, assemble the components, which are then shipped back to the lucrative US market for sale.

Maquiladora workers, who are mostly young women, seem generally satisfied because their wages are nearly double the average wage in Mexico (despite higher living costs along the border) and their jobs sometimes provide access to training programs and other benefits. Mexico is pleased with the reduced unemployment and, increased foreign exchange, but the maquiladoras' contribution to the country's economy and industrial base is minimal because their scope is so limited and they provide little prospect of long-term investment. Maquiladora wages, relatively high by Mexican standards, average about US$1 per hour.

With the implementation of the North American Free Trade Agreement (NAFTA), the border area may lose some of the economic advantages that derive from its duty-free status, but it will still benefit from its geographic proximity to the USA.

The Borderlands Economy & NAFTA

Even some Mexican professionals are poorly paid: a full-time university professor, for example, may earn as little as US$350 per month. Nevertheless, border towns make a major contribution to the economies of their US counterparts, as many residents of Tijuana, Mexicali and other settlements have special 'border crosser' status that allows them to enter USA for shopping trips and to visit relatives over the line. In November 1993, in response to anti-immigrant hysteria in mainland California, political activists in Tijuana organized a two-day boycott of San Diego businesses to accentuate the significance of the Mexican contribution to the borderlands economy.

Mexico's federal government eagerly anticipated ratification of the North American Free Trade Agreement (NAFTA), approved in late 1993 by the US Congress. This will permit Mexican goods wider access to US markets and perhaps encourage expansion of the peninsula's (and the country's) industrial base and employment, but Mexico's low wages and spotty environmental record spurred opposition to the agreement north of the border. Among opposition forces within Mexico, there is widespread concern that NAFTA and other recent economic measures mark the return and triumph of the discredited ideas of Porfirio Díaz and his científicos.

POPULATION & PEOPLE

Baja's population consists largely of *mestizos*, people of mixed Indian and European heritage, mostly immigrants, or descendants of immigrants, from mainland Mexico. Official results of the 1990 census give Baja's total population as slightly below two million – 1,661,000 in the state of Baja California (northern Baja) and 318,000 in the state of Baja California Sur (southern Baja). In southern Baja, 71% of the population was born in the state; in northern Baja, the figure was 54%, reflecting massive immigration from mainland Mexico in recent years. In northern Baja, perhaps 2% of the population is foreign, mostly US citizens residing in Tijuana.

Most *bajacalifornianos* (inhabitants of Baja California) live in cities in the extreme northern and southern parts of the peninsula. Tijuana (official population 699,000) accounts for the bulk of Baja's total population; Mexicali (officially 438,000) is the second largest city. Ensenada (officially 169,000) is third, while La Paz (officially 138,000) is the fourth largest city and the largest in Baja California Sur.

Many informed analysts suspect that official figures understate the actual figures by at least 50% and perhaps much more. Official census takers, who are poorly paid, make limited efforts to count areas like Tijuana's burgeoning and dangerous shantytowns with any accuracy. Another explanation is that the state governments of Baja California and Baja California Sur are under control of the opposition Partido de Acción Nacional (PAN), and that the Mexican federal government of the Partido Institucional Revolucionario (PRI), which has ruled Mexico in one form or another for nearly the entire century, intentionally understates population figures in order to limit the disbursement of federal assistance, which is based on these statistics, to the states. There is also widespread belief that the federal government wishes to downplay the phenomenal growth of border cities because of the sensitivity of the immigration issue across the line.

Official population figures often do not separate the city from the rest of a given municipio, substantial parts of which may be rural. Disaggregated statistics for individual census tracts are not available, which only reinforces suspicions that the numbers have been manipulated for political reasons.

Indigenous Peoples & Early Settlers

Permanent European settlements, which began in the 17th century as Jesuit missions or small military camps, exposed the indigenous population to deadly epidemics that reduced their numbers from upwards of 48,000 at contact to barely 3000 by 1820. Baja's 1500 or so remaining Indians, often known by the generic term Cochimí after the now extinct peoples of the Desierto Central, live mainly in the Sierra San Pedro Mártir, the Sierra de Juárez, and the lowlands near the Río Hardy. They belong to tribal groups like the Diegueño (Tipai), Paipai, Kiliwa, Cocopá and Kamia, but few follow the traditional subsistence economy of hunting and gathering. Nearly all speak Spanish, but indigenous language use is still vigorous among the Tipai, Paipai and Cocopá.

The past decade has seen the influx of large numbers of Indians from central Mexico to the city of Tijuana in particular, often as a staging point for crossing the border into the USA. A few hundred Indians from rural Oaxaca have settled in the San Quintín area, driven by poverty in the south and attracted by farming jobs in Baja despite relatively low wages.

In the 19th century, Baja's first fishing villages, ranchos and secular towns appeared, along with mining operations that attracted fortune-seekers from around the world. Many established bajacalifornianos are descendants of settlers whose roots were in mainland Mexico or in other parts of the world – some trace their ancestry to the USA, southern and northern Europe, and even China. Thanks to these enclaves, unexpected surnames like Smith, Jones, and even Crosthwaite and McLish are not unusual on the peninsula.

EDUCATION

Systematic formal education began with the arrival of the Jesuit missionaries in 1697. Not until 1867 did the first secular school open, in Santo Tomás, soon followed by others in Real del Castillo, San Vicente, Tecate and Rosario. After the turn of the century, educational facilities improved rapidly and by the time Baja California became a state, there were over 230 primary schools, nine secondary schools, and a university.

School attendance, obligatory throughout Mexico from the ages of 6 to 14, is increasing but still low is some rural areas. The state-run Universidad Autónoma de Baja California now has sites in Tijuana, Ensenada, and Mexicali, as does the private Centro de Enseñanza Técnica y Superior. El Colegio de La Frontera and the Universidad Iberoamericana have campuses in Tijuana, while there are also university campuses in La Paz.

Several of these institutions have exchange programs and research affiliations with institutions north of the border, including San Diego State University, the University of California at San Diego, and the Scripps Institute of Oceanography in La Jolla.

ARTS
Visual Arts
Few visitors realize what a fertile atmosphere Baja California has provided for the visual arts. Throughout the peninsula, from Tijuana to Los Cabos, evidence of cultural links with mainland Mexican movements like the muralist tradition are apparent, but sculpture and painting flourished even before the creation of the Instituto de Ciencias y Artes del Estado (ICAE, now part of the Instituto de Bellas Artes), and the Universidad Autónoma in the 1950s. Both institutions supported local artists and others who had relocated from mainland Mexico.

After the Universidad Autónoma abandoned the arts community, individual artists combined to form groups like the Círculo de Escultores y Pintores (Circle of Sculptors & Painters) and the Profesionales de Artes Visuales (Visual Arts Professionals). Since 1977, the Bienal de Artes Plásticas de Baja California has been an important competition for artists from the state.

One recent informal movement in the Baja California scene is *cholismo*, the equivalent of European or North American punk, often expressed in street murals featuring traditional Mexican figures like the Virgin of Guadalupe in unconventional contexts. The bi-national Taller de Arte Fronterizo (Border Art Workshop), with members in Tijuana and San Diego, often stages performance art shows and events with borderlands themes.

Rubén Martínez describes Tijuana's thriving independent arts community in great detail in the essay 'Tijuana Burning' in his collection entitled *The Other Side* (Vintage, 1993). Baja California Sur also has a lively arts community, revolving around the village of Todos Santos, which partly but by no means exclusively derives from expatriate North Americans who have relocated to the area. Their work, however, generally lacks the urgency of that of artists on the borderlands. It more closely resembles styles and themes of US expatriates from the New Mexican cities of Taos and Santa Fe.

Cinema & Video
Early Hollywood directors gave such insulting treatment to the Mexican borderlands, through depictions of casinos and prostitution, that Baja California's first cinematic production, *Raza de Bronce (Race of Bronze)* (1927), was a nationalist response to what director Guillermo Calles perceived as racist stereotyping. In the 1970s, authorities in the municipio of Tecate built a cinema village to attract US directors of westerns, but local talent did not flourish until the video format became an inexpensive alternative.

With support from the Universidad Autónoma de Baja California, bajacalifornianos have produced documentaries on such topics as the Jesuit colonization of the peninsula and the Chinese community of Mexicali, as well as short fictional pieces like Gabriel Trujillo's quasi-biography of the French poet Rimbaud. Since the mid-1980s, the city of Tijuana has occasionally sponsored a film and video festival to reward the efforts of emerging talent.

Dance
Since the mid-20th century, both traditional and experimental dance have prospered on the peninsula, mostly in association with

the universities and the Casa de la Cultura de Baja California. Since 1983 Mexicali's Paralelo 32 dance group, associated with the Universidad Autónoma there, has traveled widely throughout the state and the country to promote their craft.

Theater

Tijuana, Mexicali and La Paz, all with outstanding stage facilities, are the dramatic centers of Baja California. Like cinema, dance and painting, peninsular theater grew with the universities and the Casa de la Cultura; numerous theater companies have offered aspiring actors the opportunity to develop their talents. Groups like the well-established Thalía company of Mexicali and the more experimental Los Desarraigados of Tijuana have performed in Mexico City, the USA and overseas.

Music

Live musical performances take place on the streets and plazas, even on the buses, at any time. Many people play music for a living, including marimba teams with their big wooden xylophones; mariachi groups with violinists, trumpeters, guitarists and a singer, all dressed as *charros* (Mexican cowboys); *norteño* groups with guitar and accordion performing *corridos* (folk ballads); and ragged lone buskers.

In Mexico's thriving popular music industry, corridos are still popular alongside rock and even punk bands, while styles imported from elsewhere in the Americas include tango, bossa nova, salsa and Andean pan-pipe music.

CULTURE

Baja California is both a frontier region and an immigrant zone, and both US and Mexican influences are evident. Despite conscious efforts, the Mexican government never succeeded completely in removing the border region from the US economic sphere, and it now actively encourages US participation and investment through the North American Free Trade Agreement (NAFTA).

Most bajacalifornianos are city dwellers who live near the US border and work in manufacturing, agriculture and service industries like tourism. While remote from mainland Mexico, the peninsula is demonstrably Mexican even though many of its people feel ambivalent toward north-of-the-border consumerism (apparent in the US-style shopping malls in Tijuana and Mexicali), toward the dominance of US television programs and cinema, and toward the necessity of conducting much of its business and commerce in English.

Many residents also feel ambivalent, however, toward what they perceive as an unresponsive state centralized in distant Mexico City; this, in part, explains the recent electoral success of the Partido Acción Nacional (PAN), a challenger to the Partido Revolucionario Institucional (PRI), which has dominated Mexican politics for the past 70 years.

To reinforce the region's Mexican identity, for the benefit of tourists and locals, authorities have built modern cultural centers emphasizing the country's history and diverse cultural traditions, with conspicuous monuments to Mexican national heroes. Such efforts are probably superfluous; despite the pervasiveness of US influence in many spheres, Baja's inhabitants are resolutely Mexican even if they wish to share the wealth – aspiring to buy a Toyota doesn't mean the purchaser wants to be Japanese.

Nationalism

Mexican nationalism's historical roots date from a late 18th-century mestizo culture that developed along an axis running from Puebla to Mexico City and Guadalajara, but the protracted war of independence from Spain and subsequent struggles against Spanish, American and French interlopers intensified nationalist feelings. Foreign economic influence (by the British and Americans at the turn of the century and, more recently, by the Americans again) has also been an issue of contention, especially among radicals and intellectuals. But while Mexicans present a solidary front to foreigners, they also acknowledge their country's shortcomings; the typical Mexican despises corrupt politicians, police and government officials, and resents inefficiency in public organizations. Many if not most Mexicans assume that light-skinned visitors are citizens of the USA, and some resent *gringo* wealth, privilege and past military interventions in Mexican territory. Fair-skinned visitors who are not US citizens may still find themselves called *gringo*, a term that is often but not always pejorative – much depends on context and it can be purely descriptive. Another common term, which seems largely descriptive, is *güero* (blond), which is applied to virtually any fair-skinned foreigner.

Machismo

Machismo, a common trait throughout Latin America, is an exaggerated masculinity designed more to impress other men than women; it is usually innocuous if rather unpleasant, but can on occasion turn to violence. Women, in turn, exaggerate their femininity and defer to male authority in public, but exceptions to both these roles are not unusual. Foreign women, often seen as sexually available by Mexican men, often attract unwelcome attention. Most women find such attention more of a nuisance than a danger. Some women may feel more comfortable traveling with a male companion.

Sport

Baseball While soccer is more important than *béisbol* in Mexico as a whole, baseball is demonstrably more significant in Baja California: small boys, using broken table legs for bats and with balls coming apart at the stitches, play into the twilight on empty sandlots, while nearly every sizable town has a groomed sandlot field or even a stadium. Teams sometimes travel hundreds of miles for weekend games, which are social events as much as they are athletic competitions. While the winter professional leagues are worth watching, the amateurs are, in their own way, equally

interesting, and travelers should not hesitate to stop and watch a Sunday afternoon game.

While Mexican professionals have not matched the success of their Caribbean counterparts in the US major leagues, the Liga Mexicana del Pacífico offers outstanding competition, good facilities and a chance to see young players on the way up. As of the 1993-94 season, Baja California's only team was the Aguilas de Mexicali, where such US stars as Mike Piazza of the Los Angeles Dodgers and John Kruk of the Philadelphia Phillies have sharpened their skills. Mexicali's highly regarded Matías Carrillo, the league's most valuable player in the 1992-93 season, has signed with the Florida Marlins.

The league's other franchises are Los Mochis (Cañeros), Ciudad Obregón (Yaquis), Navojoa (Mayos), Culiacán (Tomateros), Hermosillo (Naranjeros), and Guasave (Algodoneros). Many hope that the Potros de Tijuana will rejoin the league in the near future.

Boxing Of all individual sports, boxing brings out the passion in Mexican audiences, whose identification with individual champions matches their allegiance to their country. When US boxer Frankie Randall won by judges' decision over Mexican super lightweight champion Julio César Chávez in January 1994 for Chávez's first career loss in over 90 matches, one Tijuana daily moaned that 'they robbed us of our hero'.

Corridas de Toros (Bullfighting) To many if not most gringos, bullfighting hardly qualifies as a sport or even entertainment, but even for Mexicans it is more properly a traditional spectacle which lends itself to a variety of symbolic interpretations. In the circular ring, the bull and the matador may be the center of the universe but, symbolism aside, the importance of the bullfight to Mexican society is underscored by the common adage that Mexicans arrive on time for only two events – funerals and bullfights.

The *corrida de toros* (literally, running of the bulls) or *fiesta brava* (wild festival) begins promptly, usually at 4 pm on winter Sundays and at 5 pm in summer. To the sound of music, usually a Spanish *paso doble*, the *matador* in his *traje de luces* (suit of lights) and his assistants *toreros* salute local authorities and the crowd in the traditional *paseíllo* (salutation). After the paseíllo, the first of six bulls is released from its pen for the first of the ritual's three *suertes* (acts) or *tercios* (parts or, more accurately, 'thirds').

The cape-waving toreros tire the bull by luring him around the ring. After a few minutes, two *picadores*, on elaborately padded horses, enter the ring with long lances called *picas* and approach the bull to jab their lances into its shoulders, weakening the bull without killing him. After the picadores leave the ring, the *suerte de banderillas* begins as the toreros attempt to stab three pairs of elongated darts into the bull's shoulders without impaling themselves on his horns. After this, the *suerte de muleta* is the climax in which the matador has exactly 16 minutes to kill the bull. Starting with fancy cape work to tire the animal, the matador then exchanges his large cape for the smaller muleta and takes sword in hand, baiting the bull to charge before delivering the *estocada* (lunge) with his sword. The matador must deliver the estocada between the horns from a position directly in front of the animal.

If the matador succeeds, as is usual, the *estoque* (death) is quick and bloody. As the bull collapses, an assistant dashes into the ring to slice the jugular and chop off the ears and the tail for the matador – should the crowd decide he is deserving (the tail is less frequently given). The dead bull is usually dragged from the ring to be butchered for sale, but in rare instances, a bull that displays *bravura* (that is, shows himself to be a real fighter) may be 'pardoned' to fight another day.

Charreadas (Rodeos) *Charreadas* Mexican rodeos, which frequently take place during fiestas and other special occasions, are particularly popular in northern Mexico, but occur throughout the peninsula. Unlike North American rodeo riders, however, *charros* (Mexican cowboys) rely on style and skill rather than speed and

strength; charreadas are competitive events, but there are no cash prizes and admission fees go to offset the costs of staging the events. Female riders, known as *escaramuzas*, play an important but different role in the charreada. While athletic, this role is ambiguous, derived from aristocratic traditions of equestrianism but also, at least symbolically, from female couriers in the Revolution of 1910. In style, escaramuzas ride sidesaddle – a dubious symbol of feminism.

Readers particularly interested in the subject should obtain Kathleen Mullen Sands' *Charrería Mexicana: An Equestrian Folk Tradition* (University of Arizona Press, Tucson, 1993).

Soccer Mexico has twice hosted the World Cup soccer finals, but on neither occasion did the home side advance beyond the quarter-finals and players lag behind other Latin American countries – the best tend to go to Europe for better competition and higher salaries. Although there's a decent professional league and several impressive stadiums, attendance is low, perhaps because the TV coverage is so extensive. América (of Mexico City) and Guadalajara are among the top clubs. A goal is a *gol*, a ball is a *pelota*, a penalty is a *penalty*, a foul is a *falta* and a referee is an *árbitro*.

Horse Racing Especially popular in border towns, horse races take place at several *hipódromos* (racetracks) around Baja. The peninsula's most famous race course, the Agua Caliente complex in Tijuana, has been closed for some time because of a labor dispute.

Jai Alai This is the Basque game *pelota*, brought to Mexico by the Spanish. Played with a hard ball on a very long court, it's a bit like squash or handball; curved baskets attached to the arm are used instead of racquets. Baja's largest jai alai *frontón* (venue) is in Tijuana; for more information, see the Tijuana section.

Tennis & Golf These sports are popular

among the handful who can afford equipment and fees. Many upscale hotels have tennis courts, and some have golf courses or putting greens, which consume inordinate amounts of precious water in unrelenting desert environments.

RELIGION
Mexicans are a religious people and religion is in evidence everywhere. Baja California lacks the monumental religious architecture of mainland Mexico, but many of the original Jesuit, Franciscan and Dominican missions still survive, at least in ruin; some of these, like Misión Santa Gertrudis in central Baja, are important pilgrimage sites despite their remoteness. Roadside shrines bear witness not just to the victims of traffic accidents but also to important religious figures like the Virgin of Guadalupe. Some of these shrines are intriguing examples of folk art and are well worth a stop on the highway.

Catholicism
Like most Mexicans, the majority of bajacalifornianos are Roman Catholic. Jesuit missionaries pioneered colonization of the peninsula and, in their domain, exercised more authority than the formal institutions of colonial government until their expulsion from the Spanish empire in 1767. Almost everyone from all social strata and racial groups belonged to the Church because, besides salvation, it offered education and other social services.

In the 19th and 20th centuries (until 1940), colonial and republican authorities enacted legislation restricting the wealth and influence of the Church. The Mexican constitutions of 1857 and 1917 included several anticlerical provisions, including obligatory civil marriage (a church marriage has no legal standing), a ban on political activity and property ownership by the clergy, and a requirement that all church buildings first be authorized and approved by the government. (Indeed, all church buildings of every denomination *belong* to the government.) Most of these provisions are still in the constitution today, but are rarely enforced.

Despite tensions with the state, the Church remains influential, especially as a symbol and an institution of social cohesion – since 1531 the dark-skinned Virgin of Guadalupe has been the most binding symbol of all. The appearance of a dark-skinned Virgin to a Christian Indian named Juan Diego, which led to construction of a landmark church, has been regarded as a link between the Catholic and non-Catholic Indian worlds, and a symbol of Mexican nationalism.

Protestantism

While Roman Catholicism is Mexico's dominant religion, evangelical Protestantism is growing here as elsewhere in Latin America. Protestantism dates from the Revolution of 1910, when many Mexicans found it an effective outlet for protesting the influence of the traditional church, but even the smallest communities now often have evangelical churches competing with the Catholics. In the larger cities, like Tijuana, these churches frequently occupy storefronts downtown and in the more established suburbs.

LANGUAGE

Spanish is the official language, but along the border and in tourist areas many bajacalifornianos speak English. In a few isolated communities, Indian languages like Tipai, Pipai and Cocopa are still common, but most speakers are bilingual in Spanish.

Every visitor should make an effort to speak Spanish, whose basic elements are easily acquired. Mexicans will normally be flattered by such attempts, so there is no need to feel self-conscious about vocabulary or pronunciation. There are many common cognates, so if you're stuck, try Hispanicizing an English word – it's unlikely you'll make a truly embarrassing error. Do not, however, admit to being *embarazada* unless you are in fact pregnant!

When asking information, avoid leading questions that may invite incorrect responses. Instead of asking, for example, 'Is this the road to San Borja?' (a question that begs a positive answer whether or not it is the correct road), ask 'Which road goes to San Borja?' – a form that gives the respondent an option. Though it's unlikely that a respondent would purposely lead you astray, a willingness to please can lead to the same results.

Phrasebooks & Dictionaries

Lonely Planet's *Latin American Spanish* phrasebook, by Anna Cody, is a worthwhile addition to your backpack. Another useful resource is the *University of Chicago Spanish-English, English-Spanish Dictionary*, whose small size, light weight and thorough entries make it very convenient for foreign travel.

Pronunciation

Spanish pronunciation is, in general, consistently phonetic. Once you are aware of the basic rules, they should cause little difficulty. Speak slowly to avoid getting tongue-tied until you become confident of your ability.

Letters Pronunciation of the letters *f*, *k*, *l*, *n*, *p q*, *s*, and *t* is virtually identical with English. *Ch*, *ll* (virtually identical to 'y' and *ñ* are separate letters, with separate dictionary entries.

Vowels Spanish vowels are very consistent and have easy English equivalents.

a is like   'a' in 'ma'
e is like   'ay' in 'say'
i is like   'ee' in 'feet'
o is like   'o' in 'go'
u is like   'u' in 'food'. After consonants other than 'q', it is more like the English 'w'.
y is a consonant except when standing alone or appearing at the end of a word, when it is identical to Spanish 'i'.

Consonants Spanish consonants generally resemble their English equivalents, but there are some major exceptions.

b resembles its English equivalent, but is undistinguished from the Spanish 'v'. For clarification, refer to the former as 'b larga', the latter as 'b corta' (the word for the letter itself is pronounced like English 'bay').

c is like the 's' in 'see' before 'e' and 'i', otherwise like English 'k'.

d closely resembles 'th' in 'feather'.

g is like a guttural English 'h' before Spanish 'e' and 'i', otherwise like 'g' in 'go'.

h is invariably silent.

j most closely resembles English 'h', but is slightly more guttural.

ñ is like 'ni' in 'onion'.

r is nearly identical to English except at the beginning of a word, when it is often rolled.

rr is very strongly rolled.

v resembles English, but see 'b' above.

x is normally like 'x' in 'taxi' except for some words in which it resembles Spanish 'j'.

z is like 's' in 'sun'.

Diphthongs Diphthongs are combinations of two vowels which form a single syllable. In Spanish, formation of a diphthong depends on combinations of 'weak' vowels ('i' and 'u') or strong ones ('a', 'e' and 'o'). Two weak vowels or a strong and a weak vowel make a diphthong, but two strong ones are separate syllables.

A good example of two weak vowels forming a diphthong is the word *diurno* ('during the day'). The final syllable of *obligatorio* ('obligatory') is a combination of weak and strong vowels.

Stress Stress, often indicated by visible accents, is very important, since it can change the meaning of words. In general, words ending in vowels or the letters 'n' or 's' have stress on the next-to-last syllable, while those with other endings have stress on the last syllable. Thus *vaca* ('cow') and *caballos* ('horses') both have accents on their next-to-last syllables.

Visible accents, which can occur anywhere in a word, dictate stress over these general rules. Thus *zócalo* (plaza), *América* and *porción* (portion) all have stress on different syllables. When words appear in all capitals, the written accent is generally omitted, but is still pronounced.

Some Useful Phrases

Below are English phrases with useful Spanish equivalents for Mexico, most of which will be understood in other Spanish-speaking countries. Words relating to food and restaurants are covered in the Food section of the Facts for the Visitor chapter.

At the Border

tourist card
    tarjeta de turista
visa
    visado
passport
    pasaporte
identification
    identificación
birth certificate
    certificado de nacimiento
driver's license
    licencia de manejar
car owner's title
    título de propiedad
car registration
    registración
customs
    aduana
immigration
    migración
the border (frontier)
    la frontera

Civilities

Like other Latin Americans, Mexicans are very conscious of civilities in their public behavior. Never, for example, approach a stranger for information without extending a greeting like *buenos días* or *buenas tardes*.

Sir/Mr	*señor*
Madam/Mrs	*señora*
Miss	*señorita*
yes	*sí*
no	*no*
please	*por favor*

thank you	*gracias*
you're welcome	*de nada*
excuse me	*perdóneme*
hello	*hola*
good morning	*buenos días*
good afternoon	*buenas tardes*
good evening	*buenas noches*
good night	*buenas noches*
goodbye	*adiós*
I understand	*Entiendo*
I don't understand	*No entiendo*
Please repeat that.	*Repítelo, por favor.*

I don't speak much Spanish.
   Hablo poco castellano or *español.*

they/them (feminine)	*ellas*
my wife	*mi esposa*
my husband	*mi esposo*
my sister	*mi hermana*
my brother	*mi hermano*
I am. . .	*Soy . . .*
a student	*estudiante*
American	*americano(a)*
citizen of the USA	*estadounidense*
British	*británico(a)*
Canadian	*canadiense*
Australian	*australiano(a)*
German	*alemán (alemana)*
French	*francés (francesa)*

Questions

Where?	*¿Dónde?*
Where is . . . .?	*¿Dónde está?*
Where are. . .?	*¿Dónde están?*
When?	*¿Cuando?*
How?	*¿Cómo?*
How much?	*¿Cuanto?*
How many?	*¿Cuantos?*
I want. . .	*Quiero*
I do not want. . .	*No quiero*
I would like . . .	*Me gustaría*
Give me	*Déme*
What do you want?	*¿Que quiere usted?*
Do you have. . .?	*¿Tiene usted. . .?*
Is/are there?	*¿Hay?*

How much does it cost?
   ¿Cuánto cuesta?

Some Useful Words

and	*y*	to/at	*a*
for	*por, para*	of/from	*de, desde*
in	*en*	with	*con*
without	*sin*	before	*antes*
after	*después*	soon	*pronto*
already	*ya*	now	*ahora*
right away	*ahorita*	here	*aquí*
there	*allí*	bad	*malo*
better	*mejor*	best	*el mejor*
more	*más*	less	*menos*

Family & Friends

I	*yo*
you (familiar)	*tú*
you (formal)	*usted*
you (plural)	*ustedes*
he/him	*él*
she/her	*ella*
we/us	*nosotros*
they/them (masculine and mixed groups)	*ellos*

Transport

airplane	*avión*
train	*tren*
bus	*autobus*
ship	*barco, buque*
car	*auto*
taxi	*taxi*
truck	*camión*
pickup	*camioneta*
bicycle	*bicicleta*
motorcycle	*motocicleta, moto*

I would like a ticket to. . .
   Quiero un boleto a. . .
What's the fare to . . . .?
   ¿Cuánto cuesta hasta. . .?
When does the next plane/train/bus leave for. . .?
   ¿Cuándo sale el próximo avión/tren/autobus para. . .?
first/last/next
   primero/último/próximo
first/second class
   primera/segunda clase
single/return (round trip)
   ida/ida y vuelta
baggage storage
   guardería, equipaje

Around Town

tourist information	*oficina de turismo*
airport	*aeropuerto*
train station	*estación del ferrocarril*
bus station	*estación del autobús, central camionera*
bathing resort	*balneario*
street	*calle*
boulevard	*bulevar*
avenue	*avenida*
road	*camino*
highway	*carretera*
corner (of)	*esquina (de)*

block	*cuadra*
to the left	*a la izquierda*
to the right	*a la derecha*
on the left side	*al lado izquierdo*
on the right side	*al lado derecho*
straight ahead	*adelante*
north	*norte*
south	*sur*
east	*este*
west	*oeste*

Post & Telecommunications

post office	*correo*
letter	*carta*
parcel	*paquete*
postcard	*postal*
airmail	*correo aéreo*
registered mail	*certificado*
stamps	*estampillas, timbres*
telephone office	*caseta de teléfono*
telephone booth	*cabina de teléfono*
local call	*llamada local*
long distance	*larga distancia*
person to person	*persona a persona*
collect call	*por cobrar*
busy	*ocupado*

At the Hotel

guesthouse
    casa de huéspedes (more modest than
    a hotel)
room
    cuarto, habitación
single room
    cuarto solo, cuarto sencillo
double room
    cuarto para dos, cuarto doble
double bed
    cama de matrimonio
with twin beds
    con camas gemelas
with private bath
    con baño
shower
    ducha
hot water
    agua caliente
air-conditioning
    aire acondicionado
blanket
    manta
towel
    toalla
soap
    jabón

toilet paper
    papel higiénico
toothpaste
    pasta dentífrica
dental floss
    hilo dental
What is the price?
    Cuál es el precio?
Does that include taxes?
    ¿Están incluídos los impuestos?
Does that include service?
    ¿Está incluído el servicio?
the bill
    la cuenta
too expensive
    demasiado caro
cheaper
    mas económico
May I see it?
    ¿Puedo verla?
I don't like it
    No me gusta.

Money

money
    dinero
bank
    banco
exchange bureau
    casa de cambio
I want to change money.
    Quiero cambiar dinero.
travelers' checks
    cheques de viajero
What is the exchange rate?
    ¿Que es el tipo de cambio?
Is there a commission?
    ¿Hay comisión?

Driving

gasoline
    gasolina
unleaded
    sin plomo
leaded
    con plomo
Fill the tank, please.
    Llene el tanque, por favor.
How much is gasoline per liter?
    ¿Cuánto cuesta el litro de gasolina?
tire
    llanta
spare tire
    llanta de repuesto
puncture
    agujero

flat tire
  llanta desinflada
My car has broken down.
  Se me ha descompuesto el carro.
I need a tow truck.
  Necesito un remolque.
Is there a garage near here?
  ¿Hay garage cerca?

Time

Telling time is fairly straightforward. Eight o'clock is *las ocho*, while 8:30 is *las ocho y treinta* (literally, 'eight and thirty') or *las ocho y media* ('eight and a half'). However, 7:45 is *las ocho menos quince* (literally, 'eight minus fifteen') or *las ocho menos cuarto* ('eight minus one quarter'). Times are modified by morning *(de la mañana)* or afternoon *(de la tarde)* instead of am or pm. It is also common to use the 24-hour clock, especially with transportation schedules. Midnight is *medianoche* and noon is *mediodía*.

While Mexicans are flexible about time with respect to social occasions like meals or parties, schedules for public events (like bullfights or movies) and transport (like airplanes and buses) should be taken very literally.

Days of the Week

Monday	*lunes*
Tuesday	*martes*
Wednesday	*miércoles*
Thursday	*jueves*
Friday	*viernes*
Saturday	*sábado*
Sunday	*domingo*

Numbers

1	*uno*	2	*dos*
3	*tres*	4	*cuatro*
5	*cinco*	6	*seis*
7	*siete*	8	*ocho*
9	*nueve*	10	*diez*
11	*once*	12	*doce*
13	*trece*	14	*catorce*
15	*quince*	16	*dieciséis*
17	*diecisiete*	18	*dieciocho*

19	*diecinueve*	20	*veinte*
21	*veintiuno*	22	*veintidós*
23	*veintitrés*	24	*veinticuatro*
30	*treinta*	31	*treinta y uno*
32	*treinta y dos*	33	*treinta y tres*
40	*cuarenta*	41	*cuarenta y uno*
42	*cuarenta y dos*	50	*cincuenta*
60	*sesenta*	70	*setenta*
80	*ochenta*	90	*noventa*
100	*cien*	101	*ciento uno*
102	*ciento dos*	110	*ciento diez*
120	*ciento veinte*	130	*ciento treinta*
200	*doscientos*	300	*trescientos*
400	*cuatrocientos*	500	*quinientos*
600	*seiscientos*	700	*setecientos*
800	*ochocientos*	900	*novecientos*
1000	*mil*	1100	*mil cien*
1200	*mil doscientos*	2000	*dos mil*
5000	*cinco mil*	10,000	*diez mil*
50,000	*cincuenta mil*	100,000	*cien mil*
1,000,000	*un millón*		

Toilets

The most common word for 'toilet' is *baño*, but *servicios sanitarios* ('services') is a frequent alternative. Men's toilets will usually bear a descriptive term like *hombres*, *caballeros*, or *varones*. Women's restrooms will say *señoras* or *damas*.

Geographical Terms

The expressions below are among the most common in this book and in Spanish language maps and guides.

bay	*bahía*
bridge	*puente*
cape	*cabo*
farm	*rancho*
island	*isla*
hill	*cerro*
lake	*lago, laguna*
marsh	*estero*
mountain	*cerro*
mountain range	*sierra, cordillera*
national park	*parque nacional*
pass	*paso*
point	*punta*
river	*río*
waterfall	*cascada, catarata, salto*

Facts for the Visitor

VISAS & EMBASSIES
Tourist Cards

By law US and Canadian citizens may cross Mexican land borders for periods of less than 72 hours with barely a glance from immigration officials and no inspection of documents (it is advisable to carry proof of US citizenship or residency in order to return to the USA, however). In practice, oversight is so limited that visitors in the immediate border zone can stay much longer almost without concern, but all visitors regardless of age need a tourist card for travel south beyond Maneadero on the Pacific coast or south beyond San Felipe on the Gulf of California, or to enter Baja by air or sea. A tourist card is also necessary for travel to mainland Mexico.

Tourist cards are issued by Mexican government tourist offices, consulates and embassies, by immigration authorities at border crossings, by airlines flying to Mexico from North America, by automobile clubs in the USA and Canada, and by some travel agencies. At the border crossing itself, *Servicios Migratorios* (Immigration) must validate the card.

Requirements for a validated tourist card at the border depend on nationality:

Travelers born in the USA need proof of US citizenship, preferably a passport or birth certificate. A birth certificate must clearly show official certification, such as an embossed seal.

Naturalized Americans need a photo and proof of US citizenship (a US passport or a certificate of naturalization from the US Immigration & Naturalization Service). Again, a US passport is preferable.

Citizens of Canada need a passport or birth certificate.

For latest requirements for citizens of other countries, contact a Mexican consulate or tourist office. As this book went to press, citizens of Western European countries, except France, needed only a passport. French citizens, Brazilians, South Africans and holders of Hong Kong passports required consular visas.

Tourist card

Visitors who overstay the time limit may be subject to a fine, but few are asked to show their tourist cards when leaving by land. On the other hand, arrivals from the south at Tijuana's Aeropuerto Internacional Abelardo L Rodríguez will probably be asked to show their card before being allowed to claim baggage. Losing your tourist card can mean a tiresome and time-consuming encounter with Mexican bureaucracy to obtain a replacement.

For short-term visitors, a driver's license or identity card issued by a department of motor vehicles is usually accepted as proof of US citizenship, but citizens of other countries must have their passports and appropriate US visas to return to the USA. Be certain of the entry and re-entry status of your US visa before departing for Mexico.

Anyone planning to live in Mexico, or to own or rent a vacation home, needs the multiple-entry, non-immigrant FM-3 visa, which is valid for one year and renewable for another five. Retirees, who are eligible for residence, require a variant on this visa.

Mexican Embassies & Consulates

Australia
> 14 Perth Ave, Yarralumla, Canberra, ACT 2600 (☎ (062) 677-520)
> Consulate: 49 Bay St, Double Bay, Sydney NSW 2028 (☎ (02) 326-1292)

Canada
> 130 Aldrich St, Ottawa KIP 5J4 (☎ (613) 233-8988)
> Consulate: 60 Bloor St W, Suite 203, Toronto, Ontario M4W 3B8 (☎ (416) 922-2718
> Consulate: 310-625 Howe St, Vancouver, British Columbia V6C 2T6 (☎ (604) 684-3547

France
> 9 Rue de Longchamps, 75116 Paris (☎ 4727-4144)
> Consulate: 4 rue Notre-Dame des Victoires, 75002 Paris (☎ 40-20-07-32/3)

Germany
> Oxfordstrasse 12-16, 5300 Bonn 1 (☎ (221) 63-1226) Consulate: Neue Mainzerstrasse 57, 6000 Frankfurt 1 (☎ (069) 23-6134)

UK
> 8 Halkin St, London SW1 (☎ (071) 253-6393)

USA
> Consular Section, 1019 19th St NW, Washington DC 20036 (☎ (202) 293-1710)

> California
> 331 W Second St, Calexico 92231 (☎ (619) 357-3863)
> 2839 Mariposa St, Fresno 93721 (☎ (209) 233-3065)
> 125 E Paseo de la Plaza, Suite 300, Los Angeles 90012 (☎ (213) 624-3261)
> 1506 South St, Sacramento 95814 (☎ (916) 446-4696)
> 588 West Sixth St, San Bernardino 92401 (☎ (714) 888-2500)
> 1549 India St, San Diego 92101 (☎ (619) 231-8414)
> 870 Market St, Suite 528, San Francisco 94102 (☎ (415) 392-5554)
> 380 N First St, Suite 102, San Jose 95112 (☎ (408) 294-3414)

Colorado
> 707 Washington St, Denver 80203 (☎ (303) 830-0523)

Florida
> 780 NW Lejeune Rd, Suite 525, Miami 33126 (☎ (305) 441-8780)

Georgia
> 410 South Tower, One CNN Center, Atlanta 30303 (☎ (404) 688-3258)

Illinois
> 300 N Michigan Ave, 2nd Floor, Chicago 60601 (☎ (312) 855-1380)

Louisiana
> 1140 World Trade Center Bldg, 2 Canal St, New Orleans 70130 (☎ (504) 522-3596)

Massachusetts
> 20 Park Plaza, Suite 321, Statler Bldg, Boston 02116 (☎ (617) 426-4942)

Missouri
> 823 Walnut St, Kansas City 64106 (☎ (816) 421-5956)
> 1015 Locust St, St Louis 63101 (☎ (314) 436-3233)

New Mexico
> Western Bank Bldg, 401 Fifth St NW, Albuquerque 87102 (☎ (505) 247-2139)

New York
> 8 East 41st St, New York 10017 (☎ (212) 689-0456)

Pennsylvania
> Independence Mall E, 575 Bourse Building, Philadelphia 19106 (☎ (215) 922-4262)

Texas
> 200 E Sixth St, Suite 200, Hannig Row Bldg, Austin 78701 (☎ (512) 478-2300)
> Elizabeth & E Seventh Sts, Brownsville 78520 (☎ (512) 542-4431)
> 800 North Shoreline, One Shoreline Plaza, 410 North Tower, Corpus Christi 78401 (☎ (512) 882-3375)
> 1349 Empire Central, No 100, Dallas 75247 (☎ (214) 630-7341)
> 1010 South Main St, Del Rio 78840 (☎ (512) 775-2352)
> 140 Adams St, Eagle Pass 78852 (☎ (512) 773-9255)

910 E San Antonio St, PO Box 812, El Paso 79901 (☎ (915) 533-3644)

4200 Montrose Blvd, Suite 120, Houston 77006 (☎ (713) 524-4861)

1612 Farragut St, Laredo 78040 (☎ (512) 723-6360)

1220 Broadway Ave, Lubbock 79401 (☎ (806) 765-8816)

1418 Beech St, No 102-104, McAllen 78501 (☎ (512) 686-0243)

127 Navarro St, San Antonio 78205 (☎ (512) 227-9145)

Washington

1411 Fourth Ave, Fourth Avenue Bldg, Seattle 98101 (☎ (206) 682-8996)

Foreign Consulates in Baja California

As might be expected, the USA maintains a greater diplomatic presence in Baja than any foreign country, with a large consulate in Tijuana and a smaller one in Cabo San Lucas. A few other countries also have representation in Tijuana; for details, see individual city entries.

DOCUMENTS

Every visitor beyond the immediate border area should carry a valid passport and a Mexican government tourist card at all times; see the Visas & Embassies section above for details. Motorists must have a valid driver's license, car registration papers and a temporary import permit for each vehicle (including motorcycles and boats), obtainable at the border. These requirements are in flux, so verify information before going.

Car Permits

For travel in only Baja California, the tourist card and the car permit are identical, and no bond or credit card deposit is required, even for additional vehicles such as a boat/trailer or motorcycle. Travelers intending to continue to mainland Mexico, however, must either post a bond for approximately one-half the value of the vehicle or else leave a nonrefundable deposit of US$10 on Visa or MasterCard. Mexican customs authorities instituted this bothersome requirement, which has drawn considerable criticism and may be changed, to prevent the illegal sale of US automobiles in Mexico.

Motorists leaving a credit card deposit may exit at any border crossing, but those leaving a bond must exit by the same border crossing at which they entered in order to redeem their bond. Do not neglect to check in with Mexican authorities on returning to the USA or your credit card may be charged for the entire value of your car – which is much higher in Mexico than in the USA.

Motorists with a clear title to their automobile or other vehicle, including boat or motorcycle, will have no difficulty obtaining a vehicle permit, but no individual may enter mainland Mexico with more than one such vehicle, even if the vehicle is in his or her name. However, with the owner's notarized permission, an accompanying passenger may obtain a permit for an additional vehicle. Drivers of vehicles they do not own, such as rental cars or those with a bank lien, require express permission of the rental company or the legal owner. This is advisable even for visitors to Baja California, where customs inspections are less stringent.

According to tourist authorities, motorists may now obtain mainland car permits at ferry terminals in Santa Rosalía and La Paz (Pichilingue), but it is still preferable to do so at the border; if regulations change, it would be a major inconvenience to have to return all the way to Tijuana or Mexicali for a permit.

Minors

Every year numerous parents run away to Mexico with their children because of legal disputes with the child's other parent in the USA. For this reason, Mexican authorities require a notarized 'Permission for a Minor to Travel in Mexico', signed by both parents, which permits children below the age of 18 to enter the country accompanied by one parent (minors traveling with both parents do not require this permission). The form is available from Mexican government tourist offices and from the California State Automobile Association (CSAA).

Fishing

Anglers 16 years or older need fishing licenses, and those importing boats need boat licenses as well. For more information, see the entries under Activities in this chapter.

Pet Permits

Travelers entering Mexico with dogs or cats must have proof of vaccination (issued within three days of crossing the border) against rabies and other contagious diseases; the proof must also be approved by the US Department of Agriculture and the Mexican Consulate (which charges US$16 for the privilege). It is also a good idea to carry an International Health Certificate, obtainable from any veterinarian.

Before taking a pet to Mexico, confirm re-importation requirements for the USA.

CUSTOMS

Since Baja is a duty-free zone, customs inspectors seldom hassle foreign visitors on entry. Firearms are prohibited, except during hunting season; acquire hunting and firearms permits from Mexican consulates. If carrying foreign-manufactured items like cameras, radios and televisions into Baja from the USA, it's a good idea to register them with US Customs before crossing the border, though registration is usually unnecessary if you have the original receipts for the items.

Each US resident returning to the USA from Baja or elsewhere in Mexico may bring in duty-free items with a total retail value up to US$400, for personal use only and not for resale. The exemption may only be used once in any 30-day period, but over 2700 items, including handicrafts, are exempt from these limits.

Limits on the importation of liquor are stricter. Adult US residents (21 years or older) crossing the California border by car or on foot may bring only one liter of hard liquor, wine or beer into mainland California every 30 days. Residents returning to mainland California by bus, taxi or airplane may bring in one liter of alcohol duty free; additional alcoholic beverages are subject to duty, but may enter in any quantity considered reasonable for personal use. Visitors to northeastern Baja California can avoid mainland California's more stringent liquor requirements by returning to the USA at San Luis Río Colorado on the Sonora-Arizona border.

There is a complex list of regulations for agricultural products, but in general plants, seeds and soil, pork and poultry, live birds and straw are prohibited. Most fruits and vegetables, except for avocados, sugarcane, potatoes, sweet potatoes, and yams are permitted. For more detailed information, ask at US Customs for the flyer 'Mexican Border: US Agricultural Quarantine Information'.

MONEY

Both Mexican pesos and US dollars are commonly used in Baja, but US dollars may not be accepted in some small towns and villages. The same symbol ($) is used for both currencies; restaurants, hotels, gas stations and other establishments which deal with North Americans will put *Dlls* or *m/n* after prices to indicate whether they are US dollars or *moneda nacional* (national money), respectively.

Under the currency reform of 1993, the Mexican government slashed three zeros off the hyperinflated peso (M$) of the 1980s to create the new peso (N$). The old system has not entirely disappeared, as coins of M$50, M$100, M$200, M$500 and M$1000 pesos remain in circulation; these are now worth N$0.05, N$0.10, N$0.20, N$0.50 and N$1 respectively. New, smaller coins have been minted in these latter denominations and are gradually replacing the former. Coins of N$2, N$5 and N$10 have also entered into circulation.

Under the old system, bills of M$2000, M$5000, M$10,000, M$20,000, M$50,000 and M$100,000 remain in circulation. New bill denominations are N$10, N$20, N$50 and N$100. Portraits are identical on corresponding denominations: the N$10 (formerly M$10,000) note features a portrait of President Lázaro Cárdenas; the N$20 (formerly M$20,000) shows Andrés Quintana Roo; the N$50 (formerly M$50,000) displays Cuauhtémoc, the last Aztec emperor; and the N$100 (formerly M$100,000) has the figure of former President Plutarco Elías Calles.

Coins and bills of the new and old system will continue to circulate side-by-side for some years, and Mexicans commonly figure prices under the old system, so don't be surprised if your bill for filling the gas tank comes to $50,000 (m/n) or more. The old and new bills are identical except for their numbers; this briefly causes confusion among visitors, who soon learn to ignore or add three zeros, depending on what happens to be in their wallets.

Exchange Rates
Between 1980 and 1993, the peso's value declined from US$1=M$22 to more than US$1=M$3100, at which point the currency reform struck three zeros from the peso, to the relief of everyone with pocket calculators. The exchange rate (US$1= N$3.38) has varied little over the past three years.

Money can be exchanged at banks, hotels and *casas de cambio* (exchange houses). Banks and cambios offer virtually identical rates and may pay less for cash than travelers' checks. Cambios are usually quicker and less bureaucratic than banks.

Banks rarely charge commissions, but may only change a certain minimum amount of foreign currency. Some cambios, mostly in the border towns on the US side, may charge a commission; those in San Ysidro (across the border from Tijuana) are notorious for cheap tricks like charging 'no commission' for pesos into dollars, but a substantial commission for dollars into pesos.

Hotels, especially at the top end of the scale, offer poor rates and often charge commissions as well.

Costs
All prices listed in this book are in US dollars, but are subject to change. Nearly everyone believes that Mexican prices are very high compared to the country's economic productivity, and there is speculation that ratification of the North American Free Trade Agreement may lead to devaluation of the peso, which in turn may lead to price fluctuations. On the other hand, the stable exchange rate's contribution to controlling inflation is a tremendous disincentive to any change in foreign exchange policies. Recent political events, most notably the Indian uprising in Chiapas and the assassination of PRI presidential candidate Luis Donaldo Colosio, may signal a period of political and, consequently, economic instability.

Food and accommodation cost more in Baja California than in the rest of Mexico, and only slightly less than in the USA. Prices are highest near the border and in tourist centers like La Paz and Cabo San Lucas. By buying food from fruit and vegetable markets or corner food stands, it is possible to eat more cheaply, but prices at better restaurants equal or even exceed those north of the border.

Accommodation is relatively costly, and it's hard to find a good double room for less than US$25 per night. Camping is the cheapest way to go – you can camp cheaply in many RV parks and for free on almost any beach.

Tipping
In restaurants, it is customary to tip about 10% of the bill. In general, waiters are poorly paid, so if you can afford to eat out, you can afford to tip. Even a small *propina* will be appreciated. Taxi drivers do not require tips, although you may round off the fare for convenience.

Bargaining
Bargaining is a way of life in Mexico, but less so in Baja than in other parts of the country. In some instances, artisan's souvenirs are open to negotiation, as are cab fares, but the market-style haggling so common in mainland Mexico is unusual.

Student Discounts
Student discounts are almost unknown.

Baja's few museums offer very small discounts on already low admission fees to students under 26 who hold a card from either the Servicio Educativo de Turismo de los Estudiantes y la Juventud de México (SETEJ) or Consejo Nacional de Recursos para la Atención de la Juventud (CREA). These cards also entitle holders to youth hostel membership and lower hostel rates. CREA cards can be obtained at their facilities in La Paz and Tijuana (CREA in Tijuana no longer functions as a youth hostel).

Both CREA and SETEJ occasionally conduct group tours of Baja and other parts of Mexico. For more information, contact the Asociación Mexicana de Albergues de la Juventud (☎ 525-2548, 525-2974), Glorieta del Metro Insurgentes, Local CC-11, Colonia Juárez, México DF 06600.

Consumer Taxes
Hotel taxes in Baja range as high as 15% for luxury lodgings, but generally do not apply to budget accommodation. Before taking a room, ask whether the price includes taxes.

WHEN TO GO
For the most part, Baja California is a winter playground whose tropical and subtropical climates appeal to escapees from the frozen north; temperatures in excess of 110° F (43°C) discourage summer visitors on the Gulf of California and the Cape Region, but mild weather on the Pacific coast of northern Baja makes it very pleasant at that time. During spring break, US university students jam Pacific and Gulf resorts like Ensenada and San Felipe – making these prime places to avoid unless you're one of the revelers. Since not all universities have identical vacation periods, this congestion can go on for weeks in March and April.

However, visitors with special interests, such as wildlife viewing, may find other seasons rewarding. The bird colonies of the Midriff Islands, from Bahía de Los Angeles south, are most active in the relatively warm month of May, and the desert big-horn sheep is easiest to spot in the blistering summer heat of the eastern escarpment of the Sierras Juárez and San Pedro Mártir, where it must frequent the few reliable water holes.

WHAT TO BRING
Clothing in Baja resembles clothing in southern mainland California – cool and casual. Men can wear jeans, shorts, tennis shoes, sandals, T-shirts or just about anything else, especially on the beach. Ties and jackets are only obligatory in the fanciest restaurants. Women can dress similarly, but may prefer conservative clothing in town or if traveling alone.

Sweaters and light jackets are often necessary in winter but only occasionally in summer. A light rain jacket, preferably a loose-fitting rain poncho, can be useful; winter storms can hit northwestern Baja hard even though it's rarely cold by continental standards, while tropical downpours sometimes happen in southern Baja's Cape Region, south of La Paz.

If you're planning to drive extensively, to camp in trailer parks or elsewhere, to backpack in the countryside or to go boating on the Gulf, consider acquiring Carl Franz's *Camping in Mexico* and *RV Camping in Mexico* (John Muir Publications, PO Box 613, Santa Fe, New Mexico 87504).

Toiletries like shampoo, shaving cream, razors, soap, dental floss and toothpaste are readily available, but bring your own contact lens solution, tampons, contraceptives and deodorant. Other desirable items include sunglasses, a flashlight (torch), a baseball cap or wide-brimmed hat, a disposable lighter, a pocket knife, a couple yards of cord, diving or snorkeling equipment, fishing equipment, sunscreen, a small sewing kit, a money belt or pouch, a small Spanish-English dictionary and lip balm.

TOURIST OFFICES
Local Tourist Offices
The federal government agency Fonatur runs the offices at Nopoló and San José, but

their sole function is to disseminate information about luxury tourist resorts at Nopoló and Los Cabos (San José del Cabo and Cabo San Lucas) and promote their development.

Secretaría de Turismo (SECTUR) offices in Tijuana, Tecate, Mexicali, Rosarito, San Felipe, Ensenada and La Paz are affiliated with either Baja California (northern Baja) or Baja California Sur (southern Baja). The staff at all these offices are helpful in providing information about those cities and any other place in Baja, and may also help make hotel reservations throughout the peninsula. They also sponsor honorary delegations in a few smaller towns, like San Quintín.

Local offices of the Cámara Nacional de Comercio (CANACO, National Chamber of Commerce) and the Comité de Turismo y Convenciones (COTUCO, Committee on Tourism & Conventions) can be found in Tijuana, Ensenada, Tecate, Mexicali, and San José del Cabo. The Ensenada office is among the best organized sources of information in Baja, while those in Tecate and Mexicali are helpful but have more limited resources.

Foreign Reps

One of the most accessible sources of information about Baja California is the Tijuana Baja Information Center (☎ (619) 298-4105; (800) 522-1516 toll-free), Suite 202, 7860 Mission Center Court, San Diego, California 92108. Providing information about Tijuana is their main function, but the staff also answers questions about the rest of Baja, makes reservations for hotels and Aero California flights, and issues insurance policies. However, they are unprepared and even reluctant to provide budget travel information.

Mexican government tourist offices outside Mexico know little about Baja California, but they do have the latest information on matters like tourist card requirements, and can also issue tourist cards and automobile permits. Mexican government tourist offices abroad include:

Canada
    1 Place Ville Marie, Suite 2409, Montreal, Quebec M5H 3M7 (☎ (514) 871-1052)
    181 University Ave, Suite 1112, Toronto, Ontario M4W 3E2 (☎ (416) 364-2455)
France
    34 Avenue George V, 75008 Paris (☎ (1) 47-20-69-07)
Germany
    Wiesenhüttenplatz 26, D6000, Frankfurt-Am-Main 1 (☎ (69) 25-3413)
Italy
    Via Barberini No 3, 00187 Rome (☎ (6) 474-2986)
Japan
    2-15-2 Nagata-Cho, Chiyoda-Ku, Tokyo 100 (☎ 580-2961)
Spain
    Calle de Velázquez 126, Madrid 28006 (☎ (1) 261-1827)
UK
    7 Cork St, London W1X 1PB (☎ (071) 734-1058)
USA
    10100 Santa Monica Blvd, Suite 2204, Los Angeles, California 90067 (☎ (310) 203-8151)
    Two Illinois Center, 233 N Michigan Ave, Suite 1413, Chicago, Illinois 60601 (☎ (312) 565-2785)
    405 Park Ave, Suite 1002, New York, New York 10022 (☎ (212) 755-7261)
    2707 North Loop West, Suite 450, Houston, Texas 77008 (☎ (713) 880-5153)
    1615 L St NW, Suite 430, Washington, DC 20036 (☎ (202) 659-8730)

Tourist Publications

The *Baja Times* and the *Baja Sun* are English-language publicity rags distributed free at hotels, restaurants, souvenir shops and tourist offices throughout Baja. Though both provide information about events, restaurants and tourist-related news in northern Baja, they are probably most useful for their discount coupons for restaurants and bars. *Baja Visitor* is a *Baja Sun* clone newsletter that appears in several different giveaway versions that cover Tijuana, Mexicali, Ensenada, San Quintín, and San Felipe.

Other sources of current information include: newsletters published by Sanborn's Mexico Club (Sanborn's Insurance,

PO Box 310, McAllen, Texas 78502) and distributed at most of their border offices; the Mexico West Travel Club (PO Box 1646, Bonita, California 92002); and *Los Cabos News*, a newsletter focussing on southern Baja, published by Vagabundos del Mar (PO Box 824, Isleton, California 95641). A new source of information is the Discover Baja Travel Club (☎ (619) 275-4225, 3065 Clairemont Drive, San Diego, California 92117), which publishes perhaps the highest quality newsletter of any such organization.

In the Los Cabos-La Paz region, several other publications (wholly or partially in English) provide information useful to travelers. These are mostly free and available in restaurants and hotel lobbies; see the Cabo San Lucas entry for more information.

BUSINESS HOURS & HOLIDAYS
Most major national and Catholic holidays are observed throughout Baja California, but special festivities and fairs such as Carnaval and patron saints' days are usually only celebrated in major towns and cities. Additional events that take place only in Ensenada are listed in the Ensenada section of the Tijuana & the Pacific Coast chapter.

Travelers expecting to stay at hotels in Tijuana, Tecate, San Felipe, Ensenada, Mulegé, La Paz or Los Cabos during religious holidays, special fairs or US holidays such as Thanksgiving and Memorial Day should make reservations.

Businesses are generally open weekdays 9 am to 2 pm and 4 to 7 pm. Banking hours are 9 am to 1:30 pm weekdays. Siesta, or break time, is between 2 and 4 pm.

Banks, post offices and government offices are closed on most holidays, celebrations and events listed below.

1 January
    Año Nuevo (New Year's Day)
5 February
    Día de la Constitución (Constitution Day)
24 February
    Día de la Bandera (Flag Day)
Late February to early March
    Carnaval (Carnival) – celebrated in Ense-

nada and La Paz, usually the week before Lent, with parades, music, food and fireworks
2 March
    Natalicio de Juárez (Benito Juárez' Birthday)
19 March
    Día del Señor San José (St Joseph's Day) – Bajacalifornios celebrate the festival of St Joseph, the patron saint of San José del Cabo, with street dances, horse races, cockfights, food fairs and fireworks.
21 March
    Cumpleaños de Juárez (Birthday of President Benito Juárez)
March/April
    Semana Santa (Holy Week) – Starting on Palm Sunday, a week before Easter, Holy Week is celebrated in every church in Baja California on variable dates in March and April; some areas become so overrun that gasoline may be rationed.
1 May
    Día del Obrero (Labor Day)
5 May
    Cinco de Mayo – anniversary of victory over the French at Puebla (1862)
10 May
    Día de la Madre (Mother's Day)
1 June
    Día de la Armada (Navy Day)
8 September
    Día de Nuestra Señora de Loreto (Our Lady of Loreto) – festival of founding of Loreto
15 to 16 September
    Día de la Independencia – Commemoration of Mexican independence from Spain (1821). The biggest celebrations take place in Tijuana and La Paz with fireworks, horse races, folk dances and mariachi bands.
12 October
    Día de la Raza (Columbus Day) – Mexican holiday celebrating Spanish heritage of the country
1 to 2 November
    Todos Santos (Day of the Dead) – Festivities take place throughout Baja, but are especially colorful in La Paz. Breads and sweets made to resemble human skeletons are sold in almost every market and bakery, and papiermâché skeletons and skulls appear everywhere.
20 November
    Día de La Revolución (Anniversary of the Revolution of 1910)
12 December
    Día de Nuestra Señora de Guadalupe (Festi-

val of Our Lady of Guadalupe) – Tecate hosts one of the most interesting celebrations of this day. Groups come from all over Baja to display their costumes and dancing, while Mexicali holds colorful nightly processions from the first of the month.

25 December

Navidad (Christmas Day) – Marks the end of a week of *posadas*, parades of costumed children re-enacting the journey of Mary and Joseph to Bethlehem. The children also celebrate by breaking a *piñata* (a papier-mâché animal) full of candy.

CULTURAL EVENTS

While not official holidays, events like the Baja 1000 (an annual off-road motor race) are good excuses to celebrate. For details, see individual city entries.

POST & TELECOMMUNICATIONS

The Servicio Postal Mexicano (the formal name for Mexico's national postal service) sells postage stamps and sends and receives mail at every *oficina de correos* (post office) in Baja California. Its snappy new logo is no reflection of its efficiency – letters from Tijuana, for instance, arrive in San Diego only after passing through Mexico City.

Sending Mail

Airmail letters to North and Central America cost about US$0.30, to Europe US$0.50 and to Australasia US$0.60. Service is not always dependable – an airmail letter from Cabo San Lucas to Los Angeles, via Mexico City, may take anywhere from four days to a fortnight. Mail to Europe takes one to three weeks.

When sending a parcel or letter via airmail, mark it conspicuously with the phrase 'Por Avión'. To guarantee that it will arrive, send it registered or, better yet, entrust it to a private service like UPS or Federal Express.

Receiving Mail

Receiving mail can be somewhat tricky. You can send or receive letters and packages care of a post office if the letter or package is addressed as follows:

John SMITH (capitalize surname)
Lista de Correos
Town/City Name, State (Baja California or Baja
California Sur) 00000 (postal code if known)
MÉXICO

When the letter arrives at the locale's central post office, the postmaster places it on an alphabetical list that is updated daily. Ask the sender to mark the letter or package *favor de retener hasta llegada* ('please hold until arrival'); otherwise, it may be returned to sender after 15 days.

If expected correspondence does not arrive, ask the clerk to check under every possible combination of your initials, even 'M' (for Mr, Ms, etc). There may be particular confusion if correspondents use your middle name, since Mexicans use both paternal and maternal surnames for identification, with the former listed first. Thus a letter to Mexican 'Carlos Salinas de Gortari' will be found under 'S' rather than 'G', while a letter to North American 'William Jefferson Clinton' may be found under 'J' even though 'Clinton' is the proper surname.

Telephone

Local and domestic long-distance calls are moderately priced and easy to place from a *caseta de teléfono*, a telephone office which is usually part of a shop or pharmacy, which is easily identified by its telephone-shaped symbol. Except for large border cities like Tijuana and Mexicali, public telephones are few, frequently out of order and often located at the noisiest intersections.

From standard telephones, dial 02 for domestic long distance; 04 for information; and 09 for international service. From the newer Larga Distancia Automática (Automatic Long Distance, or 'Ladatel') phones, dial 91 for domestic long distance, 95 for the USA and Canada, 96 for the USA and Canada collect or person-to-person, and 98 for other countries. After dialing that number, dial the area code and number within the country you're calling.

International calls can still be time-consuming, but services have improved and some formerly isolated locations, such as Bahía de Los Angeles, now have telephone service. Approximate rates are US$1.20 per minute to the USA, US$6 per minute to Western Europe. Collect or credit card calls are generally cheaper, but not all offices permit collect calls; those which do usually levy a surcharge of up to US$2, so truly destitute travelers will not be able to place a call. The best sites to place long-distance calls are the casetas or *cabinas* at larger bus terminals, like Tijuana's Central Camionera, where bank cards like Visa may be used to charge the call.

Mexico's newly privatized telephone system is being revamped, with fiber-optic lines replacing copper wire and line-microwave systems. At first, these improvements will affect only long-distance services, but improvements to local lines should take place in the near future.

Fax & Telegraph

Most larger post offices offer fax services, as do telegraph offices, major hotels, larger bus terminals and private operators. Telégrafos Nacionales sends cables both within Mexico and overseas; charges depend on whether the telegram is *ordinario*, *urgente* or *extra urgente*.

TIME

The northern State of Baja California is on Pacific Standard Time (PST), while Baja California Sur is on Mountain Standard Time (MST), which is one hour ahead of PST. In summer, PST is moved ahead one hour for Pacific Daylight Time (PDT) and thus becomes the same as MST. Northern Baja is always on the same time as the US state of California. PST is eight hours behind GMT/UTC, while MST is seven hours behind GMT/UTC.

ELECTRICITY

Electrical current, plugs and sockets in Mexico are the same as in the USA and Canada: 110 volts, 60 cycles and flat, two-prong plugs.

LAUNDRY

US-style laundromats are becoming more common, at least in larger cities and tourist destinations; travelers can either do the wash themselves or leave it for the staff for a nominal additional charge. Figure about US$3 to US$4 per load.

WEIGHTS & MEASURES

In Mexico, the metric system is official, but in Baja California the colloquial use of US measures, especially miles and gallons, is very widespread. Because so many people drive to Baja California in cars manufactured north of the border whose odometers read in miles, this book uses both miles and km to indicate distance. Landmarks along the Transpeninsular and other main roads may be indicated by the appropriate roadside km marker (placed by the Mexican highway department).

Temperatures, weights and liquid measures are also given in both US measures and their metric equivalents. See also the conversion table at the back of this book for further information.

BOOKS

The available books on Baja are quite numerous, so readers can afford to be selective. From the early Jesuit journals to the latest guidebook, quality varies, but for a more enjoyable experience, learn before you go.

Prehistory Baja

California's cave paintings have attracted the attention of both popular and academic writers; a basic overview is Campbell Grant's *Rock Art of Baja California* (Dawson's Bookshop, Los Angeles, 1974), which also reproduces French explorer Léon Diguet's 'Notes on the Pictographs of Baja California', dating from 1895.

Harry Crosby's *Cave Paintings of Baja California* (Copley Books, 1975) is a more detailed effort by an enthusiastic aficionado which contains excellent color and B&W photographs, plus several fairly general maps. Clement Meighan's and V L Pontoni's *Seven Rock Art Sites in Baja California* (Ballena Press, Socorro, New Mexico, 1978) is an edited collection of systematic archaeological assessments of specific sites. Readers who understand Spanish might acquire María del Pilar Casado's & Lorena Mirambell's *El Arte Rupestre de México* (México D F, INAH, 1990), which contains a major chapter on Baja California.

General History
Available in paperback, Michael C Meyer & William L Sherman's *The Course of Mexican History* (Oxford, 1986) is one of the best general accounts of Mexican history and society.

For a general introduction to Baja, see W W Johnson's *Baja California* (Time-Life Books, New York, 1972). Alexander S Taylor, a 19th-century court clerk, reporter and historian, wrote *A Historical Summary of Baja California* (Socio-Technical Books, Pasadena, California, 1971) to summarize the history of Baja 'from its discovery in 1532 to 1867'.

Colonial Baja & the Missions
Several classic studies of colonial Baja make fascinating reading, and are still available in university libraries and occasionally in specialist bookshops. Among them are Peveril Meigs's *The Dominican Mission Frontier of Lower California* (University of California, 1935), and Homer Aschmann's *The Central Desert of Baja California: Demography and Ecology* (University of California, 1959), both of which focus on pre-Columbian peoples and their contact with the missions. For the perspective of an early Jesuit father, obtain Johann Jakob Baegert's *Observations in Lower California* (University of California, 1952; reprinted 1979), originally published in Germany in 1771, only three years after the Jesuits' expulsion from the peninsula. A new and comprehensive history of early colonial Baja is Crosby's *Antigua California: Mission and Colony on the Peninsular Frontier, 1697-1768* (University of New Mexico Press, Albuquerque, 1994).

On the subject of piracy and the Manila galleons, see Peter Gerhard's succinct and readable *Pirates of the Pacific, 1575-1742* (University of Nebraska Press, 1990).

Post-Independence Baja
William Walker's adventures in Baja (and elsewhere) are the subject of Albert Carr's *The World of William Walker* (Harper & Row, New York, 1963). Views of the peninsula in the late 19th century are apparent in Edward Nelson's *Lower California and Its Natural Resources* (Manessier Publishing, Riverside, California, first published 1892, reprinted 1966).

Modern History
James Blaisdell's *The Desert Revolution* (University of Wisconsin, 1962) tells the story of Ricardo Flores Magón's quixotic attempt to influence the Mexican revolution from the Baja periphery. James Sandos's *Rebellion in the Borderlands: Anarchism and the Plan of San Diego, 1904-1923* (University of Oklahoma Press, 1992) provides more detail on the Magonista movement and some of its offshoots.

Norris Hundley's *Dividing the Waters* (University of California, 1966) details the controversy over the Colorado River delta between the US and Mexico.

Contemporary Baja & the Borderlands
In recent years, the US-Mexico borderlands have drawn an extraordinary amount of attention from both academic and popular writers. This section presents both general books on the region and others dealing specifically with Baja California.

Ted Conover's *Coyotes* (Vintage, New York, 1987) is a compellingly readable account of undocumented immigrants by a writer who befriended Mexican workers while picking fruit with them in the orchards of Arizona and Florida, lived among them in their own country, and accompanied them across the desert border despite concerns about his (and their) personal safety at the hands of the police and other unsavory characters in the business of illegal transport. He concludes that 'the majority (of laborers) would make good neighbors; I'd welcome them as mine'. Another recent book on similar themes is Luis Alberto Urrea's grim but fascinating *Across the Line: Life and Hard Times on the Mexican Border* (Anchor Books, New York, 1993), which focuses on the problems of immigrants and shantytowns in a Tijuana which very few tourists ever see.

Rubén Martínez's *The Other Side* (Vintage, New York, 1993) is a collection of essays, plus a few poems, on Mexican and Mexican-American culture which includes a lengthy piece on Tijuana. *Troublesome Border* (University of Arizona, 1988), by Oscar Martínez, deals with current borderlands issues like population growth, economic development and ecology, and international migration.

Mexican Border Cities (University of Arizona, 1993), by Daniel Arreola & James Curtis, analyzes urban economic and cultural development south of the border, with illuminating essays on topics like the infamous *zonas de tolerancia* of sex, drink and gambling. Less rigorously academic, but perhaps more accessible, is Alan Weisman's *La Frontera: The United States Border with Mexico* (University of Arizona, 1986), which explores all aspects of border life and culture, from the shining skyscrapers of San Diego and Tijuana to poverty-stricken shantytowns and the seedy zona of Nuevo Laredo. Exceptional B&W photos by Jay Dusard further enhance an often eloquent text.

Edited by Stanley Ross, *Views across the Border* (University of New Mexico Press, 1978) is a worthwhile collection of essays on borderlands culture, politics, economics and ecology by leading US and Mexican academics and intellectuals. Lawrence Herzog's *Where North Meets South* (University of Texas Press, 1990) is a more unified account of the region by a single author with considerable experience in the area. Abraham F Lowenthal's & Katrina Burgess' *The California-Mexico Connection* (Stanford University Press, 1993), an edited collection of essays, analyzes many aspects of the intertwined eco-

nomic, social and cultural relations between mainland California and its neighbor to the south.

Travel Literature

John Steinbeck's classic combination of travelogue and natural history essay, *The Log from the Sea of Cortez* (Penguin, New York, 1977), was one of the earliest studies of marine life in the Gulf of California. Steinbeck's biologist companion, Ed Ricketts, was the model for Doc in the novelist's famous *Cannery Row*.

The late Ray Cannon's *The Sea of Cortez* (Lane Books, Menlo Park, California, 1966) is a coffee-table format book, with first-rate photos, published by a lifelong Baja enthusiast. Literary naturalist Joseph Wood Krutch wrote *The Forgotten Peninsula* (University of Arizona, 1988; originally published in 1962), recently reissued in paperback, about his own travels in pre-Transpeninsular Baja.

Graham Mackintosh's self-published *Into a Desert Place*, a narrative of his two-year, 3000-mile (5000-km) walk around the Baja coast, has been called 'the best Baja book ever published' *(Western Outdoor News)* 'one of the finest pieces of travel writing of recent times' *(Irish Independent)*, and 'one of the most grueling and challenging solo bipedal treks ever taken' (Sierra Club). Mackintosh lived off the desert and the sea, eating rattlesnakes, cacti and abalone, and drinking distilled salt water; this hardback book is available for US$24.95, including postage and handling, from Graham Mackintosh, PO Box 1196, Idyllwild, California 92349.

General Interest & Guidebooks

Carl Franz's *The People's Guide to Mexico* (John Muir Publications, Santa Fe, New Mexico, 1992) is the 9th edition of an irreverent classic whose attitude is summarized by the motto 'Wherever you go, there you are'. It is an essential complement to books like this one, which deal more with specific destinations.

If you are traveling further afield Lonely Planet also has guidebooks to Mexico, Costa Rica, Guatemala, Yucatan & Belize, and a shoestring guide to Central America.

The annual *Mexico & Central America Handbook* (Trade & Travel Publications, Bath, England) is a clone of the well-established *South American Handbook* and contains a chapter on Baja California. Joe Cummings' unrelated *Baja Handbook* (Moon Publications, Chico, California, 1992) is a comprehensive guide to the peninsula.

Long out of print but still available from specialist bookshops, is Peter Gerhard & Howard Gulick's informed and intelligent *Lower California Guidebook* (Arthur H Clark Company, Glendale, California, 1962). It's a classic guide to driving the peninsula prior to the completion of the Transpeninsular, and it's still a worthwhile companion on the road.

Intended primarily for motorists, the Automobile Club of Southern California's *Baja California* is available free to members of the club and its affiliates, but is also available in commercial bookshops for US$7.95. A more recent and valuable entry, well worth acquiring, is John Minch & Thomas Leslie's *The Baja Highway* (John Minch & Associates, San Juan Capistrano, California, 1991), which logs Baja's main roads with exceptionally informative commentary on the geographical, geological and biological features along the way. Its shortcomings are rather mediocre sketches of landforms and animals, the absence of a glossary for terms which may be unfamiliar to general audiences and the absence of a bibliography (despite bibliographical references in the text).

For a variety of outdoor activities, easily the best choice is Walt Peterson's *The Baja Adventure Book* (Wilderness Press, Berkeley, California, 1992), which covers fishing, boating, kayaking, rock climbing, backpacking, wind surfing and many other possibilities. It also contains many useful maps, but its oversize format makes it unwieldy for backpackers.

Tom Miller's *The Baja Book III* (Baja Trail Publications, Huntington Beach, California, 1992) is a mile-by-mile guide which uses a series of maps consisting of satellite photographs with superimposed cultural features like roads and campsites. Unfortunately, the photographs' greenish tint depicts Baja's complex topography worse than the original B&W photos, and considerable cloud cover on some photographs further diminishes their utility.

Bicycling Bonnie Wong's *Bicycling Baja* (Sunbelt Publications, Santee, California, 1988) is the only guidebook to bicycling the peninsula, but its coverage rarely addresses unpaved roads except in the far north; mountain bikers will in most instances have to be pioneers.

Boating Leland Lewis & Peter Ebeling's well-illustrated *Baja Sea Guide* (Hearst Marine Books, New York, 1985) charts yacht anchorages on Baja's Pacific and Gulf coasts. Jack Williams's two-volume *Baja Boaters Guide* (H J Williams, Sausalito, California, 1988) covers practically every possible mooring along the Pacific coast (Vol I) and the Sea of Cortés (Vol II).

Camping *Camping in Mexico* and *The People's Guide to RV Camping in Mexico*, both by Carl Franz and published by John Muir Publications, are excellent practical guides. The latter has a lengthy, detailed chapter on every RV park and camping area in Baja.

Diving *Baja California Diver's Guide* (Marcor Publishing, Calistoga, California, 1991), by Michael & Linda Farley, is a detailed guide to diving off the Pacific and Gulf coasts.

Fishing The 4th edition of Tom Miller's *Angler's Guide to Baja California* (Baja Trail Publications, Huntington Beach, California, 1993) is packed with information on identifying various fish species and where, when and how to catch them. It includes several maps, drawings and charts.

Flora & Fauna Norman C Roberts's *The Baja California Plant Field Guide* (Natural History Publishing Co, La Jolla, California, 1989) describes over 400 plants on the peninsula. For US$25, it is available from Natural History Publishing Co, PO Box 962, La Jolla, California 92037. Specialists should consult Ira L Wiggins's voluminous *Flora of Baja California* (Stanford University Press, 1980).

Ann Zwinger's *A Desert Country near the Sea* (University of Arizona, 1983) is an unusual first person natural history of Baja's Cape Region. Interspersed with descriptions and attractive illustrations of flora and fauna are informative historical vignettes of people and places, but her style is a bit florid.

A Field Guide to Mexican Birds (Houghton-Mifflin, Boston, 1973), by R T Peterson & E L Chaliff, covers both the mainland and Baja California. Sanford Wilbur's *Birds of Baja California* (University of California, 1987) is more specialized, but its handful of illustrations show only those birds unique to the peninsula.

Marine Animals of Baja California: A Guide to the Common Fish & Invertebrates (Western Marine Enterprises, Marina del Rey, California, 1988) by Daniel Gotshall, has lavish color photographs of Baja's sea life. *The Sierra Club Handbook on Whales & Dolphins* (Sierra Club Books, San Francisco, 1983), by S Leatherwood & R R Reeves, is useful for whale-watchers. Ted Case & Martin Cody's *Island Biogeography in the Sea of Cortéz* (University of California Press, 1983) is a collection of essays for specialists or enthusiastic amateurs in the fields of oceanography, geology, botany, mammalogy, ornithology, herpetology (the study of reptiles and amphibians) and ichthyology (the study of fishes), as well as those interested in the human impact on the Gulf environment.

Other recommended books include *Reef Fishes of the Sea of Cortés* by D Thompson (John Wiley & Sons, New York, 1979) and *Guide to the Coastal Marine Fish of California* by D J Miller & R N Lea (California Resources Agency, Department of Fish & Game, 1972).

Flying Arnold Senterfitt's *Airports of Baja California* (Arnold Senterfitt Publications, PO Box 11950, Reno, Nevada 89510) is extremely useful for people flying their own airplanes; it includes information such as airport radio frequencies, map coordinates and airstrip lengths.

Hiking Jim Conrad's *Hiking in Mexico* (Bradt Publications, 1992) contains a brief chapter on Baja written by Graham Mackintosh, author of *In a Desert Place*. Unfortunately, this chapter contains no maps and only brief trail descriptions. Parts of Walt Peterson's *The Baja Adventure Book* (Wilderness Press, Berkeley, California, 1992) do a much better job; its size and weight make it unwieldy for hikers, but features like the 1:50,000 contour map of the trail up the Picacho del Diablo in Parque Nacional Sierra San Pedro Mártir are very useful.

Kayaking Andromeda Romano-Lax's *Sea Kayaking in Baja* (Wilderness Press, Berkeley, California, 1993) describes a handful of good kayaking routes, mostly on the Gulf of California.

Mexico Book Service

To order books on Mexico which are unavailable in your area, try the Mexican Book Service in the USA (☎ (205) 265-7153, PO Drawer 6161, Montgomery, Alabama 36106).

Bookshops

Dawson's Book Shop (☎ (213) 469-2186, 535 North Larchmont Blvd, Los Angeles, California 90004) publishes a set of 47 books called the Baja California Travel Series that addresses a variety of topics both historical and contemporary.

Few Baja bookshops specialize in English-language material, but most major cities and towns have a *librería* (bookshop) which stocks some books and magazines in English. Baja's many trailer parks are full of North Americans who may be willing to swap reading material. Try also trailer park offices, some of which have accumulated many shelves of books that can be traded. Hotels catering to tourists also carry English-language books and publications.

MAPS

The *Baja Explorer Topographical Atlas Directory* (Alti Publishing, 4180 La Jolla Village Drive, La Jolla, California 92037) contains over 200 pages of topographical maps in a ring binder at a scale of 1:100,000. It is now out of print, but a handful of bookshops, such as the Map Centre in San Diego and the Museo de la Naturaleza y de la Cultura in Bahía de Los Angeles may still have copies.

Perhaps the best practical road map of Baja is published by the Automobile Club of Southern California, available free of charge to members of the American Automobile Association (AAA); nonmembers can try asking a member for help in getting a copy or can purchase a copy for US$3.95. Several Baja bookshops and other tourist-oriented enterprises, such as Mulegé Divers, carry the AAA map, which is not totally reliable off main roads.

International Travel Map Productions (PO Box 2290, Vancouver B C V6B 3W5) publishes the finely annotated *Baja California* at a scale of 1:1,000,000, that sells for about US$7.95; while excellent for planning trips and background information, it's a bit cluttered for field use.

Ediciones Corona (☎ 52-88-06, Calle G 175, Mexicali) now publishes the Guías Urbanas series of very detailed maps and directories for Mexican cities, including Tijuana, Mexicali, Tecate, Ensenada, San Felipe, the Valle de Mexicali and La Paz. While these maps are very up to date, a gray and light blue color scheme makes some of them difficult to read.

For map orders, try the Map Centre (2611 University Ave, San Diego, California 92104) or Maplink (☎ (805) 963-4438, 529 State St, Santa Barbara, California 93101). The latter publishes an extensive mail-order catalogue.

MEDIA
Newspapers & Magazines

Baja California has a rich journalistic heritage and a thriving local press in addition to national newspapers. Of the nine main dailies in Baja California, those with the highest circulation are Mexicali's *La Voz de la Frontera* (65,000) and Tijuana's *El Mexicano* (80,000). Tijuana's *El Heraldo de Baja California* (25,000), the state's first daily, dates from 1941.

Other daily newspapers include *ABC*, with a circulation of 50,000 in Mexicali and Ensenada, Tijuana's *El Día* (20,000) and *Diario de Baja California* (22,000), Mexicali's *El Centinela* (15,000), *Novedades de Baja California* (25,000 in Mexicali, Tijuana and Ensenada) and Tijuana's *Ultimas Noticias* (45,000).

Though published locally, *Diario 29* is a regional edition of *El Nacional*, a Mexico City paper which generally supports the PRI. In addition to the daily press, there are numerous magazines of varying content, including cultural supplements to the daily papers.

Tijuana-based *Zeta* (125,000), a weekly alternative to the rather conservative daily press, also publishes a Mexicali edition. Extensive readers' letters give a good sampling of the most articulate public opinion in the state.

In Baja California Sur, the main dailies are the La Paz-based *Diario Peninsular* and *El Sudcaliforniano*.

Baja California's free English-language papers, the *Baja Sun* and *Baja Times*, are thinly disguised publicity rags which promote the peninsula as a tourist destination and as an area for real estate investment – or speculation. They do, however, have occasional articles of interest to travelers, as well as coupons for hotel and restaurant discounts and free drinks.

Television & Radio

Four television stations operate in Baja California (Norte), two in Mexicali and one each in Tijuana and Ensenada, but cable and satellite TV services are now widely available throughout the peninsula.

Of the 41 radio stations in Baja California (Norte), 26 are on the AM band and 15 on the FM band. All are commercial except for four FM stations, mostly associated with the Universidad Autónoma, which emphasize cultural programming.

FILM & PHOTOGRAPHY

Mexican customs laws theoretically permit an individual to import a maximum of one camera and 12 rolls of film, but enforcement is so lax as to be nonexistent.

Most types of film are available, but it is generally better to bring it from the USA; beware of out-of-date film. Color-print film is plentiful but slide (transparency) film is difficult to find, especially in smaller locales. Film prices are higher than in Canada or the USA.

Color print film tolerates a wide variety of conditions, but lacks the resolution of slide film. Kodachrome, which portrays reds and nearby colors of the spectrum exceptionally well, is ideal for desert scenery, but Fujichrome is much cheaper and by no means inferior. For certain subjects, such as cave paintings and the interiors of historic buildings like the missions, you should carry high-speed (ASA 400) film to avoid using the flash, which is not permitted at these sites.

Always protect camera lenses with an ultraviolet (UV) filter. In tropical light conditions, the UV may not be sufficient to prevent washed out photos; a polarizing filter can correct this problem and, incidentally, dramatically emphasizes cloud formations, improving results on mountain and shoreline landscapes. If shooting in proximity to salt water, as for instance on whale-watching excursions, take special precautions to protect your equipment from corrosion; plastic grocery bags are an inexpensive safeguard.

HEALTH

Travel health depends on your predeparture preparations, your day-to-day health care while traveling and how you handle any medical problem or emergency that does develop. For extended stays in Baja or elsewhere in Mexico, medical insurance is advisable. Many US insurance companies, like Blue Cross, will extend their coverage to travel in Mexico.

While the list of potential dangers can seem quite frightening, with a little luck, some basic precautions and adequate information, few travelers experience more than upset stomachs.

Travel Health Guidebooks

Probably the best all-round guide is *Staying Healthy in Asia, Africa & Latin America* (Volunteers in Asia). It's compact but very detailed and well organized. Dr Richard Dawood's *Travelers' Health* (Oxford University Press, 1989) is comprehensive, easy to read, authoritative and highly recommended, but rather large to lug around. David Werner's *Where There Is No Doctor* (Hesperian Foundation) is a very detailed guide, more suited to those working in undeveloped countries than to travelers.

Travel with Children by Maureen Wheeler (Lonely Planet) offers basic advice on travel health for younger children.

Predeparture Preparations

Health Insurance A travel insurance policy covering theft, loss and medical problems is a wise idea. There is a wide variety of policies and your travel agent will have recommendations. The international student travel policies handled by STA (Student Travel Association) or other student travel organizations are usually good value. Some offer lower and higher medical expenses options, but the higher one is more appropriate for countries like the USA where medical costs are extremely high. Check the small print:

1. Some policies specifically exclude 'dangerous activities' like scuba diving, motorcycling and even trekking. If these activities are on your agenda, avoid this sort of policy.
2. You may prefer a policy which pays doctors or hospitals directly, rather than you having to pay first and file claims later. If you have to file a claim later, keep all documentation. Some policies ask you to call back (reverse

charges) to a center in your home country for an immediate assessment of your problem.

3. Check whether the policy covers ambulance fees or an emergency flight home. If you have to stretch out, you will need two seats and somebody has to pay for it!

Medical Kit It's useful to carry a small, straightforward medical kit. This should include:

1. Aspirin or panadol, for pain or fever;
2. Antihistamine (such as Benadryl), which is useful as a decongestant for colds, and to ease the itch from allergies, insect bites or stings and to help prevent motion sickness;
3. Antibiotics, which are useful for traveling off the beaten track, but they must be prescribed and you should carry the prescription with you;
4. Kaolin preparation (Pepto-Bismol), Imodium or Lomotil, for stomach upsets;
5. Rehydration mixture, to treat severe diarrhea, which is particularly important if traveling with children;
6. Antiseptic such as Betadine, which comes as impregnated swabs or ointment, and an antibiotic powder or similar 'dry' spray, for cuts and grazes;
7. Calamine lotion, to ease irritation from bites or stings;
8. Bandages, for minor injuries;
9. Scissors, tweezers and a thermometer (airlines prohibit mercury thermometers);
10. Insect repellent, sunscreen lotion, lip balm and water purification tablets.
11. A couple of syringes, in case you need injections. Ask your doctor for a note explaining why they have been prescribed.

Ideally, antibiotics should be administered only under medical supervision and should never be taken indiscriminately as they are specific to the infections they can treat. Overuse of antibiotics can weaken your body's ability to deal with infections naturally and can reduce the drug's efficacy. Take only the recommended dose at the prescribed intervals and continue taking it for the prescribed period, even if the illness seems to be cured earlier. Stop taking antibiotics immediately if you have any serious reactions and don't use them at all if you are not sure that you have the correct one.

In many countries if a medicine is available at all, it will generally be available over the counter and the price will be much cheaper than in Europe or North America. However, check expiration dates and try to determine whether storage conditions have been adequate. In some cases, drugs which are no longer recommended, or have even been banned elsewhere, are still being dispensed in Third World countries.

Vaccinations Vaccinations are not required for travel anywhere in Mexico, including Baja California, but if you plan to spend more than a week, it is a good idea to be up to date on at least your tetanus vaccine. A gamma globulin injection is also recommended for protection against infectious hepatitis.

Infectious hepatitis is the most common travel-acquired illness which can be prevented by vaccination. Protection can be provided in two ways – either with the antibody gammaglobulin or with a new vaccine called Havrix.

Havrix provides long term immunity (possibly more than 10 years) after an initial course of two injections and a booster at one year. It may be more expensive than gammaglobulin but has many advantages, including length of protection and ease of administration. It is important to know that being a vaccine it will take about three weeks to provide satisfactory protection – hence the need for careful planning prior to travel.

Gammaglobulin is not a vaccination but a ready-made antibody which has proven very successful in reducing the chances of hepatitis infection. Because it may interfere with the development of immunity, it should not be given until at least 10 days after administration of the last vaccine needed; it should also be given as close as possible to departure because it is at its most effective in the first few weeks after administration and the effectiveness tapers off gradually between three and six months.

If you plan to travel into small towns and

villages on the mainland, polio and typhoid shots are recommended.

Other Preparations Make sure you're healthy before traveling. If embarking on a long trip, make sure your teeth are OK; there are lots of places where a visit to the dentist would be the last thing you'd want to do. If you wear glasses, take an extra pair and your prescription. Losing your glasses can be a real problem, although in many places you can get new spectacles made up quickly, cheaply and competently.

If you require special medication which may not be available locally, carry an adequate supply. Take the prescription, with the generic rather than the brand name, as it will facilitate obtaining replacements. It's a wise idea to have the prescription with you to show you legally use the medication, as over-the-counter drugs from one place may be illegal without a prescription, or even banned, in another.

Food & Water

Many people traveling in Baja are worried about potential health problems from food and water. The common problems – upset stomachs and diarrhea – can be minimized or even avoided by taking a few precautions.

It is generally safe to eat cooked food as long as you don't punish your stomach by consuming large portions immediately upon arrival. Take it easy – you may even want to have your first Baja meal in one of the many restaurants which cater mainly to North Americans. Do not avoid the local restaurants, taco stands and street-corner fish and fruit carts – just introduce yourself to them gradually. Eating a clove of raw garlic every day for a week prior to your trip has also been highly recommended by many travelers, who say that it staves off stomach problems.

Try to avoid uncooked or unpasteurized dairy products like raw milk and home-made cheeses. Dairy products from supermarkets are usually *pasteurizado* but, in a restaurant, you can't be sure. *Licuados con leche* (milk shakes) from juice stands are

usually safe because the government requires the use of pasteurized milk and purified water.

Avoid most raw fruits and vegetables unless you can wash and/or peel them yourself. In tourist-oriented hotels and restaurants, you can usually eat the salads. If thoroughly cooked, meat, chicken and most types of seafood are safe.

Everyone has heard the infamous warning about Mexico: don't drink the water, and it's often true – the water can be potable, but bacterial differences can still make you sick. Generally, it is best to avoid tap water for drinking, brushing your teeth, washing fruit and vegetables or making ice cubes. *Agua purificada* (purified water) and *hielo* (ice) are available throughout Baja from supermarkets, *ultramarinos* (small grocery stores) and *licorerías* or *vinos y licores* (liquor stores).

If you travel off the main roads and into the 'boonies', some sort of water purification system is advisable, unless you take enough bottled water with you. You can purify water with *yodo* (iodine), which is sold in pharmacies; add about seven drops per quart of water. Otherwise, use *gotas* (water purification drops) or *pastillas para purificar agua* (pills) sold in pharmacies and supermarkets. Hidroclonazone water-purification tablets are usually sold in supermarkets.

Another alternative is to boil the water vigorously for at least five minutes or use a portable water filter. Compact water filters are available from major US camping supply stores like Recreational Equipment Inc (REI), which has many branches throughout the country.

These precautions are important because contaminated food and water can cause dysentery, giardia, hepatitis A and, in extremely rare instances, typhoid and polio.

Basic Rules

A normal body temperature is 98.6°F (37°C); more than 3.5°F (2°C) higher is a 'high' fever. A normal adult pulse rate is 60 to 80 per minute (children 80 to 100, babies 100 to 140). You should know how to take a temperature and a pulse. As a general rule, the pulse increases about 20 beats per minute for each 2°F (1°C) rise in fever.

Your respiration rate can also be an indicator of illness. Count the number of breaths per minute: from 12 to 20 is normal for adults and older children, up to 30 for younger children and 40 for babies. People with high fever or serious respiratory illnesses like pneumonia (acute lung infection) breathe more quickly than normal. Over 40 shallow breaths a minute usually means pneumonia.

Many health problems can be avoided by basic hygiene. Wash your hands frequently, as it's easy to contaminate your own food. Clean your teeth with purified water rather than tap water. Avoid climatic extremes: avoid the sun when it's hot, dress warmly when it's cold. It is also important to dress sensibly. You can get worm infections from walking barefoot or dangerous cuts from walking barefoot over coral. Avoid insect bites by covering bare skin when insects are around, by screening windows or beds or by using insect repellents. Seek local advice: if you're told the water is unsafe because of jellyfish or sharks, don't go in. In situations where there is no information, play it safe.

Medical Problems & Treatment

Potential medical problems can be broken down into several areas: extremes of temperature, altitude or motion; insanitation; insect bites or stings, and animal or human contact; and simple cuts, bites or scratches.

Self-diagnosis and treatment can be risky, so seek qualified help if possible. Treatment dosages indicated in this section are for emergency use only. Seek medical advice before administering any drugs.

Embassies and consulates can usually recommend a good place to go for such advice. So can five-star hotels, which often recommend doctors with five-star prices (this is when medical insurance is really useful!).

Hospitals & Clinics Almost every town and city in Baja has either a hospital or medical clinic and Cruz Roja (Red Cross) emergency facilities, all of which are indicated by road signs showing a red cross. Hospitals are generally inexpensive and can be relied on for typical ailments (such as diarrhea or dysentery) and minor surgery (such as stitches). On the other hand, clinics are often understaffed and too overburdened with local problems to be of much help, though they are linked by a government radio network to emergency services.

For serious medical problems needing immediate treatment at more sophisticated facilities, San Diego-based Air-Evac International (☎ (800) 854-2569 toll-free in the USA, or (619) 292-5557 or 278-3822) can arrange flights to the USA at any time of the day or night.

Taking the Heat & Cold

Fungal Infections Hot weather fungal infections are most likely to occur on the scalp, between the toes or fingers (athlete's foot), in the groin (jock itch or crotch rot) and on the body (ringworm). You get ringworm (a fungal infection, not literally a worm) from infected animals or by walking on damp areas, like shower floors.

To prevent fungal infections, wear loose, comfortable clothes, avoid artificial fibers, wash frequently and dry carefully. If infected, wash the area daily with a disinfectant or medicated soap and water, and rinse and dry well. Apply an antifungal powder like the widely available Tinaderm. Try to expose the infected area to air or sunlight as much as possible. Wash all towels and underwear in hot water and change them often.

Heat Exhaustion Dehydration or salt deficiency can cause heat exhaustion. Take time to acclimatize to high temperatures and make sure that you get enough liquids. Salt deficiency is characterized by fatigue, lethargy, headaches, giddiness and muscle cramps. Salt tablets may help. Vomiting or diarrhea can also deplete your liquid and salt levels. Anhydrotic heat exhaustion, caused by an inability to sweat, is quite rare. Unlike other forms of heat exhaustion it is likely to strike people who have been in a hot climate for some time rather than newcomers.

Heat Stroke Long, continuous periods of exposure to high temperatures can leave you vulnerable to this serious, sometimes fatal, condition, which occurs when the body's heat-regulating mechanism breaks down and body temperature rises to dangerous levels. Avoid excessive alcohol intake or strenuous activity when you first arrive in a hot climate, and do drink other liquids well before you desperately need them.

Symptoms include feeling unwell, lack of perspiration and a high body temperature of 102°F to 105° F (39°C to 41°C). When sweating ceases, the skin becomes flushed and red. Severe, throbbing headaches and lack of coordination will also occur, and victims may become confused or aggressive. Eventually they become delirious or go into convulsions. Hospitalization is essential, but meanwhile get them out of the sun, remove their clothing, cover them with a wet sheet or towel and fan them continually.

Hypothermia At high altitudes in the mountains, cold and wet can kill. Changeable weather can leave you vulnerable to exposure: after dark, temperatures in the mountains or desert can drop from balmy to below freezing, while a sudden soaking and high winds can lower your own body temperature so rapidly that you may not survive. Disorientation, physical exhaustion, hunger, shivering and related symptoms are warnings that you should seek warmth, shelter and food. If possible, avoid traveling alone; partners are more likely to avoid hypothermia successfully. If you must travel alone, especially when hiking, be sure someone knows your route and when you expect to return.

Seek shelter when bad weather is unavoidable. Woolen clothing and synthetics, which retain warmth even when wet, are superior to cottons. A quality sleeping bag is a worthwhile investment, although goose down loses much of its insulating qualities when wet. Carry high-energy, easily digestible snacks like chocolate or dried fruit.

Prickly Heat Prickly heat, an itchy rash caused by excessive perspiration trapped under the skin, usually strikes people who have just arrived in a hot climate and whose pores have not yet opened sufficiently to cope with greater sweating. Keeping cool, bathing often, using a mild talcum powder or even resorting to air-conditioning may help until you acclimatize.

Sunburn In the desert climate of Baja California, you can get sunburnt very quickly, even on cloudy days. Use a sunscreen and take extra care to cover areas which don't normally see sun – your feet, for example. A hat provides added protection, and use zinc cream or some other barrier cream on your nose and lips. Calamine lotion or cold tea are good for mild sunburn.

Remember: the sunshine on the beach and in the water is deceptive and will burn you quickly. Wear a T-shirt while snorkeling or swimming.

Motion Sickness

Eating lightly before and during a trip will reduce the chances of motion sickness. If you are prone to motion sickness, try to find a place that minimizes disturbance, for example, near the wing on aircraft, close to midships on boats, and near the center on buses. Fresh air usually helps, while reading or cigarette smoke don't. Commercial anti-motion sickness preparations, which can cause drowsiness, have to be taken before the trip commences; when you're feeling sick it's too late. Ginger, a natural preventative, is available in capsule form.

Diseases of Insanitation

Diarrhea Almost every traveler to Baja fears and loathes diarrhea, more commonly

Street Market, Calle Madero, La Paz

Algodones, Baja California Norte

Rancher, interior of Llano de Magdalena

Spices & condiments, Mercado Hidalgo, Tijuana

La Chinesca, Mexicali

Produce packers with tomatillos, Mercado Hidalgo, Tijuana (RR)

Tijuana-San Ysidro border

Burnt Microbus (JH)

known as Montezuma's Revenge or *la turista*. Stomach problems can arise from dietary changes – they don't necessarily mean you've caught something. Introduce yourself gradually to exotic and/or highly spiced foods.

Avoid rushing to the pharmacy and gulping antibiotics at the first signs. The best thing to do is to avoid eating and to rest, drink plenty of liquids (tea or herbal solutions, without sugar or milk). Many cafés serve excellent chamomile tea *(agua de manzanilla)*; otherwise, try mineral water *(agua mineral)*. About 24 to 48 hours should do the trick, but if symptoms persist, see a doctor. If you must eat, keep to bland foods.

After a severe bout of diarrhea or dysentery (see below), you will probably be dehydrated and suffering from painful cramps. Relieve these with fruit juices or tea, with a tiny bit of dissolved salt. Lomotil or Imodium can be used to bring relief from the symptoms, although they do not actually cure the problem. Only use these drugs if absolutely necessary – eg, if you *must* travel. For children Imodium is preferable, but under all circumstances fluid replacement is the main message. Do not use these drugs if the person has a high fever or is severely dehydrated.

In certain situations antibiotics may be indicated:

- Watery diarrhea with blood and mucous. (Gut-paralyzing drugs like Imodium or Lomotil should be avoided in this situation.)
- Watery diarrhea with fever and lethargy.
- Persistent diarrhea for more than five days.
- Severe diarrhea, if it is logistically difficult to stay in one place.

The recommended drugs (adults only) would be either norfloxacin 400 mg twice daily for three days or ciprofloxacin 500 mg twice daily for three days.

The drug bismuth subsalicylate has also been used successfully. It is not available in Australia. The dosage for adults is two tablets or 30 mls and for children it is one tablet or 10 mls. This dose can be repeated every 30 minutes to one hour, with no more than eight doses in a 24-hour period.

The drug of choice for children would be co-trimoxazole (Bactrim, Septrin, Resprim) with dosage dependent on weight. A three-day course is also given.

Ampicillin has been recommended in the past and may still be an alternative.

Dysentery Fortunately, dysentery is less common in Baja than in the rest of Mexico. This serious illness, caused by contaminated food or water, is characterized by severe diarrhea, often with blood or mucus in the stool.

There are two kinds of dysentery. Bacillary dysentery is characterized by a high fever and rapid development; headache, vomiting and stomach pains are also symptoms. It generally lasts no longer than a week, but is highly contagious. Amoebic dysentery develops more gradually and causes no fever or vomiting, but will persist until treated and can recur and cause long-term damage.

A stool test is necessary to diagnose which kind of dysentery you have, so seek medical help quickly. In case of emergency, note that norfloxacin or ciprofloxacin can be used as presumptive treatment for bacillary dysentery, and metronidazole (Flagyl) for amoebic dysentery.

For bacillary dysentery, norfloxacin 400 mg twice daily for seven days or ciprofloxacin 500 mg twice daily for seven days are the recommended dosages.

If you're unable to find either of these drugs then a useful alternative is co-trimoxazole 160/800 mg (Bactrim, Septrin, Resprim) twice daily for seven days. This is a sulfa drug and must not be used by people with a known sulfa allergy.

In the case of children the drug co-trimoxazole is a reasonable first line treatment. For amoebic dysentery, the recommended adult dosage of metronidazole (Flagyl) is one 750 mg to 800 mg capsule three times daily for five days. Children aged between eight and 12 years should have half the adult dose; the dosage for younger children is one-third the adult dose.

An alternative to Flagyl is Fasigyn, taken as a two gram daily dose for three days. Alcohol must be avoided during treatment and for 48 hours afterwards.

Giardia This intestinal parasite is present in contaminated water. The symptoms are stomach cramps, nausea, a bloated stomach, watery, foul-smelling diarrhea and frequent gas. Giardia can appear several weeks after exposure to the parasite; symptoms may disappear for a few days and then return, a pattern which may continue. Metronidazole (Flagyl) is the recommended drug, but should only be taken under medical supervision. Antibiotics are useless.

Hepatitis Hepatitis A is a very common problem amongst travelers to areas with poor sanitation. With good water and adequate sewage disposal in most industrialized countries since the 1940s, very few young adults now have any natural immunity and must be protected. Protection is through the new vaccine Havrix or the antibody gammaglobulin. The antibody is short-lasting.

The disease is spread by contaminated food or water. The symptoms are fever, chills, headache, fatigue, feelings of weakness and aches and pains, followed by loss of appetite, nausea, vomiting, abdominal pain, dark urine, light colored feces, jaundiced skin and the whites of the eyes may turn yellow. In some cases you may feel unwell, tired, have no appetite, experience aches and pains and be jaundiced. You should seek medical advice, but in general there is not much you can do apart from rest, drink lots of fluids, eat lightly and avoid fatty foods. People who have had hepatitis must forego alcohol for six months after the illness, as hepatitis attacks the liver and it needs that amount of time to recover.

Hepatitis B, which used to be called serum hepatitis, is spread through contact with infected blood, blood products or bodily fluids, for example through sexual contact, unsterilized needles and blood transfusions. Other risk situations include having a shave or tattoo in a local shop, or having your ears pierced. The symptoms of type B are much the same as type A except that they are more severe and may lead to irreparable liver damage or even liver cancer. Although there is no treatment for hepatitis B, an effective prophylactic vaccine is readily available in most countries. The immunization schedule requires two injections at least a month apart followed by a third dose five months after the second. Persons who should receive a hepatitis B vaccination include anyone who anticipates contact with blood or other bodily secretions, either as a health care worker or through sexual contact with the local population, particularly those who intend to stay in the country for a long period of time.

Hepatitis Non-A Non-B is a blanket term formerly used for several different strains of hepatitis, which have now been separately identified. Hepatitis C is similar to B but is less common. Hepatitis D (the 'delta particle') is also similar to B and always occurs in concert with it; its occurrence is currently limited to IV drug users. Hepatitis E, however, is similar to A and is spread in the same manner, by water or food contamination.

Tests are available for these strands, but are very expensive. Travelers shouldn't be too paranoid about this apparent proliferation of hepatitis strains; they are fairly rare (so far) and following the same precautions as for A and B should be all that's necessary to avoid them.

Worms These parasites are most common in rural, tropical areas and a stool test when you return home is not a bad idea. They can be present on unwashed vegetables or in undercooked meat, and you can pick them up through your skin by walking in bare feet. Infestations may not show up for some time, and although they are generally not serious, if left untreated they can cause severe health problems. A stool test is necessary to pinpoint the problem, and medication is often available over the counter.

Diseases Spread by People & Animals
Rabies Dogs are noted carriers of rabies, which is caused by a bite or scratch by an infected animal. Any bite, scratch or even lick from a mammal should be cleaned immediately and thoroughly. Scrub with soap and running water, and then clean with an alcohol solution. If there is any possibility that the animal is infected, you should seek medical help immediately. Even if the animal is not rabid, all bites should be treated seriously as they can become infected or can result in tetanus. A rabies vaccination is now available and should be considered if you are in a high-risk category, eg, if you intend to explore caves (bat bites could be dangerous) or work with animals.

Sexually Transmitted Diseases Sexual contact with an infected partner spreads these diseases. While abstinence is the only 100% effective preventative, using condoms is also a significant deterrent. Gonorrhea and syphilis are the most common of these diseases; sores, blisters or rashes around the genitals, discharges or pain when urinating are common symptoms. Symptoms may be less marked or not observed at all in women. Syphilis symptoms eventually disappear completely, but the disease continues and can cause severe problems in later years. The treatment of gonorrhea and syphilis is by antibiotics.

There are numerous other sexually transmitted diseases, for most of which effective treatment is available. However, there are no cures for herpes or AIDS *(la SIDA)*. Using condoms is the most effective preventative.

HIV/AIDS HIV, the Human Immunodeficiency Virus, may develop into AIDS, Acquired Immune Deficiency Syndrome. HIV is a major problem in many countries. Any exposure to blood, blood products or bodily fluids may put the individual at risk. In many developing countries transmission is predominantly through heterosexual sexual activity. This is quite different from industrialized countries where transmission is mostly through contact between homosexual or bisexual males or contaminated needles in IV drug users. Apart from abstinence, the most effective preventative is always to practice safe sex using condoms. It is impossible to detect the HIV-positive status of an otherwise healthy-looking person without a blood test.

HIV/AIDS can also be spread through infected blood transfusions; most developing countries cannot afford to screen blood for transfusions. It can also be spread by dirty needles – vaccinations, acupuncture, tattooing and body piercing can potentially be as dangerous as intravenous drug use if the equipment is not clean. If you do need an injection, buy a new syringe from a pharmacy and ask the doctor to use it. You may also want to take a couple of syringes with you, in case of emergency. The AIDS Foundation in San Diego, California has a hotline number: call ☎ (619) 686-5000.

Tetanus Difficult to treat but preventable with immunization, this potentially fatal disease is found in the rural tropics. Tetanus occurs when a wound becomes infected by a germ which lives in the feces of animals or people, so clean all cuts or animal bites. Tetanus is known as lockjaw, and the first symptom may be discomfort in swallowing, or stiffening of the jaw and neck; this is followed by painful convulsions of the jaw and entire body.

Cuts, Bites & Stings
Cuts & Scratches Cuts easily become infected in hot climates and may heal slowly. Treat any cut with an antiseptic solution such as Betadine. Where possible, avoid bandages and Band-Aids, which can keep wounds wet. Coral cuts are notoriously slow to heal, as the coral injects a weak venom into the wound; avoid such cuts by wearing shoes when walking on reefs, and clean any cut thoroughly.

Bites & Stings Bee *(abeja)* and wasp *(avispa)* stings are more painful than dangerous. Use calamine lotion for relief and

ice packs to reduce the swelling. There are some spiders with dangerous bites, but antivenom is usually available. Scorpions often shelter in shoes or clothing and their stings are notoriously painful – check your shoes and clothing in the morning. Various sea creatures can sting or bite dangerously or are dangerous to eat. Again, seek local advice about potentially dangerous areas.

Snakes Rattlesnakes *(cascabeles)* are common in the Baja deserts. To minimize chances of being bitten, always wear boots, socks and long trousers when walking through undergrowth where snakes may be present. Keep your hands out of holes and crevices, and be cautious when collecting firewood.

Though painful, rattlesnake bites do not cause instantaneous death, rarely kill healthy adults under any circumstances and antivenom is usually available. Keep the victim calm and still, wrap the bitten limb tightly, as you would for a sprained ankle, and then attach a splint to immobilize it. Don't attempt to catch the snake if there is even a remote chance of being bitten again. Seek medical help; tourniquets and sucking out the poison are now completely discredited.

Bedbugs & Lice Bedbugs *(chinches)* live in various places, but particularly in dirty mattresses and bedding. Spots of blood on bedclothes or on the wall around the bed can serve as a suggestion to find another hotel. Bedbugs leave itchy bites in neat rows. Calamine lotion may help.

All lice *(piojos)* cause itching and discomfort. They make themselves at home in your hair (head lice), your clothing (body lice) or in your pubic hair (crab lice). You catch lice through direct contact with infected people or by sharing combs, clothing and the like. Powder or shampoo treatment will kill the lice, after which infected clothing should be washed in very hot water.

Ticks Ticks *(garrapatas)* may be present in chaparral vegetation, where hikers often get them on their legs or in their boots. Pulling them off increases the likelihood of infection, but an insect repellent may keep them away. Vaseline, alcohol or oil will induce ticks to let go.

Jellyfish Local advice is the best way of avoiding contact with these sea creatures and their stinging tentacles. Stings from most jellyfish *(medusas)* are not dangerous, just painful. Dousing in vinegar *(vinagre)* will deactivate any stingers that have not 'fired'. Calamine lotion, antihistamines and analgesics may reduce the reaction and relieve the pain.

Women's Health
Gynecological Problems Poor diet, lowered resistance due to the use of antibiotics for stomach upsets and even contraceptive pills can lead to vaginal infections when traveling in hot climates. Keeping the genital area clean, wearing cotton underwear and skirts or loose-fitting trousers will help prevent infections.

Yeast infections, characterized by rash, itch and discharge can be treated with a vinegar or even lemon juice douche (diluted with water) or with yogurt containing active cultures. Nystatin suppositories are the usual medical prescription. Trichomonas is a more serious infection with a discharge and a burning sensation when urinating. Male sexual partners must also be treated; if a vinegar-water douche is not effective, seek medical attention. Flagyl is the prescribed drug.

Pregnancy Most miscarriages occur during the first three months of pregnancy, so this is the most risky time to travel as far as your own health is concerned. Miscarriage is not uncommon, and can occasionally lead to severe bleeding. The last three months should also be spent within reasonable distance of good medical care. A baby born as early as 24 weeks stands a chance of survival, but only in a good modern hospital. Pregnant women should avoid all unnecessary medication, but vaccinations and malarial prophylactics should still be taken where possible. Additional care should be taken to prevent illness and particular attention should be paid to diet and nutrition. Alcohol and nicotine, for example, should be avoided.

Women travelers often find that their periods become irregular or even cease while they're on the road. Remember that a missed period in these circumstances doesn't necessarily indicate pregnancy. There are health posts or Family Planning clinics in many small and large urban centers in developing countries, where you can seek advice and have a urine test to determine whether you are pregnant or not.

WOMEN TRAVELERS

In a land of machismo, women should strongly consider making some concessions to local custom. Mexicans generally believe in the *difference* rather than equality between the sexes, and women who are on their own may have to put up with numerous men attempting to chat them up. Mexican men may assume that unaccompanied foreign women are fair game; this can get pretty tiresome, but the best discouragement is a cool but polite initial response and a consistent, firm 'No!'

If you choose to do things an average Mexican woman would not do, such as challenging a man's masculinity, drinking in a cantina or hitchhiking alone, you are likely to be the target of unwanted attention, significant hostility or even violence. Although informal 'dress codes' are more permissive than in the recent past, avoid clothing which Mexican men may interpret as provocative. Wearing beach attire in town is not appropriate.

Police in Tijuana are known for harassing unaccompanied women on their early morning 'disco patrol'; to avoid one of these unpleasant encounters after a night of dancing, take a taxi back to the border instead of driving. In a serious emergency, seek help at a consulate in Tijuana or Cabo San Lucas.

DANGERS & ANNOYANCES
Safety & Theft

Thanks mainly to stereotyped foreign movies and machismo, Mexico has something of a reputation as a violent country, but there is really little to fear in terms of physical safety, unless you somehow get deeply involved in a quarrel – dangerous weapons like handguns are much less common south of the border. More at risk are your possessions – particularly those you carry around with you. Reports of theft from rooms are rare, but there have been instances of thefts from tourist vehicles, usually when left alone for substantial periods in remote areas.

Legal Matters

The Mexican judicial system is based on the French Napoleonic Code, which presumes that a person is guilty until proven innocent. There is no jury trial; if you have problems such as a car accident (and the police arrive on the scene), everyone involved is considered guilty and liable until proven otherwise. If you have no car insurance, you will be detained until fault has been established. Prior to arriving in Baja, consider purchasing legal or juridical insurance, which covers you against damage caused to federal property (like street signs) or injury to a person. This allows the insurance adjuster to get you out of jail without having to post a bond.

If you encounter legal hassles with public officials or local businesspeople in Baja, contact La Procuraduría de Protección al Turista (Attorney General for the Protection of the Tourist, ☎ 84-21-38 in Tijuana, 6-36-86 in Ensenada, 2-57-44 in

Mexicali and 7-11-55 in San Felipe). Each office has English-speaking aides.

Police & Other Officials

Some Mexicans call the *judiciales* (state and federal police) a 'mafia with badges' who view their positions as a license to extort money and favors from ordinary citizens or, worse, to torture and even kill those who run afoul of their caprice; see Ted Conover's *Coyotes* (Vintage, 1987) for a harrowing story of their treatment of undocumented workers trying to cross the US border.

Immigration officers and similar officials may also subtly (or openly) seek bribes (see 'La Mordida', below), but the federal government has made a genuine attempt to limit the practice; in late 1991, it took the unprecedented step of replacing all officials on the US border with ostensibly uncorrupted novices. Nobody, however, expects corruption to disappear very soon.

Travelers returning north across the border should not assume that US Immigration & Customs officials are virtuous in this regard. Corrupt US officials often traffic in drugs and take advantage of powerless immigrants, but abuses against all classes of border-crossers are well documented.

La Mordida

Historically, Mexico is notorious for *la mordida* (literally, 'the bite', or bribe). The most frequent opportunity for the mordida is a traffic violation, such as driving the wrong way on a one-way street or running a stop sign. Realists do not expect the mordida to disappear from Mexican life at any time in the near future, but petty harassment of tourists for minor matters is likely to decline.

Tourists should never directly offer money to a police officer, because that is illegal; one current strategy is to tell the officer that, if he forgives you, you will be extremely grateful *(Si me perdona, se lo podría agradecer)*. This is a very circumlocutious but effective way of sounding out the situation, and courteous travelers have

escaped awkward situations without paying anything. Alternatively, make a subtle suggestion such as offering a few pesos to purchase a *refresco* (soft drink) or *caguama* (large bottle of beer) because you're thirsty and you wonder if the officer is also.

In an unambiguously desperate situation, some motorists hand over a US$20 bill (or more) beneath their driver's license when the officer requests the license. Motorists should know that the Mexican drivers' manual *(reglamento de tránsito)* explicitly limits the offenses for which a driver may be taken into police custody. Each state has its own reglamento; try obtaining one at bookstores or from street vendors.

Natural Hazards

The Pacific coast of Baja California is part of the 'ring of fire', which stretches from Asia to Alaska and Tierra del Fuego. Active vulcanism is minimal in Baja, but earthquakes can be very serious, since they strike without warning and rustic construction often does not meet seismic safety standards. Travelers staying in budget accommodation should make contingencies for safety and even evacuation before going to sleep at night. Adobe buildings are especially vulnerable.

While rain is rare in the Baja desert, flash floods are a serious hazard in the backcountry and even on paved highways like the Transpeninsular. If weather is threatening, seek high ground away from watercourses, which can fill instantly with runoff. Wait for low water before attempting to cross any swollen stream – even if you must wait for days. If your vehicle becomes stuck under such conditions, abandon it rather than risk drowning.

Recreational Hazards

Many of Baja's Pacific beach areas have dangerous offshore rip currents, so ask before entering the water and be sure someone on shore knows your whereabouts; surfers and swimmers should also beware of sharks. In wilderness areas like Parque Nacional San Pedro Mártir, the consequences of an accident can be very serious, so inform someone of your route and expected return.

WORK

Except for those directly involved in tourist specialties, like natural history tours or diving, work is not an attractive alternative in Baja. Wages are low by US or European standards, and permits are hard to obtain, but this does not seem to stop the slimy real estate speculators of Cabo San Lucas. English tutoring may be feasible in Tijuana or Mexicali, but competition is stiff because of the proximity of the border.

Anyone interested in establishing a business in Baja must establish a Mexican corporation; to do so, consult a Mexican attorney on the proper immigration and business procedures.

ACTIVITIES

Mexicans are less enamored of outdoor activities like camping and hiking than they are of hunting and fishing, but visitors will find some mountain areas suitable for the former activities. Campgrounds that are not also trailer parks are rare, though tent camping is possible at most trailer parks and beaches. In some areas, horses are available for rent. Cycling is increasingly popular as both bicycles and Baja roads

improve, but lack of water in some areas can be a serious drawback without logistical support.

Water Sports & Diving

Most resorts and surrounding towns have shops that will arrange boats and hire out equipment such as snorkels, masks, fins and other diving paraphernalia, but serious participants may prefer to bring their own equipment.

Surfing

Surfers enjoy Baja's Pacific coast and even parts of the far southern Gulf of California, but be aware that the entire coastline between Tijuana and Ensenada is heavily polluted, and that areas farther to the south are more suitable for this sport. To reach the best spots, surfers need sturdy vehicles and should carry extra parts and gasoline, plenty of water and all supplies, and should be especially conscientious about carrying out their trash.

Surfers who speak Spanish will find that local fishermen are good sources of information, since they know where to find the *olas* (waves). For more detailed surfing information, consult individual geographical entries in this book.

Some businesses, such as surf shops in

Rosarito and San José del Cabo, cater specifically to surfers, and major surfing sites are less crowded and competitive than in southern mainland California. US periodicals like *Surfer* (☎ (714) 496-5922, 33046 Calle Aviador, San Juan Capistrano, California 92675) often contain material on both Baja California and Baja California Sur; by calling the above number, surfers can get the most current information.

Fishing & Fishing Regulations
Sport fishing is especially popular off the Pacific and in the Gulf of California. Tom Miller's *Angler's Guide to Baja California* (Baja Trail Publications) is a worthwhile acquisition for fishing enthusiasts. Another is the recently updated *The Baja Catch* by Neil Kelly & Gene Kira, available from Apples & Oranges, PO Box 2296J, Valley Center, California 92082. The price is US$22.95, postage and handling included (plus US$1.66 sales tax for mainland California residents).

Anyone 16 years or older who plans to do any beach or offshore fishing in Baja will need a fishing license; for an application, contact the Secretaría de Pesca (☎ (619) 233-6956), Mexican Fisheries Department, 2550 Fifth Ave, Suite 101, San Diego, California 921030. Do not fish any species, such as the popular but endangered *totuava* of the Gulf of California, which are in *veda*.

According to the California Department of Fish & Game, any fish or game obtained legally in Mexico may enter California upon submission of its form FG 901; contact them (☎ (619) 525-4215, 1350 Front St, San Diego, California 92101) for information about declaration forms, permits and limits. For other US states or Canadian provinces, check with the respective authorities.

For seasonal suggestions on fishing, see individual geographical entries.

Language Courses
Ensenada is the best option for travelers wishing to learn or improve their Spanish. Travelers have enthusiastically recommended the Center of Languages & Latin American Studies (☎ 7-18-40, Riveroll 1287), whose US contact (☎ (619) 279-0996 or toll-free (800) 834-2256) is at 5666 La Jolla Blvd, No 116 La Jolla, California 92037. Besides its standard courses, the Center offers specialized instruction for professionals in nursing, teaching and law enforcement. It can also arrange community college or university credit in the USA.

Regular students pay a one-time registration fee of US$100, plus US$125 per week (30 hours instruction) from September to June; in the summer months of June, July and August, the weekly charge is US$145. After two consecutive weeks, rates fall to US$100 per week except in summer, when the rate is US$110. Weekend courses cost US$75. The Center will arrange housing with Mexican families for US$20 to US$25 per day, including meals.

The Colegio de Idiomas de Ensenada (☎ 6-01-09, 6-65-87), Blvd J A Rodríguez 377 also offers intensive instruction in classes of no more than five students for US$100 weekly (30 hours instruction) or US$50 weekends (eight hours both Saturday and Sunday), plus a one-time registration fee of US$100. There is a 10% Mexican government tax on tuition only. Accommodation with a Mexican family is available for about US$20 per day with meals, but students may also choose hotel accommodation. Their US contact is the International Spanish Institute (☎ (619) 472-0600), PO Box 536, Bonita, California 91908.

Language instruction is also available in La Paz, the capital of Baja California Sur; see the La Paz section for details.

Study Programs & Expeditions
Many educational institutions and organizations based in mainland California offer programs, research expeditions and tours to Baja. Tour operators are listed in the Getting There & Away chapter.

Colleges and universities often conduct short research trips to study flora, fauna, gray whales, ancient cave paintings and various other topics. The itineraries and academic department sponsors change every year; write to the following addresses or to individual colleges and universities for current information:

Office of the Chancellor, California Community Colleges, 1107 9th St, Sacramento 95814 (☎ (916) 445-8752)

Office of the Chancellor, California State University, 400 Golden Shore, Long Beach 90802 (☎ (213) 590-5506)

Extension Division, University of California Los Angeles, 405 Hilgard Ave, Los Angeles 90024 (☎ (213) 825-1024)

Off-campus Research Expeditions, University of California Berkeley, Berkeley 94720 (☎ (510) 642-6586)

The Smithsonian Institution also organizes expeditions and study tours to Baja. Write to National Associates, Capital Gallery 455, Smithsonian Institution, Washington, DC 20560 (☎ (202) 287-3362 for tour brochures; (202) 357-1350 for seminar brochures).

The Foundation for Field Research (☎ (619) 450-3460), PO Box 910078, San Diego, California 92121 is a nonprofit organization which arranges field research expeditions to Baja California and elsewhere. Their principal Baja projects include an ongoing study of endangered sea turtles at Bahía de Los Angeles and a study of a rare subspecies of deer found only on Isla Cedros. Volunteers assist the researchers with their work and pay a reasonable tax-deductible amount for taking part. Trips are open to scientists and non-scientists; participants are expected to consider the trips as expeditions, not vacations.

HIGHLIGHTS

Some of Baja California's finest experiences are not the ones that tourist offices usually promote.

Tecate

Unlike the typical border crossing, this modest manufacturing center more closely resembles a mainland Mexican town than any other settlement in the entire state of Baja California (Norte).

Puertecitos-Laguna Chapala Road

In dry weather, at least, any vehicle with reasonable clearance and a relatively short wheelbase can recreate the nostalgic feeling of driving the peninsula before the paving of the Transpeninsular – so long as the driver(s) are willing to devote at least one full day to a route that can be hell on tires.

San Borja

Founded by Jesuits and finished by Dominicans, this remote mission village occupies a scenic oasis reached by a spectacular road from the Transpeninsular or from the paved lateral to Bahía de Los Angeles.

Islas San Benito

Visitors to Isla Cedros, itself an off-the-beaten-track destination, can sometimes catch a lift on a fishing boat to the elephant seal colony on the westernmost island of this tiny, remote archipelago.

Sierra de San Francisco

Recently declared a UNESCO World Heritage Site, this dissected volcanic plateau contains the most extraordinary rock art sites of the many which dot the peninsula from the borderlands to the Cape Region. The muleback descent from the village of San Francisco de la Sierra, north of San Ignacio, is an unforgettable experience.

Santa Rosalía

Aficionados of industrial archaeology will find this former French company town worth exploring for the ruins of its massive copper smeltering operation, as well as its unusual residential architecture and a church designed by the famous Eiffel, of Tower fame.

San Evaristo

The drive north along the west side of the Bahía de La Paz is like viewing a cutaway of Arizona's Grand Canyon of the Colorado. Ordinary passenger cars can go as far as Punta El Mechudo, where the route starts to climb, but high-clearance, short-wheelbase vehicles can continue to some of the most secluded camping and fishing areas on the peninsula.

Todos Santos
Limited beach access has kept this artists' colony in the Cape Region from suffering the relentless overdevelopment of the nearby Los Cabos area. The gringo presence, while palpable, is more subdued and refined than almost anywhere else on the peninsula.

Sierra de la Laguna
The most worthwhile sight in the Cape Region, this interior mountain range is a botanical wonderland where aspens, cacti, oaks and palms grow in close proximity, refreshing mountain streams rush through granite canyons, and 7000-foot peaks offer relief from the tropical heat of the lowlands. No other place on the peninsula is more deserving of national park status, as it provides what is probably Baja's best hiking and backpacking.

TOURIST TRAPS
Like every destination, Baja California has its share of places that are overrated or simply distasteful.

La Bufadora
Scads of souvenir stands overwhelm the modest significance of this seaside blowhole south of Ensenada. Everybody goes here, nobody knows why.

San Felipe
On the Gulf side of the peninsula, two hours south of Mexicali, this ear-splitting resort belongs to low-life real-estate speculators, roaring ATVs and, during spring break, US university students taking advantage of Mexico's lenient liquor laws. In summer, it's insufferably hot.

Nopoló
South of Loreto, the 'mother of the missions', this presumptuous resort has no reason to exist except for the ambitions of

Fonatur bureaucrats, and it squanders resources, particularly fresh water, that could be utilized much better elsewhere.

Cabo San Lucas
If chugging 28 post-dinner shots of tequila (a posted record at one waterfront bar/restaurant) is your idea of a good time, Cabo San Lucas is for you. If you survive that experience, an aggressive salesman will probably get your signature on a time-share contract.

ACCOMMODATION
Accommodation in Baja ranges from luxury resorts, tourist vacation hotels, and budget hotels and motels to *casas de huéspedes* (guesthouses). Camping both in and out of RV parks is the most popular alternative for budget travelers. There is a single *villa deportiva juvenil* (youth hostel) in La Paz, Baja California Sur.

Camping
Camping is free on almost any beach in Baja, but wherever formal facilities are available, expect to pay from US$3 to US$20 per night; most sites are in the US$8 to US$12 range. Many have full hook-ups for electricity, water and sewerage.

If planning to camp extensively, acquire Carl Franz's *Camping in Mexico* and *RV Camping in Mexico* (John Muir Publications, PO Box 613, Santa Fe, New Mexico 87504) for suggestions on what to bring, how and where to camp, cooking and many other camping topics. Many of the RV guide's descriptions of Baja RV parks and campgrounds are out of date, but it's still a worthwhile acquisition. For more current campground information, check the AAA Baja California guidebook.

Youth Hostels
Aside from camping, the most inexpensive option is the villa deportiva juvenil (youth hostel), but only La Paz now has one. The Consejo Nacional de Recursos para la Atención de la Juventud (CREA), associated with the International Youth Hostel Federation (IYHF), charges from US$6 per

night for members and nonmembers. You can use an IYHA card or obtain a CREA card at the hostel.

Guesthouses

Casas de huéspedes (guesthouses) are usually houses converted wholly or partially into simple guest lodgings. A double room can cost anywhere from US$8 to US$15, with or without meals. Unfortunately casas de huéspedes are few in Baja, but in the Gulf resort of Mulegé they are a real bargain.

Hotels & Motels

By US or European standards, many hotels and motels are in the budget range, with double-room rates starting around US$20 to US$25, but a handful are cheaper and still tolerable. Standards vary and room rates and external appearance are not always accurate indicators of quality. Go inside, ask to see a room, sniff around and sit on a bed to see how much it sags.

Tourist vacation hotels are often affiliated with chains based in the USA and Mexico, such as Quality Inns, Comfort Inns, Travelodge and Holiday Inn. Their Baja rates tend to be somewhat lower than those for comparable accommodation in the USA, from US$50 to US$100 for a double room.

The principal Mexican chains, with standards equivalent to their US counterparts, include La Pinta, El Presidente and Castel hotels. Rates for doubles start around US$50 per night.

Most luxury resort hotels are south of La Paz along the eastern and southern shores of the Cape Region. Double-room rates start around US$80 per night and reach US$250 or even higher.

FOOD

Mexicans generally eat three meals a day: *desayuno* (breakfast), *almuerzo* (lunch) and *cena* (dinner). All usually include one or more of the following national staples:

Tortillas are thin, round patties of pressed corn or wheat-flour dough cooked on griddles.

Harina (flour) tortillas are common in northern Mexico and Baja, but *maíz* (corn) tortillas are more traditional. Both can be served under, on or wrapped around just about any type of food.

Frijoles are beans – boiled, fried, refried, in soups, on tortillas or with eggs as part of almost every meal.

Chiles come in numerous varieties. Some, such as the *habanero* and *serrano*, are almost always hot, while others, such as the *poblano*, vary in spiciness according to when they were picked. If your tolerance is limited, ask whether the chile is *picante* (spicy hot) or *muy picante* (very spicy hot). If you exceed your tolerance and start to choke, start eating or drinking sugar, beer, milk, bread or anything else that might extinguish the fire. Note, however, that water usually worsens the pain.

Breakfast is usually *café* (coffee) or *jugo* (juice), a *bolillo* (sweet roll) or *pan tostado* (toast) and eggs. Eggs are served in a variety of ways; when ordering eggs, never say *¿Tiene huevos?* (Do you have eggs?) because *huevos* are slang for testicles. Instead, ask *¿Hay huevos?* (Are there eggs?).

Huevos fritos are fried eggs, while *huevos rancheros* are also fried, but smothered with tomato sauce and served on a tortilla. *Huevos revueltos* are scrambled eggs, sometimes served with *chorizo* (sausage) or *frijoles* (refried beans). *Huevos revueltos estilo Mexicano*, also known as *huevos estrellados*, contain tomato, onion, chile and garlic.

Lunch, the day's biggest meal, is usually served about 2 pm. Dinner, a lighter version of lunch, is served about 7:30 pm. In restaurants that do not cater primarily to tourists, lunch and dinner menus (if available) may change daily, weekly or not at all. Meals may be ordered á la carte or on a fixed price basis. A fixed price *comida corrida* (a bargain meal) sometimes costs as little as US$1. Most fixed price meals include soup, a main dish, one or two side dishes and dessert. Dishes for either lunch or dinner can include the following *antojitos* (traditional dishes):

burrito – any combination of beans, cheese, meat, chicken and seafood, seasoned with salsa or chile and wrapped in a flour tortilla

chilaquiles – a scrambled concoction of eggs, chiles and bits of tortillas

chiles rellenos – poblano chiles stuffed with cheese, meat or other foods, dipped in egg whites, fried and baked in salsa

enchilada – ingredients similar to tacos and burritos are wrapped in a flour tortilla, dipped in sauce and then baked or fried

machaca – cured, dried and shredded beef or pork mixed with eggs, onions, cilantro and chiles

quesadilla – flour tortilla topped or filled with cheese, and occasionally other ingredients, then heated

taco – ingredients similar to the burrito are wrapped in a soft or crisp corn tortilla

tamales – steamed corn dough stuffed with meat, beans or chile and wrapped in corn husks

tostada – a flat, crisp tortilla topped with meat or cheese, tomatoes, beans and lettuce

Soups

sopa – soup

sopa de arroz – rice soup, really more rice than soup, commonly served at lunch

sopa de pollo – chicken soup

pozole – hominy soup with some meat and vegetables

menudo – tripe

gazpacho – a chilled vegetable soup spiced with hot chiles

Seafood

Baja's seafood is varied and excellent, consisting of both finfish and shellfish. It is available in restaurants most of the year. Clams, oysters, shrimp and prawns are also often available as *cocteles* (cocktails) from roadside stands in almost every city and town. Note that fish which is alive in the open water is referred to as *pez*, while fish after it has been caught is called *pescado*.

abulón – abalone

atún – tuna

ceviche – raw seafood marinated in lime and mixed with onions, chiles, garlic and tomatoes

filete de pescado – fish fillet

huachinango or *pargo* – red snapper

jurel – yellowtail

cabrilla – sea bass

lenguado – flounder or sole

pescado al mojo de ajo – fish fried in butter and garlic

pez espada – swordfish

sierra – mackerel

tiburón – shark

trucha de mar – sea trout

mariscos – shellfish

abulón – abalone

almejas – clams

callos – scallops

camarones – shrimps

camarones gigantes – prawns

cangrejo – large crab

jaiva – small crab

langosta – lobster

ostiones – oysters

Meat & Fowl

asado – roast

barbacoa – barbecued by placing under hot coals

biftec – beefsteak

birria – barbecued lamb or goat on a spit

cabra – goat

carne – meat

carne al carbón – charcoal-grilled meat

carne asada – grilled meat

carnitas – deep-fried pork

chicharrones – deep-fried pork rinds

chorizo – pork sausage

chuletas de cerdo – pork chops

conejo – rabbit

cordero – lamb

costillas de puerco – pork ribs or chops

hígado – liver

jamón – ham

milanesa – breaded beefsteak

patas de puerco – pig's feet

puerco – pork

pato – duck

pavo or *guajolote* – turkey

pollo – chicken

pollo asado – grilled chicken

pollo con arroz – chicken with rice

pollo frito – fried chicken

tocino – bacon or salted pork

Fruit

coco – coconut

dátil – date

fresa – strawberry; often used to refer to any berry

frutas – fruits

guayaba – guava

higo – fig

limón – lime or lemon

mango – mango

melón – melon
naranja – orange
papaya – papaya
piña – pineapple
plátano, banana – banana
toronja – grapefruit
uva – grape

Vegetables

Vegetables are rarely served as separate dishes; instead, they are often mixed into salads, soups and sauces.

aceituna – olive
aguacate – avocado
calabaza – squash or pumpkin
cebolla – onion
champiñon – mushroom
chícharo – pea
ejote – green bean
elote – corn on the cob
jícama – popular root crop, resembling a potato and an apple, eaten with a sprinkling of lime, chile and salt
lechuga – lettuce
papa – potato
papitas fritas – potato chips
tomate – tomato
verduras or *legumbres* – vegetables
zanahoria – carrot

Desserts

bolillo or *birote* – French-style rolls, sometimes sweet
flan – custard
helado – ice cream
nieve – flavored ice, Mexican equivalent of US 'snow cone'
paleta – flavored ice on a stick, equivalent to US popsicle, Australian icy-pole or UK ice-lolly
pan dulce – sweet roll
pastel – cake
postre – dessert

Other Food

azúcar – sugar
crema – cream
guacamole – mashed avocados mixed with onions, chile sauce, lemon, tomato and other ingredients
leche – milk
mantequilla – butter
mole – popular sauce made from numerous ingredients, including unsweetened chocolate, chile and many spices, often served over chicken or turkey

pimienta negra – black pepper
queso – cheese
salsa – sauce made with chiles, onions, tomato, lemon or lime juice and spices
sal – salt

At the Table

cuenta – bill
cuchara – spoon
cuchillo – knife
menú – menu
plato – plate
propina – the tip, usually about 10% to 15% of the bill
servilleta – serviette or napkin
tasa – cup
tenedor – fork
vaso or *copa* – glass

DRINKS
Tea & Coffee

Té and *café* are available throughout Baja California, but *té de manzanillo* (chamomile) is more common in restaurants than standard *té negro* (black tea). Regular coffee is mostly instant Nescafé but sometimes ground, and will almost always be served heavily sweetened unless requested otherwise. In restaurants, coffee or tea rarely arrives before the meal unless you ask for it.

In some tourist centers like Rosarito, Ensenada and Cabo San Lucas, capuccino and other espresso drinks are becoming more widely available.

café con crema – coffee with cream; cream is usually served separately
café con leche – about half hot milk and half coffee
café negro or *café americano* – black coffee with nothing added except sugar
café sin azúcar – coffee without sugar; this keeps the waiter from adding heaps of sugar but doesn't mean that coffee won't taste sweet – sugar is often added to coffee beans during processing

Juices

Fresh fruit and vegetable *jugos* (juices), *licuados* (shakes) and *aguas frescas* (flavored waters) are all popular. All the fruits and a few of the squeezable vegetables mentioned below are used either individually (as in jugos or aguas frescas) or in some combination (as in licuados). At reputable chains like La Michoacana, these are made with purified water.

A basic licuado is a blend of fruit or juice, water and sugar. Other items can be added or substituted: raw egg, milk, ice and flavorings like vanilla or nutmeg. Delicious combinations are practically limitless.

Aguas frescas are made by mixing fruit juice or syrup (made from mashed grains or seeds) with sugar and water; look for them in big glass jars on the counters of juice stands. Try the delicious *agua fresca de arroz* (rice water), which has a sweet, nutty taste; it is sometimes called *horchata*. *Cebada*, made with barley, is also surprisingly tasty and refreshing.

Soft Drinks

Almost every *refresco* (soft drink) available in the USA can also be found in Baja; two of the better Mexican brands are apple-flavored Sidral and Manzanita. Other flavors, like *fresa* (strawberry), *limón* (lime) and *cereza* (cherry) tend to be too sweet, but Peñafiel is a generally acceptable local brand.

Alcoholic Beverages

Mezcal, Tequila & Pulque Mezcal, tequila and pulque are all made from the sap of the *maguey (Agave* spp), a fibre plant with long, wide, slightly curved spikes which is a Mexican domesticate. Mezcal and tequila are made in similar ways. Mezcal can be made from any species of maguey, but tequila is made only from *Agave tequilana*, which grows in and around the mainland town of Tequila. The plant's spikes are stripped away to expose the plant's *piña* (core), which is chopped, roasted, shredded and then pressed to remove the juice. Sugar is added to the juice and, after the resulting mixture has fermented four days, it is twice distilled. Following distillation, the mezcal and tequila are aged in wooden casks for periods ranging from four months to seven years. The final product is a potent, golden-colored liquid, bottled and priced according to its age – the longer the aging, the higher the price.

The traditional manner of drinking mezcal or tequila involves licking the back of your hand and sprinkling salt on it, licking the salt, downing the shot of mezcal or tequila in one gulp, and sucking on a lime. When the bottle is empty, you are supposed to eat the worm (preferably fried), which is traditionally added to each bottle before it is filled.

Foreigners unaccustomed to the potency of straight tequila often take it in a mixed drink called a *margarita*. There are more than 100 types of margarita, most of them made by adding lime juice and orange liqueur to tequila in a salt-rimmed glass; fresh fruit, often strawberries or peaches, may be added.

When shopping for tequila, look for the letters 'DGN', which stand for Dirección General de Normas (Bureau of Standards), certifying that the tequila is made with agave tequilana rather than other species.

Pulque is a mildly alcoholic drink extracted directly from the sap of the maguey. Because this foamy, milky liquid spoils quickly, it cannot be bottled and easily shipped long distances; since most pulque is produced near Mexico City, it is difficult to find it in Baja bars and homes.

Liquor & Liqueurs Baja is a shopper's paradise for inexpensive liquors and liqueurs made in Mexico: Bacardi Rum, brandy (the Pedro Domecq brand is produced in Baja), Controy (Cointreau, an orange liqueur), Kahlua (coffee liqueur, extremely popular with North Americans) and Oso Negro vodka.

Remember that US Customs permits the importation of only one liter of liquor per person (over 21 years of age) every 30 days into mainland California, unless crossing by common carrier (bus, taxi or airplane). Common carrier passengers may import any amount of alcohol destined for 'personal use', a vague term meaning more than a single bottle but much less than a truckload. Duty, payable on quantities in excess of one bottle, is higher for hard liquor than for beer and wine.

Beer Baja's landmark Tecate brewery, the only one in Baja, now belongs to Cervecería Cuauhtémoc, Mexico's second largest brewery conglomerate, and also produces other brands like Carta Blanca.

Late 19th-century German immigrants first established breweries in Mexico, and their techniques and technology have probably been a major factor in making Mexican beer so popular throughout North America. Tecate is still one of the most popular beers in Baja, but other popular brands include Corona, Carta Blanca, Dos Equis and Sol Especial.

In restaurants and bars unaccustomed to tourists' tastes, beer may be served at room temperature. If you want cold beer, order *una cerveza fría, por favor*.

Wine Wine is less popular than beer and tequila, but Baja has several significant wineries, all in and around Ensenada: Vinícolas Domecq, Formex-Ybarra and Bodegas de Santo Tomás. Domecq is renowned in Mexico for its Los Reyes table wines, while Formex has over 800 acres (320 hectares) of vineyards in the Valle de Guadalupe and is known for its Terrasola table wine. L A Cetto has recently opened its Tijuana installations for tours and tasting.

Run by the mainland California-based Tchelistcheff family, Santo Tomás hopes to produce wines that can compete with the northern product. They have planted several varieties of grape from mainland California and recently started producing pinot noir, chardonnay and cabernet wines.

ENTERTAINMENT

Historically Baja California has a reputation for border-town bawdiness, but this notoriety is largely outdated despite the continued existence of Tijuana's Zona Norte and the tawdrier parts of Mexicali's Chinesca.

Both Tijuana and Mexicali are increasingly cosmopolitan cities with a variety of nightlife activities, ranging from spectator sports like baseball and horse racing, to glitzy discos and pop music concerts, to symphony orchestras and serious drama. In tourist resorts like San Felipe and Cabo San Lucas, bars and discos stay open nearly all night for live music and dancing. Sports bars with satellite TV connections, even in very remote places, attract tourists to Monday night football and other athletic events.

The cinema was once a dominant form of entertainment throughout Mexico, but the video revolution has subverted the big screen almost everywhere in Baja; only in Tijuana, Mexicali, Ensenada and La Paz will movie goers still find first-run features.

THINGS TO BUY

Baja's tourist centers – Tijuana, Mexicali, Ensenada, La Paz and Los Cabos – are full of souvenirs from throughout Mexico, but relatively few crafts come from Baja California itself. A few jewelry stores carry traditional silver jewelry and cutlery from Taxco. Carved doors and other woodwork from Guadalajara can be bought or ordered in Ensenada. A variety of other crafts are also available: woven baskets, colorful *rebozos* (shawls), brightly painted ceramic animals, hand-painted tiles, intricately decorated leather boots and wrought-iron staircases.

Many crafts sold in Baja qualify as junk or kitsch, like wrought-iron cages with stuffed birds, black velvet paintings, oversized embroidered sombreros, bull horns, and onyx chess sets. The exceptions to this general rule are Paipai, Kumiai and Cucupá Indian basketry, pottery and jewelry, which is available in those communities as well as in major tourist cities like Ensenada.

Travelers should know that the importation into the USA of black coral jewelry, a specialty from Baja's Cape Region, is restricted under Appendix II of the Convention on International Trade in Endangered Species (CITES). (See page 28 for more information about CITES). Export permits for black coral can only be obtained from Dr Exequiel Ezcurra (Dirección General de Aprovechamiento Ecológico de los Recursos, Río Elba 20, 10° Piso, Co y Delegación Cuauhtémoc, 06500 México, Distrito Federal, México).

It is much better, however, not to encourage the destruction of such endangered habitats by purchasing items made of coral, which is dredged from the reefs at great ecological cost. Other products regulated under either Appendix I (absolutely prohibited) or Appendix II (permitted with formal export permit only) include cacti, sea turtles and marine mammal products. These products can be confiscated and those in possession of them can be prosecuted under civil and criminal laws.

Baja's best bargains are medical services such as dentistry and optometry, and prescription pharmaceuticals. Because Mexican prices for such services and products are typically a fraction of their cost north of the border, some US insurance companies have begun to pay claims for medical services on the other side. Remember, of course, to declare to US Customs that gold crown fitted in Tijuana or Mexicali!

Pharmaceuticals require some caution. Self-medication is a risky business; the Tijuana weekly *Zeta* recently reported that only a handful of the 540 pharmacies in Tijuana, Tecate and Rosarito comply with regulations requiring a qualified doctor or pharmacist on duty, and that some pharmacies promote outdated or inappropriate medications as 'impulse' items. Analgesics, antiparasitics, antibiotics and the like require particular attention.

Border towns like Tijuana and Mexicali do a thriving business in auto body repair, painting and upholstery at prices from one-third to one-half of their cost north of the border. Mufflers, brakes and similar repairs are equally inexpensive.

Getting There & Away

FROM THE USA
Air
From the USA, the main carriers are Alaska Airlines, Mexicana de Aviación (Mexicana) and Aero California. Each offers different routes, fares and packages to Loreto, La Paz and Los Cabos (Cabo San Lucas and San José del Cabo). A recent entry is AirLA, which offers service to Tijuana, Ensenada, Mexicali and San Felipe; it also coordinates schedules and fares to mainland Mexico with Aeroméxico. Taesa has flights from Chicago to Tijuana, but the route is interrupted by a rather awkward connection via Zacatecas. Continental Airlines may institute service from Houston to Los Cabos. Morris Air of Salt Lake City runs charters to Cabos San Lucas in the winter months.

The main addresses and telephone numbers of these companies in the USA and Canada are:

Aero California
  1960 East Grand Ave, El Segundo, California 90245 (☎ (310) 322-2644, (800) 237-6225 toll free)
  Suite 640, 2425 Camelback Rd, Phoenix, Arizona 85016 (☎ (602) 224-5457)
AirLA
  6151 W Century Blvd, Suite 1114, Los Angeles, California 90045 (☎ (310) 215-8234, (800) 933-5952 toll free)
Alaska Airlines (☎ (800) 426-0333 toll free from the USA or Mexico) serves 30 cities in North America and, through its subsidiary, Horizon Air, 30 smaller cities and towns in the Pacific Northwest and just about every place with an airstrip in Alaska.
Mexicana (☎ (800) 531-7921 toll free)
  Suite 1004, 60 Bloor St West, Toronto, Ontario, Canada M4W 3B8 (☎ (416) 961-2080)
  Suite 1760, Oceanic Plaza, 1066 West Hastings St, Vancouver, British Columbia, Canada V6E 3X1 (☎ (604) 682-8364)
  Suite 314, 9841 Airport Blvd, Los Angeles, California 90045 (☎ (213) 646-9500)
  433 California St, San Francisco, California 94104 (☎ (800) 531-7921 toll free)

  55 East Monroe, Chicago, Illinois 60603 (☎ (312) 346-6805)
  Suite 1717, 500 5th Ave, New York, New York 10110 (☎ (212) 840-2344)
  Adolphus Hotel, 1303 Commerce, Dallas, Texas 75202 (☎ (214) 651-8303)
  Suite 203, 701 5th Ave, Seattle, Washington 98104 (☎ (206) 441-5480)
Morris Air (☎ (800) 444-5660 toll free)
Taesa (☎ (708) 686-7622, (800) 328-2372 toll free)

When booking flights with Mexicana or Aero California, check special fares and combined airfare and hotel packages. Fares are generally US$20 to US$30 lower on flights that arrive and depart Monday to Thursday. Accommodation at resort-style hotels in Baja is often much cheaper if arranged through an airline or travel agency.

To Tijuana, Mexicali & San Felipe
AirLA has three or four flights daily from Los Angeles International Airport (LAX) to Aeropuerto Internacional Abelardo Rodríguez in Tijuana, where it is possible to make many connections to Mexicali, San Felipe and mainland Mexico.

To Loreto & La Paz
Aero California is the only airline with direct flights from the USA (Los Angeles only) to Loreto, which cost about US$205 to US$225 return. This flight continues to La Paz for a fare of US$144/225 one way/return (Los Angeles to La Paz).

Mexicana and Aero California have daily flights from Tijuana to La Paz for US$200 to US$239 return. No other North American cities have direct connections to Loreto or La Paz; these must be made through Los Angeles or Tijuana.

To Los Cabos (San José del Cabo & Cabo San Lucas)
Mexicana, Alaska Airlines and Aero California all fly to Los

Cabos. Mexicana flies to Los Cabos from Los Angeles (daily) and San Francisco.

Return fares with Mexicana can be as low as US$185 from Los Angeles and US$349 from San Francisco but are usually higher. These airlines and several California-based travel agencies and tour operators, like Suntours (☎ (800) 786-8687), offer bargain packages for short-term visitors.

Alaska Airlines has two flights daily to Los Cabos from Los Angeles, usually in the morning and afternoon. Fares range from US$223 (restricted) to US$564 (1st class).

Aero California flies daily from Los Angeles, Phoenix and Denver to Los Cabos. Los Angeles one-way fares start at US$158 and return fares range from US$196 to US$249. Fares for the daily flight from Phoenix are US$154/205, while those from Denver are US$228 one way, US$305 return during the week (Monday to Thursday) and US$328 return on weekends (Friday to Sunday).

Morris Air flies charters from Salt Lake City to Cabo San Lucas between Christmas and April; prices range from US$299 to US$419 depending on departure dates.

Holiday Packages If flying to San Felipe, Loreto, La Paz or Los Cabos, check specials offered by Mexicana and various travel agencies for stays at resort-style or tourist-class hotels. Aero California works with many agencies and tour operators, including the following in southern mainland California:

Baja Holidays (☎ (714) 826-3877, (800) 326-2252 toll free in the USA) offers packages including air fares from Los Angeles and three nights at San José del Cabo's Hotel Palmilla (US$323 per person) or Cabo San Lucas' Hotel Finisterra (US$295 per person).

Barvi Tours (☎ (310) 474-4041, (800) 824-7102 toll free) offers three nights at the Posada Real Los Cabos (US$225 per person) or Meliá San Lucas (US$437 per person). The staff are Mexico travel specialists; most were born in Mexico and are thoroughly familiar with the country. Special fishing trips can be arranged throughout Baja, mostly in Los Cabos and La Paz.

Island Flight Vacations (☎ (310) 477-5858, (800) 426-4570 toll free) offers air fares and three nights at the Plaza Las Glorias (US$376 per person) or the Meliá Cabo Real (US$375 per person) in Cabo San Lucas.

Alaska Airlines offers a midweek four-night package, including air fare and accommodation at an unspecified hotel in Los Cabos, for US$299 per person.

Check Sunday travel sections of major US newspapers for additional listings. Before committing to one of these packages, confirm hotel and airline reservations that the operator has supposedly made for you. Although problems are unlikely, you don't want to show up at the airport or hotel and find yourself without tickets or reservations.

Border Crossings

From west to east, there are five official border crossings from mainland California to Baja: Tijuana, Otay Mesa, Tecate, Mexicali and Algodones. The Otay Mesa crossing is open daily from 6 am to 10 pm, and Tecate and Algodones are open daily from 7 am to midnight. Mexican immigration at any crossing will validate tourist cards and process car permits free of charge.

San Ysidro to Tijuana Open 24 hours, this is one of the most heavily traveled border crossings in the world.

Mesa de Otay Opened to relieve the pressure on the San Ysidro-Tijuana crossing, Mesa de Otay is open daily from 6 am to 10pm. For motorists it offers a far less congested port-of-entry, accessed via California State Highway 117.

Tecate (California/Baja California) Open daily from 7 am to midnight, Tecate is about 30 miles (50 km) southeast of San Diego via California state highways 94 and 188.

Calexico to Mexicali Open 24 hours, this crossing is about 8 miles (13 km) south of

El Centro via California State Highway 111. The city of Calexico recently approved a bond issue for construction of a new rail station, and train service from Los Angeles may soon follow.

Andrade to Algodones The least frequently used border crossing between mainland California and Baja California is nevertheless bustling. It's located about 7 miles (11 km) west of Yuma, Arizona, via Interstate 8 and California State Highway 186. It's open from 6 am to 8 pm daily.

Bus & Trolley
Travelers can enter Baja by land at any of the crossings mentioned above. There are frequent buses and trains (light rail) to the San Ysidro crossing. Buses also run to Calexico/Mexicali and to Yuma in Arizona (the closest US city to the Andrade/Algodones crossing).

Greyhound is the major bus operator from the USA to the border. If planning to travel extensively by bus in the USA, consider Greyhound's Ameripass or International Ameripass; the former costs US$250 for seven days of travel, US$450 for 15 days or US$550 for 30 days.

The International Ameripass is available to foreign students, research scholars and lecturers (and their families) who have been in the USA less than a year. If you qualify, it is a better deal for US$140 for seven days, US$225 for 15 days and US$280 for 30 days; extra days can be added for US$15 per day.

The Ameripass is sold at every Greyhound terminal, while the International Ameripass can only be bought at Greyhound terminals in the US cities of New York, Miami, Hollywood (Los Angeles) and San Francisco, after completion of an affidavit and presentation of your passport to the appropriate Greyhound officials.

To Tijuana Many buses run daily from San Diego and Los Angeles to Tijuana. A new light-rail trolley line also runs from central San Diego to the border.

The San Diego Trolley (☎ (619) 231-1466), a modernized version of what once was San Diego's only mass transit system, runs every 15 minutes from 5 am to 1 am from downtown San Diego to the border crossing at San Ysidro. Fares range up to US$1.75 according to the length of the trip.

Greyhound Bus Lines (☎ (800) 231-2222 toll free) departs frequently from its central Los Angeles terminal at 1716 E Seventh St en route to its San Diego terminal at 120 W Broadway (US$12 one way) and to Tijuana's bus terminal at the corner of Avenida México and Avenida Madero (US$27 one way). Buses start as early as 6 am and run until about 10 pm.

Mexicoach (☎ (619) 232-5049 in San Diego, ☎ 85-69-13 in Tijuana) has daily buses at 9, 10 and 11 am, noon, and 2, 4 and 6 pm to and from San Diego's Amtrak station to central Tijuana's Plaza La Jolla, directly behind the Jai Alai Palace. One-way/return fares are US$6.25/12 for adults, with a small discount for seniors (60 and over); children under 12 travel free.

Mexicoach will also arrange taxis from Plaza La Jolla to the airport, but you can organize this more cheaply yourself, either by hailing a cab at Plaza La Jolla or phoning the government-run taxi service (☎ 83-10-20). See the Tijuana Getting There & Away section for more information on fares and schedules.

ATC/Vancom (☎ (619) 427-6438) runs buses from the corner of Broadway and Third Ave or Broadway and Front St in downtown San Diego to the US side of the border for only US$1.50. It takes 80 minutes to reach the border.

To Calexico/Mexicali Greyhound also runs buses from San Diego and Phoenix (via Yuma) to Calexico and El Centro. One-way/return fares from San Diego are US$16/24 to El Centro and US$14/22 to Calexico. The fare from Los Angeles to Calexico is US$23/39.

Phoenix departures are at 7:40 am (arriving Calexico/Mexicali at 12:50 pm) and 5:45 pm (arriving Calexico/Mexicali at 10:30 pm). One-way/return fares from Phoenix are US$31/51.

Taxi

Taxis are available on both sides of the border in San Diego/Tijuana and Calexico/Mexicali, and on the Mexican side in Tecate and Algodones. There is a singular advantage in taking a taxi across the border from Baja California into mainland California: passengers on common carriers are not subject to import limitations on alcoholic drinks, including beer, wine and spirits, as long as those spirits are for personal use. For more information, see the Customs section in the Facts for the Visitor chapter.

Train

Amtrak runs eight passenger trains daily from its Los Angeles terminal at 800 N Alameda St to its San Diego terminal at 1050 Kettner Blvd, near Broadway. One-way/return fares are US$24/31. For latest fare and schedule information, phone Amtrak (☎ (800) 872-7245 toll free). From the San Diego terminal, trolleys go directly to the border at San Ysidro.

Train service from Los Angeles to Calexico may begin in the near future, thanks to a bond issue recently approved by Calexico residents.

Driving

Countless visitors drive their own vehicles into Baja California from the USA. Those traveling no farther south than Mexicali or Ensenada and staying less than 72 hours do not need a tourist card or car permit, but those continuing to mainland Mexico, either by ferry from Baja or overland from Mexicali, will need a car permit/tourist card (for the driver) or a tourist card for all passengers.

Car insurance, purchased from a Mexican company, is essential for driving in Mexico; policies from other countries are not valid. While insurance is not obligatory, it can prevent serious legal problems for anyone involved in an accident.

According to Mexican law, the principals in an accident are guilty until proven innocent. Regardless of details, foreigners are more likely to be considered guilty than locals, especially if they have no insurance, in which case police detention is probable until fault is established. Understandably, it is common for the victims of a nonlethal accident to leave the scene before the police arrive.

For more information about car permits, tourist cards and insurance, see the Visas and Documents sections in the Facts for the Visitor chapter.

Sea

From California Cruise ships, private yachts and a shuttle boat between San Diego and Ensenada are the only ways to travel by sea to Baja.

The cruise ship *Jubilee*, belonging to Carnival Cruise Lines (☎ (800) 327-9501 toll free) sails every Sunday from Pier No 93-A at the Port of San Pedro, near Los Angeles. Week-long cruises visit Cabo San Lucas, Puerto Vallarta and Mazatlán; prices start at US$899 per person, with air fares additional.

Starlite Cruises (☎ (619) 338-1100), 1150 North Harbour Drive in San Diego, organizes luxury, Vegas-style day cruises to Ensenada for US$59 (US$69 Saturdays), plus US$19.50 port charges. Its *Pacific Star* leaves San Diego at 9 am and returns to San Diego by 10:30 pm; visitors have the afternoon in Ensenada or, for an additional charge, can stay overnight in Ensenada with accommodation included.

Transportation-only arrangements are possible for longer stays. One-way passengers pay US$49 plus US$9.75 port charges.

If you know something about boats and sailing, look for a crew position on one of the many boats that sail south from mainland California. Marinas at Dana Point, Newport Beach, Belmont Shores and Marina del Rey are all good places to ask, but one correspondent has offered these detailed suggestions for southbound travelers on the Pacific coast:

From October through February sailboats converge on San Diego to rest, make repairs and purchase provisions. Crews also frequently change, and it is a perfect place for crew to be added. Crews with experience are in demand, and just about any type of deal they want with regard to costs is possible. There is a place for the novice. A person who is willing to ask questions and learn can also do quite well. Many of the skippers are engaged in their first open ocean experience and may not be all that relaxed. I would encourage potential crews to have frank discussions about costs, equipment, safety, nudity and expectations. The last is very important for females (crew) and male skippers.

Shelter Island in San Diego is where almost all skippers meet and are available. Throughout the boating communities, we are linked via radio for news and information. The radio networks are referred to as UHF nets or simply local nets. The key is that you do not need to have a radio to participate. Yachties are more than happy to broadcast that potential crew is available. Shyness has no place.

There are two stores that cater to the cruising community. Make inquiries and/or send three-by-five cards for posting on the bulletin board to Downwind Marine (☎ (619) 224-2733, fax (619) 224-7683), 2819 Canon St, San Diego, California 92106. The local net is operated by Mike at Pacific Marine Supply (☎ 223-7194, fax (619) 223-9054), 2804 Canon St, San Diego, California 92106.

For vessels in Baja, Downwind is a supplier of spare parts. If ocean travel is not your bag, drivers buying parts will often take riders as far as La Paz to share gas.

Mexico Services (☎ (310) 398-5797, fax (310) 398-2048) at 12601 Venice Blvd, Los Angeles, California 90066 can arrange full boating insurance packages as well as car insurance. Any vessel traveling south along the Baja coast beyond Ensenada or staying more than three days in Ensenada must file a crew list with a Mexican consulate before entering Mexican waters. All registration papers and other relevant documentation must also be on board.

The Secretaria de Pesca (Mexican Fisheries Department, ☎ (619) 233-6956, 2550 Fifth Ave, Suite 101, San Diego, California 92101) can also provide necessary forms and information.

FROM THE UK & EUROPE

There are no direct flights from Europe to Baja California – you must first fly to North America or Mexico City and from there to Baja. The cheapest alternative is probably to fly to Los Angeles and then head south, rather than fly to Mexico City and travel north. Excursion return fares from London to Los Angeles are around UK£420 (UK£459 to Mexico City).

For cheaper fares from London, check the many 'bucket shops' that advertise in the daily newspapers, giveaway papers or the weekly magazine *Time Out*. Two reliable agents for discounted tickets are Trail Finders, (☎ (071) 938-3366) 46 Earls Court Rd, London W8 and STA Travel, (☎ (071) 581-4132) 74 Old Brompton Rd, London SW7.

FROM AUSTRALIA & NEW ZEALAND

The cheapest and most direct route across the Pacific is to fly to the US Pacific Coast (Los Angeles or San Francisco) and continue to Mexico from there.

Direct discount fares from Australia to Los Angeles range from A$950 to A$1100 one way and from A$1250 to A$1700 return, depending on season of travel. Airfares from New Zealand range from NZ$1250 one way and NZ$1800 to NZ$1950 return. If you wish to stopover in Hawaii or plan to stay abroad for more than two months, you will generally pay more.

FROM MAINLAND MEXICO
Air

Internal Mexican flights are a bit cheaper than comparable flights in the USA. There are direct daily flights from several mainland Mexican cities to Tijuana, Mexicali, Loreto, La Paz and Los Cabos. Consult Aeroméxico, Aero California or Mexicana for specific route information.

Bus

Buses run regularly from major centers throughout Mexico to Mexicali. From Mexicali, you can continue to other Baja cities and towns (see the Mexicali Getting There & Away section for details).

Train

Mexican railways offer daily service from Guadalajara to Mexicali, with intermediate stops including Tepic, Mazatlán, Culiacán, Hermosillo and Guaymas. In some cases, it is necessary to change trains at Benjamín Hill, in the state of Sonora.

Ferry

One alternative between mainland Mexico and Baja is the ferry across the Gulf of California. Boats sail between Guaymas and Santa Rosalía, La Paz and Topolobampo (near Los Mochis), and La Paz and Mazatlán at least weekly.

Although the schedules and fares listed here will probably change, they will give you at least some idea of departure times and costs:

To/From La Paz

Class	To/From Mazatlán	To/From Topolobampo (Los Mochis)
	(daily)	(daily)
salón	US$14.50	US$10
turista	US$29	US$20
cabina	US$43.50	US$29
especial	US$58	US$38.50

Vehicle Rates

Length*	To/From Mazatlán	To/From Topolobampo
Up to 5 meters	US$106	US$64.50
5 to 6½ meters with trailer up to	US$138	US$84
9 meters	US$190.50	US$116
9 to 17 meters	US$360	US$219
bus	US$180	US$110.25
motorcycles	US$14	US$8.25

(*1 meter = 3 feet 3 inches)

A ferry departs La Paz at 7 pm daily for Mazatlán (arriving 9 am) and at 8 pm for Topolobampo (arriving 7 am). Ferries leave Mazatlán at 7 pm (arriving in La Paz at 9 am) and leave Topolobampo at 8 pm (arriving in La Paz at 7 am).

Travelers have recently reported mixed experiences on the ferry service from Baja to the mainland. Fares were rising rapidly and the availability of accommodation was becoming increasingly unpredictable. Recently, Grupo Sematur de California, a Mexico-based conglomerate, was operating the service, which seems to have improved conditions.

TOURS

General and special interest tours are an increasingly popular way to explore Baja California. Whale-watching expeditions, desert bicycling trips, kayaking and windsurfing in the Gulf of California, beach camping trips and fishing trips are only a few of the many types of tours available. The following lists may help you determine tour operators' specialties (see the Tour Companies section later in this chapter for more information):

Astronomy
    Baja Expeditions, Forum Travel International
Bicycling
    Baja Expeditions
Bird Watching
    Biological Journeys, Oceanic Society Expeditions
Horseback Treks
    Baja Expeditions
Kayaking
    Baja Expeditions, Baja Tropicales (see Baja Fishing Resorts later), Mountain Travel Sobek, Southwest Sea Kayaks
Mountain Biking
    Baja Expeditions, Vela's Baja Highwind Center
Scuba Diving
    Baja Expeditions
Snorkeling
    Baja Expeditions, Oceanic Society Expeditions, Vela's Baja Highwind Center
Surfing
    Baja Expeditions
Whale-Watching
    American Cetacean Society, Baja Discovery, Baja Expeditions, Biological Journeys, Foundation for Field Research, Green Tortoise, Nature Expeditions International, Oceanic Society Expeditions, Pacific Sea Fari Tours, San Diego Natural History Museum
Wind Surfing
    Vela's Baja Highwind Center

Some activities can be combined in a single trip. For example, Baja Expeditions has a sea kayaking trip that can also include some snorkeling, camping and whale-watching.

Pacific Sea Fari Tours runs several sea tours from San Diego to several Pacific Coast and Sea of Cortés destinations. A few of these tours are specially designed for whale-watching. Their itineraries include the following:

Laguna San Ignacio (seven to eight days)
    San Diego-Isla Todos Santos/Ensenada-Islas San Benito-Laguna San Ignacio-Isla Cedros-Isla San Martín-San Diego
Baja West Coast (eight to nine days)
    San Diego-Isla Todos Santos/Ensenada-Islas San Benitos-Laguna San Ignacio-Bahía Magdalena-Puerto San Carlos-La Paz
Baja Offshore Islands (three days)
    San Diego-Isla Coronado Norte-Isla Coronado Sur-Isla Todos Santos-San Diego
Sea of Cortez (11 days)
    San Diego-Islas San Benito-Laguna San Ignacio-Bahía Magdalena-Cabo San Lucas-Isla Espíritu Santo-Isla San José-Isla Santa Catalina-Isla Ildefonso-La Paz

Pacific Sea Fari Tours uses two boats for these trips: the 30-passenger MV *Spirit of Adventure* and the 20-passenger MV *Big Game*. Whale-watching expeditions (their specialty) take place annually from late December to April. For more details, contact Paul C Robbins, Natural History Coordinator, Pacific Sea Fari Tours (☎ (619) 226-8224, fax (619) 222-0784), 2803 Emerson St, San Diego, California 92106. Costs range from US$300 for weekend trips to US$1895 for longer excursions.

Spirit of Adventure Charters (☎ (619) 226-1729) runs trips of similar itineraries and duration for whale-watching at comparable prices. Their mailing address is 1938 Catalina Blvd, San Diego, California 92107.

Affiliated with the environmental organization Friends of the Earth, Oceanic Society Expeditions is a nonprofit enterprise specializing in natural history trips to Baja's Pacific and Gulf coasts. Whale-watching, snorkeling, bird-watching and camping trips range from seven to 11 days, all led by experienced naturalists. On a few tours, they use the 86-foot *Spirit of Adventure*. One-week overland trips cost US$950, while week-long whale-watching cruises cost US$1635. Contact them at ☎ (415) 441-1106 or by writing to Oceanic Society Expeditions, Fort Mason Center, Bldg E, San Francisco, California, USA 94123.

Whale-Watching

It is possible to arrange informal full or half-day whale-watching trips on local fishing boats at Scammon's, Guerrero Negro and San Ignacio lagoons and Magdalena Bay, but these are generally less extensive and informative than organized trips arranged in the USA.

Tour Companies

The following list contains addresses for and additional information about US tour companies operating in Baja:

American Cetacean Society, PO Box 2639, San Pedro, California 90731 (☎ (213) 548-7821), a nonprofit whale-conservation group, organizes several whale-watching trips every year to help support its activities, publishes the quarterly journal *Whalewatcher* and a newsletter *Whale News* for its members and also produces two information kits about whales and dolphins (US$5 each, plus tax and shipping).

Arrow to the Sun Bicycle Touring Company offers tours for periods ranging from a weekend to 25 days, at various prices and levels of ability. One offering is a mountain bike excursion into the mountains west of Loreto. Owner Michael Sobrero has led cycling trips into Baja California for over a decade. For more information, contact him at PO Box 115, Taylorsville, California 95983 (☎ (916) 284-6263).

Backroads Bicycle Touring, Suite Q-417, 1516 Fifth St, Berkeley, California 94710 (☎ (510) 527-1555, (800) 462-2848 toll free outside California) has five and six-day mountain bike loops of southern Baja's Cape Region, starting in San José del Cabo and ending in Cabo San Lucas. While most routes are not difficult, van shuttle support is available in a pinch. With accommodation in hotels, trip prices start at US$1245 per person; with camping, prices are around US$700.

Backroads also offers five and six-day hiking trips in the Cape Region, costing US$698 for campers; trips with hotel accommodation cost US$1095.

Baja Discovery runs five to eight-day whale-watching trips, starting around US$1450 per person, which combine comfortable hotels (usually the La Pinta chain) with beach camping. Small 22-foot *pangas* (skiffs) allow passengers to get close enough to pet the whales. Baja Discovery also runs personalized van trips to Bahía de Los Angeles on the Sea of Cortés for about US$950 per person, and spring and autumn hiking trips from about US$650. For further information, contact Karen Ivey at PO Box 152527, San Diego, California 92195 (☎ (619) 262-0700, (800) 829-2252 toll free).

Baja Expeditions (☎ (619) 581-3311, fax (619) 581-6542), (800) 843-6967 toll free), 2625 Garnet Ave, San Diego, California 92109, is Baja's oldest and largest natural history and adventure travel company, emphasizing whale-watching, scuba diving and sea kayaking. Knowledgeable naturalists and guides accompany every trip to explain the flora, fauna and environment. Trips start at US$750 for five-day kayak trips and run as high as US$2495 for 10-day diving expeditions in the Sea of Cortés. A few Baja Expeditions' trips, such as the 'Sea of Cortés Cruise' and whale-watching cruises, take place aboard the fully equipped schooner *Copper Sky* and the MV *Don José*.

Baja Fishing Resorts (☎ (818) 591-9463, (800) 368-4334 toll free in the USA) offers packages of four and five days with lodging, meals and fishing in the East Cape area, from US$238 per person. Their mailing address is PO Box 9016, Calabasas, California 91372.

Baja Tropicales offers local kayak trips from Playa Santispac, near Mulegé, for US$35 per person, including meals and beverages; they require a minimum of four persons. In addition, they offer five and six-day trips around Bahía Concepción and to spots like Isla San Marcos, Bahía Magdalena and Laguna Ojo de Liebre (Scammon's Lagoon). Prices range from US$290 to US$340. Rental equipment is also available for experienced kayakers. For more detailed information, inquire at Hotel Las Casitas (☎ 3-00-19, fax 3-03-40 in Mulegé) or write to Baja Tropicales,

Apartado Postal 60, Mulegé, Baja California Sur, México.

Biological Journeys specialize in natural history expeditions, offering about half a dozen whale-watching trips yearly to San Ignacio, Scammon's Lagoon, and the Sea of Cortés, from February to mid-March. For more information, write to 1696 Ocean Dr, McKinleyville, California 95521 (☎ (707) 839-0178, (800) 548-7555 toll free). Prices range from US$795 for short trips to US$2995 for more extensive tours.

The Foundation for Field Research, PO Box 910078, San Diego, California 92121 (☎ (619) 450-3460), arranges natural study trips to Baja and elsewhere; see also the listing in the Activities section in the Facts for the Visitor chapter.

Forum Travel International offers several trips to Baja, including whale-watching and special astronomy-oriented trips at very reasonable prices. For more information and a list of trips, contact Forum Travel International, Suite 21, 91 Gregory Lane, Pleasant Hill, California 94523 (☎ (510) 671-2900, (510) 946-1500).

Green Tortoise Alternative Travel, PO Box 24459, San Francisco, California 94124 (☎ (310) 392-1990, (805) 569-1884, (408) 462-6437, (415) 821-0803, (503) 937-3603, (503) 225-0310, (206) 324-7433, (604) 732-5153, (212) 431-3348, (617) 265-8533, (310) 392-1990, (800) 227-4766 toll free for all other areas) offers Baja bus trips with two or three weeks of beach camping and sea kayaking, usually between November and April. Nine-day trips cost around US$300, meals included, while 14-day trips cost around US$420, meals included. Meals are mostly vegetarian.

Mountain Travel Sobek, 6420 Fairmount Ave, El Cerrito, California 94530 (☎ (510) 527-8100, (800) 227-2384 toll free) offers six-day kayak trips in the Gulf of California, starting at US$890.

Nature Expeditions International, PO Box 11496, Eugene, Oregon 97440 (☎ (503) 484-6529), conducts nine-day cruises in the Gulf of California, visiting several hard-to-reach islands to view birds, whales and other wildlife. Costs start around US$2500.

Oceanic Society Expeditions, Fort Mason Center, Building E, San Francisco, California 94123 (☎ (415) 441-1106), runs 11-day motor yacht expeditions along the Pacific and Gulf coasts from San Diego to La Paz, visiting Laguna San Ignacio for the whale-watching season. It also offers one-week cruises to Laguna San Ignacio, which include stops at Islas San Benito and Isla Cedros, and a week-long exploration of the Gulf from a base camp in Bahía de Los Angeles.

Point South RV Tours conducts tours for recreational-vehicle enthusiasts, organizing caravans from San Diego to Cabo San Lucas that can be extended to mainland Mexico. It also offers special insurance policies for assistance during mechanical breakdowns, which cover towing, parts shipping, hospital costs and other matters not normally covered by Mexican car insurance policies. Their address is 11313 Edmondson Ave, Moreno Valley, California 92555 (☎ (909) 247-1222, (800) 421-1394 toll free).

The San Diego Natural History Museum, PO Box 1390, San Diego, California 92112 (☎ (619) 232-3821, ext 201), offers eight-day overland whale-watching safaris for US$925 per person on a car-pool basis. Its eight-day natural history cruises of the Gulf of California, stopping at both mainland and island destinations of difficult access, cost from US$2170 per person.

The Sierra Club conducts occasional trips to Baja. For details, write to 730 Polk St, San Francisco, California 94109 or contact a local branch in the USA or Canada.

Southwest Sea Kayaks, 1310 Rosecrans St, San Diego California 92106 (☎ (619) 222-3616) arranges kayaking excursions in the Ensenada area, the Midriff Islands of the central Gulf of California, and southern Baja, including whale-watching trips at Laguna Ojo de Liebre. It also publishes a useful quarterly newsletter.

The Touring Exchange, PO Box 265, Port Townsend, Washington 98368 (☎ (206) 385-0667) leads one to two-week bicycle and mountain bike excursions of varying difficulty from January to April. Its 'Baja Challenge' is a two-week, 1145-mile (1843 km) ride from Tijuana to Cabo San Lucas, definitely not for beginners. Prices range from US$450 to US$795.

Vela's Baja Highwind Center is part of Vela Highwind Centers, based in the San Francisco area. Each winter (November to April) it relocates to the Hotel Playa del Sol in Los Barriles (south of La Paz), where the season's highlight is an annual windsurfing championship race, usually held in early January. World-class windsurfing instructors hold weekly classes with prototypes of the latest equipment direct from the manufacturers. Mountain biking, snorkeling, horseback riding and fishing are also possible. Week-long trips start around US$700 per person, double occupancy. For further details, contact Vela Highwind Centers, 351-C Foster City Blvd, Foster City, California 94404 (☎ (415) 525-2070, (800) 223-5443 toll free).

Viajes Guaycura (☎ 8-16-41, 8-10-45), Alvarado 95, Suite 4, Ensenada, organizes overnight packages from San Diego from US$88 per person. These packages include round-trip bus transport between San Diego's Amtrak station and Ensenada, transfers to and one night's accommodation at one of several featured hotels, an Ensenada city tour, one free margarita and discount coupons. Departures are at 9 am and 1 pm daily. Their US contact is (☎ (800) 628-3475).

Worldwide Sportfishing Adventures, PO Box 13896, Scottsdale, Arizona 85267 (☎/fax (602) 948-7707) offers five-day, four-night fishing excursions from Phoenix for US$595 per person, plus tax; this includes air fare, accommodation at Hotel Plaza Las Glorias, and two full days of fishing with guides, tackle and licenses.

Getting Around

The opening of the 1050-mile (1700-km) *Carretera Transpeninsular Benito Juárez* (Transpeninsular Highway) in 1973 eliminated the major obstacle to large-scale tourism on the peninsula – its very bad roads. Less than a year later, Baja California Sur (southern Baja California) became a separate, bona fide Mexican state.

Joseph Wood Krutch, in his classic *The Forgotten Peninsula*, remarked that 'Baja is a splendid example of how much bad roads can do for a country' in preserving it much as it was when Europeans first saw it. Today, however, Baja has a transpeninsular bus system, six international airports, over 40 airstrips, taxis and rent-a-car agencies in major cities and towns, and plenty of donkeys, mules and horses.

In areas on or near paved highways, the car is the principal mode of transport. Off these main roads, travel on gravel roads or corrugated dirt tracks requires caution, but 4WD vehicles are essential only in truly extreme cases. Nevertheless, if you have any doubts, be cautious when heading off the main routes.

AIR

Three major domestic carriers, and several smaller ones, connect the peninsula's five major airports (Tijuana, Mexicali, Loreto, La Paz and Los Cabos) and the Mexican mainland. In addition, Ensenada, Guerrero Negro, Isla Cedros and Bahía Tortugas have very limited commercial aviation; for information on these destinations, see the appropriate sections. Many towns have air taxi charter services; some resorts, especially in the Los Cabos area, provide air taxis for their guests.

For addresses and telephones of Aero California and Mexicana, which have direct flights to the USA, see the Getting There & Away chapter. Aeroméxico (☎ (800) 237-6639 in the USA) has no flights from the USA to Baja California,

but offers an extensive network of flights within Baja California and to the mainland.

With air fares more erratic than other prices in the travel business, the sample fares in the accompanying table are approximations based on purchasing a ticket at the airport without a reservation. Most carriers have significantly cheaper fares with advance reservations, even for one-way flights; some routes, such as Tijuana-Guadalajara, have very inexpensive promotional fares (as low as US$78), but available seats may be limited.

From Tijuana

To one-way/return	Airline	Frequency
La Paz US$168/336	Aero California	daily
La Paz US$203/386	Aeroméxico	daily
Los Mochis US$140/280	Aero California	daily
Los Mochis US$167/334	Aeroméxico	daily
Guadalajara US$186/372	Taesa	daily
Guadalajara US$242/484	Aero California	daily
Guadalajara US$260/468	Aeroméxico	daily
Guadalajara US$260/468	Mexicana	daily
Mexico City US$220/440	Taesa	daily
Mexico City US$282/564	Aero California	daily
Mexico City US$307/614	Aeroméxico	daily
Mexico City US$307/614	Mexicana	daily

From La Paz

To one-way/return	Airline	Frequency
Loreto US$52/104	Aero California	daily
Los Mochis US$67/134	Aero California	daily
Mazatlán US$96/192	Aero California	daily

Guadalajara	Aero California	daily
US$144/288		
Guadalajara	Aeroméxico	daily
US$156/312		
Mexico City	Aero California	daily
US$230/460		
Mexico City	Aeroméxico	daily
US$253/506		

Aero California's flights from Loreto to La Paz are extensions of its Los Angeles to Loreto flights.

Nearly every town and village in Baja California has an airstrip, though most are only large enough for small private aircraft. Private pilots should consult Arnold Senterfitt's *Airports of Baja California* (Arnold Senterfitt Publications, PO Box 11950, Reno, Nevada 89510) for detailed information about every airstrip and airport on the peninsula.

BUS

Air-conditioned buses, operate daily between Tijuana and La Paz for about US$56 one way (a trip that takes 22 to 24 hours), are fairly comfortable but stop in almost every town and city between Tijuana and La Paz to let off and pick up passengers. Since it is impossible to predict how many seats will be available at any given stop, there is no guarantee of a seat at intermediate stops, however, it is rare not to get a seat except on holidays. See the Tijuana and La Paz Getting There & Away sections for specific departure information. Some *elite* or *especial* services, only slightly more expensive, now serve meals and show films.

Buses (some air-conditioned) also run frequently between La Paz and Cabo San Lucas (via San José del Cabo or Todos Santos), Tijuana and Ensenada, Tijuana and Rosarito, Tijuana and Mexicali (via Tecate), and Ensenada and San Felipe. See the Getting There & Away sections for these cities/towns for schedules and fares.

Tickets can be bought just before departure, but to be assured of getting a seat on long-distance trips, it's a good idea to purchase a ticket in advance. Advance purchase is unnecessary for short trips, especially from Tijuana, Mexicali and Ensenada, because departures are frequent.

CAR

Travel by car is usually more convenient than going by bus, and it's often the only way to reach Baja's more isolated towns, villages, mountains and beaches. Many North Americans take large RVs, but such vehicles mostly limit them to the few paved highways.

Driver's License

To drive in Baja California, you need a valid US or Canadian driver's license or an International Driving Permit. US and Canadian licenses are widely recognized, but the International Driving Permit may require some explanation, since Baja police are unaccustomed to it.

A car permit is only required for mainland Mexico; it also serves as a tourist card for the driver. It is preferable to validate them at the border, but it may be possible to do so in Ensenada or at ferry terminals at Santa Rosalía and La Paz. For more information about car permits and tourist cards, see the Visas and Documents sections in the Facts for the Visitor chapter.

Car Permits

Motorists planning to take the ferry from Baja to the mainland should get their permit form stamped at the border after paying the US$10 fee by Visa or Master-Card, though it is now presumably possible to do so at ferry terminals in Santa Rosalía and La Paz (Pichilingue). The Tijuana office is on the right-hand side of the border post just beyond the crossing, adjacent to the immigration office, but the less congested Mesa de Otay office is more expeditious. Permits are valid for 90 days.

To obtain an auto permit, show proof of citizenship (such as a passport or birth certificate) and the original current registration or notarized bill of sale for each vehicle, including motorcycles and boats. If the vehicle belongs to or is registered to a bank or company, you will need these documents plus a notarized affidavit of authorization. This affidavit is also required if the vehicle will be driven by someone without the registered owner present. The original current registration is also still necessary.

You must have a permit for each vehicle that you bring into mainland Mexico, and no individual may obtain a permit for more than one vehicle. Thus, if you bring a motorcycle as well as a car, a companion will have to obtain a permit for the motorcycle with your authorization. These regulations also apply to boats, but are subject to change; contact a Mexican consulate or AAA before going.

Drivers in mainland Mexico may not leave the country without their vehicle, even if it breaks down, without permission from either the Registro Federal de Vehículos in Mexico City or a *registro* or *hacienda* (treasury department) in another city or town. This is to reduce the illegal importation of vehicles for resale in Mexico as well as auto theft.

Occasionally visitors are asked to show their tourist cards on leaving the country, but this is unusual except on arrival at the Tijuana or Mexicali airports from some other point in Mexico.

Car Insurance

Mexican law only recognizes Mexican car insurance – non-Mexican insurance policies are not valid anywhere in the country. Though not obligatory, insurance is highly recommended because all parties in a car accident are considered guilty until proven innocent. This means that you must be able to prove to the police that you have the means to pay all injuries and damages or wait in jail until the case goes to court. Insurance prevents your detention.

There are many insurance offices at every Baja border crossing, some of them open 24 hours a day. Rates are government controlled and thus fairly standard on both sides of the border, but policies may also be arranged through representatives in the USA. Most major US insurance companies and automobile clubs (which usually require membership) can help arrange cov-

erage. If you're planning to spend more than a few days in Baja, contact representatives offering group coverage, whose rates may be 20% to 30% lower than standard policies.

US-based organizations offering Mexican insurance policies include Mexico Services, McAfee & Edwards, International Gateway and Sanborn's:

Mexico Services (☎ (310) 398-5797, fax (310) 398-2048) is at 12601 Venice Blvd, Los Angeles, California 90066. Owner-manager Raúl Martinez will arrange insurance policies for automobiles, airplanes or boats and help with any permits, licenses or documents, whether for automobiles, fishing or pets. He also runs a reservation service for hotels throughout Mexico.

MacAfee & Edwards Mexican Insurance Specialists (☎ (213) 388-9674), Suite 1018, 2500 Wilshire Blvd, Los Angeles, California 90057, offer insurance policies for automobiles, airplanes and boats. Maps and tourist cards are also available.

International Gateway Insurance Brokers (☎ (619) 422-3057, (619) 585-3033, (800) 423-2646 toll free in California) is at Suite 107, 3450 Bonita Rd, Chula Vista, California 92013. A typical three-day policy for an automobile worth US$8000 costs US$25; insurance for aircraft, homes, recreational vehicles and motorcycles is also available. Gateway claims to be the sole US representative of Mexico's largest insurance agency, Asemex, and shares offices with the Mexico West Travel Club.

Sanborn's, a Texas-based company in the Mexican insurance business since 1948, has offices at many border crossings, but for Baja-bound travelers, their only alternative is at 444 S Fourth St, El Centro, California (☎ (619) 352-4647).

Sanborn's represents Seguros Del Centro, a major Mexican insurance company. Rates are competitive with other insurance companies and agencies, and claims are promptly processed and settled in the USA.

Unlike most insurance agencies, Sanborn's also provides clients with extremely detailed mile-by-mile Travelogs, custommade for each traveler's trip. A typical Travelog describes, down to a tenth of a mile, every bump, stop light and gasoline station, as well as other road-related details. It also offers a listing service for riders and drivers who want to share a trip through Baja and/or other parts of Mexico.

Frequent travelers and others planning extensive trips through Mexico might consider joining Sanborn's Mexico Club. Membership includes special annual group insurance rates, a quarterly newsletter, accommodation discounts, health tips and plenty of information about campgrounds and recreational-vehicle (RV) parks. If one of the local Sanborn's offices doesn't have complete information, contact the Travelog editor, 'Mexico Mike' Nelson, at the main office (☎ (210) 686-0711), PO Box 310, McAllen, Texas 78502.

A one-year third-party liability policy costs about US$275, while a full-coverage policy on a vehicle valued from US$2000 to US$20,000 will cost from US$420 to US$1200 per year. A three-day premium for a vehicle valued at US$8000 is about US$25. After 30 days of coverage, the daily premium drops; the longer the coverage, the lower the daily premium.

Gasoline

The oil industry is still a Mexican government monopoly, and gasoline is officially available only at Pemex (Petróleos Mexicanos) stations throughout the peninsula. In some towns, private individuals sell fuel out of drums, usually at a considerable markup.

Unleaded Magna Sin gasoline is now widely available, but it's still a good idea to carry at least a five-gallon spare can if you plan to leave the paved roads. Extra fuel is also a good idea because massive caravans of 20 or more RVs can deplete gas supplies at Transpeninsular stations such as the one in Cataviña or at the Bahía de Los Angeles junction, in the Desierto Central.

Except in the immediate border area, where gasoline prices are lower, Magna Sin costs US$1.61 per gallon (N$1.31 per liter) throughout the peninsula. Leaded Nova, which is not suitable for vehicles with catalytic converters, is about 20% cheaper.

Road Conditions

In towns and cities, beware of potholes, *alto* (stop) signs and *topes* (speed bumps).

Wide one-way streets in Tijuana, for example, are renowned for stop signs placed on one street corner or the other, but not both. Consequently, drivers in the far-left lane may not see a stop sign on the right corner until they are already in the intersection. Sometimes stop signs are not posted on corners but painted in bold letters on the street, just before the intersection, and drivers looking on the corner can miss the painted letters. Driving slowly and carefully should eliminate the danger of overlooking stop signs.

Speed-bump signs, speed bumps and potholes can also be easy to miss until it's too late, but highway driving has its own set of problems and challenges. The toll portion of the Transpeninsular between Tijuana and Ensenada is the best maintained highway in Baja – four lanes wide, smooth and fast, with spectacular coastal views. Baja's other highways offer equally spectacular scenery – polychrome desert landscapes, dark, craggy volcanoes, verdant valleys, vineyards – but the landscape can distract your attention from sharp curves and narrow lanes. Keep your eyes on the road between glances at the landscape, and take all road signs seriously.

If you must leave the road and go onto the shoulder, slow down and ease your car off the pavement; the narrow shoulder is several inches below the pavement and slopes steeply downward.

Driving off the main roads presents special problems. Many unpaved roads are graded and passable even for ordinary passenger vehicles, but sharp stones and other hazards can shred even heavy-duty tires, forcing wise drivers to travel at much slower speeds than on paved roads. Mexican drivers regularly deflate their tires in such circumstances, to as little as 22 or even 20 lbs per square inch, in order to avoid punctures and smooth out the rough surfaces. This obviously reduces fuel efficiency, but gas is cheaper than a set of new tires.

Anyone planning more than a day trip off paved roads should carry extra food, fuel, water and sleeping bags. Remember that

STOP

ESCUELA
School

PUENTE
ANGOSTO
Narrow
Bridge

GANADO
Cattle

CRUCE F.C.
Railroad
Crossing

YIELD
Right
of Way

CURVA
PELIGROSA
Dangerous
Curve

VADO
dip

ZONA DE
DERRUMBES
Slide Area

CAMINO
SINUOSO
Winding Road

HOMBRES
TRABAJANDO
Men Working

be fixed efficiently and inexpensively by mechanics in Baja's towns and cities if parts are available. On the other hand, don't expect miracles if your problems are linked to state-of-the-art computerized systems or other features foreign to Mexican mechanics. Volkswagens (without fuel injection engines) are the most common cars and thus the easiest to have repaired in Baja.

Because Baja's notoriously bad roads take a heavy toll on tires, *llanteras* (tire repair shops) are ubiquitous, even in many out-of-the-way spots, but they cannot work miracles on a tire that has been shredded by sharp rocks or other hazards, so avoid driving too fast. Ordinary llanteras, especially those in remote areas, may have only a limited selection of spares. Other than major cities like Tijuana, Ensenada, Mexicali and La Paz, the best places to buy tires along the Transpeninsular are Guerrero Negro, Santa Rosalía and Ciudad Constitución.

Off-Highway Driving

Hundreds of miles of rough dirt roads and tracks crisscross Baja's backcountry. Many are passable in an ordinary passenger car, but others require a 4WD vehicle with high clearance. You must be well prepared, however, and your vehicle must be in excellent condition; some areas are so isolated that getting stuck can be dangerous. Heat, drought, rain, flash floods and snakes are among the hazards that may bedevil an unprepared motorist. Some travelers may prefer to form an informal convoy with other vehicles.

many, if not most, unpaved roads quickly become impassable after rain, and even locals avoid them until they've had a chance to dry out. If in doubt, stop the car, get out, check the road and, if not absolutely certain you can continue, turn back.

Help!

Organized to deal with tourists' car problems on the highways, the Mexican government's Angeles Verdes (Green Angels) are teams of bilingual mechanics in bright-green trucks who patrol each stretch of highway in Baja at least twice each day. They can make minor repairs, replace small parts, provide gasoline and oil and arrange towing or other assistance by short-wave and citizen-band radio if necessary. Service is free and parts, gasoline and oil are provided at cost. If a telephone is nearby, contact their national 24-hour emergency hot line (☎ 5-250-0123).

Most serious mechanical problems can

Essentials for excursions off paved highways include water, a first-aid kit, tools, flares, matches and a disposable lighter. For more information, consult the *Baja California Guidebook* published by the Automobile Club of Southern California, which also publishes a detailed map of Baja that shows almost every off-road route described in the book. Once available to club members only, the map can be purchased in many Baja shops for about US$4; the book is also for sale at club offices and bookstores in the USA for US$7.95.

Car Rental

Rental cars are available in Mexicali, Tijuana, Ensenada, La Paz, San José del Cabo and Cabo San Lucas from major agencies like Hertz, Avis, Budget and National. Small private car-rental agencies also operate in these cities.

Daily rates from international rental agencies start at around US$45, depending on the agency, when and how long you rent the car, the amount of insurance you want, the number of miles you plan to drive, whether you make your reservation in the USA or in Baja, where you return the car and so on. Note that travelers who wish to rent a car in one location and drop it off in another (for example, rent in San Diego and drop off in La Paz), will usually pay high drop-off charges, maybe as much as an additional US$20 per day. Since rates and specials change almost daily, call each agency toll free in the USA for the latest information:

Avis (☎ (800) 331-2112)
Budget (☎ (800) 527-0700)
Hertz (☎ (800) 654-3131)
National (☎ (800) 328-4567)

Local agencies' rates tend to be slightly lower but, like those of US-based companies, they change frequently. Shop around if you decide to rent a car on arrival.

No agency in Baja allows its cars to be taken to the USA, but some San Diego-based agencies do permit their rental cars to be taken into Mexico. National, for example, allows cars as far south as Ensenada, but charges an additional US$16 per day for Mexican insurance. Avis will allow its vehicles to be driven 450 miles into Mexico, but drivers must pay US$11 to US$14 per day for supplementary Mexican insurance.

MOTORCYCLE

Traveling on Baja California's paved roads and highways by motorcycle is fast, thrilling and economical but recommended only for experienced motorcyclists. The challenges of traveling by car in Baja become dangers on a motorcycle. A good helmet and protective clothing are advisable because the gravelly, potholed roads can easily cause a spill.

Exercise extreme caution on corners, especially those marked ¡Peligro! (Danger!) – gasoline often sloshes out of Pemex trucks on curves and makes the roads slippery. Livestock on the road can also pose a serious hazard.

Carry extra water and food if traveling alone because, if you have mechanical problems on an isolated stretch of road, you should avoid leaving your bike unattended. An experienced, well-prepared rider can cover the Transpeninsular from Tijuana to La Paz in three days.

Venturing off the paved roads and onto the trails and tracks of the peninsula requires careful preparation and a machine suitable for off-road travel. Many street bikes are not suitable for off-road riding. Parts are scarce, although street mechanics are geniuses at repair and improvisation. For other motorcyclists' perspectives on touring Baja, read Alex Kinglake's article 'Biker's Guide to Baja' in the January 1989 issue of *Road Rider* magazine.

BICYCLE

Bicycling is an increasingly popular way to tour Baja. In northern Baja, annual summer races and recreational rides on the paved routes between Tecate and Ensenada, Tijuana and Ensenada and Playas de Rosarito and Ensenada attract more and more people, mostly mainland Californians.

Many others are riding the entire length of the peninsula, occasionally solo, but such a trip requires a tent, sleeping bag, tools, spare tubes and tires, food, several water jugs, a first-aid kit and other supplies. Cyclists should be in top physical shape, have excellent equipment and be prepared to handle their own repairs, even in the middle of nowhere. Small towns and villages often have bicycle mechanics, but they may lack replacement parts for complex repairs.

Racing bicycles are suitable for paved roads like the Transpeninsular, but potholes

Sierra San Francisco (JH)

Cuesta El Mechudo, North of La Paz

San Javier Rd, near Loreto

Picacho del Diablo, Parque Nacional Sierra San Pedro Mártir

El Pilón, La Purísima

are numerous and highway shoulders are very steep and narrow; even though most Mexican drivers are courteous to cyclists, there are likely to be anxious moments when that 18-wheeler blows by at 70 mph (112 kph). On the graveled or dirt roads which crisscross much of the peninsula, a mountain bike *(todo terreno)* is a much better choice, but even then thorns are a major hazard to bicycle tires.

Some companies are now offering bicycle tours of isolated areas like Península Vizcaíno; see the Tours section in the Getting There & Away chapter for details.

HITCHING

Hitching is never entirely safe in any country in the world, and we don't recommend it. Travelers who decide to hitch should understand that they are taking a small but serious risk. You may not be able to identify the local rapist/murderer before you get into his vehicle. However, many people do choose to hitch, and the advice that follows should help to make their journeys as fast and safe as possible.

For those with no fixed schedule, hitchhiking is possible on Baja's main roads and highways. Displaying your destination on a readable sign is a good idea. The temperature can plunge in the desert at night and being stranded is no picnic; hitchers should anticipate long waits and carry sun protection in addition to warm, wind-proof clothing. A water bottle and snack food are imperative. Always, of course, use your judgment in deciding whether to accept a lift or not; hitching is definitely not advisable for single women, but anyone could fall into a difficult or unpleasant situation.

WALKING

Anyone contemplating hiking or walking around any part of Baja should read Graham Mackintosh's *Into a Desert Place*, the story of his two-year, 3000-mile (5000-km) walk around the coast of Baja Califor-

nia. Macintosh lived off the sea and desert, eating rattlesnakes, cacti and abalone and drinking distilled sea water. The book is an entertaining read, informative and useful even for much shorter trips; for more information, see the Books section of the Facts for the Visitor chapter.

LOCAL TRANSPORT
Bus

Intracity buses exist only in and around Tijuana, Ensenada, San Quintín, Mexicali and La Paz. These buses are cheap (around US$0.40), often dilapidated and not too crowded.

Taxis

Every large town and city in Baja California has a taxi service. Most are private taxis with government-regulated fares, though haggling over fares is still the rule. In Tijuana, Loreto, San José del Cabo and Cabo San Lucas, you'll also find bright-yellow, government-run minivans called Aeroterrestre taxis that serve as transport to and from major airports; fares are government-controlled and not subject to bargaining.

In Tijuana and other large cities, route taxis, usually painted in white and another primary color, are only slightly more expensive than local buses and are much faster. Look for the destination painted on the taxi's body.

Donkeys, Mules & Horses

In isolated parts of Baja California, away from paved roads, people still depend on donkeys, mules and horses. But unless you are on an organized backcountry tour, renting a horse at the beach or looking to buy a donkey or mule, you're unlikely to be traveling on these animals. One major exception is the Sierra San Francisco, in the Desierto Central, where the only access is by mule; for details, see the Desierto Central chapter.

La Frontera & the Desierto del Colorado

La Frontera is that part of the State of Baja California (Baja California Norte) which corresponds roughly to the Dominican mission frontier; over two centuries since the establishment of their missions, the main lines of communication still follow El Camino Real, the route of the missionaries. It is also the area most heavily frequented by visitors from north of the border. Many if not most visitors view its cities and beaches as hedonistic enclaves established for the benefit of roving libertines, but this superficial image hides a more complex and interesting reality.

Northern Baja is, undeniably, a playground for mainland Californians. Only three hours' drive from populous Los Angeles, it attracts large numbers of US citizens in search of inexpensive holidays south of the border. The Mexican federal government's *fideicomiso*, a 30-year bank trust, has eased restrictions on property ownership and promoted the construction of resort complexes and time-share condominiums all along the coast. Some US citizens also find Baja's low rents attractive – in Tijuana, substantial numbers of them rent apartments for a fraction of the cost of comparable housing in San Diego and commute to jobs just across the border.

This approach, however, gives an incomplete picture of the border region's vitality. The conspicuous urban tourist enclaves and idyllic beach resorts on the Pacific and the Gulf mask the fact that this is one of Mexico's fastest growing, most innovative and most prosperous areas, and not only because of US influence. Tijuana and Mexicali are major cities and important manufacturing centers in their own right, while Mexicali's Río Colorado hinterland resembles mainland California's Imperial Valley as an agricultural producer. Unlike most US cities, whose centers are virtually empty after dark, the border towns enjoy a lively street life in which the tawdry attractions of the zonas de tolerancia play only a

minimal role. One ironic observer has remarked that downtown San Diego, with its strip joints and porn houses, more closely resembles the Tijuana of the past than of the present.

Many travelers are surprised that Tijuana has a flourishing arts community, officially symbolized by the federal government's Centro Cultural Tijuana, an ambitious project with first-rate facilities which are little frequented by foreigners. The Programa Nacional Fronterizo (PRONAF), evincing Mexico City's apprehension that *fronterizos* (inhabitants of the border region) may identify more readily with the nearby USA than the distant capital, has also erected conspicuous monuments to Mexican heroes like Benito Juárez and Miguel Hidalgo to promote nationalism along the border. Richard Rodríguez, a US writer of Mexican ancestry, has remarked that Tijuana's imposing statues 'were set down upon the city like paperweights upon a map. They are reminders from the capital'.

There is also, however, a thriving alternative arts scene; Rubén Martínez, a Los Angeles-based writer of Mexican and Salvadorean heritage, has written that the city's young artists are producing work that 'reflects the clashing, the melding, the hybridization of culture that is taking place here, virtually invisible to the Northern eye'.

Commerce is booming as well, due in part to foreign investors (mostly US and Japanese) who have underwritten the construction of new factories, commercial centers, shopping centers and housing complexes. Baja's duty-free status permits the sale of many imported goods at prices lower than those in the USA, and has also attracted US, European, South Korean and Japanese manufacturers who have established over 500 maquiladoras (twin assembly plants) which, as of 1990, employed nearly 60,000 people in and around Tijuana. Maquiladoras are equally important to the economies of

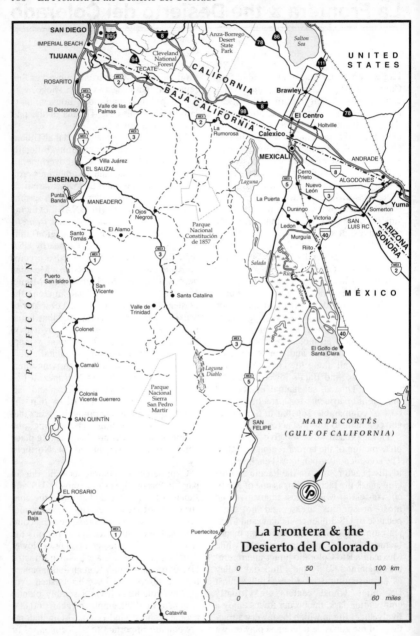

La Frontera & the Desierto del Colorado

Mexicali, Tecate and border towns in other Mexican states.

At these plants, raw materials or components for items such as TV sets and compact refrigerators can be imported duty free and then exported back to the USA with duty payable only on the value added to the original materials. Mexico's low labor costs – a fraction of those in the USA – are a major incentive to foreign investors. They are also a matter of controversy, as well-paid workers north of the border worry that the recently approved North American Free Trade Agreement (NAFTA) may intensify the movement of manufacturing jobs south of the border. It has been written that the US-Mexico border is the only place where the First World borders the Third

These new business developments have attracted many immigrants, primarily from Mexico City and the states of Jalisco, Michoacán, Sinaloa and Sonora. For some, the border region is a way station en route to the USA; the US Immigration & Naturalization Service claims that 5000 undocumented people cross the permeable international border every week, with and without the help of coyotes or polleros. These smugglers' clients are a mix of circular migrants who traditionally spend part of the year north of the border but have been shut out of their traditional livelihood by restrictive US immigration laws, novices who have no idea what to expect across the frontier and political refugees from Central American wars and other upheavals who have found Mexico an ambivalent host.

Because of this continuing problem, both documented and undocumented immigrants, as well as US citizens of Mexican heritage, have found themselves targets of attacks by mainland California politicians like US Senator Dianne Feinstein, who proposed a US$1 'admission' charge on legal border crossers in order to finance increased police and paramilitary surveillance on the US side of the border. One newspaper columnist observed ironically that 'she forgot to mention the two-drink minimum'.

Tijuana & the Northern Pacific Coast

TIJUANA

Fast growing Tijuana (official population 698,752) suffers from an exaggerated, largely outdated reputation as a tawdry booze-and-sex border town, a gaudy place whose curio shops overflow with kitschy souvenirs like wrought-iron bird cages and ceramic burros. That Tijuana still exists, but the developing cityscape of modernistic office buildings, housing developments and maquiladoras marks Baja California's largest border city as a place of increasing sophistication. Certain areas, such as the Zona Río southeast of downtown, may sink under the weight of shopping centers that make it seem an extension of mainland southern California's mall culture.

At the same time, impoverished immigrants inhabit 'suburban' hillside dwellings of scrapwood and cardboard, where retaining walls of worn tires keep the soil from washing away during winter storms. These dwellings lack basic services like potable water and trash collection (except for those who actually live at the dump). The city is notorious, of course, for masses of undocumented immigrants who, at nightfall, intrepidly cross the Río Tijuana and other permeable points along the US border. Most of these desperate, impoverished families and individuals come from regions like the Bajío (in the states of Jalisco, Michoacán, Guanajuato and Querétaro), and the states of Oaxaca, San Luis Potosí, Guerrero and México. The indigenous presence in Tijuana is more conspicuous than ever, as Mixtecs from Oaxaca and Mayas from Chiapas and the Yucatán line the sidewalks.

Nevertheless, Tijuana is one of Mexico's most prosperous cities, thanks in part to its proximity to southern mainland California's large retail markets and the heavy influx of US tourists. Local retail activity has also expanded as maquiladora wages circulate in the local retail sector, supporting additional employment. Recent figures suggest that nearly 70% of the economic activity derives from 'frontier transactions' (including exports and tourism), about 17% from maquiladoras, 5% from local commerce, 4% from various services, 3% from local industry, and 1% from agriculture and fishing.

Tijuana has also become a major educational center, thanks to the growth of institutions like the Universidad Autónoma de Baja California and the Universidad Iberoamericana del Noroeste. The city's cultural importance extends to the arts, an influence that derives in part from establishments like the Centro Cultural de Tijuana, as well as from individuals and groups who lack state sponsorship or encouragement.

History

In colonial times, the area which is now Tijuana fell under the jurisdiction of Misión San Diego, Alta California, but with the secularization of the missions in 1834, the Kumiai neophytes of Punta Tía Juana became peons. At the end of the Mexican-American War in 1848, the newly relocated international border turned the modest rancho of Tijuana into a port of entry overnight, but it remained a backwater even after the government built a formal customs depot in 1874.

Subdivision of the rancho in 1889 created Pueblo Zaragoza (Tijuana's official name until 1929), but the population grew very slowly to only 242 in 1900 and less than 1000 at the end of WW I. The fledgling city, however, drew upscale tourists from north of the border to facilities like the US-owned Tijuana Hot Springs Hotel, and soon became a center for gambling, greyhound racing, boxing matches and cockfights. Other facilities, like bars and bordellos, further 'diversified' the local economy.

Tourist development suffered a setback in 1911 when the forces of anarchist leader

Ricardo Flores Magón's Liberal Party tried to use Baja as a territorial foothold during the Mexican Revolution. After holding the town for six weeks, however, the indecisive rebels fled Federal reinforcements. Rebel commander Caryl Pryce, a Welshman, was detained for violating US neutrality laws when he fled north; the intellectual Flores Magón, who remained in exile in Los Angeles where he edited a weekly newspaper, was later tried for espionage in the USA. Convicted on flimsy evidence, he died years later in prison in Leavenworth, Kansas.

After 1915, despite restrictive US wartime measures, Tijuana's tourist industry recovered; during Prohibition, it positively flourished as thirsty US residents flocked to Tijuana for alcohol, gambling and sex – and displaced US businesses flocked there to offer these services. During these years, the municipal administration paved streets, improved the water system, built schools and attracted industries like breweries, distilleries and even an aircraft factory (headed by one-time Mexican President Abelardo Rodríguez, after whom Tijuana's international airport is named). Foreign businesses, however, were slow to employ Mexican workers in responsible positions.

After Prohibition, President Lázaro Cárdenas outlawed casinos and prostitution – Tijuana's main casino became a high school, the Instituto Tecnológico Industrial Agua Caliente – but the Great Depression of the 1930s in the USA probably had a greater impact than executive intervention. As bankrupt US-owned businesses reverted to Mexican control, and northern Baja became a customs free zone, jobless Mexican returnees from the USA remained in Tijuana rather than return to their hometowns, doubling the city's population (to about 16,500) by 1940. The presently notorious borderside Colonia Libertad dates from this period.

During WW II, with the US Army absorbing nearly all able-bodied American males, the US and Mexican governments established the *bracero* program which

Ricardo Flores Magón

allowed Mexican laborers north of the border to alleviate serious wartime labor shortages. This program, which lasted until 1964, led to major growth in border-area commerce, and by 1960 Tijuana's population had grown tenfold to over 180,000.

In each succeeding decade, the city's population has probably doubled, although truly reliable statistics are hard to find. Many observers believe it is at least double the Mexican government's official figure of just below 700,000; it almost certainly exceeds a million. Uncontrolled growth has brought serious social and environmental problems, as the municipal administration has failed to provide adequate housing, potable water and public health services for many parts of the city; contamination of the Río Tijuana, which enters the USA west of the San Ysidro border crossing, is one of several serious international ecological issues.

Tijuana has never completely overcome its image as a paradise for sinners. During and immediately after WW II, the city probably experienced its seamiest era as the infamous Avenida Revolución attracted US servicemen from nearby San Diego. In recent years, the city has cleaned up its act considerably, although the Zona Norte at the north end of Avenida Revolución retains some of the style (and substance) of the post-war era.

Most of 'La Revo', however, now appeals to a younger crowd of US university students and their cohorts who take advantage of Mexico's permissive drinking laws (18-year-olds may purchase alcohol and frequent bars) to party until dawn. At the same time, families feel more comfortable in the city's streets and shops than they did in sleazier times.

Orientation

Tijuana parallels the US border for about 12 miles (20 km) from west to east. Flowing northwest across the border before emptying into the Pacific Ocean, the Río Tijuana divides the older part of the city to the south and southwest, and the newer Mesa de Otay sector, on a broad hilltop to the northeast. Mesa de Otay contains the international airport, most of the city's maquiladoras, newer residential neighborhoods and major shopping areas.

Central Tijuana features a regular grid pattern of north-south avenidas (avenues) and east-west calles (streets), but often lacks street signs; most streets have numbers that are more frequently used than their names. The city's intended center was Plaza Zaragoza, now Parque Vicente Guerrero, but Avenida Revolución (ex-Avenida Olvera), five blocks to the east, soon became the city's commercial heart.

A new numbering system for street addresses has created some confusion. Since the transition is likely to be a very slow one, and since most tijuanenses still rely on the old system, this chapter uses the old system but also locates places such as hotels and restaurants by their cross streets. In some instances, the new street address, in parentheses, follows the old one.

The San Ysidro-Tijuana border crossing is north of the river, about a 10-minute walk from downtown. Taxis are numerous, but any bus with a 'Central Camionera' placard goes downtown and costs about US$0.40. To reach the commercial center by foot, continue through the Plaza Viva Tijuana shopping mall to the pedestrian bridge over the river, cross the street and proceed to Calle 1a (Comercio or, west of Avenida Revolución, Artículo 123). Most of Tijuana's seedier bars and clubs are in the area north of Calle 2a (Juárez) and west of Avenida Revolución.

South of Calle 1a, Revolución is the city's tourist center, where many visitors purchase cheap liquor, imported goods and Mexican handicrafts. Its major landmark is the Palacio Frontón Jai Alai (Jai Alai Palace), but the surrounding area also contains many bungalows moved intact from San Diego and other north-of-the-border communities during the construction of US Interstate 5. Unlike US cities, commercial, industrial and residential uses exist side by side.

Directly east of the Frontón, Tijuana's 'new' commercial center straddles the Río Tijuana. Paseo de los Héroes, Paseo de Tijuana and Via Oriente, the principal streets in this part of town, all parallel the river. West of the Frontón, between downtown and the Pacific Ocean, lie both spiffy suburbs and hillside shantytowns known as *asentamientos irregulares* (irregular settlements). Formally, all of these neighborhoods are known as *colonias* and addresses are much easier to locate if one knows the name of the colonia.

Information

Border Crossings One of the busiest borders in the world, the San Ysidro-Tijuana port of entry is open 24 hours. Two emergency gates (the second gate on the far left and Gate No 1) allow immediate entry to the USA for Americans and Mexicans needing urgent medical attention. For general information about immigration, customs and car permits, see the Visas and Documents entries in the Facts for the Visitor chapter.

In 1991 nearly 19 million foreigners entered Tijuana via San Ysidro, but the alternative border crossing at Mesa de Otay, east of downtown near Tijuana's airport, has relieved some of the pressure by absorbing about 20% of the total cross-border traffic. Motorists wishing to avoid the perpetual backup at San Ysidro will usually find the Otay crossing much

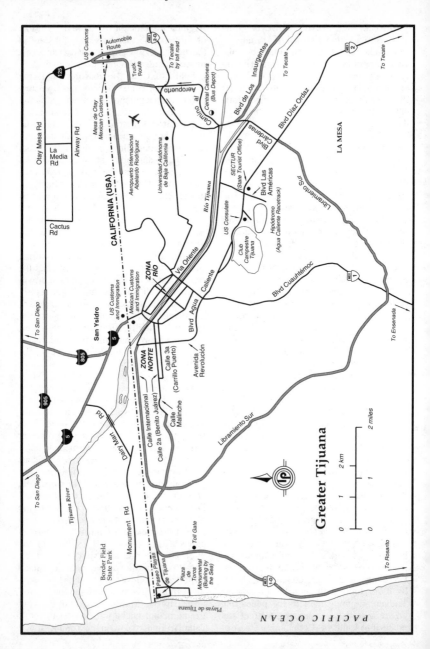

Greater Tijuana

quicker, but the time it takes to drive to Otay and to return to Interstate 5 after crossing the border, may be a drawback for some. The Otay border crossing is open from 6 am to 10 pm.

Arrange automobile insurance either before crossing the border or at the border (Otay is much quicker than San Ysidro). See the Car Insurance section in the Getting Around chapter for details.

Tourist Office Tijuana has several tourist offices in the border area, downtown, and the newer suburbs to the southeast. None of them has a very satisfactory map of the city; the best available is the Guías Urbanas map published by Ediciones Corona in Mexicali.

The Cámara Nacional de Comercio, Servicios y Turismo de Tijuana (CANACO, the Tijuana Chamber of Commerce Tourism office, ☎ 85-84-72, 88-16-85) is the Tijuana city office. At the corner of Avenida Revolución and Calle 1a (Comercio), it's open 9 am to 7 pm daily. It has helpful, gregarious English-speaking staff and a wide selection of printed matter on Baja California and, to some degree, the rest of Mexico.

The Secretaría de Turismo del Estado de Baja California (SECTUR, Secretary of Tourism of the State of Baja California, ☎ 81-94-92, fax 81-95-79) is on the 3rd floor of the Edificio Plaza Patria at the corner of Blvd Díaz Ordaz and Avenida Las Américas. The English-speaking staff answers queries relating to northern Baja and has a rather mediocre tourist map of the state and several important cities and towns. The central office hours are 8 am to 3 pm and 5 to 7 pm weekdays.

If you have any legal problem while touring northern Baja, contact Auxilio Turístico (☎ 81-94-92), formerly the Procuraduría de Protección al Turista, in the same offices as the Secretaría de Turismo. Hours are 8 am to 7 pm, but they can be reached 24 hours.

For most visitors, the SECTUR office (☎ 88-05-55) in the Plaza Santa Cecilia, diagonally across from CANACO and alongside Hotel Nelson, will be much more convenient than the one at Plaza Patria. It's open daily 9 am to 7 pm, has capable staff, and will also handle legal problems.

There are also branches of Tijuana's Comité de Turismo and Convenciones (COTUCO) at the border (very inconspicuous) and at the airport. After passing through Mexican customs, look for the building on your left as you approach the Plaza Viva Tijuana. Hours are about 7 am to 9 pm daily.

Money Tijuana's countless cambios keep long hours; banks offer slightly better rates but are much slower and more bureaucratic. In Tijuana, almost everyone accepts US dollars, except for bus drivers.

The cambio outside Hotel Nelson is open until midnight, but charges 10% commission on travelers' checks. Beware cambios on the US side, which advertise 'no commission' on exchanges of pesos for US dollars, but charge up to 8% for converting US-dollar travelers' checks into pesos. Change money on the Mexican side instead.

For those heading south into Baja California or east into mainland Mexico, there's also a cambio at the Central Camionera.

Post & Telecommunications Tijuana's central post office is at the corner of Avenida Negrete and Calle 11a (P E Calles). Hours are 8 am to 4 pm weekdays.

Telnor is on Avenida Pío Pico just south of Calle 10a (Sarabia), but Tijuana has many public telephones and long-distance offices both downtown and in the outskirts. The Central Camionera has several booths with an operator in attendance, and a public fax machine as well. Tijuana's area code is 66.

Foreign Consulates The US consulate (☎ 86-00-01/5) is at Tapachula 96, Colonia Hipódromo, just behind the Club Campestre Tijuana (Tijuana Country Club). The Canadian consulate (☎ 84-04-61) is at Calle Gedovius 5-202 in the Zona Río.

Cultural Centers Dating from 1929, the Casa de la Cultura de Tijuana (☎ 37-31-22), formerly the Escuela Alvaro Obregón, is an imposing neoclassical brick building on pleasant grounds at Calle Lisboa 5, in Colonia Altamira. It presents lectures, art exhibitions and film festivals; its small Café Literario is open weekdays from 1 to 8 pm. Take any blue-and-white taxi (Colonia Altamira) westbound from Calle 3a (Carrillo Puerto), or walk up Calle 4a (Díaz Mirón); instead of the busy street, try the hillside staircase, which offers fine views of the city.

The Instituto de Cultura de Baja California (☎ 84-26-91) holds film festivals and other cultural events at its Sala de Usos Múltiples, Avenida Centenario 460 in the Zona Río. See also the separate entry for the Centro Cultural Tijuana (CECUT), below.

Travel Agencies Viajes Honold's (☎ 88-11-11), Avenida Revolución 602 at the corner of Calle 2a (Juárez), is one of the most established travel agencies in town. There are many others both downtown and in the Zona Río.

Bookshops Sanborn's, at the corner of Avenida Revolución and Calle 8a (Hidalgo), is a Mexican institution known for its food and sundries, but also has a good book department with a large selection of US and Mexican newspapers and magazines.

Librería El Día (☎ 84-09-08), Blvd Sánchez Taboada 61-A (10080) in the Zona Río, has a good choice of books on Mexican history and culture, including a section on Baja California, and a handful of books in English. Librolandia (☎ 85-36-58), Calle 2a (Juárez) No 130, is also worth a visit. In the Galería de Arte de la Ciudad, at the corner of Calle 2a (Juárez) and Avenida Constitución, are two small but worthwhile academic bookshops, UNAM and Educal-Sebs, which also have some bilingual coffee-table-format books on Mexico.

In the Plaza Fiesta mall, at the corner of Paseo de los Héroes and Avenida Independencia, La Capilla de Frida (☎ 34-14-19) has a good selection of new Baja books (in Spanish) and an upstairs art gallery with second-hand selections.

Medical Services The Cruz Roja (☎ 132) is at the corner of Calle 10a (Sarabia) and Avenida Pío Pico. Tijuana's Hospital General (☎ 84-09-22) is north of the Río Tijuana on Avenida Padre Kino, west of the junction with Avenida Rodríguez, but Tijuana has many other medical facilities that cater to visitors from north of the border.

Emergencies The central police station is at the corner of Avenida Constitución and Calle 8a (Hidalgo); the fire station is next door. Tijuana's police emergency number is (☎ 134); for fire it is (☎ 136).

Dangers & Annoyances Coyotes, polleros and their clients congregate in the area along the Río Tijuana, west of the San Ysidro border crossing, especially around twilight. After dark this area can be unsafe and is better avoided. The same is true of Colonia Libertad, east of the border crossing.

Motorists at stop lights may find that street children wash your windscreen first and ask questions later. If you don't need a wash, a wagging finger is a good deterrent.

La Revo

Avenida Revolución, popularly known as 'La Revo', is the tourist heart of Tijuana, especially between Calle 1a (Artículo 123) and Calle 8a (Hidalgo). Virtually everyone who visits Tijuana has to experience at least a brief stroll up this raucous avenue of futuristic discos, bellowing hawkers outside seedy strip bars, brash taxi drivers, tacky souvenir shops, street photographers with zebra-striped burros, discount liquor stores and first-rate restaurants. If the sensory overload from clashing high-tech sound systems is too overpowering, but you still need to walk from north to south, try the more normal shopping street of

Avenida Constitución, which parallels La Revo one block to the west.

Frontón Palacio Jai Alai (Jai Alai Palace)

Jai alai, a fast-moving game played in a long, walled-in court, in either a singles or doubles format, originated in the Basque borderlands of France and Spain. The very agile and highly skilled *pelotaris* (players) wear an elongated wicker basket on one arm to catch and throw a hard rubber ball with a tightly woven goatskin casing – roughly akin to an outfielder catching a rocketing line drive with his gloved hand and throwing it in the same motion.

However, the game more closely resembles a hybrid between tennis and handball, as pelotaris alternatively serve and then play the caroms off the very high front and rear walls. Six or eight individual pelotaris or two-man teams play to win, place or show for the benefit of spectators who bet on each game; some spectators find doubles more interesting, as the volleys last much longer.

The individual or team remains on court until losing a point, when the next in the rotation takes the court. The first to score six points wins; after the first round, if there is no winner (as is usually the case), each point counts double. The next two highest scorers play off for second and third. Frontón staff are on hand to explain details to neophytes, and the bilingual narration is very helpful in elucidating the game's intricacies.

A Tijuana landmark, begun in 1926 but not completed until 1947, the baroque-style Frontón (☎ 85-25-24) is on Avenida Revolución between Calle 7a (Galeana) and Calle 8a (Hidalgo); a connecting door leads to the LF Caliente Sports Book, with multiple giant TV screens for watching team sports, horse racing, boxing and other athletic events, mostly from north of the border.

Jai alai matches start Mondays and Tuesdays at 1 pm, and Thursday through Sunday at 8 pm; doors open about an hour earlier and players start warming up around 7:30 pm. General admission is US$2. The Frontón is closed Wednesdays.

Zona Norte

This area west of Avenida Revolución and north of Calle 1a (Artículo 123) preserves the unsanitized atmosphere of Tijuana's tawdriest times. Municipal and tourist officials prefer not to dwell on its continued existence, but the area is of sufficient economic importance that authorities cannot, or will not, eradicate it.

The Zona Norte is also an infamous haven for coyotes and undocumented border crossers, and is not a recommended destination for foreigners who lack street savvy, at least after dark. Most hotels in the area are very cheap and equally disreputable.

Vinícola L A Cetto

Still run by descendants of Italian immigrants who arrived in Baja California in 1926, the L A Cetto winery (☎ 85-30-31, fax 85-35-52) has recently opened its Tijuana facilities at the south end of Avenida Constitución to tours and tasting. With vineyards in the Valle de Guadalupe between Tecate and Ensenada Cetto produces a variety of tasty red and white varietals, as well as sparkling wines, at reasonable prices.

For US$1 without tasting or US$2 with a sampling of four different wines, tours take place on demand between 10 am and 5:30 pm, Tuesday through Sunday; there is no minimum group size. Tours for large groups can be arranged in advance, however. There is also a boutique with Cetto wines and souvenirs for sale, but remember that pedestrians and motorists can only take one liter of wine across the border into mainland California.

Cetto's local address is Cañón Johnson 2108 (8151), a diagonal in Colonia Hidalgo, just south-west of Avenida Constitución; its US mailing address is PO Box 434260, San Ysidro, California 92143.

Galería de Arte de la Ciudad

Only a block from the rowdiness of La

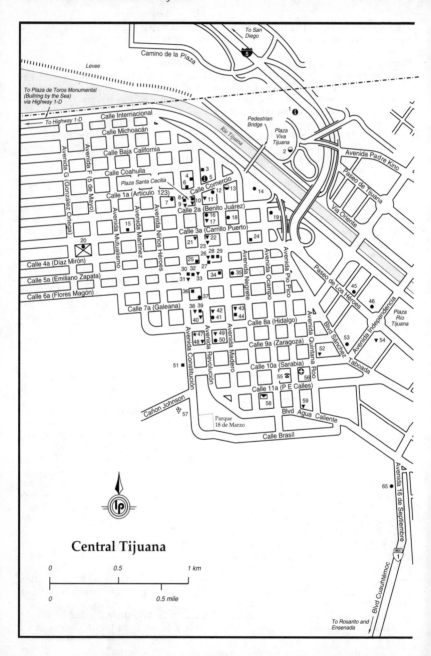

To San Diego

5

Camino de la Plaza

Levee

To Plaza de Toros Monumental
(Bullring by the Sea)
via Highway 1-D

To Highway 1-D

Calle Internacional

Calle Michoacán

Calle Baja California

Calle Coahuila

Plaza Santa Cecilia

Calle 1a (Artículo 123)

Calle 2a (Benito Juárez)

Calle 3a (Carrillo Puerto)

Calle 4a (Díaz Mirón)

Calle 5a (Emiliano Zapata)

Calle 6a (Flores Magón)

Calle 7a (Galeana)

Calle 8a (Hidalgo)

Calle 9a (Zaragoza)

Calle 10a (Sarabia)

Calle 11a (P E Calles)

Avenida G (González Ortega)

Avenida F (5 de Mayo)

Avenida Mutualismo

Avenida Martínez

Avenida Niños Héroes

Avenida Constitución

Avenida Revolución

Avenida Madero

Avenida Negrete

Avenida Ocampo

Avenida Pío Pico

Avenida Quintana Roo

Avenida Independencia

Río Tijuana

Pedestrian Bridge

Plaza Viva Tijuana

Calle Comercio

Avenida Padre Kino

Paseo de Tijuana

Vía Oriente

Paseo de Los Héroes

Blvd Sánchez Taboada

Plaza Río Tijuana

Cañón Johnson

Parque 18 de Marzo

Blvd Agua Caliente

Calle Brasil

Avenida 16 de Septiembre

Blvd Cuauhtémoc

To Rosarito and Ensenada

1

Central Tijuana

0   0.5   1 km

0   0.5 mile

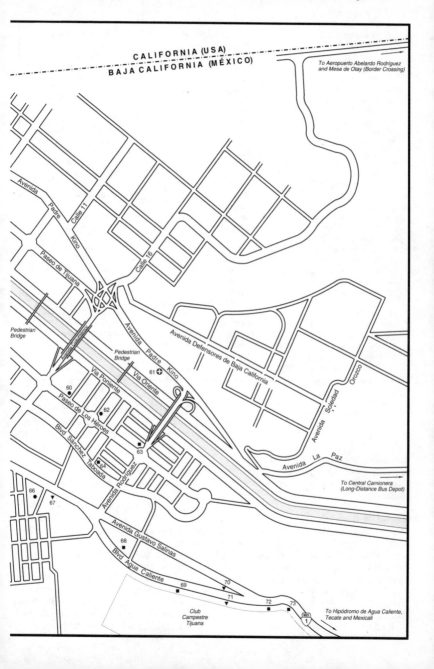

	PLACES TO STAY	22	Margarita's Village	12	Museo de Cera (Wax
3	Motel Díaz	23	Café La Especial		Museum)
4	Motel Alaska	26	La Leña (downtown)	13	Downtown Bus Terminal
6	Hotel del Mar	31	La Torta	14	Mercado de Artesanías
8	Hotel San Jorge	33	Tilly's Fifth Avenue	16	Honold's Viajes (travel
10	Hotel Nelson	38	La Costa		agency)
15	Hotel Villas Veracruz	40	Pedrín's	18	Route Taxis to Central
24	Hotel Terrazas	42	Tía Juana Tilly's		Camionera
25	Hotel Caesar	43	Tortas Ricardo	19	Mexitlán
27	Hotel Arreola	48	Vittorio's	20	Parque Vicente Guerrero
28	Hotel Adelita	49	Sanborn's	35	Route Taxis to Rosarito
29	Hotel Rey	52	El Molino	37	Fiesta Mexicana
30	Hotel del Prado	54	Plaza Fiesta mall	41	Frontón Palacio Jai Alai
32	Hotel París	59	Dionnysos		(Jai Alai Palace)
34	Hotel Catalina	67	La Baguette	45	Taesa (airline)
36	Hotel Tecate	70	Boccacio's Nuevo	46	Centro Cultural Tijuana
39	Motel León		Marianna		(CECUT)
44	Hotel Villa de Zaragoza	71	La Leña (Agua Caliente	47	Police Station
51	Motel Plaza Hermosa		branch)	50	Aeroméxico
63	Hotel Lucerna			53	Mercado Hidalgo
64	Hacienda del Río		OTHER	55	Telnor (long-distance)
68	Hotel El Conquistador	1	Comité de Turismo y	56	Cruz Roja (Red Cross)
69	Hotel Fiesta Americana		Convenciones (COTUCO)	57	Vinícola L A Cetto (winery)
72	Motel Padre Kino		(tourist office)	58	Post Office
73	Hotel Paraíso Radisson	2	Border Bus Terminal,	60	Budget Rent-A-Car
			Plaza Viva Tijuana	61	Hospital General
	PLACES TO EAT	5	Cámara Nacional de	62	Baby Rock (dance club)
9	Jugos Los Norteños		Comercio (CANACO)	65	Hertz Rent-A-Car
10	Restaurant Hotel Nelson		(tourist office)	66	Toreo de Tijuana (bullring)
11	Bol Corona	7	Galería de Arte de la		
17	Woolworth's		Ciudad		
21	Tequila Circo				

Revo, the municipal art gallery occupies the former city hall (from 1921 to 1986) at the corner of Avenida Constitución and Calle 1a (Artículo 123). At the entrance are two modest but interesting murals; the interior gallery is open weekdays 9 am to 7 pm. There are also two small but worthwhile bookshops.

Museo de Cera

Strategically placed at the corner of Avenida Madero and Calle Comercio to attract foot traffic en route from the border to La Revo, Tijuana's new wax museum is a monument to kitsch. Admission is US$3 for adults, US$2 for children.

Mexitlán

It's tempting to suggest that Tijuana's latest self-consciously nationalist tourist attraction, which features diorama scale models of many of the Mexico's most significant archaeological monuments and distinguished public buildings (plus more than a handful of less distinguished ones), could draw bigger crowds by laying down some Astroturf, drilling a few holes, buying a few putters and reopening as a miniature golf course. It has an upstairs restaurant, but nearly all the street level shops are vacant, and the impression is one of a clever but costly white elephant.

Situated atop a parking garage at the corner of Avenida Ocampo and Calle 2a (Juárez), Mexitlán (☎ 38-41-01) is open 10 am to 6 pm Tuesday to Friday, noon to 8 pm weekends. Admission is US$3.25 for adults; children under 12, who get in free, seem irresistibly tempted to play with (and potentially destroy) everything within their reach, which means nearly all the exhibits.

Mercado Hidalgo

Sprawling Mercado Hidalgo, which borders Avenida Independencia and Blvd Sánchez Taboada, is Tijuana's major city market for fruit, vegetables and, to a lesser degree, for souvenirs and other odds and ends. It also has a handful of decent but inexpensive restaurants and juice bars.

Centro Cultural Tijuana (Cultural Center)

Mexico's federal government built Tijuana's modern cultural center (☎ 84-11-11) at the corner of Paseo de los Héroes and Avenida Independencia to reinforce the Mexican identity of its border populations with exhibits chronicling mainland Mexican history. Often known by its acronym CECUT, it houses the **Museo de Las Identidades Mexicanas** (Museum of Mexican Identities), an art gallery with rotating exhibitions, a 1000-seat theater with frequent major performances, as well as the globular **Cine Planetario**, an Omnimax cinema with all the architectural charm of the Three Mile Island nuclear power plant (it is colloquially known as *La Bola* – 'The Ball').

The Cine Planetario presents three short films on a 180° screen. *El Pueblo del Sol*, a cinematic tour of Mexico in English, is shown Fridays, Saturdays and Sundays at 2 pm; admission is US$4.50. The other two films, in Spanish, change periodically; among the most recent entries were *Anillo de Fuego*, about vulcanism on the Pacific Rim, and *Selva Tropical*, on the situation of the world's rainforests.

Admission to the Museo de Las Identidades Mexicanas is US$1, while the art gallery is free of charge. Among recent museum exhibits was an elaborate display of charro horsegear and related artifacts; there are also permanent exhibits on pre-Columbian, colonial and republican Mexico, as well as the history of Tijuana. The gallery's most recent exhibition,

'Talleres en Fronteras' (Workshops on the Frontier), displayed works of artists from Texas and Baja California, stressing common themes like the indigenous tradition (rock art), the landscape (both urban and rural), and the border itself (one particularly powerful painting showed the area as a human torso, red, white and blue above the waist and red, white and green below the waist, with a belt of barbed wire).

The center also contains a bookshop with a good general selection of works in Spanish on Mexico and Baja California in particular, plus a few coffee-table photo books. Hours are 11 am to 8 pm on weekdays and to 9 pm on weekends. From the city center, catch any southbound bus on Avenida Constitución at Calle 3a (Carrillo Puerto). From the border bus lot, catch a 'Baja P' bus.

Corridas de Toros (Bullfights)

Bullfights take place every Sunday from May to September at two bullrings, from 4 to 6 pm. The larger, more spectacular venue is the Plaza de Toros Monumental, the renowned bull-ring-by-the-sea, only a short distance from the border fence.

The other bullring, El Toreo de Tijuana, is at Blvd Agua Caliente 100, between central Tijuana and the Agua Caliente racetrack. Corridas take place here from May to August and at the Monumental ring for the rest of the season; in Tijuana phone ☎ 85-22-10 or ☎ 85-15-72 for reservations; in San Diego, phone ☎ (619) 231-3554.

Tickets, ranging from US$4.50 to US$16 (those in the shade are costlier), are available from Ticketron outlets in the USA, at a kiosk on Avenida Revolución between Calles 4a and 5a, and at the bullrings themselves.

Hipódromo de Agua Caliente

At present, because of a sustained labor dispute, the ponies no longer circle this famous track (☎ 26-20-02), so the place has literally gone to the dogs. Greyhound races with pari-mutuel wagering take place at 7:45 pm Wednesday to Sunday and at 2 pm Monday, Thursday, Friday and Sunday.

Open all year, it's just south of the Club Campestre Tijuana; admission and parking are both free.

The track places retired dogs with adoptive owners; for more information, phone the greyhound manager (☎ 81-78-11, X342 or 451).

Playas de Tijuana

Popular with locals, Tijuana's beaches tend to get crowded, especially during bullfights. A blue-and-white bus marked 'Playas' runs along Calle 3a (Carrillo Puerto) and westward to the beach.

Places to Stay – bottom end

Tijuana has a wealth of accommodation in all categories, from the really seedy to the truly luxurious. Tourist authorities try to steer visitors away from less expensive, but often very acceptable, alternatives.

Camping Unofficial free camping is possible on any public beach, but the further from Tijuana, the better. The coastal *KOA Trailer Park/Campground* (☎ 86-14-12), about 12 miles (20 km) south of Tijuana and 7 miles (11 km) north of Rosarito, has all the typical facilities and recreational-vehicle hookups common at KOA campgrounds in the USA and charges about US$16 per night for two persons, US$1 for each additional person. Take the San Antonio del Mar exit off the Ensenada toll road.

Hotels & Motels *Hotel del Mar* (☎ 85-73-02) at Calle 1a (Artículo 123 or Comercio) 1948 (8170) across from Hotel Nelson, is only half a block from Avenida Revolución but borders on a sleazy part of town. The rooms (even the communal bathroom) are clean, a double room costs only US$17, and the English-speaking manager is obliging to travelers. Basic *Hotel Tecate* (☎ 85-92-75), Calle 6a (Flores Magón) No 1907 at the corner of Avenida Constitución, charges only US$17 for doubles.

For a clean, basic place with no frills, try *Hotel Adelita* (☎ 85-94-95) at Calle 4a (Díaz Mirón) 2017 between Avenidas Revolución and Madero, whose only amenity is its hot showers. Rooms are a bit shabby, with peeling paint and sagging beds, for US$17 single/double. Perhaps a better bargain is the *Motel Plaza Hermosa* (☎ 85-33-53) at Avenida Constitución 1012, corner of Calle 10a (Galeana), which has doubles for US$17. *Hotel del Prado* (☎ 88-23-29), at Calle 5a (Zapata) No 1929 between Avenida Revolución and Avenida Constitución, is clean and comfortable despite the graffiti on the interior walls. Rates average about US$13/17 single/double. Next to the Club Campestre Tijuana and only a short walk from the racetrack, *Motel Padre Kino* (☎ 86-42-08), at Blvd Agua Caliente 3 just beyond the junction with Avenida Gustavo Salinas, is popular among gringos with cars. Singles/doubles start at US$20.

Hotel Arreola (☎ 85-26-18), very centrally located at Revolución 826 (1080), corner of Calle 5a (Zapata), has carpeted rooms with a B&W TV and telephone for US$20 single or double. The older *Hotel Rey* (☎ 85-14-26), very central at Calle 4a (Díaz Mirón) 2021 between Revolución and Madero, has sagging mattresses in rooms that are otherwise acceptable. Singles/doubles cost US$20/30.

One-star *Hotel Catalina* (☎ 85-97-48), Calle 5a (Zapata) No 2039, has singles/doubles for US$20/25. *Hotel San Jorge* (☎ 85-85-40), Avenida Constitución 506 between Calle 1a (Artículo 123) and Calle 2a (Juárez) resembles Hotel del Mar, but is rather dearer at US$25 for a single/double. Rooms are old but clean, and the paint is not yet peeling off the walls. *Hotel Villas Veracruz* (☎ 85-90-30), Calle 3a (Carrillo Puerto) No 1642 between Avenida Martínez and Avenida Mutualismo, charges about the same for singles/doubles with telephone and color TV.

The 74-room *Motel Alaska* (☎ 85-36-81), on Avenida Revolución between Calle 1a (Artículo 123) and Calle Coahuila, is a reliable, aging motel with clean, basic singles/doubles for US$28, but other places offer better services for the same price. Across the street, dingy *Motel Díaz* (☎ 85-

71-48) has adequate singles/doubles for US$25.

Places to Stay – middle

Hotel Nelson (☎ 85-43-03, fax 85-43-02), Avenida Revolución 503 (721), has long been a favorite with budget travelers because of its central location and 92 clean, basic and carpeted rooms, plus a bar and an inexpensive coffee shop. Windowless interior singles/doubles with telephone and spotless toilets cost US$22, but may not be suitable for claustrophobics; a room with a view, color TV and the less than soothing sounds of La Revo will cost US$32.

Similarly priced *Motel León* (☎ 85-63-20), Calle 7a (Galeana) No 1939 (8151) between Revolución and Constitución, is a convenient central motel with telephone, restaurant room service and parking. *Hotel París* (☎ 85-30-23), Calle 5a (Zapata) No 1939 between Revolución and Constitución, has singles/doubles with telephone, color TV and air-conditioning for US$30.

Hotel Caesar (☎ 88-16-66), at the corner of Calle 5a (Zapata) and Avenida Revolución, has great character, with rooms painted in varied shades of green and hallways featuring hundreds of posters and photographs of matadors and bullfights; its restaurant created the Caesar salad. Singles/doubles cost US$30. At *Hotel Villa de Zaragoza* (☎ 85-18-32), a newer brown stucco motel at Avenida Madero 1120 directly behind the Frontón Palacio Jai Alai, all rooms include TV, telephone, heat and air-conditioning. Singles/doubles cost about US$38. *Hotel Terrazas* (☎ 88-27-11), at Calle 4a (Díaz Mirón) No 2206 between Avenidas Negrete and Ocampo, has doubles with color TV, air-conditioning and room service for US$42.

Places to Stay – top end

The *Country Club Hotel* (☎ 81-77-33), at Calle Tapachula 1 across from the Hipódromo Agua Caliente, has gone through several renovations and upgrades. Most suites and other rooms overlook the golf course and the city. All rooms and suites have full carpeting, air-conditioning, cable TV, telephone and private bathroom. Singles/doubles cost US$56, including all taxes and charges. The two-story main section has rooms with parking spaces in front. Adjacent are a swimming pool, coffee shop/ restaurant and a smaller building with suites and junior suites. The coffee shop serves typical Mexican breakfasts for about US$5 or more.

The 120-room *Hotel La Mesa Inn* (☎ 81-65-22) is at Blvd Díaz Ordaz 50, a continuation of Blvd Agua Caliente. Singles/doubles cost US$54/58; all have carpets, satellite TV, telephone and air-conditioning. Facilities include a coffee shop, a Chinese restaurant, a pizza parlor, two bars and a swimming pool. Rooms in the newer section are larger.

The *Hacienda del Río* (☎ 84-86-44), at Blvd Sánchez Taboada 10606, charges US$66 for singles/doubles, but offers occasional specials from US$51; it also has a restaurant and swimming pool. Reservations for the Country Club, La Mesa and Hacienda del Río, which are affiliated with the US Best Western chain, can be made in the USA through the Tijuana Baja Information Center (☎ (619) 299-8518, (800) 522-1516 toll free).

The *Hotel Paraíso Radisson* (☎ 81-72-00, (800) 333-3333 toll free in the USA), at Blvd Agua Caliente 1, caters primarily to businesspeople, with singles/doubles starting at US$87. All rooms have color TV, air-conditioning and telephone. Its King Jester's Disco is popular with local university students.

At Blvd Agua Caliente 4500, the *Hotel Fiesta Americana* (☎ 81-70-00) is Tijuana's most prominent hotel. Its shiny 23-story towers, the tallest buildings in town, house a shopping mall and many offices and restaurants. Additional attractions include a swimming pool, golf course and various convention facilities. Room rates are US$77, but ask for AAA or Baja Times Club member discounts.

Hotel El Conquistador (☎ 86-48-01) is across from the Club Campestre Tijuana at Blvd Agua Caliente 700 – look for the pseudo-colonial architecture. All 110 rooms have air-conditioning, cable TV and telephones; rates start around US$60 single or double.

Modern *Hotel Lucerna* (☎/fax 84-20-00), Paseo de los Héroes 10902 at the corner of Avenida Rodríguez, primarily caters to visiting businesspeople. Singles/doubles, all with air-conditioning, color TV and telephone, cost US$63/68 weekdays, but are slightly discounted on weekends. Continental breakfast is included. It has a restaurant, piano bar and swimming pool.

Places to Eat

Tijuana's multitudinous restaurants serve everything from traditional antojitos to Italian, Swiss and Chinese food. At the foot of the stairs at Revolución 718, near the corner of Calle 3a (Carrillo Puerto), *Café La Especial* (☎ 88-66-54) has very decent Mexican food at reasonable prices and is far quieter than the average eatery on La Revo. *La Torta*, on Avenida Constitución between Calle 5a and Calle 6a, is part of a chain specializing in tortas of a very high standard at reasonable prices; it also serves a surprisingly rich chocolate cake at a very low price of just over US$1. On the east side of Avenida Constitución, between Calle 1a (Artículo 123) and Calle 2a (Juárez), *Jugos Los Norteños* is a popular juice bar and taco stand.

Restaurant Hotel Nelson, at the corner of Avenida Revolución and Calle 1a (Artículo 123), is a sterile coffee shop with cheap but mediocre meals for as little as US$1.50. Among their standards is a breakfast of eggs, toast, beans and coffee and, at lunch time, they serve inexpensive fixed-price meals. Seats near the window are good for people watching.

The renowned *Bol Corona* (☎ 85-47-08), across from Hotel Nelson on Avenida Revolución, was once a traditional Mexican restaurant but is now a two-story complex with a bar and family-style coffee shop at street level, plus a candle-lit steakhouse and thunderous disco upstairs. The coffee shop serves varied, inexpensive Mexican food (burritos are a specialty), but the steakhouse has obsequious English-speaking waiters and far higher prices (starting around US$10 for a steak dinner). One block south, *Woolworth's* is a time-warp department store with an inexpensive lunch counter of a type which was once common north of the border.

At the southwest corner of Calle 3a (Carrillo Puerto) and Avenida Revolución *Tequila Circo*, better known for its beer and margaritas than for its food, is a 2nd-story place wrapped around a corner balcony. Across the street, *Margarita's Village* (☎ 85-73-62) is similar in decor and purpose; it also has a branch at the Plaza Viva Tijuana, a short walk from the San Ysidro border crossing.

La Leña, downstairs on Avenida Revolución between Calle 4a (Díaz Mirón) and Calle 5a (Zapata), serves some of Tijuana's best Sonoran beef, particularly its carne asada. Lunch or dinner costs between US$10 and US$25. Another branch (☎ 86-29-20) operates at Blvd Agua Caliente 4560 next to the Fiesta Americana Hotel. Two of downtown's best seafood restaurants are *Pedrín's* (☎ 85-40-62), on Avenida Revolución between Calles 7a (Galeana) and 8a (Hidalgo), and nearby *La Costa* (☎ 85-84-94), on Calle 7a (Galeana) between avenidas Revolución and Constitución. Across the street from La Costa is *Fiesta Mexicana*, an attractive new place.

Tía Juana Tilly's is one of Tijuana's most popular gringo hangouts; one location (☎ 85-24-77) is next to the Palacio Jai Alai on Avenida Revolución, while the related *Tilly's Fifth Avenue* is near the corner of Revolución and Calle 5a (Zapata). Both food and drinks seem overpriced (a plate of nachos costs about US$3), but most people come for the booze and party atmosphere. At the corner of Avenida Revolución and Calle 8a, *Sanborn's* (☎ 88-14-62), the local branch of the famous Mexican department store, has both a bar and a good restaurant. For generous portions of good, reasonably priced pizza and pasta, try *Vittorio's* at Revolución 1269, at the corner of Calle 9a (Zaragoza).

Another moderately priced place near the city center is *Tortas Ricardo* (☎ 81-86-

55), at the corner of Avenida Madero and Calle 7a (Galeana), which is popular with local businesspeople for dishes like New York steak with enchiladas and guacamole. Their Mexican combination plate is also a good choice.

For baked goods *El Molino*, on Calle 10a (Sarabia) at the corner of Avenida Quintana Roo, is open 24 hours. In continuous operation since 1928, it makes everything from ordinary bolillos to elaborate wedding cakes. *La Baguette*, on Blvd Agua Caliente a short distance east of the Toreo de Tijuana bullring, is the local branch of a popular Baja chain that offers good croissants and other pastries.

Although Blvd Agua Caliente is distant for pedestrians, it has several restaurants worth trying. *Dionnysos* (☎ 84-85-08), at the corner of Avenida Pío Pico and Blvd Agua Caliente, serves Greek specialties like souvlaki, gyros, spanakopita and moussaka at moderate prices. Pizza and pasta are available at *Giuseppi's* (☎ 84-10-18), on Blvd Agua Caliente at the corner of Avenida Querétaro.

Burritos del Bol Corona, near the corner of Avenida Cuauhtémoc and Blvd Agua Caliente, is a branch of Avenida Revolución's landmark eatery, with a variety of inexpensive take-out burritos. *Boccaccio's Nuevo Marianna* (☎ 86-22-66), supposedly one of the best restaurants in town, serves Italian and seafood dishes; it's at Blvd Agua Caliente 2500 near the Club Campestre Tijuana, but some consider it poor value for money (it's not cheap).

The Plaza Fiesta mall, at the corner of Paseo de los Héroes and Avenida Independencia, features several restaurants and cafes serving food and drink from various countries. Well worth a splurge, *Saverio's* (☎ 84-73-72) is an outstanding Italian restaurant with pizza, pasta and seafood (prices are much higher than the more modest Vittorio's, above), open daily except Monday from 7:30 am to 10 pm. In the same complex, try also Argentine-run *Buenos Aires* (closed Sundays) for beef or *Taberna Española* (☎ 84-75-62) for Spanish meals and tapas.

Entertainment

Baseball Temporarily suspended from the Liga Mexicana del Pacífico for financial reasons, Los Potros de Tijuana (Tijuana Colts) normally play at Estadio de los Potros in Cerro Colorado (formerly known as La Mesa), east of the city along Blvd Los Insurgentes. The winter professional season lasts from October to January

For information about the Potros' reinstatement, ask at the tourist office; for more information about Mexican baseball, see the Facts for the Visitor chapter and the separate Mexicali entry in the Mexicali & the Northern Gulf chapter.

Charreadas Usually free of charge, charreadas (rodeos) take place every Sunday afternoon from May to September at one of four venues in the Tijuana area – ask the tourist office for latest details. One popular charro ground is in Playas de Tijuana, just south of the Plaza de Toros Monumental.

Cinemas In central Tijuana, the few remaining cinemas show cheap Mexican porno, but in and around the shopping centers in the Zona Río and on Mesa de Otay it is still possible to see first-run films from Mexico, the USA and Europe. The Multicinemas Río (☎ 84-04-81) are in the Plaza Río Tijuana, at the corner of Paseo de los Héroes and Avenida Independencia, while the related Multicinemas Otay (☎ 23-23-70) are in the Centro Comercial Otay, on Carretera Aeropuerto in Mesa de Otay. The Cinemas Gemelos Hipódromo (☎ 81-40-36), a two-screen cinema, are on Blvd Agua Caliente, just east of the racetrack.

Discos Rowdy Avenida Revolución is the home of venues for earsplitting live and recorded music at places like the Bol Corona, the local branch of the Hard Rock Café and many others.

Most of Tijuana's fancier discos are in the Zona Río, such as the kitschy Baby Rock at Diego Rivera 1482 (correspondents to the Tijuana weekly *Zeta* have complained of its discriminatory admission policies). Single women from north of the border should beware the city police department's notorious 'disco patrol', which reportedly hangs around the area at closing time; for the unsavory details, see Luis Alberto Urrea's *Across the Wire* (Anchor Books, New York, 1993).

Jazz Tijuana's only jazz club is Jazz Alley (☎ 81-87-30), in the Edificio Gallegos at Blvd Agua Caliente 3401, Colonia Chapultepec. Doors open at 8 pm Wednesday, Friday and Saturday nights; there is no cover charge.

Soccer Inter-Tijuana, the city's professional soccer team, is a second-division unit; matches take place in summer.

Things to Buy

Avenida Revolución and Avenida Constitución are the main shopping streets. Because Baja is a duty-free zone, it offers good deals on some imported goods. Calvin Klein, Ralph Lauren and several other top-name designers have opened stores in Tijuana, but most of their merchandise is manufactured in Mexico.

Local handicrafts are plentiful, especially jewelry, wrought-iron furniture, baskets, silver, blown glass, pottery and leather goods; bargaining is the rule in smaller shops. Try also the municipal market on Avenida Niños Héroes between Calle 1a (Artículo 123) and Calle 2a (Juárez) or the sprawling **Mercado de Artesanías** at Calle 1a (Comercio) and Avenida Ocampo, just south of the northernmost pedestrian bridge over the Río Tijuana.

Mexican liquor and beer are popular buys, though prices are higher than in other border cities. Remember that US Customs regulations allow only one liter of liquor and six bottles of beer per adult (21 years or older) to be taken into the USA, unless you arrive by common carrier (bus or taxi).

Many visitors take advantage of Tijuana's low-priced auto body and upholstery repair shops, along Avenida Ocampo, where prices are typically less than half those north of the border. Most of these shops have English-speaking staff and do good work, but clarify your expectations beforehand and get a written estimate before committing yourself to repairs.

Other visitors frequent Tijuana's equally low-priced dentists for fillings, crowns, bridges and dentures. Cut-rate pharmaceuticals and physicians also attract refugees from the avaricious drug companies, insurers and doctors of the USA.

Getting There & Away

Air Mexico's fourth busiest air terminal, Aeropuerto Internacional Abelardo L Rodríguez (☎ 83-20-21, 83-21-18) is on Mesa de Otay, east of downtown; it has become a popular departure and arrival point, but except for occasional promotions, fares are now only slightly cheaper than similar US-based fares.

Aeroméxico (☎ 85-15-30; ☎ 83-27-00 at the airport), at Avenida Revolución 1236 (1668) between Calle 8a (Hidalgo) and Calle 9a (Zaragoza), flies to Acapulco, Cancún, Guadalajara, Los Angeles, Los Mochis, Mazatlán and Mexico City.

Mexicana (☎ 82-41-83 at the airport), which no longer has offices downtown or in the Zona Río, serves Guadalajara, Mexico City and Zacatecas, with connections to Acapulco, Cancún, León, Puerto Vallarta, San Luis Potosí, Tepic and Villahermosa.

Taesa (☎ 84-84-83, ☎ 83-55-93 at the airport), at Paseo de Los Héroes 9288 almost next door to the Centro Cultural Tijuana, flies mostly to Mexican destinations, but has Monday and Friday connections to Chicago via Ciudad Juárez; Thursday, Saturday and Sunday service to Chicago is via Zacatecas.

Aero California (☎ 84-21-00), in the Plaza Río Tijuana at the corner of Paseo de los Héroes and Avenida Independencia, flies from Tijuana to Aguas Calientes, Colima, Culiacán, Durango, Guadalajara, La Paz/Los Cabos, Los Mochis, Mazatlán, Mexico City, Puebla, Tepic and Torreón. Fares to Los Mochis are about US$116 (one way) and US$210 (return).

AirLA (☎ (800) 010-0413 in Mexico, ☎ (800) 933-5952 in the USA, both toll free) provides international service to Los Angeles, four times every weekday, twice daily weekends. Round-trip fares start at US$118, with some restrictions. Like Mexicana, its only office is at the airport, but downtown travel agents can make reservations and sell tickets.

Bus Tijuana has three bus stations. Only ABC (local buses) and US-based Greyhound use the handy but dilapidated downtown terminal, at the corner of Avenida Madero and Calle 1a (Comercio). Both ABC (☎ 86-90-10) and Greyhound also use the less convenient Central Camionera, the departure point for nearly all long-distance buses. From the Plaza Viva Tijuana, just south of the San Ysidro border crossing, ABC and Autotransportes Aragón offer convenient services to Ensenada; in Ensenada, Aragón makes easy connections to points south as far as San Quintín.

The Central Camionera (☎ 26-17-01) is a cavernous building on the outskirts of Tijuana, about 3 miles (5 km) southeast of the city center where Blvd Lázaro Cárdenas becomes the airport road. From Calle 2a (Juárez) east of Avenida Constitución, take any 'Buena Vista', 'Centro' or 'Central Camionera' bus (US$0.40), which also stop at the border bus lot. Quicker and more convenient are the gold-and-white cabs (Mesa de Otay) from Avenida Madero between Calle 2a (Juárez) and Calle 3a (Carrillo Puerto) for US$0.50.

To/From the USA Several companies, including Greyhound, Intercalifornias, Mexicoach and ATC/Vancom offer services between San Diego and Tijuana; Greyhound and Intercalifornias offer long-distance services. Greyhound has several depots in the San Diego area, and fares to Tijuana from each depot are:

San Diego
    120 West Broadway, cnr 1st Ave (☎ (619) 239-3266); US$4/8 one way/return
Chula Vista
    Atlas Travel Service, 234 3rd Ave (☎ (619) 422-9211); US$4/8

San Ysidro
    799 East San Ysidro Blvd (☎ (619) 428-1194); US$6.50/12.35. (Yes, it costs more to go to Tijuana from San Ysidro than from San Diego or Chula Vista!)

Buses from San Diego and San Ysidro depart almost every hour between about 5:30 am and 12:30 am; there are only two or three Chula Vista departures daily. Check with Greyhound for the latest schedules.

Intercalifornias, on the east side of the road just south of the San Ysidro border crossing, goes to Los Angeles and points in mainland California's Central Valley.

Mexicoach (☎ (619) 232-5049 in San Diego; ☎ 85-69-13 in Tijuana) has daily buses at 9, 10 and 11 am, noon, and 2, 4 and 6 pm to and from San Diego's Amtrak station to central Tijuana's Frontón Palacio Jai Alai, on Avenida Revolución between Calle 7a and Calle 8a. One-way/return fares are US$6.25/12 for adults, with a small discount for seniors (60 and over); children under 12 travel free.

ATC/Vancom (☎ (619) 427-6438) runs buses from the corner of Broadway and 3rd Ave or Broadway and Front St in downtown San Diego to the US side of the border for only US$1.50. It takes 80 minutes to reach the border.

A variety of minivans operate between the border and local San Ysidro area communities. Most vans terminate next to the end of the trolley line; fares average US$1 to US$2.

To/From Elsewhere in Mexico Tres Estrellas de Oro's Servicio Elite offers 1st-class buses with air-conditioning and toilets throughout the country. Autotransportes del Pacífico and Autotransportes de Baja California (ABC) operate mostly 2nd-class buses to various destinations on mainland Mexico's Pacific Coast (Autotransportes del Pacífico and Norte de Sonora) and in Baja California (ABC). ABC's Servicio Plus is comparable to Tres Estrellas's Servicio Elite.

Buses leave Tijuana's dilapidated downtown bus station, at the corner of Calle 1a (Comercio) and Avenida Madero, en route to:

Ensenada
(1½ hours, US$5) at least hourly from 5 am to 6 pm.
Rosarito
(½ hour, US$1) about every 40 minutes from 6 am to 8 pm. Rosarito-bound passengers can also catch route taxis on Avenida Madero between Calle 5a and Calle 6a.
Tecate
(one hour, US$1.75) half-hourly from 5:30 am to 8 pm.
Los Angeles
(3½ hours, US$18) at least hourly from 6:30 am to 12:30 pm with Greyhound. Greyhound starts from the Central Camionera, on the eastern outskirts of Tijuana, and also has connections to cities and towns in mainland California's Central Valley. The fare to San Diego is US$4.

From the Central Camionera (☎ 21-29-82, ask for appropriate extension), about 3 miles (5 km) southeast of the city center, there are services to:

Ensenada
(1½ hours, US$5) at least hourly from 5 am to midnight with ABC, and three times daily with slightly cheaper Tres Estrellas.
Tecate
(1½ hours, US$1.75) at least hourly from 5:30 am to 10 pm.
Mexicali
(four hours, US$7.50) at least hourly from 5:30 am to 10 pm.
San Felipe
(six hours, US$17) once daily at 8 am with ABC, more frequently from Ensenada.
San Quintín
(six hours, US$15) twice daily at 12:30 and 4 pm with ABC.
Bahía de Los Angeles
(8½ hours, US$27) Saturday at 6 am. This new service constitutes the only public transport to Bahía de Los Angeles.
Guerrero Negro
(10 hours, US$13.50) once daily at 7 pm with ABC.
Santa Rosalía
(12 hours, US$34) once daily at 4:30 pm with ABC.

La Paz
(22 to 24 hours, US$56) daily at 8 am, noon and 4 pm with ABC.
Express to Guadalajara/Mexico City
(36/46 hours, US$78/101) several times daily with Tres Estrellas del Norte. Transportes del Pacífico and Norte de Sonora are a few dollars cheaper, but much less comfortable than Tres Estrellas' Servicio Elite. All three lines stop en route at most major towns and cities in mainland Mexico, including San Luis Río Colorado (US$12), Sonoita (US$19), Nogales (US$33), Guaymas (US$35), Hermosillo (US$38), Ciudad Obregón (US$46), Los Mochis (US$56), Culiacán (US$65), Mazatlán (US$68), Tepic (US$71), Querétaro (US$92) and Morelia (US$110).

Norte de Sonora also runs three buses daily to Puerto Peñasco, Sonora, on the mainland coast of the Gulf of California. Turismo y Pasajes (TYPS) has six direct buses daily to Ciudad Obregón and Culiacán.

From the Plaza Viva Tijuana, only a few minutes' walk south of the border, Autotransportes Aragón and ABC (☎ 83-56-81) offer convenient and inexpensive service to Ensenada. Aragón leaves hourly between 8 am and 9 pm for US$5 one way, US$7.50 return, with connections to points south as far as San Quintín.

Train Amtrak (☎ (800) 872-7245 toll free in the USA) runs daily trains between San Diego and Los Angeles. For schedule information, see the Train section in the Getting There chapter. The San Diego Trolley runs from San Diego's Amtrak station directly to San Ysidro.

Trolley For fares ranging from US$0.50 to US$1.50, the San Diego trolley (☎ (619) 233-3004) is one of the cheapest ways from San Diego's Center City to the San Ysidro border. Trolleys depart from stations every 15 minutes or so from about 5 am to midnight. A leaflet with full schedule and fare information is available at each station (see the From the USA section in the Getting There chapter for details).

From San Diego's Lindbergh Field airport, city bus No 2 goes directly to the trolley stop at Plaza America, across from the Amtrak depot. There is also a second trolley line from El Cajón and eastern San Diego to transfer stations at Plaza America and Imperial Ave & 12th St. In San Ysidro, the trolley stops on the east side of the border station near a pedestrian bridge into Mexico.

Car Rental Rental cars are cheaper in San Diego, where some companies permit their cars to be taken across the border. Locally, however, try Central Rent de Mexicali (☎ 84-22-57), Paseo de Los Héroes 104, Zona Río.

National (☎ 86-21-03) is at Blvd Agua Caliente 5000, with a branch at the airport (☎ 82-44-33). Avis (☎ 86-40-04) is at Blvd Agua Caliente 3310-1, while Hertz (☎ 86-43-71) is at the Hotel Palacio Azteca, Avenida 16 de Septiembre 213. Budget (☎ 84-02-53) is at Paseo de los Héroes 77 in the Zona Río, one block east of Avenida Cuauhtémoc.

Getting Around
To the Airport Phone the government-regulated taxi service (☎ 83-10-20) for an airport cab from central Tijuana, or else grab one on the street; fares are about US$10. Sharing the ride can reduce the cost to about US$2 per person for up to five.

From the border, take any bus marked 'Aeropuerto' from the street just past the taxi stand, for about US$0.40; from downtown, catch the airport bus on Calle 5a (Zapata) between Constitución and Los Héroes.

Bus From the border, just about any bus from the taxi lot will drop passengers downtown near the Frontón Palacio Jai Alai on Avenida Revolución. At the bus stop, there is usually a man with a notebook who directs people towards the right bus to any destination in town.

The 'Baja P' bus goes to the Centro Cultural de Tijuana and the Plaza Río and Plaza Fiesta shopping centers. Standard fares are about US$0.40.

Taxi Tijuana taxis have no meters, and cabbies sometimes overcharge gringos, especially for the five-minute trip from the border to central Tijuana – about US$5 per person for a trip that should only cost about US$3. Try out your bargaining skills; in general, expect to pay anything from US$2 to US$5 for most city taxi rides.

Route taxis (about US$0.50) are only slightly dearer, and much quicker, than city buses. From Avenida Madero and Calle 3a, gold-and-white station-wagon cabs (Mesa de Otay) go frequently to the Central Camionera.

TECATE
Tecate (official population 40,240) is a somnolent but growing border town about 34 miles (55 km) east of Tijuana and 90 miles (150 km) west of Mexicali. Far enough from Tijuana to be off the main tourist route, it more closely resembles a mainland Mexican *pueblo* (town) than any other town in northern Baja California. Known for its family life, it even lacks the dubious attractions of a zona de tolerancia (an apparent arson fire once destroyed a nearly completed casino).

Most mainland Mexican cities and towns have a zócalo, a central plaza decreed by the Spanish colonial Laws of the Indies, around which the major public buildings are clustered. Even post-colonial cities like Tijuana, Ensenada and Mexicali have similarly picturesque plazas, but they are often remote from the centers of activity. Tecate's Parque Hidalgo, though, has long been the town's social center for both visitors and locals. On weekends mariachi bands play here, and fiestas take place throughout the year.

Across the US border, Tecate's mainland California namesake is barely a wide spot in the road, but a major discount shoe retailer has recently set up here to take advantage of the growing Mexican market. With approval of NAFTA, this trend is likely to continue.

History
Tecate's origins derive from an 1831 land

Tecate

UNITED STATES

CALIFORNIA
BAJA CALIFORNIA

US Customs

Avenida México

Mexican Customs

To Calif 94 and
San Diego

To Mexicali
90 miles (145 km)

To Ensenada
66 miles (106 km)

To Tijuana
34 miles
(54 km)

Calle Portes Gil
Calle Rodríguez
Calle Ortiz Rubio
Calle Lázaro Cárdenas
Calle Elias Calles
Calle Alvaro Obregón
Calle de la Huerta
Calle Aldrete
Calle Santana
Calle Esteban Cantú
Calle 15

Callejón Madero
Avenida Revolución
Callejón Reforma
Avenida Benito Juárez
Callejón Libertad
Avenida Hidalgo
Calle Carranza

Avenida Benito Juárez

Rail Station
(No Passengers)

Vía de Ferrocarril

Rio Tecate

N

500 m

0.25 mile

250

0

grant to a Peruvian named Juan Bandini (later mayor of San Diego, immediately before the US takeover of Alta California), but the establishment of early businesses and the development of agriculture in the 1880s really put the town on the map. The surrounding countryside yielded both grains and fruit crops, like grapes and olives.

In 1911 Ricardo Flores Magón's Liberal Party army occupied Tecate before marching west to Tijuana, but the federal government regained control after six weeks. After 1915, the railroad linked Tijuana, Tecate and Tucson (Arizona, USA), but the former passenger line now carries only eastbound freight. Completion of México 2, the last link on the Tijuana-Mexico City highway, was a further boost to the economy.

Tecate's one time whiskey factory, a major employer, folded with the repeal of US Prohibition, but businessman Alberto Aldrete's malt factory, founded in 1928, expanded into a major brewery by 1944 but soon went bankrupt. Acquired by a Mexican conglomerate after several years' management by the Banco de México, it is still an important employer, producing up to 1200 cans per minute of two of Mexico's best known beers, Tecate and Carta Blanca. Maquiladoras, however, are now the major

source of employment; the largest is Schlage Locks, which employs about 3000 people. In 1986, the Universidad Autónoma de Baja California opened an extension center which has enhanced the town's cultural environment.

Like other Baja California border towns, Tecate has sprawled dramatically over the past decade, in part because presumptive border crossers have remained in the area; some claim the actual population is at least double the official figure. This seems too high, but growing numbers have clearly stressed local resources and accentuated social problems that barely existed a decade ago – town residents now lock their doors against thieves, for example. Still, by border town standards, Tecate is an atypically placid and appealing destination.

Orientation

México 2, the east-west route linking Tijuana and Mexicali, is divided into Avenida Benito Juárez to the north and Avenida Hidalgo two blocks south. Avenida Juárez runs past Parque Hidalgo (Tecate's main square) and the bus station, while Avenida Hidalgo runs parallel to it and past the brewery.

Calle Lázaro Cárdenas runs north from Avenida Hidalgo, past the western side of Parque Hidalgo and straight to the border

■	PLACES TO STAY		OTHER	21	Instituto de Cultura de
1	Hotel Frontera	2	CANACO (tourist kiosk)		Baja California
6	Motel El Dorado	3	Post Office	24	Cervecería
8	Motel Paraíso	5	Cruz Roja (Red Cross)		Cuauhtémoc-Moctezuma
19	Hotel México	9	Multibanco Comermex		(brewery)
22	Motel Hacienda	10	L F Caliente Foreign	27	Iglesia Nuestra Señora de
26	Hotel Tecate		Sports Book		Guadalupe
		12	Multi-servicio Cox's	28	SECTUR (tourist office)
▼	PLACES TO EAT		(money exchange)	29	Viajes Segovia (travel
4	Mariscos Chemel	13	Viajes Tecate		agency)
6	El Tucán	14	Banamex	31	Baseball Park
7	La Carreta	15	Banco Internacional	32	Parque Adolfo López
11	El Mejor Pan	16	Bancomer		Mateos
18	Taquería La Placita	17	Parque Hidalgo	33	Universidad
23	Dragón Cuchumá	20	Terminal de Autobuses;		Autónoma/Museo de Arte
25	Passeto		Long-distance	34	Tile Workshop
30	La Escondida		Telephone/Fax		

crossing. Calle Ortiz Rubio runs parallel to and one block east of Cárdenas, passes the eastern edge of Parque Hidalgo and heads south to become México 3 to Ensenada. Just south of the river are Tecate's baseball stadium, the university extension center, and the larger square of Parque Adolfo López Mateos.

Information

Border Crossing Immigration and customs on both sides of the border are open 6 am to midnight daily, but Mexican officials issue car permits only from 8 am to 4 pm. In 1991, over 1.7 million foreigners entered Mexico through Tecate. Saturday is the busiest day; Sunday, surprisingly, is relatively quiet.

Tourist Office SECTUR's cramped offices (☎ 4-10-95), at Callejón Libertad 1305 on the south side of Parque Hidalgo, have little printed matter and English-speaking staff are not always available. Office hours are 9 am to 7 pm weekdays, 10 am to 3 pm weekends.

At the border, the Cámara Nacional de Comercio (CANACO) has a small but helpful information kiosk with decent maps of the town, open 9 am to 2 pm and 3 to 6 pm daily except Sundays, when it is closed. Its staff speak English.

Money Most businesses readily accept US dollars, but Tecate also has several banks on Avenida Benito Juárez and around Parque Hidalgo. These include Banamex, Bancomer, Banco Internacional, Banca Serfin and Multibanco Comermex.

Multi-servicio Cox's operates exchange services on Avenida Juárez, between Aldrete and Santana; it's open daily except Sunday from 9 am to 7 pm.

Post & Telecommunications Tecate's new post office is at the corner of Calle Ortiz Rubio and Callejón Madero, three short blocks north of Parque Hidalgo.

The Telnor office at the corner of Calle Alvaro Obregón and Callejón Libertad is now purely a business office. Tecate has

plenty of public telephones, but the best place to make a long-distance call is the bus station, which has several cabinas and a fax machine. Tecate's area code is 665.

Cultural Centers The Instituto de Cultura de Baja California (☎ 4-14-83), at Blvd Morelos 511 in Colonia Cantú, at the eastern approach to town, offers film series and other cultural events. The Universidad Autónoma's Centro de Extensión, just south of the bridge over the Río Tecate, hosts occasional traveling exhibitions of bajacaliforniano art.

Travel Agencies Viajes Tecate (☎ 4-13-14, 4-13-41) is on the south side of Avenida Juárez, between Aldrete and Santana. Viajes Segovia (☎ 4-27-55, fax 4-27-56) is at Calle Ortiz Rubio 260-2, south of Parque Hidalgo.

Medical Services The Cruz Roja (☎ 132) is at the west end of Avenida Juárez. Tecate has numerous medical clinics, dentists and pharmacies that serve visitors from north of the border.

Cervecería Cuauhtémoc-Moctezuma

Tecate's landmark brewery (☎ 4-20-11, X299), on Avenida Hidalgo between Calle Lázaro Cárdenas and Calle Alvaro Obregón, offers daily tours by reservation only and preferably for at least five people. It's best to call far in advance for reservations – at least two weeks is desirable, but it's worth calling to see if you can hook up with another tour or persuade Señor Peñaloza, who is in charge of publicity, to offer a tour on the spot. The brewery, the largest building in Tecate, produces some of Mexico's best known beers, including Carta Blanca and the town's namesake Tecate.

Behind the brewery, the deserted station of the Ferrocarril Tijuana-Tecate, a key segment of the San Diego & Arizona Eastern Railway line which ran along and across the border for over 60 years, dates from 1915. There are speculative plans to restart the rail line for both passenger and freight service; for details, see the aside on 'Rails Across the Border' in the Mexicali chapter.

Festivals & Events

While less extroverted than Tijuana and Ensenada, Tecate holds several festivals that are more frequented by locals than foreigners. Double-check with the tourist offices, since recent problems associated with several events may lead to major changes.

March
   Biatlón Internacional (International Biathlon)
May
   Cinco de Mayo
   Carrera Ciclísta Tecate-Ensenada (Tecate-Ensenada Bicycle Race) – Up to 15,000 cyclists participate in one of Tecate's biggest annual events, usually held in mid-May but sometimes postponed. For more information, contact the local offices of SECTUR or CANACO.
   Maratón de Relevos (Relay Marathon to Ensenada)
June
   Gran Charreada (Rodeo) – Several other charreadas take place throughout the year.
July
   Tecate en Marcha (Tecate in Progress), also known as *La Romería* (the Pilgrimage) – Celebrated with parades and rodeos; sometimes held in September, but possibly under suspension because recent festivals have lost money.
August
   La Pamplonada (Running of the Bulls) – Resembling the running of the bulls in Pamplona, Spain, this was suspended after the event of 1989, when disorderly gringos caused a near riot and major fire. Despite considerable local opposition, it was a commercial success and may be revived soon.
September
   Fiesta Mexicana y Charreada (Mexican Fiesta & Rodeo)
December
   Posadas de Tecate (Annual Pre-Christmas Parades)

Places to Stay

Hotel México, at Avenida Juárez 230 almost next door to the bus terminal, is reportedly frequented by *polleros* (smugglers) who help *pollos* ('chickens' or undocumented Mexicans) across the border. Dark, gloomy doubles with private bath are about US$15, but rooms with shared bath cost only US$8/10.

For the budget-minded, friendly *Hotel Frontera* (☎ 4-13-42), Callejón Madero 131, is probably a better choice, with basic but tidy rooms for US$13. *Motel Paraíso* (☎ 4-17-16), Calle Aldrete 83 just north of Avenida Juárez, is ragged around the edges but very hospitable for US$15 single or double. The spartan, unheated singles/doubles at *Hotel Tecate*, on Lázaro Cárdenas half a block south of Parque Hidalgo, are a poorer value for US$22 (the hot showers are dependable and the toilets very clean, however); similar rooms with color TV cost US$32.

Motel Hacienda (☎ 4-12-50), at Avenida Benito Juárez 861, west of the town center, offers clean, carpeted, air-conditioned doubles with TV and swimming pool for US$38. The 41-room *Motel El Dorado* (☎ 4-13-33, 4-11-02), Avenida Benito Juárez 1100, has comfortable singles/doubles with air-conditioning, cable TV, telephone and wall-to-wall carpeting for US$50. Its US mailing address is PO Box 160, Tecate, California 91980.

Places to Eat

Despite its modest size, Tecate has a number of good restaurants. *Passeto*, at Callejón Libertad 200 less than a block west of Parque Hidalgo, serves moderately priced Italian dishes like spaghetti and ravioli. *El Tucán*, at Motel El Dorado, serves various continental and Mexican dishes; lunch costs an average of US$6 and dinner about US$10. *Dragón Cuchumá*, on Calle Alvaro Obregón between Avenida Hidalgo and Callejón Libertad, is a Chinese restaurant named after the mountain that straddles the nearby border.

La Placita, a sidewalk taco stand on the east side of Parque Hidalgo, serves some of Tecate's juiciest tacos. The south side of Avenida Juárez, between the bus terminal and Parque Hidalgo, supports wall-to-wall taco stands of good to excellent quality, but the real prize is *Mariscos Chemel*, on Calle Obregón between Avenida Revolución and Callejón Reforma, where locals swarm for succulent fish tacos costing less than US$1 each.

La Carreta, at the corner of Avenida Juárez and Calle Santana, has reasonably priced seafood dishes and cheap margaritas, and offers both indoor and outdoor seating. Inconspicuous *La Escondida* almost lives up to its name ('the hidden'), but has good antojitos in a pleasant environment if you can locate the entrance, on Callejón Libertad between Calles Ortiz Rubio and Rodríguez. It's open daily except Sunday, from 7 am to 5 pm.

El Mejor Pan, open 24 hours at Avenida Juárez 331 half a block west of the bus terminal, is a bakery renowned for its fresh, steaming breads and *pan dulce* (pastries). Locals call it the best bread in Baja.

Entertainment
LF Caliente Sports Book has opened a betting salon with big-screen TVs at the corner of Avenida Juárez and Calle Rodríguez.

Things to Buy
Hand-painted clay tiles and Tecate beer are the town's specialties; both are much cheaper than in the USA, but ask US customs about tiles before purchasing any quantity. There's a tile workshop a short distance south of town via México 3.

Many US citizens also cross the border for groceries and pharmaceuticals because prices are much lower here.

Getting There & Away
Bus Tecate's Terminal de Autobuses is at the corner of Avenida Juárez and Calle Rodríguez, one block east of Parque Hidalgo. ABC buses to Tijuana (US$1.75) leave almost every half hour, while ABC and Transportes Norte de Sonora go to Mexicali (US$5.50) at least hourly between about 6 am and midnight. There are also at least five buses daily to Ensenada (US$7). ABC has three buses daily to Puerto

Peñasco, located on the Gulf Coast of the state of Sonora.

México 2 is a key route for every major bus company in Baja California and northwest Mexico; for an idea of services which pass through Tecate, see the Getting There & Away section for Tijuana

AROUND TECATE
Rancho Tecate Country Club
On México 3, approximately 6 miles (10 km) south of Tecate in the Tanama Valley is the *Rancho Tecate Resort & Country Club* (☎ 4-00-11, fax 4-02-41), with a hotel, a golf course (only three of nine holes are presently ready for play, and there is no projected date for completion), tennis courts, a restaurant, two artificial lakes and a swimming pool. Rooms range from US$50 to US$90 per night. Its US Customer Relations Office (☎ (619) 234-7951) is at 2550 5th Ave, Suite 136, San Diego, California 92103, but they usually refer potential customers to the Tecate number.

Rancho La Puerta
On México 2, 3 miles west of Tecate, luxuriously landscaped *Rancho La Puerta* (☎ 4-11-55) is a health spa and resort for patrons who can afford at least US$1350 per person, double-occupancy for the minimum one-week stay – only slightly less than a year's wages for a maquiladora laborer. Founded in 1940 by self-improvement gurus Deborah and Edmund Szekely, the resort boasts that its location at the foot of border-straddling Mount Cuchumá is 'the south rim of the last surviving Southern California "safe zone" for the environmentally sensitive'. It features two staff members for each guest.

According to its brochure, the resort does not cater to those 'guests who weigh 35% more than the accepted norms, or guests who have difficulty in walking, or seeing, or those with serious health problems'. Vacancies are booked as far as a year in advance; for reservations in the USA, contact Rancho La Puerta (☎ (619) 744-4222 or (800) 443-7565 toll free), PO Box

463057, Escondido, California 92046. The Rancho provides free transportation to and from San Diego's Lindbergh Field Airport, Saturdays only, and handles immigration formalities on the spot.

Budget-conscious travelers with hunger pangs can probably afford the antojitos at *Café Sierra Bonita*, next to Rancho La Puerta's entrance.

Hacienda Santa Verónica

Climbing to a high plateau, México 2 passes through a zone of small farms and ranches where *Hacienda Santa Verónica* (☎ (66) 85-97-93 in Tijuana), about 32 miles (50 km) southeast of Tecate via a lateral off the main highway, offers rooms with fireplace and patio, a swimming pool, six tennis courts and an RV park/campground. Visitors in search of peace and quiet should know that Santa Verónica simultaneously boasts of the 'first all-purpose off-road and dirt-racing facility in the world', which will showcase 'Gran Prixs, ATVs, sprint cars and super modifieds'.

Rooms cost US$50 per night for a double, with seasonal packages also available. An RV space costs US$15 per night with full hookups, access to restrooms, showers, laundry and sports facilities. Santa Verónica's US contact is the Tijuana Baja Informaton Center (☎ (619) 298-4105; (800) 522-1516 toll free in California, Arizona and Nevada; (800) 225-2786 toll free in the rest of North America), 7860 Mision Center Court, Suite 202, San Diego, California 92108.

Paraíso Los Alisos

At Km 40 of México 2, about 9 miles (15 km) west of Tecate, Los Alisos (☎ 4-21-38) is a modest private recreational and sports center with a swimming pool, basketball, tennis and volleyball courts, soccer fields, barbecue pits and a restaurant. It is much more frequented by Mexicans than by gringos.

La Rumorosa

East of Tecate, for about 40 miles (65 km),

México 2 passes through an imposing panorama of immense granite boulders to La Rumorosa, where it descends the precipitous Cantú Grade, with extraordinary views of the shimmering Colorado Desert. Mexico's federal government has improved the highway and plans to charge a heavy toll along this route; the state government of Baja California and many citizens' groups have objected vigorously, since the only free alternative, the parallel US Interstate 8, is limited to those with border-crosser passports
.

SOUTH OF TIJUANA

México 1-D, a divided toll road, can be reached directly from the international border at Tijuana by following the 'Ensenada Toll Road' signs along Calle Internacional, which runs along the border fence almost to the ocean (see the Around Tijuana map). The road turns south just before the exit for Playas de Tijuana and passes through the first of three toll gates. This route is both fast (about 1½ hours) and scenic as it follows the coast to Ensenada.

Tolls for the entire 68-mile (110-km) stretch from Tijuana to Ensenada are about US$7 for an ordinary passenger vehicle or motorcycle, twice that for a motorhome and three times as expensive for vehicles with trailers. One-third of the toll is charged at each of three gates – Playas de Tijuana, Rosarito and San Miguel – though there are several other exits along the route.

Two-lane México 1, which is toll free, passes through equally spectacular scenery but heavy traffic makes it much slower. From the Tijuana border crossing, follow the signs to central Tijuana and continue straight (west) along Calle 3a (Carrillo Puerto) and turn left (south) at Avenida Revolución. Follow Avenida Revolución to the end, where it veers left (east) and becomes Blvd Agua Caliente. Turn right at Blvd Cuauhtémoc, just before the twin towers of the Fiesta Americana Hotel, and head south.

At Rosarito on the coast, the roads run

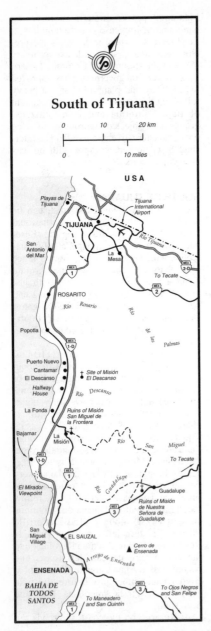

South of Tijuana

```
0          10        20 km
├─────────┼─────────┤

0              10 miles
├─────────────────┤
```

USA

Playas de Tijuana
Tijuana International Airport
TIJUANA
Río Tijuana
San Antonio del Mar
La Mesa
To Tecate
ROSARITO
Río Rosario
Río de las Palmas
Popotla
Puerto Nuevo
Cantamar
El Descanso
Halfway House
Río Descanso
La Fonda
Ruins of Misión San Miguel de la Frontera
Bajamar
La Misión
Río San Miguel
To Tecate
Site of Misión El Descanso
El Mirador Viewpiont
Río Guadalupe
Guadalupe
Ruins of Misión de Nuestra Señora de Guadalupe
San Miguel Village
EL SAUZAL
Cerro de Ensenada
Arroyo de Ensenada
ENSENADA
BAHÍA DE TODOS SANTOS
To Maneadero and San Quintin
To Ojos Negros and San Felipe

parallel for several miles. Just past La Fonda, México 1 turns inland and zigzags through the countryside for another 21 miles (35 km) before crossing the toll road again.

Tourist Office
Just beyond the Playas de Tijuana toll gate, there's a tourist information booth with a few brochures and maps of Tijuana and Rosarito.

San Antonio del Mar
One of the first communities south of Playas de Tijuana, San Antonio is overrun with condominiums and houses for US holiday makers and retirees. A small mobile-home park accommodates transients.

On a hill east of the condominium complex is the *KOA Campground* (☎ 86-14-12), which has a pleasing ocean view but costs US$16 per site. The campground caters mostly to long-term trailer-laden campers, and 'Farmer John' hot dogs, hot coffee, hot showers and a host of other amenities are available to keep them happy.

La Costa, a pleasant restaurant with thickly padded booths, white tablecloths and similar ocean views, serves rather expensive shrimp, lobster, king crab and similar seafood specialties.

El Oasis
Beautifully landscaped *El Oasis*, an RV-park resort (☎ 3-32-53) at Km 25 south of Tijuana, has easy beach access. All 126 sites are paved with small patios, brick barbecues and full hookups, including cable TV. Facilities include a nine-hole golf course, tennis courts, swimming pool, spa and grocery as well as a club house with bathrooms, sauna, TV, laundry and weight room. Rates are US$25 per night and US$2 for cable TV.

El Camello, an ocean-view restaurant which is also part of the resort, has a good but rather pricey menu of items like crab hors d'oeuvres, Manhattan clam 'showder' and shrimp in garlic sauce. Most entrees include soup or salad and garlic bread.

Centro Cultural Tijuana

Plaza de las Tres Cabezas (Three Heads Plaza), Ensenada

Christmas decorations, Mexicali

Christmas decorations, Mexicali

ROSARITO
History

In 1827, José Manuel Machado obtained a grant of 11 leagues south of Rancho Tijuana which, now divided into several ranchos, also includes the city of Rosarito, officially founded in 1885. The valley of Rosarito marks the original boundary between Alta and Baja California, which after the Mexican-American War was moved north to Tijuana.

In 1916 the Compañía Explotadora de Baja California purchased 14,000 acres of the Machado concession; in 1927 this became Moreno & Compañía, which began the Hotel Rosarito. Completed by Manuel Barbachano, it became the landmark Rosarito Beach Hotel.

A few years ago, Rosarito (estimated population 40,000-plus) was a modest fishing village with its single posh resort hotel (known to a few Hollywood stars), long sandy beaches (frequented only by a handful of surfers) and a few taco stands, but its recent 'discovery' has fostered a noisy commercial strip with several resort-style hotels and fine restaurants. Signs are now as likely to be in English as in Spanish. Its beach, fishing, organized bicycle rides and races and horseback riding are the main attractions. Beach-goers who fall asleep in the sun, however, may awake with tread marks on their backs or chests from the three-wheelers that speed up and down the firm sand.

Orientation

Rosarito's main street, Blvd Benito Juárez, is a segment of México 1. On weekends, it becomes a two-way traffic jam, due mostly to traffic from southern mainland California. Nearly all Rosarito's hotels and restaurants are on the west side of this boulevard, some of them directly fronting the beach. While many places do have street addresses, the numbering system is very erratic and most people use landmarks like the Rosarito Beach Hotel as points of reference. Since most east-west streets crossing the central section of Blvd Juárez are named, this section uses those cross streets to indicate directions whenever possible.

Information

Tourist Office SECTUR (☎ 2-10-05, 2-02-00), the local representative of the state-run tourist agency, is on the east side of Blvd Benito Juárez, next to the police station. It has a modest selection of English-language brochures and leaflets, along with recent issues of *Baja Times*, an English-language newspaper; the English-speaking staff will deal with tourist hassles and may help find accommodation in Rosarito or Ensenada. It's open from 9 am to 7 pm daily except Sunday, when it is open 10 am to 6 pm.

For the latest parties, look for *Too Much Fun News*, a monthly newsletter that sponsors events like bicycle races, duathlons, and motocrosses. Their Rosarito address, which is also a beachwear shop, is Blvd Juárez 294-1; the US contact is PO Box 120089, Chula Vista, California 91912.

Money Nearly all merchants accept US dollars in payment or will exchange them for pesos. Banks will not change travelers' checks and, in any event, offer poor rates, but cash advances are possible at Banco Internacional at Avenida Benito Juárez 52-13, Banco Nacional de México at the corner of Juárez and Calle Ciprés, or Multibanco Comermex at Juárez 300.

Post & Telecommunications Rosarito's post office is on Calle Acacias, east of the tourist office. Several pharmacies and other shops along Blvd Juárez have private phone facilities. Rosarito's area code is 661.

Immigration Like the post office, Servicios Migratorios is on Calle Las Acacias, directly behind the tourist office. If you haven't obtained a tourist card to travel south beyond Ensenada, you can do so here.

Travel Agencies Expediciones Ecotur (☎ 3-11-83), north of town at Km 18 on

México 1, organizes backcountry excursions, including hiking, mountain biking, climbing and similar activities. Their US contact address is 482 W Border Village Rd, Suite 244, San Ysidro, California 92173.

Medical Services Hospital Santa Laura (☎ 2-04-40), open 24 hours, is on Avenida Mar del Norte, behind the police station. The Clínica Santa Verónica, on Calle Nogal just west of Blvd Juárez, is also open 24 hours.

Emergency The police station is at Blvd Juárez and Las Acacias. For the Cruz Roja, dial ☎ 132.

Laundry There's a Lavamática at the Quinta Plaza shopping center, at the north end of town, and another on the east side of Blvd Juárez, between Calle Acacias and Calle Roble.

Emiliano Zapata

Museo Wa-Cutai

Rosarito's small historical and anthropological museum, a few doors north of the Rosarito Beach Hotel, offers a good introduction to the area from pre-Columbian times to the present, with a selection of indigenous artifacts and good historical photographs. It also offers occasional traveling exhibitions from mainland Mexico and is open daily 9 am to 5 pm. Admission is free.

Parque Municipal Abelardo L Rodríguez

The amphitheater at Rosarito's beachfront plaza contains the impressive 1987 mural 'Tierra y Libertad' (Land and Liberty) by Juan Zuñiga Padilla, proof that the celebrated muralist tradition is still alive and well in Mexico. Traditional motifs include the eagle and plumed serpent, and Emiliano Zapata and his followers.

Water Sports

Both swimmers and surfers should know that Playa Rosarito and the entire coastline between Tijuana and Ensenada are heavily polluted, and that neither activity is advisable in the area.

Tony E Surf Shop (☎ 2-11-92), at Blvd Juárez 312 opposite Ortega's Place (see Places to Eat, below) is at the north end of town; only a single copy remains of a useful surfer's map of Baja California, but they'll loan it out for photocopies.

Riding

Horses can be hired on the west side of México 1 through Rosarito. From the highway, most people gallop towards the beach and, when appropriate, off into the sunset. Rates average about US$5 to US$10 per hour.

Places to Stay – bottom end

Because it's a resort town and so close to the USA, Rosarito lacks consistent budget accommodation; rates vary both seasonally and between weekdays and weekends, making it difficult to categorize hotels and motels by price.

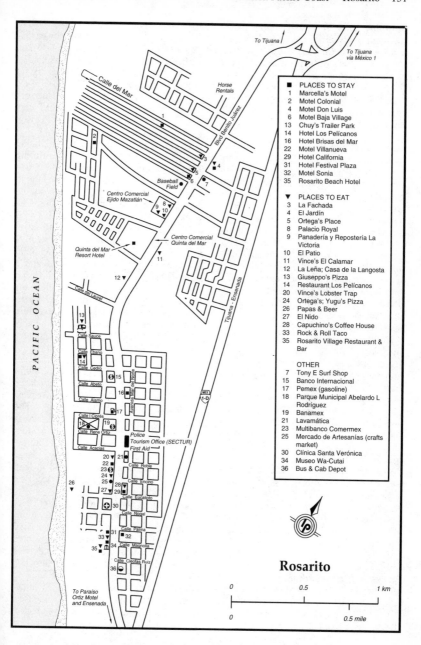

PLACES TO STAY
1   Marcella's Motel
2   Motel Colonial
4   Motel Don Luis
6   Motel Baja Village
13 Chuy's Trailer Park
14 Hotel Los Pelícanos
16 Hotel Brisas del Mar
22 Motel Villanueva
29 Hotel California
31 Hotel Festival Plaza
32 Motel Sonia
35 Rosarito Beach Hotel

PLACES TO EAT
3   La Fachada
4   El Jardín
5   Ortega's Place
8   Palacio Royal
9   Panadería y Repostería La Victoria
10 El Patio
11 Vince's El Calamar
12 La Leña; Casa de la Langosta
13 Giuseppo's Pizza
14 Restaurant Los Pelícanos
20 Vince's Lobster Trap
24 Ortega's; Yugu's Pizza
26 Papas & Beer
27 El Nido
28 Capuchino's Coffee House
33 Rock & Roll Taco
35 Rosarito Village Restaurant & Bar

OTHER
7   Tony E Surf Shop
15 Banco Internacional
17 Pemex (gasoline)
18 Parque Municipal Abelardo L Rodríguez
19 Banamex
21 Lavamática
23 Multibanco Comermex
25 Mercado de Artesanías (crafts market)
30 Clínica Santa Verónica
34 Museo Wa-Cutai
36 Bus & Cab Depot

Rosarito

0   0.5   1 km

0   0.5 mile

Camping Most cheaper camping places are south of Rosarito; the only alternative in town itself is *Chuy's Trailer Park* (☎ 2-16-08), at the west end of Calle Sauce behind Giuseppo's Pizza, which charges US$30 per night with full hookups, but only US$20 for self-contained campers. This is no bargain, but it has good beach access.

Hotels & Motels Two very basic, inexpensive, phoneless motels are worth a try for the financially challenged: *Motel Villanueva*, on the west side of Avenida Juárez at Calle Roble, and *Motel Sonia*, on the east side of Juárez at Calle Palma. Both cost around US$20 single or double.

Among Rosarito's budget favorites is the 24-room *Marcella's Motel* (☎ 2-04-68) at Calle del Mar 75, a dirt road half a mile west of Blvd Juárez and a few blocks north of the baseball field. Clean, carpeted rooms with wood panelling and large beds cost US$20 weekdays, US$35 weekends. *Motel Don Luis* (☎ 2-11-66), Blvd Juárez 272-A, has singles/doubles for US$25.

Motel Colonial (☎ 2-15-75), about half a mile west of Blvd Juárez at the end of the first dirt road south of the baseball field, is an aging, pseudo-colonial building whose lobby fixtures give it some character – lots of wrought iron, pastel paintings and a giant antique jukebox. Most rooms are suites with separate living/dining areas, full kitchens, a double bed and enough space for cots and sleeping bags. Prices start around US$28.

The sparkling new *Hotel California* (☎ 2-25-50), at Blvd Juárez 32, has found a niche among college students during spring break, when its American owner more or less gives them the run of the place; the rest of the year it's more sedate. Single/double rates are US$26/34.

Places to Stay – middle
Motel Baja Village (☎ 2-00-50), on the corner of Calle Vía de las Olas and Blvd Juárez, has singles/doubles from US$31 to US$49. Its US contact address is PO Box 309, San Ysidro, California 92143. One of Rosarito's better values is the newer, 39-room *Hotel Los Pelícanos* (☎ 2-04-45), on the beach at the end of Calle Ebano, adjacent to Restaurant Los Pelícanos. Basic singles or doubles cost US$35 to US$45, plus US$7.50 for each additional person. Rooms with ocean-view balconies cost US$55. The US contact address is PO Box 433871, San Diego, California 92143.

The *Paraíso Ortiz Motel* (☎ 2-10-20; PO Box 435349, San Ysidro, California 92143), ½ mile (1 km) south of the Rosarito Beach Hotel, has rooms resembling small cabins for US$25 single/double during the week, but rates rise to US$35 on weekends and US$45 in summer. It's a bit quieter than accommodations in Rosarito proper. The very new, high-rise *Hotel Festival Plaza* (☎ 2-29-50, ☎ (800) 453-8606 toll free in the USA), on Avenida Juárez a short distance north of the Rosarito Beach Hotel, has studio singles/doubles for US$25, regular doubles for US$39 weekdays and US$49 weekends, plus more expensive suites and villas. Rates are likely to rise as this Best Western place becomes more established.

The rambling, motel-style *Hotel Baja del Sol* (☎ 2-13-50; PO Box 548, San Ysidro, California 92073), at Km 26.8, south of the Paraíso Ortiz, has singles/doubles/triples/quadruples for US$35/40/50/60. The *Quinta Chica Motel* (☎ 2-13-00), across from the Baja del Sol, is a modern, stuccoed place popular with mainland Californians, especially on weekends; large double rooms cost around US$38 in high season, but it's a bargain for US$20 on winter weekdays.

The *Quinta del Mar Resort Hotel* (☎ 2-13-01, ☎ (619) 428-5500 for reservations in the USA), a tourist complex on Blvd Juárez in the center of town, contains three restaurants and bars and a commercial center. Motel rooms, all with showers, color TV and telephone, cost US$39 to US$47, but there are also one- to three-bedroom condominiums and townhouses, some with fireplaces and beachfront barbecues, from US$89 to US$161. The costliest option is a beachfront townhouse for four to six people.

South of town, *Castillos del Mar* (☎ 2-10-88) offers moderately priced rooms and suites fronting a tranquil, sandy beach. Double rooms/suites, some with fireplaces and wet bars, cost from US$50 to US$69. For reservations or more information, write PO Box 93, San Ysidro, California 92143.

Hotel Brisas del Mar (☎ 2-25-47), Blvd Juárez 22 between Calles Alamo and Abeto, has off-season doubles from US$43, but rooms with ocean views start at US$53, plus US$10 for each additional person. Summer and weekend rates are US$10 more per room. Special rooms with whirlpools are available at premium prices. Its US mailing address is PO Box 1867, Chula Vista, California 91912 (☎ (619) 685-1246 or toll free (800) 697-5223).

Places to Stay – top end

Facing the ocean, at the south end of Blvd Juárez, the *Rosarito Beach Resort Hotel* (☎ 2-11-06) opened in the late 1920s during the Prohibition era in the USA, and quickly became a popular watering hole and gambling haven for Hollywood stars like Orson Welles and Mickey Rooney. Larry Hagman of *Dallas* fame, Vincent Price, and Mexican presidents Miguel Alemán, Adolfo López Mateos and Adolfo Ruiz Cortines have also been guests.

The best rooms are suites in the new building closest to the beach. Despite its popularity and prestige, room rates remain surprisingly modest – US$59 for doubles on weekends, with occasional special rates of US$39 for doubles during the week, plus 10% tax. Prices include access to all facilities: restaurant, swimming pool, racquetball courts and gymnasium. In the USA, call (☎ (619) 498-8230 or toll free (800) 343-8582) between 7:30 am and 7:30 pm, or write to PO Box 430145, San Ysidro, California 92143 for more information.

La Paloma Beach & Tennis Club (☎ 2-00-74, 2-13-16), at Km 26 on the toll free road south of Rosarito, is an extravagantly landscaped complex of pseudo-Spanish villas, swimming pools, tennis courts, a gymnasium and small library. Most of the villas are individually owned, but several are available for daily and weekly use, starting from US$69 for a three-person studio to US$225 for a fully furnished two-bedroom condo.

At Km 37 on the toll free road is *Hotel Las Rocas* (☎ 2-21-40), whose balconied suites and rooms overlook the ocean; all have fireplaces, kitchenettes and satellite TV. Double-room rates range from US$70 to US$230 Friday and Saturday nights and from US$49 to US$154 the rest of the week (plus 10% tax). For more information and reservations, contact Pipeline Reservations (☎ (619) 428-5500), 223 Via de San Ysidro, San Ysidro, California 92173.

Places to Eat

At Blvd Juárez 2884, at the north end of town, upscale *La Fachada* gets rave reviews from almost everyone for specialties like steak and lobster. *Ortega's Place*, just south of La Fachada, serves great lobster dinners; its weekly Sunday champagne brunch is also a big attraction for US$9. Another *Ortega's* is on Blvd Juárez at Calle Roble; next door is *Yugu's Pizza*. *El Jardín*, alongside Motel Don Luis, serves Chilean and Argentine food.

El Patio, more a coffee shop, is at the south corner of the Centro Comercial Ejido Mazatlán, about one block north of the Quinta del Mar Resort Hotel; its standard Mexican breakfast (eggs with ham or chorizo, tortillas and coffee) costs US$4 to US$5. Alongside El Patio, the *Panadería y Repostería La Victoria* sells sugar-laden Mexican pastries and cookies. Across the parking lot, *Palacio Royal* is a huge, conspicuous Chinese restaurant.

La Leña, just south of the Hotel Quinta del Mar, specializes in beef; at the same location is *Casa de la Langosta*, a seafood restaurant which serves lobster. A short walk from the beach is *Giuseppo's Pizza*, a pleasant Italian place on Calle Sauce, specializing in shrimp pizza and pasta entrees at moderate prices.

Near the beach on Calle Ebano, *Los Pelícanos Restaurant & Bar*, just south of

Giuseppo's, serves a variety of excellent seafood and steak specials at some higher prices; also try their quail in garlic sauce. *El Nido* (part of a popular Baja chain) and *La Misión*, both on Blvd Juárez, belong to the same owner and have similar menus.

Vince's Lobster Trap, Blvd Juárez 39, has been highly recommended for lobster dinners; the same owner runs *Vince's El Calamar* in the northern part of town, opposite the Centro Comercial Quinta del Mar. On the beach, a few blocks southwest of the Lobster Trap, *Papas & Beer* is one of a chain of brightly decorated watering holes better known for partying than dining – there's a US$1 cover charge, and a hefty bouncer keeps rowdies, minors (under 18) and other undesirables from entering this outdoor bar and its sandlot volleyball court. A similar crowd hangs out at *Rock & Roll Taco*, on Blvd Juárez just north of Rosarito Beach Hotel.

Rosarito Village Restaurant & Bar, part of the Rosarito Beach Hotel, is known for massive margaritas and weekend mariachis. The weekend brunch is excellent value for US$9. For espresso drinks and pastries, a good choice is *Capuchino's Coffee House* on Blvd Juárez, between Encino and Eucalipto.

Entertainment

Every Friday night the Rosarito Beach Resort Hotel presents performances by mariachis, singers and gaudy charros (who do rope tricks). Performances happen constantly from 7 pm to 2 am, but the main show starts at 9 pm.

Things to Buy

At Blvd Juárez 306, near the intersection with Calle Encino, is the Mercado de Artesanías, a handicraft market with 200 shops and stalls, where you can haggle for serapes, wind chimes, hats, T-shirts, dresses, Batman piñatas, ceramic Buddhas and clay pots. It's open from 9 am to 6 pm daily.

Getting There & Away

Rosarito's bus depot is across from the Rosarito Beach Hotel. Buses leave for Tijuana (US$1) every 20 minutes from 6 am to 9 pm and for Ensenada (US$5) at least six times daily between 5:30 am and 6:30 pm. Route taxis, slightly more expensive but faster than buses, also connect Rosarito with Tijuana.

AROUND ROSARITO

Popotla

About 5 miles (8 km) south of Rosarito on México 1, *Popotla Trailer Park* (☎ 2-15-02) caters mostly to long-term campers, but about 30 spaces are available to short-termers for US$14 a night. The park has an ocean-view restaurant, a clubhouse, showers, toilets and easy beach access.

South of Popotla, at Km 37.6, *Surfpoint Camping* welcomes surfers for US$5 per person. Showers are only tepid, but the toilets are very clean. At Km 55, *Park 'n' Surf* has barebones camping on a barren coastline, with rustic toilets – bring all supplies, including water.

Puerto Nuevo

If tectonic uplift were not raising this section of the coastline from the sea, the village of Puerto Nuevo, about 13 miles (21 km) south of Rosarito, might sink beneath the sea under the weight of its 30 or so seafood restaurants. All of them specialize in lobster, usually cooked in one of two ways: *ranchera* (simmered in salsa) or *frito* (buttered and grilled or fried). All have similar prices, about US$15 for a full lobster dinner and US$10 for a grilled fish dinner. Garlic shrimp is also popular.

Ortega's is one of the largest and best known in Puerto Nuevo – look for the shiny, modern building that towers over every other in town. Señor Ortega owns five restaurants in Puerto Nuevo and two others in Rosarito. Don't judge these restaurants by their decor; the *Miramar*, for example, looks very ordinary but its food, particularly lobster, is exceptional.

The *New Port Baja Hotel* (☎ 4-11-88), at Km 45 on México 1 just south of Puerto Nuevo, has single/double rooms for US$55 except on weekends, when rates climb to

US$65. Make reservations in the USA by writing PO Box 2776, Chula Vista, California 92012, or phoning ☎ (800) 582-1018 toll free. Rates at the *Grand Baja Resort* (☎ 4-214-84), at the next lot south, start at US$36.

Misión del Descanso
(San Miguel Nuevo)
Just south of Puerto Nuevo is **Cantamar**, in the Valle de los Médanos (Valley of the Dunes), where ATV assaults have nearly destroyed the fragile dune ecology. About 1.6 miles (3 km) south of Cantamar, a gravel road off México 1 passes east, beneath the toll road, to the site of the Dominican **Misión del Descanso**, one of the last missions founded in California; to find the road, look for the greenhouses at Vivero La Central on the north side of the Río Descanso.

When Misión San Miguel, about 5 miles (8 km) south, lost its irrigable lands to floods, Fray Tomás de Ahumada moved part of its operations north to this site around 1817. The two missions operated simultaneously for some time, but Descanso was also known as San Miguel Nuevo. As of Peveril Meigs' visit in 1927, adobe ruins still existed. On the south side of the valley, on a 150-foot (45-meter) slope, was an apparent guardhouse.

The present church, dating from the turn of the century, occupies the site of the mission, which is commemorated by a large marker. Fridays a priest opens the church and may have more detailed information. An abandoned adobe house, on a knoll to the east, was part of the Machado grant which later assumed control of the mission lands.

The original boundary between the Dominican and Franciscan mission provinces, and thus between Baja and Alta California before the Treaty of Guadalupe Hidalgo, was just north of here, but was later moved north to the vicinity of Rosarito.

Places to Stay & Eat
The *Halfway House*, a small but popular restaurant about 3 miles (5 km) south of Puerto Nuevo, serves typical antojitos, a steak-and-eggs special, hamburgers and hot dogs. It's well known among mainland Californians who surf the reef breaks at nearby Punta Mesquite.

Overlooking the ocean, a small but pleasant garden on the north side of the house is a great viewpoint for afternoon photographs. Free camping is possible on a beautiful beach at Km 71 on México 1-D, the toll road.

The *Baja Ensenada RV Resort* has 136 landscaped spaces with full hookups on an attractive stretch of beach 17 miles (29 km) north of Ensenada. There is a restaurant, a swimming pool, tennis courts, a laundry, a small grocery and a clubhouse with a big-screen TV. Rates range from US$22 to US$28 per night. For more information, phone ☎ (800) 982-2252 (toll free in southern California only) or write to Outdoor Resorts, Suite 214, 1105 Broadway, Chula Vista, California 92011.

La Misión
The seaside village of La Misión is most notable as the site of the Dominican **Misión San Miguel de la Frontera**, also known as San Miguel Encino and San Miguel Arcángel. Founded in 1787 at a site unknown today, it depended on a spring; when the spring dried up, the mission moved up the valley of the Río San Miguel. This valley dissects a broad fault surface known locally as a mesa, which is surrounded by higher lava flows.

Fishing from balsa rafts, local Indians relied mostly on seafood for their subsistence, but the mission also grew wheat, maize, barley and beans, and grazed over 1600 cattle and 2100 sheep at its peak. The maximum Indian population, about 400, occurred in 1824 – a fairly large number at this late date. In the late 19th century, Russian immigrants moved into the area.

The few remaining ruins, protected under a tiled roof behind the Escuela Primaria La Misión (the elementary school) at Km 65.5, about 1 mile (1.6 km) south of the bridge over the Río San Miguel, include the foundations and some adobe walls of the church and adjacent buildings.

Places to Stay & Eat

La Fonda, an oceanfront resort motel and restaurant 19 miles (32 km) south of Rosarito, also resembles a mission with its tiled roof, banana trees and flower-lined paths. The restaurant's specialties include prime rib, lobster, shrimp and scallops. It has live music several nights weekly; Wednesday is blues night.

Detached from the bar and restaurant, the motel is very quiet. Rates average about US$40 per night for a room and US$60 for an apartment (which sleeps four). Make reservations at least two weeks in advance by sending a deposit for one or more nights to PO Box 430268, San Ysidro, California 92143.

Hotel La Misión (☎ (310) 420-8500 in mainland California), overlooking a broad sandy beach at Km 59 on the Carretera Libre, has bargain doubles for US$29 weekdays, US$45 weekends, plus 10% tax. Suites with jacuzzis cost US$56 weekdays, US$75 weekends, plus tax. It also has a restaurant/bar with very cheap dinner specials (as low as US$2 for spaghetti and salad on Thursdays), plus live music on weekends. Its US contact address is PO Box 439060, San Ysidro, California 92143.

El Mirador

El Mirador, a roadside viewpoint about 17 miles (29 km) north of Ensenada and about 11 miles (18 km) south of La Fonda, is spectacularly sited above the ocean. A few small stands sell soft drinks and occasionally coconuts.

Bajamar

On a headland just north of Punta Salsipuedes and about 7½ miles (12 km) south of La Fonda, *Bajamar* is a Mediterranean-style resort complex with an 18-hole golf course, three swimming pools, tennis courts, a clubhouse and bicycle rentals. There are 100 privately owned villas, 20 of which are available for daily or weekly rental, with one to four bedrooms, wood-burning fireplaces, fully equipped kitchens, partial or full views of the ocean or golf course, and daily maid service.

Daily rates range from US$50 for a guest room without kitchen to US$250 for a four-bedroom villa, plus 10% tax. Weekly rates are also available. In the USA, phone the Tijuana Baja Information Center (☎ (619) 299-8518, (800) 522-1516 toll free) or write to Suite 202, 7860 Mission Center Court, San Diego, California 92108 for information and reservations.

San Miguel Village

San Miguel is a small beach community about 5 miles (8 km) north of Ensenada that consists mostly of US retirees in mobile homes, but also offers surfers a good right break. Down by the beach, where full hookups, showers and rustic toilets are available, you can camp for US$5 per night. There's a small seafood restaurant at the entrance to the mobile-home park.

El Sauzal

The seafood cannery at sedate El Sauzal, about 2 miles (3 km) north of Ensenada, gives off a powerful fishy odor, but several trailer parks and campgrounds charge about US$4 to US$10 a night, though it's becoming difficult to find a trailer park that does not cater mostly to long-term RVers. Try camping for free on any unclaimed stretch of beach, but these are not easy to find; for hotels, check the Places to Stay entry for Ensenada.

ENSENADA

In the daytime, hundreds of aging Americans stroll the tranquil streets of the erstwhile capital of Baja California territory with shopping lists of prescription pharmaceuticals, but the state's third-largest city (official population 170,000, probable population closer to 250,000) is also its biggest party town, whose main attractions are food, drink and fiestas (Ensenada hosts many special events every year). Outdoor activities like fishing and surfing are also popular, and it's the locus of Baja's advancing wine industry.

Because of the large number of US visitors from mainland California, Ensenada is also a reluctant host for spontaneous Fourth of July celebrations, a fact which many local residents resent. At this time of year in particular, visitors from north of the border should take special care to refrain from offensive behavior. Many fireworks which are now illegal in mainland California are obtainable in Mexico, but this does not imply permission to use them indiscriminately.

History

Sited on the harbor of Bahía de Todos Santos, Ensenada has sheltered explorers, freighters and fishing boats for over four centuries. Juan Rodríguez Cabrillo, searching for the Strait of Anián (the mythical Northwest Passage) with his caravels *San Salvador* and *Victoria*, entered the bay to replenish his water supply in September 1542, encountering a small group of Indian hunter-gatherers.

In 1602 Sebastián Vizcaíno named Ensenada de Todos los Santos after All Saints Day, 1 November. During colonial times, the harbor was an occasional refuge for Spanish *naos* (galleons) returning to Acapulco from Manila. Naos usually passed the area once or twice yearly, loaded with Oriental treasures such as silks, spices, Japanese artwork and jewels; the last one sailed through in 1815.

Far northern Baja was the last part of the peninsula to be missionized; Dominican Padre Juan Crespí passed through Ensenada on his Expedición Sagrada (Sacred Expedition) of 1769, but a shortage of irrigation water prevented the establishment of any mission on the site. The nearest missions were San Miguel de la Frontera (founded 1787) 30 miles (50 km) north, Guadalupe (founded 1834) 25 miles (40 km) northwest and Santo Tomás (founded 1791), about 30 miles (50 km) south.

Ensenada's first permanent settlement was established in 1804, when the Viceroy of New Spain granted the surrounding area to José Manuel Ruiz, whose Rancho Ensenada became a prosperous cattle ranch. It was purchased in 1824 by Francisco Gastelum, whose family consolidated farming and ranching interests in the area.

In 1870, discovery of gold at Real del Castillo, 22 miles (35 km) inland, transformed a sleepy backwater. Todos Santos was the closest harbor, the ranchos the closest food suppliers, and Ensenada boomed with an influx of miners, merchants and hangers-on. After this initial prosperity attracted investors, the Mexican government designated Ensenada the capital of Baja territory from 1882 to 1915.

In the 1880s the US-owned International Company of Mexico attempted to attract agricultural colonists to the region, but failed to live up to its contract (fraud was apparent) and sold out to a British concern, the Mexican Land & Colonization Company. Around this time, Ensenada had five general stores, three hotels, two dress shops, two hardware stores, a mattress factory, a tannery, a fruit cannery, a brewery and several miscellaneous industries (as well as Hussong's renowned cantina, which opened in 1892), but closure of the mines and failure of agricultural colonization ended the boom.

Ensenada briefly revived in the spring of 1911 when a splinter group of anarchist Magonistas occupied the mining hamlet of El Alamo, 40 miles (65 km) southeast. Their presence so alarmed George Schmucker, the hysterical US consul in

Ensenada, that he cabled the US State Department with exaggerations of the rebels' importance and sophistication, linking them to an international conspiracy and calling for warships to protect US citizens. State Department officials ignored most of his communications, and Schmucker, who fantasized a Biblical Armageddon in Baja California, suffered a nervous breakdown.

Ensenada lost its political primacy during the Revolution, when Colonel Estéban Cantú, concerned over the anarchist Magonistas and an increasing US influence in the border region, shifted the territorial capital to Mexicali. After the Revolution Ensenada, like Tijuana, began to cater to the 'sin' industries of drinking, gambling and sex during US Prohibition. The Playa Ensenada Hotel & Casino opened in the early 1930s but closed when Mexico's federal government outlawed gambling in the late 1930s. Renamed the Riviera del Pacífico, the Spanish-style hotel tried to function as a resort for another decade; today it's a cultural center which also offers facilities for wedding receptions and similar social occasions.

As more visitors came to Ensenada, entrepreneurs built more hotels and restaurants and the town became a major tourist resort and weekend retreat for more than four million visitors annually – mostly southern mainland Californians.

Orientation

Ensenada, 68 miles (110 km) south of Tijuana and 119 miles (192 km) north of San Quintín, is a major fishing and commercial port on the sheltered Bahía de Todos Santos. Many of the city's best hotels and restaurants line the waterfront Blvd Costero, also known as Blvd Lázaro Cárdenas. Blvd Costero is also the site of the Plaza Cívica, known colloquially as the 'Plaza de Las Tres Cabezas' (Three Heads Plaza) for its massive busts of Mexican heroes Benito Juárez, Miguel Hidalgo, and Venustiano Carranza. Avenida López Mateos (also known as Calle 1a) parallels

Blvd Costero for a short distance, one block inland (north).

A few blocks further inland is the business center, along Avenida Benito Juárez and side streets, an area that includes Ensenada's 'party district' – Avenida Gastelum and Avenida Ruiz (the Ruiz and Gastelum families founded Ensenada). Several bars and cantinas, such as the legendary Hussong's, are located here.

At the north end of town, Colinas de Chapultepec (Chapultepec Hills) is an exclusive residential zone that usurped the name of an even more exclusive residential zone in Mexico City. Just north of the city, México 3 heads east and then north through the Valle de Guadalupe to the pleasant border town of Tecate. At the south end of town, Calzada Cortez leads east toward Ojos Negros and Laguna Hanson (Parque Nacional de Constitución de 1857), and south to the Valle de Trinidad before descending the eastern scarp of the Sierra de Juárez and connecting with México 5, the north-south route between Mexicali and San Felipe.

Information

Tourist Office Ensenada's municipal Comité de Turismo y Convenciones (COTUCO, ☎ 8-24-11, fax 8-36-75), is at Blvd Costero 540 and Avenida Gastelum across from the Pemex station. The staff are particularly helpful, offering a wide selection of maps, brochures and current hotel information (such as rates and ratings). Open hours are 9 am to 7 pm Monday to Saturday, 9 am to 2 pm Sunday.

The Secretaría de Turismo del Estado (SECTUR, ☎ 2-30-22 or ☎ 2-30-00, X3081-4) has moved to Blvd Costero 1477, at the corner of Calle Las Rocas, just south of the Riviera de Pacífico. Though less well provided with printed matter than the municipal office, the staff are friendly, obliging and well informed. It's open from 9 am to 7 pm weekdays, 10 am to 3 pm Saturday and 10 am to 2 pm Sunday.

Another source of information is the local Cámara de Comercio (CANACO, ☎ 8-37-70) at Avenida López Mateos near

Avenida Macheros. Open hours are weekdays, 8:30 am to 2 pm and 4 to 6:30 pm.

The local English-language monthly *Baja Sun* (☎ 8-73-33), Calle Obregón 1099, is composed primarily of promotional literature, but it's still a good source of information about the Tijuana-Ensenada coastline. Free copies are available at tourist offices and tourist-oriented businesses throughout the peninsula. Another freebie is *Ensenada Happenings*.

Businesses interested in local investment might consult *Enlace*, a publication of the Centro Empresarial de Ensenada (☎ 6-19-77, fax 6-00-60), Obregón 206 at the corner of Calle 2a.

Money Most banks and cambios are on Avenida Ruiz and Avenida Juárez; the cambios are more useful for changing money, but banks can provide cash advances on credit cards. Servicio La Comercial, on Uribe just north of Gastelum, cashes travelers' checks charging a 1.5% commission. Cambio Yesan, Ruiz 201, charges 2%.

If you need to conduct other bank-related business, try Bancomer at Ruiz 500 or Banamex at Calle 3a 279. The latter has an ATM machine.

Post & Telecommunications Ensenada's main post office, at the corner of Avenida López Mateos and Avenida Riviera, is open weekdays 8 am to 7 pm, weekends 9 am to 1 pm.

Public telephones are now widespread in Ensenada, and it is no longer essential to visit a central telephone office; however, the Computel Ensenada office at the bus terminal conveniently allows payment by Visa or MasterCard. Rates are about US$0.40 to Tijuana, Tecate and other nearby Baja locations; US$1.20 per minute to the USA; and US$6 per minute to Western Europe. Ensenada's area code is 617.

Immigration At Avenida Tte Azueta 100, around the corner from the municipal tourist office, Servicios Migratorios (☎ 4-

10-64) is open daily, 8 am to 8 pm. Travelers and motorists who have failed to obtain or validate their tourist cards or vehicle permits may do so here.

Travel Agencies Inter Voyage (☎ 6-00-00), at Avenida Floresta and Calle 3a, opposite the telegraph office, arranges plane, train and bus tickets, hotels, car rentals and tours.

Viajes Guaycura (☎ 8-16-41, 8-10-45) is at Alvarado 95, Suite 4. Besides weekend excursions from San Diego (see the Getting There & Away chapter), it arranges area tours that include the Santo Tomás winery and La Bufadora (US$18, four hours), horseback riding on the beach (US$25, 3½ hours), a cultural tour of the city (US$25, four hours), sport fishing trips (US$35, six hours) and golf at the Baja Country Club (US$45).

Bookshops Librería España (☎ 4-09-66), Avenida Ruiz 217, has a good selection of books on the Baja peninsula in both English and Spanish. An anonymous real estate office on the west side of Avenida Ruiz, just south of López Mateos, also sells Baja books and souvenirs.

Medical Services Ensenada's Hospital General (☎ 6-76-00) is at Km 111 of the Transpeninsular, south of the city. Hospital Las Américas (☎ 6-03-01) is at Avenida Las Dunas 130.

Like other large cities, Ensenada also has numerous private doctors and dentists.

Emergency The Procuraduría de Protección al Turista (☎ 2-30-22), now in the same office as SECTUR (see Tourist Offices, above), helps tourists with legal problems.

Other emergency numbers are the Bomberos (Fire Department, ☎ 136), Cruz Roja (Red Cross, ☎ 132), and the Policía (Police, ☎ 134).

Laundry Lavamática Blanca is in the mall at the corner of Avenida Reforma and Calzada Cortez.

El Mirador

Atop the Colinas de Chapultepec, El Mirador offers spectacular panoramic views of the city and Bahía de Todos Santos. Climb or drive up Avenida Alemán from the western end of Calle 2a in central Ensenada to the highest point in town.

Bodegas de Santo Tomás

Santo Tomás (☎ 8-33-33, 8-25-09), at Avenida Miramar 666, is one of Baja's premier wineries, founded in 1888 near the vineyards of the Valle de Santo Tomás, 27½ miles (44 km) south. After purchasing the winery in 1937, former Mexican president Abelardo Rodríguez moved it to Ensenada to facilitate shipping; today, it is owned and operated by the Corporación Elías Pando, a Mexico-based multinational.

Trucks haul the grapes from Santo Tomás to a building across the street from the winery, where they are crushed and the juice is piped into stainless steel fermentation vats for about 25 days. It is then pumped into huge, wooden vats, where the juice (not quite wine at this point) stays for varying periods, depending on the type of wine.

Varieties produced here include Pinot Noir, Chardonnay and Cabernet. Up to 120,000 cases are shipped annually throughout Mexico and to Western Europe; Santo Tomás wines are not exported to the USA. Daily tours, which include wine tastings, take place at 11 am, and 1 and 3 pm. Admission costs US$2.

Cavas Valmar

This smaller but still respectable winery (☎ 8-64-05, 4-24-69), at Calle 19 (also known as Calle Ambar) No 810 at the north end of Avenida Miramar, offers free tours and tasting by appointment.

Centro Social, Cívico y Cultural de Ensenada (Riviera del Pacífico)

In an extravagant but still distinguished Spanish-style building on the waterfront, the Riviera del Pacífico first opened in the early 1930s as the Hotel Playa Ensenada and gambling casino. In a bid to attract wealthy American gamblers, the management hired the famous US boxer Jack Dempsey as manager, but the hotel and casino closed in 1938 when President Lázaro Cárdenas outlawed casino gambling.

Open to the public and well worth exploring, the building now offers various cultural events, such as retrospective film series, and hosts weddings, conventions, meetings and art exhibitions. The lobby features an impressive three-dimensional mural of the Californias, emphasizing the mission sites of both Baja and Alta California. A museum at the north end of the building was under renovation at the time of writing.

With its long wooden bar, a rather goofy mural, magnificent tilework and outstanding historical photos, the *Bar Andaluz* is a great place for a quiet drink. Contrast its subdued elegance with the gaudiness of Las Vegas to comprehend the decline of the casino as an institution since the days of Prohibition.

Museo (ex-Aduana Marítima de Ensenada)

Ensenada's new historical and cultural museum, operated by the Instituto Nacional de Historia y Antropología (INAH), is Ensenada's oldest public building. Built in 1886 by the US-owned International Company of Mexico, it passed into the hands of the British-owned Mexican Land & Colonization Company before coming under control of Mexican customs in 1922.

At Avenida Ryerson 1, corner of Virgilio Uribe, it offers traveling exhibitions and is open daily, except Monday, 10 am to 5 pm. Admission is free.

Museo de Ciencias

The Museo de Ciencias de Ensenada (☎ 8-71-92), Avenida Obregón 1463, contains exhibits on both the natural and physical sciences, and also organizes whale-watching cruises in the winter months. It's open 9 am to 5 pm Tuesday to Friday, noon to 5 pm weekends. Admission costs US$1.

Mercado Los Globos

Antique collectors may want to explore Ensenada's largest outdoor market at Los Globos, an area of eight square blocks on Calle 9a, east of Avenida Reforma, where vendors sell everything from old radios and typewriters to fruit and vegetables. It's open daily, but there are many more vendors on weekends.

Activities

Diving Buceo Almar (☎ 8-30-13), Avenida Macheros 149, is the local dive shop, but there's another at Punta Banda, the most popular diving area in the Ensenada area (see the 'Around Ensenada' section).

Para-Sailing Baja Para-Sail (☎ 8-18-79), at Blvd Costero 609-14 across from the tourist office, offers half-hour parachute rides 300 feet above the bay for US$30; sailing 500 feet above the bay costs US$40. The company also organizes mountain bike rides, with all gear provided, in the Ensenada area.

Fishing Many shops on Avenida López Mateos offer fishing trips, and there are also charter-boat offices next to the port and fish market. You can join an organized group for about US$35 a person per day or charter an entire boat (charter rates and vessels vary dramatically, so shop around).

One alternative is the Ensenada Clipper Fleet (☎ 8-21-85), which also has north of the border offices at 2530 E Beyer Blvd, San Ysidro, California 92143. It will also arrange multi-day charters, but these are very expensive.

Among the popular species in the area are albacore, barracuda, bonito, halibut, white sea bass and yellowtail, depending on the season. For more specific information, consult Tom Miller's *Angler's Guide to Baja California* (Baja Trail Publications, PO Box 6088, Huntington Beach, California 92646) or Neil Kelly & Gene Kira's *The Baja Catch* (Apples & Oranges, PO Box 2296-J, Valley Center, California 92082).

Whale-Watching

Whale-Watching Between December and March, the Museo de Ciencias de Ensenada (☎ 8-71-92), Obregón 1463, arranges short whale-watching cruises between Ensenada and the offshore Islas de Todos Santos.

Language Courses

The Colegio de Idiomas de Ensenada (☎ 6-01-09, 6-65-87), Blvd J A Rodríguez 377, offers intensive Spanish instruction, as does the highly regarded Center of Languages & Latin American Studies (☎ 7-18-40), Riveroll 1287. For more details and their US contacts, see the Activities section in the Facts for the Visitor chapter.

Festivals & Events

Over 70 sporting, tourist and cultural events take place in Ensenada each year; the ones listed below are only a sample. Dates are subject to change, so contact the tourist office or event organizers for specific details.

February
> *Carnaval* – Mardi Gras (third week)
> *Circuito Off-Road La Lágrima 250* – off-road race (4th week)

March
> *Tijuana-Rosarito-Ensenada Paseo Ciclista* – bicycle ride (late March)

April
> *Muestra Gastronómica* – CANIRAC Food Fair (mid-April)
> *Paseo Ciclista Rosarito-Ensenada* – bike ride (mid-April)
> *Regata Newport Beach-Ensenada* – yacht race (late April)

May
> *Tecate Mexican Surfing Fiesta* (mid-May)
> *Paseo Ciclista Tecate-Ensenada & Relevos* – bike ride and relay race (third week)

June
> *Carrera Fuera de Carretera Baja 500* – SCORE-sponsored off-road race (early June)
> *Torneo de Volleyball Playero Estero Beach* – beach volleyball tournament (late June)

July
> *Regata Todos Santos* – yacht race (late July)

August
> *Fiesta de la Vendimia* – wine harvest (2nd or 3rd week)
> *Circuito Off-Road Ensenada 300* – off-road race (late August)

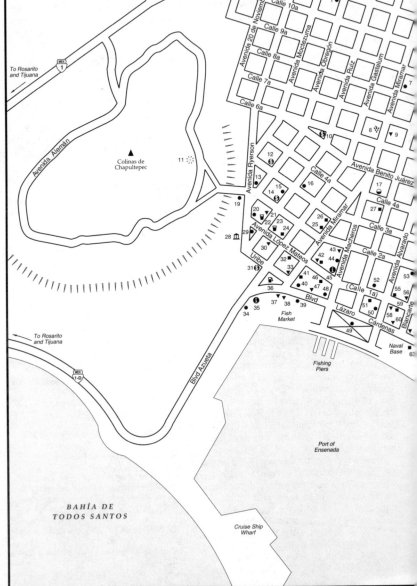

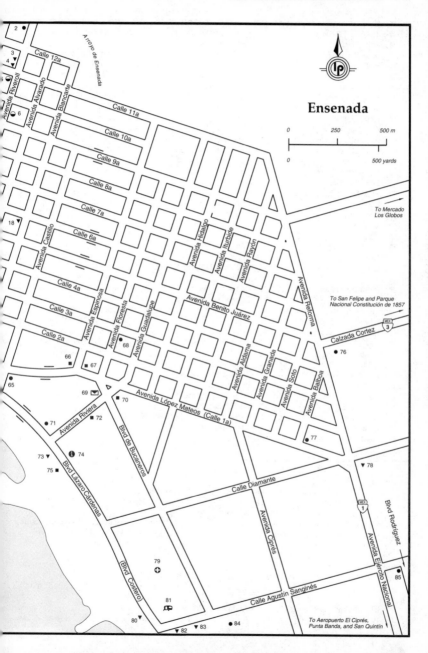

Ensenada

	PLACES TO STAY	60	Casamar/El Galeón	29	Real Estate Office (books,
■	PLACES TO STAY	62	La Baguette		souvenirs)
24	Hotel Royal	73	La Fábula Pizza	31	Servicio La Comercial
25	Hotel Perla del Pacífico	78	Muy Lam		(money exchange)
26	Hotel de Río	80	Cha Cha Burgers No 1	34	Servicios Migratorios
27	Hotel del Valle	82	La Casa del Abulón		(Immigration)
32	Hotel Plaza	83	Kiki's Las Cazuelas	35	COTUCO (tourist office)
41	Hotel Santo Tomás			36	Pemex station
42	Motel Caribe (annex)		OTHER	39	Bananas
46	Motel Caribe	1	Baja Sun	40	Baja Para-Sail
51	Hotel Bahía	2	Center of Languages &	44	Buceo Almar (diving)
54	Ensenada Travelodge		Latin American Studies	45	CANACO (tourist office)
55	Hotel El Cid	5	Central de Autobuses;	48	Plaza México
57	Hotel Casa del Sol		Computel Ensenada	49	Plaza Cívica (Plaza de las
59	Hotel Villa Fontana		(long-distance telephone)		Tres Cabezas)
61	Hotel Villa Marina	6	Autotransportes Aragón	50	Viajes Guaycura (travel
63	Hotel Misión Santa Isabel		(buses to Tijuana & San		agency); Ensenada Rent-
64	Hotel Cortez		Quintín)		A-Car; Scorpio Rent-A-Car
66	Motel Coronado	7	Aerotaxis Peninsulares	52	Artesanías Los Castillo
67	Motel América	8	Bodegas de Santo Tomás	53	Lienzo de Charros (rodeo
70	Hotel San Nicolás		(winery)		grounds)
72	Hotel La Pinta	10	Bancomer	65	Centro Artesanal de
75	Hotel Corona	11	El Mirador (vista point)		Ensenada
81	Campo Playa RV Park	12	Banamex	68	Inter Voyage (travel
		13	Centro Empresarial		agency)
▼	PLACES TO EAT	14	Cambio Yesan (money	69	Post Office
3	China Land		exchange)	71	Riviera del Pacífico
4	All-night Taquería	15	Librería España		(Cultural Center &
9	La Vieja Embotelladora	16	Aeroméxico		Museum)
18	Panificadora Bahía	17	Transportes Brisa (rural	74	SECTUR (tourist office)
21	Café El Portal		buses)	76	Lavamática Blanca
30	Las Brasas	19	Sociedad Cooperativa de	77	Cinemas Gemelos
33	Anthony's		Producción Pesquera	79	Hospital Las Américas
37	Plaza del Marisco		(fishing coop)	84	Plaza de Toros
38	La Palapa Bahía	20	Plaza Hussong mall	85	Colegio de Idiomas de
42	Corralito	22	Hussong's Cantina		Ensenada (language
43	El Pollo Real	23	Papas & Beer		school)
47	Cha Cha Burgers No 2	28	Museo (ex-Aduana		
56	El Rey Sol		Marítima)		
58	Mesón de Don Fernando				

September
  Paseo Ciclista Rancho Sordomudo – bike ride (mid-September)
  Exposición Canófila – international dog show (mid-September)
  Fiestas Patrias – Mexican independence days (mid-September)
  Paseo Ciclista Rosarito-Ensenada – bike ride (late September)
  Muestra Gastronómica – food fair (late September)
October
  Regata Southwestern Yacht Club – yacht race (early October)

Annual Juan Hussong International Chili Cook-off (mid-October)
  Exposición Fiesta Viva (mid-October)
November
  Baja 1000 – Unlike races before completion of the Transpeninsular, this is now only a 689-mile (1100-km) loop starting and finishing in Ensenada; in theory, it now keeps to established routes instead of tearing up virgin desert. In 1993, it started and ended in Mexicali, but local authorities hope it will return to the coast (mid-November).
December
  Desfile Navideño Club Amigos de

Ensenada – Annual Christmas Parade (mid-December)

Feria Internacional del Pescado
Usually held in late summer, the Feria is an annual international seafood fair organized by CANIRAC (Chamber of Restaurants, ☎ 4-04-48) and judged by the Chefs de Cuisine Association of San Diego. The purpose of the fair is to celebrate, stimulate and promote the art of preparing and presenting fine seafood dishes. Chefs compete to prepare the best dishes, and visitors can sample the results. Folkloric dancing and ice sculpture are also featured. For latest information, contact CANIRAC.

Places to Stay
Although Ensenada has many hotels, demand can exceed supply at times – on weekends and in summer, reservations are advisable. Unless there's a special event, finding accommodation during the week is not a problem, but as in Rosarito, rates vary both seasonally and between weekdays and weekends, making it difficult to categorize hotels by price.

Guaranteed reservations at several mid- to upper-range hotels and motels in Ensenada can be made through the Tijuana Baja Information Center (☎ (619) 222-9099, (800) 522-1516 toll free in the USA).

Places to Stay – bottom end
Camping *Campo Playa RV Park* (☎ 8-37-68) has over 100 small, grassy sites, mostly with full hookups, for pitching a tent or parking a camper or motorhome. It's at the south end of central Ensenada, at the corner of Calle Agustín Sanginés and Blvd Costero. A notable plus is hot showers. Fees are US$10 per night.

Many 'official' campgrounds and trailer parks north and south of Ensenada offer basic facilities like toilets, sinks, showers, water taps and electrical outlets – try those on Punta Banda and Playa Estero. Parks north of Ensenada increasingly cater to long-term RV campers. Rates range from US$5 to US$10 per night.

Hotels & Motels Several cheap hotels dot a seedy area of Avenida Miramar, just north of Avenida López Mateos, where rooms cost as little as US$8, but don't expect to get much sleep among the strip joints and rowdy bars. *Hotel de Río* (☎ 8-37-33), Miramar 231, may be the best of this bunch, but Avenida Macheros has similar accommodation. A conspicuous placard at *Hotel Perla del Pacífico* (☎ 8-30-51), Miramar 229, warns guests that it will tolerate 'no bad behavior, no alcohol' – which may be an idea of what to expect.

Probably the best bargain in central Ensenada is *Motel Caribe* (☎ 8-34-81), Avenida López Mateos 628, which has single/doubles with private bath as cheap as US$15/20 (these are across the street at López Mateos 627). *Hotel Royal* (☎ 8-27-21), Gastelum 127, is a very modest six-room place charging US$17/20 single/ double. *Hotel Plaza* (☎ 8-27-15), at Avenida López Mateos 540, has rather dark, spartan and gloomy rooms, but is generally clean for about US$17/20. Rooms away from the street are much quieter.

Motel América (☎ 6-13-33), at the corner of Avenida López Mateos and Avenida Espinosa, south of the dry bed of the Arroyo de Ensenada, has clean, simple singles/doubles with kitchenettes for US$20/30. The kitchenettes make this a good deal, but otherwise it's nothing special. For US$18/20 single/double, nearby *Motel Coronado* (☎ 6-14-16), an older place with firm beds at López Mateos 1275, resembles the América but lacks kitchenettes.

Places to Stay – middle
Both affiliated with the US-based Best Western chain, the *Hotel Casa del Sol* (☎ 8-15-70) at Avenida López Mateos 1001 (corner of Avenida Blancarte) and the *Hotel Cortez* (☎ 8-23-07) at Avenida López Mateos 1089 (corner of Avenida Castillo) offer similar amenities. A double room with air-conditioning, TV and access to a swimming pool costs US$23/32 at the Casa del Sol and US$41 at the Cortez; singles

are slightly cheaper. The more popular Cortez is often completely booked on summer weekends.

Hotel del Valle (☎ 8-22-24), at Riveroll 367 between Calle 3a and Calle 4a, is really a motel with 21 carpeted singles/doubles with cable TV for US$27/32. *Hotel Santo Tomás* (☎ 8-15-03), conveniently central at Blvd Costero 609 between Miramar and Macheros, has doubles from US$45 weekdays; rates rise by about 10% weekends.

The renovated and upgraded *Hotel Villa Fontana* (☎ 8-34-34), centrally located on Avenida López Mateos between Avenida Blancarte and Avenida Alvarado, has a bar, coffee shop, swimming pool with sun deck, jacuzzi and parking. Comfortable rooms with full carpeting, air-conditioning, color cable TV and balconies cost from US$45 to US$55 for a single/double. Weekend prices are 10% higher.

At López Mateos 993, across from the Villa Fontana, *Hotel El Cid* (☎ 8-24-01, fax 8-36-71) offers singles/doubles from US$41/57 weekdays, US$52/72 weekends, plus taxes; it has a swimming pool, a restaurant and a disco. The popular *Hotel Bahía* (☎ 8-21-03), around the corner from the Villa Fontana, covers a whole block on Avenida López Mateos and Blvd Costero, between Avenida Riveroll and Avenida Alvarado. Clean, carpeted single/doubles with balconies, heaters and small refrigerators cost US$32/45 during the week, rising to US$38/45 weekends.

East of Hotel Bahía, at the corner of Blvd Costero and Avenida Castillo, is the 52-room colonial-style *Hotel Misión Santa Isabel* (☎ 8-36-16, fax 8-33-45), with a restaurant, swimming pool and a convention room. Rooms with telephone, TV and spotless bathrooms cost US$50 single (with king-size bed) weekdays, while doubles (with two double beds) cost US$66, tax included, but some travelers have complained that the rooms are cramped. Weekend rates are about 20% higher; the mailing address is Apartado Postal 76, Ensenada, Baja California, México.

At Avenida Blancarte 130, near López Mateos, the 52-room *Ensenada Travelodge* (☎ 8-16-01) has a swimming pool, jacuzzi, restaurant and bar – upon arrival, every guest receives one hour of free margaritas. Comfortable rooms with air-conditioning, cable TV, shower baths and telephones cost US$36/45 single/double weekdays, US$45/55 weekends. In the USA, phone (800) 255-3050 for information and reservations.

Hotel La Pinta (☎ 6-26-01), at the corner of Blvd de Bucaneros and Avenida Riviera across from the post office, is one of a chain of hotels on the peninsula. Singles/doubles cost US$43/45 weekdays, US$55/65 weekends; facilities include a swimming pool and restaurant. For information and reservations, contact the Tijuana Baja Information Center in mainland California (see above).

Hussong's Quintas Papagayo Resort (☎ 4-41-55), about 1 mile (1.6 km) north of Ensenada on México 1, has large, airy rooms with balconies overlooking the ocean, macramé wall hangings, terracotta floors and hand-carved furniture. One- and two-bedroom apartments are also available. All guests have access to the resort's tennis courts and Hussong's Pelícano Restaurant & Oyster Bar (see the Places to Eat, below). Double rooms cost about US$40, suites US$55 to US$65, and two-bedroom cabañas US$85.

Places to Stay – top end

Ensenada's high-rise *Hotel Villa Marina* (☎ 8-33-21, 8-33-51), at the corner of Avenida López Mateos and Avenida Blancarte, offers a swimming pool, restaurant and great harbor views from many of its rooms. Singles/doubles start at US$45/55 weekdays, but climb to US$77/88 weekends.

At Blvd Costero 1442, facing the harbor and across from the Riviera del Pacífico, the tile-roofed *Hotel Corona* (☎ 6-09-01) has 100 rooms, all with balconies, color TV and air-conditioning at US$46 for singles/doubles, plus taxes; rates rise to US$65 on weekends, but there are occasional specials as cheap as US$29. For reservations and information, contact Pipeline Reservations (☎ (619) 428-5500, (800) 659-7457 toll free in the USA), 223 Via de San Ysidro, Suite 10, San Ysidro, California 92173.

Half a block from La Pinta, at the corner of Avenida Guadalupe and Avenida López Mateos, *Hotel San Nicolás* (☎ 6-19-01) caters mostly to groups and has a coffee shop, restaurant and swimming pool with a waterfall and Aztec-style decor. Singles/ doubles cost from US$61/65 weekdays to US$81/97 weekends.

One of the area's most spectacular hotels is the elegant *Hotel Las Rosas* (☎ 4-43-20) at Km 105, 4 miles (6.5 km) north of Ensenada on an oceanside bluff. All rooms have balconies, minibars, cable TV, cushy beds and telephones; there are also exercise rooms and a racquetball court. Singles/ doubles start at US$101/108.

Places to Eat
Ensenada's 200-plus restaurants (not including taco stands) serve everything from typical antojitos and seafood to Chinese and French cuisine. For more restaurant information, see current issues of the *Baja Sun* and *Baja Times*.

City Center At Ensenada's seafood market just south of Blvd Costero, try the famous deep-fried fish or shrimp tacos. *Plaza del Marisco*, on Blvd Costero across from the Pemex station, is a similar collection of seafood taco stands. For carnitas (pork) or carne asada (beef) tacos, the all-night stand at the corner of Avenida Riveroll and Calle 11a is very popular.

La Baguette, a French-style bakery with branches throughout Baja, is a good place to sample typical pan dulce (sweet pastry), a croissant or two-foot baguettes. It's across from the navy base and hospital, near the corner of Avenida Blancarte and Blvd Costero.

One of the largest and most popular bakeries is *Panificadora Bahía* on the corner of Calle 6a and Avenida Blancarte. Over three dozen types of pan dulce are baked here

daily, as well as *bolillos* (typical Mexican bread). The modest *Corralito*, alongside the annex of the Motel Caribe at López Mateos 627, is a good breakfast spot.

Café El Portal, up the block from Hussong's Cantina, is a quiet sidewalk café at Ruiz 153, luring caffeine junkies with satisfying cappuccinos, mochas and lattés at north-of-the-border prices. Their desserts are also appealing.

La Palapa Bahía, next door to the Plaza del Marisco on Blvd Costero, is a moderately priced seafood restaurant. On the north side of Blvd Costero, near Avenida Alvarado, *Casamar* (☎ 4-04-17) is a more expensive alternative specializing in items like lobster salad and Filet Manila (a broiled fish fillet smothered in mango sauce), a variety of shrimp dishes, fried frogs' legs and octopus. The upstairs bar, *El Galeón*, presents live entertainment.

Mesón de Don Fernando, on Avenida López Mateos at the corner of Alvarado, is a good place for breakfast – huevos rancheros with salsa, refried beans and bacon costs about US$5. For lunch and dinner, they serve lobster tacos and burritos and several other seafood dishes.

El Rey Sol (☎ 8-17-33), Avenida López Mateos 1000 at Avenida Blancarte, is an elegant, venerable French-Mexican restaurant that won highest honors at the International Seafood Fair. It specializes in seafood, chicken and vegetable dishes, and breakfast omelettes; there are also more unusual dishes like manta ray, and the health-conscious can get yoghurt and granola for breakfast. Full dinners run around US$20 or above, but it's worth considering for a splurge.

Across the street from the Santo Tomás winery, at the corner of Avenida Miramar and Calle 7a, *La Vieja Embotelladora* (☎ 4-08-07) was never really a bottling plant despite its name. The cavernous building, modernized for upscale dining with its huge wooden wine casks and other unique features intact, provides great atmosphere; the cheapest lunches or dinners cost about US$10, while lobster dishes run about US$25.

Kiki's Las Cazuelas (☎ 6-10-44), at Calle Sanginés and Blvd Costero across from Campo Playa RV Park, has an appealing but expensive menu of seafood dishes like abalone and lobster, but the antojitos are more reasonably priced. *La Casa del Abulón* (☎ 6-54-60), also on Calle Sanginés near Blvd Costero, features moderately priced breakfasts, including 10 varieties of omelette. Breakfast is served from 7 am to noon, while an international menu of beef, poultry, seafood and Mexican dishes is available until 11 pm weekdays and midnight on weekends.

For marinated Mexican-style chicken, grilled or roasted over an open flame, try *Las Brasas* at Avenida López Mateos 486 near Avenida Gastelum, or *El Pollo Real* on Calle 2a at the corner of Avenida Macheros. At either place, a half (US$4) or whole (US$8) chicken includes salsa, tortillas and condiments. El Pollo Real serves very greasy chips, but the tortillas are good.

Cha-Cha Burgers (☎ 6-54-51), on Blvd Costero near Calle Sanginés, caters to a mostly Mexican clientele craving US-style fast food. Although most ingredients come from north of the border, prices are reasonable for burgers, fries and shakes. There is also a branch on Blvd Costero between Avenida Macheros and Avenida Miramar. Pizza lovers can try *La Fábula*, at the corner of Blvd Costero and Avenida Riviera.

Ensenada has a dozen or more Chinese restaurants, but *Muy Lam*, at the corner of Avenida Ejército and Calle Diamante, and *China Land* (☎ 8-66-44), Avenida Riveroll 1149 near the corner of Calle 11a, are favorites. Menu choices range from a simple, inexpensive chop suey to far more elaborate dishes like Peking duck.

South Ensenada *La Cueva de los Tigres* (☎ 6-64-50) is a popular seafood restaurant on Playa Hermosa, about a mile south of the intersection of Avenida Reforma and Calle Agustín Sanginés; a sign on the Transpeninsular indicates the road. An abalone steak dinner costs upwards of US$20, but is not a great value.

North of Ensenada *Hussong's El Pelícano Restaurant & Oyster Bar* (☎ 4-45-75), 1 mile north of Ensenada on México 1, serves abalone with crab-meat sauce, and it is the only restaurant in town serving chili con carne – owner Juan Hussong organizes the annual International Chili Cookoff. The Mexican combination is reasonably priced. All meals include soup or salad, fresh vegetables and bread or tortillas.

Entertainment
Bars & Cantinas Potent, tasty and inexpensive beer, margaritas and other liquors are prime attractions for gringos, especially those who have not yet reached the mainland California drinking age of 21. On weekends, most of Ensenada's bars and cantinas are packed from early afternoon to early morning.

Thanks in part to bumper stickers and T-shirts widely disseminated on the Pacific Coast, Hussong's, Avenida Ruiz 113, is probably the best known cantina in the Californias – though their namesake beer is brewed in Mazatlán. After arriving from Germany in the late 19th century, the Hussong family used their knowledge of traditional German brewing to establish one of Ensenada's first cantinas. Their early clientele were miners and ranchers, now replaced by college students, mariachi bands and tattooed bikers. Open hours are 10 am to 2 am.

Nearby Papas & Beer, at the corner of Avenida López Mateos and Avenida Ruiz, caters mostly to college students on holiday. Roaring music drowns out conversations, but the margaritas are sweet and fruity. Open hours are 10 am to 3 am. Anthony's, at the corner of Uribe and Avenida Miramar, just north of Blvd Costero, is a rowdy place that attracts a broader clientele.

Bananas is a noisy high-tech disco on Blvd Costero between Avenida Miramar and Avenida Macheros. Plaza México, an outdoor bar at the corner of Avenida Macheros and Blvd Costero, is also a popular gringo hang out and streetside taco stand, but it has been criticized for making inaccurate change. Their strong margaritas are very cheap; buy drink 'tickets' from the waiter if you think you'll want more than one.

Bullfights Bullfights take place in summer at the Plaza de Toros on Avenida Sanginés between Blvd Costero and Avenida Ciprés. Look for posters on city streets or inquire at the tourist offices.

Cinemas The Cinemas Gemelos (☎ 6-36-16) are at the corner of López Mateos and Balboa.

Rodeos Stylish charreadas take place almost every summer weekend at the Lienzo de Charros, near the corner of Calle 2a and Avenida Blancarte, with typical rodeo feats like bull riding and calf roping. Check with one of the tourist offices for schedules.

Things to Buy

Many items sold in Tijuana shops are available here at slightly lower prices (see the Tijuana Things to Buy section), but the selection is smaller. Wine is fairly reasonable because of the nearby Santo Tomás winery. Liquors and beers from all over Mexico are also available at discount prices.

Shops along Avenida López Mateos overflow with colorful serapes, wrought-iron bird cages, silver jewelry (and cheap imitations), wood carvings, leather goods and other crafts from throughout Mexico; very few items actually come from Baja itself. Artesanías Los Castillo at López Mateos 815 sells silverwork from Taxco.

Galería de Pérez Meillon, in the Plaza Hussong at Avenida López Mateos 335-13, sells first-rate indigenous pottery and other crafts from Baja California's indigenous Paipai, Kumiai and Cucapah peoples, as well as from the Tarahumara of mainland Mexico. There's a smaller branch at the Centro Artesanal de Ensenada, Blvd Costero 1094-39, corner of Castillo.

Galería 19, on Avenida Riveroll between Calle 11 and Calle 12, exhibits and sells the work of local artists and photographers.

For those interested in antiques see the section on Mercado Los Globos above.

Getting There & Away

Air AirLA offers daily flights from the military Aeropuerto El Ciprés, south of Ensenada, to Los Angeles at 5:45 pm; the one-way fare is US$79. AirLA has no Ensenada facilities except at the airport, but downtown travel agencies sell tickets.

The Sociedad Cooperativa de Producción Pesquera (☎ 8-11-66), Avenida Ryerson 117, has information on flights to offshore Isla Cedros, near the border between Baja California and Baja California Sur. These flights leave at least twice weekly and cost US$95 one way, but tickets must be purchased at the military Aeropuerto El Ciprés (☎ 6-60-76, ask for Joel or Maricruz), south of Ensenada. Scheduled flights leave Wednesday and Saturday at 9 am, and must usually be booked at least a week in advance; cheaper and more frequent flights are available from Guerrero Negro (see the Central Baja chapter).

Aerotaxis Peninsulares (☎ 8-27-89, fax 8-32-13), Avenida Miramar 832-B, operates charter flights to peninsular destinations. AirLA plans to introduce service from Los Angeles to Ensenada.

Aeroméxico has no flights from Ensenada, but maintains an office at the corner of Avenida Ruiz and Calle 3a.

Bus Ensenada's Central de Autobuses (☎ 8-65-50) is at Avenida Riveroll 1075, at the corner of Calle 11a, 10 blocks north of Avenida López Mateos. Tres Estrellas de Oro (☎ 8-67-70) and Transportes Norte de Sonora (8-66-77) operate from the same counter, with buses to mainland Mexican destinations like Guaymas (US$42), Mazatlán (US$65), Guadalajara (US$82) and Mexico City (US$104). Norte de Sonora fares on 2nd-class buses are up to 15% cheaper.

Autotransportes de Baja California (ABC, ☎ 8-66-80) is the main peninsular carrier, with numerous buses to Tijuana as well as points south:

La Paz
(23 hours, US$50) at least four times daily from 12:15 pm to midnight
Mexicali
(3½ hours, US$10) at least four times daily
Rosarito
(1 hour, US$3) almost every half hour from 6 am to 7:45 pm
San Felipe
(5 hours, US$10) twice daily, at 8 am and 6 pm
Tecate
(1½ hours, US$4) at least five times daily
Tijuana
(1½ hours, US$5) almost every half hour from 6 am to 7:45 pm

Between 6 am and 7 pm, Autotransportes Aragón (☎ 4-04-86), at Avenida Riveroll 861 just south of the main bus station, goes hourly to Tijuana for US$7 round trip; it also links up with Intercalifornias buses to Santa Ana (US$18), Los Angeles (US$18), San Fernando (US$24), Bakersfield (US$37), Delano (US$40) and Fresno (US$48). Ask about direct service to Tijuana's airport.

Transportes Brisa (☎ 8-38-88), at Calle 4a No 771, serves nearby rural destinations like Maneadero (US$2), Sauzal and Ejido Uruapán.

Sea Starlite Cruises (☎ (619) 338-1100), 1150 North Harbor Drive in San Diego, offers luxury, Vegas-style day trips to Ensenada for US$59 (US$69 Saturdays), plus US$19.50 port charges. Their *Pacific Star* leaves San Diego daily at 9 am and returns to San Diego by 10:30 pm; visitors have the afternoon in Ensenada or, for an additional charge, can stay overnight with accommodation included.

Transportation-only arrangements are possible for longer stays. One-way passengers pay US$49 plus US$9.75 port charges.

Getting Around
Taxi Taxis are available 24 hours a day at several corner stands along Avenida López

Mateos – one major stand is at the corner of Avenida Miramar.

Car Rental Renting a car is only necessary for convenient transport to isolated beaches, Punta Banda and Agua Caliente (the hot springs). The two local agencies, Ensenada Rent-a-Car (☎ 8-18-96) at Avenida Alvarado 95 and next-door Scorpio Rent-a-Car (☎ 8-32-75), both charge similarly extortionate rates of US$53 per day, plus US$0.35 per km, plus gasoline. It's much cheaper to rent a car in San Diego, even with additional daily charges for Mexican insurance.

AROUND ENSENADA
Islas Todos Santos
Professional surfers frequent these two offshore islands, about 12 miles (20 km) west of Ensenada, especially when winter storms bring towering surf to the smaller Isla Norte. Todos Santos Tours (☎ (714) 721-8747 in the USA) runs surfing trips to the islands, but it's also possible to hire a launch out to the islands from Ensenada; to do so, ask around the harbor.

Playa El Faro
Playa El Faro, about 2 miles (3 km) north of the turn-off to Estero Beach (follow the signs) has a small motel, *El Faro Beach Motel*, and a trailer park/campground. The motel has eight clean, simple rooms with bath and shower for US$30, but proximity to the beach is its main attraction. Camping is also possible on a sandy lot next to the beach, with electricity, water, showers and toilets for US$7.50. The mailing address for both the campground and the motel is Apartado Postal 1008, Ensenada, Baja California, México.

Estero Beach Resort
The *Estero Beach Resort* (☎ 6-62-25, fax 6-69-25), 6 miles (10 km) south of Ensenada and immediately south of Playa El Faro, is a gringo enclave (*all* signs are in English, and the grounds are so extensive that it issues its own map). Besides a luxury hotel, it also includes a campground and RV park

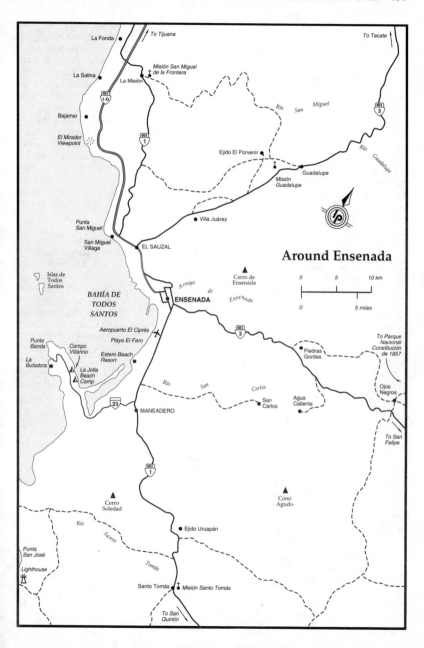

Around Ensenada

To Tijuana
To Tecate
La Fonda
La Salina
Misión San Miguel de la Frontera
La Misión
MEX 1-D
Bajamar
MEX 1
Río San Miguel
MEX 3
El Mirador Viewpoint
Ejido El Porvenir
Guadalupe
Río Guadalupe
Misión Guadalupe
Punta San Miguel
Villa Juárez
San Miguel Village
EL SAUZAL
Islas de Todos Santos
Arroyo de Ensenada
Cerro de Ensenada
BAHÍA DE TODOS SANTOS
ENSENADA
0   5   10 km
0   5 miles
Aeropuerto El Ciprés
Playa El Faro
MEX 3
Punta Banda
Campo Villarino
Piedras Gordas
To Parque Nacional Constitución de 1857
La Bufadora
Estero Beach Resort
La Jolla Beach Camp
Río San Carlos
San Carlos
Agua Caliente
Ojos Negros
23
MANEADERO
To San Felipe
MEX 1
Cerro Soledad
Cono Agudo
Río Santo
Punta San José
Ejido Uruapán
Lighthouse
Tomás
Santo Tomás
Misión Santo Tomás
To San Quintín

which charges US$12 a night for two people, plus US$1 for each extra person. Most sites have full hookups, and hot showers and clean toilets are also available.

Hotel doubles range from US$48 to US$64 in the off-season (October through March), but rise to US$78 to US$94 the rest of the year. Cottages with two queen beds and kitchenettes cost from US$82 to US$220. For information and reservations, write Apartado Postal 86, Ensenada, Baja California, México.

Horses can be hired next to the RV park. The complex also includes tennis courts, a recreation hall and restaurant; its **Museo de la Naturaleza y de las Culturas Precolombinas** contains quality replicas of ceramics and statuary from various Mexican cultures, including the Aztecs, Olmecs, Mayas and Teotihuacán; it also displays an exceptional collection of seashells, which is well arranged but lacks any explanation of their biological or ecological context.

Southwest Sea Kayaks (☎ (619) 222-3616), 1310 Rosecrans St in San Diego, offers introductory weekend sea kayaking classes here for US$125 including kayak rental; three-day courses cost US$200.

Baja Beach & Tennis Club

About 10 miles (16 km) south of Ensenada and 1 mile (1.6 km) before La Jolla Beach Camp is the *Baja Beach & Tennis Club*, a major hotel resort complex with 93 hotel rooms, tennis courts, a swimming pool, a marina, jet ski and sailboat rentals, a charter fishing boat, three bars, a restaurant and a coffee shop.

The club now admits nonmembers, who pay US$62 for doubles weekdays and US$88 weekends. In the USA, phone ☎ (800) 842-3118 (toll free in southern California only) or ☎ (619) 283-8519 for more information.

Punta Banda & La Bufadora

Many visitors enjoy a side trip from Ensenada to Punta Banda and La Bufadora, although their attractions are less than exceptional. BCN-23, the paved road to the

Punta Banda Peninsula, leaves the Transpeninsular at Maneadero and passes several campgrounds and roadside stands selling chile peppers and olives. Beyond the Baja Beach & Tennis Club are a few isolated campsites and, at the end of the road past several taco stands and souvenir stalls, the overrated **La Bufadora**.

A tidal blowhole that spews water and foam through a V-shaped notch in the headlands, La Bufadora is the Ensenada area's most popular weekend destination for tourists and locals; unless the sea is really rough, it's a pretty tame sight, and the endless souvenir stands are a blight on the coastline. Sandy lots sporadically collect US$1 for parking.

Diving Below Los Gordos is La Bufadora Dive Center, which offers underwater excursions to see sea anemones, sea urchins and other sea life. Canadian operator Dale Erwin has three boats, two compressors, complete sets of diving gear and many wet suits for rent at reasonable prices. Air fills cost US$3, while boat rental is US$20 per person for half a day. Boat trips to La Bufadora can also be arranged for US$5 per person. For more information, write La Bufadora Dive Center at Apartado Postal 102, Maneadero, Baja California, México. The shop is closed Tuesdays and Wednesdays.

Places to Stay Camping at *Rancho La Bufadora*, with a view, outhouse access and use of a few fire rings, costs US$5 per night for two people. Bring water, which is trucked into the settlement from time to time. There is no electricity. Local ejidos rent slightly cheaper sites.

Most houses on the hill above belong to gringos who favor the spectacular view and inexpensive lot rents (from about US$50 per month). For further information about the lots and the campground, contact José León Toscano at Apartado Postal 300, Ensenada, Baja California.

The other two main campgrounds on Punta Banda, *La Jolla Beach Camp* (US$6 per person) and next-door *Campo Villarino*

(☎ 6-13-09, US$5 per person), have attracted many permanent mobile-home residents. La Jolla has sites overlooking the beach and is the only place on the point with hot (but salty) showers. Both campgrounds have electricity and small grocery stores with canned goods, milk and purified water. Every summer, a catamaran race takes place in front of the two campgrounds.

Places to Eat Many stalls near La Bufadora serve fish tacos, shrimp cocktails and *churros* (deep-fried dough dipped in sugar). There are also seafood restaurants with lower prices and better ocean views than Ensenada.

Salvador Padilla, owner-chef of *Los Panchos*, serves up specialties like mesquite grilled fish, breaded shrimp, Pacific lobster and a savory 'Siete Mares' (Seven Seas) soup chock full of shrimp, octopus, fish, crab claws and other fresh seafood. It's open from 9 am to sunset, but closed Thursdays.

Near the entrance to Rancho La Bufadora is *Restaurant Los Gordos*, where photographs, memorabilia and graffiti cover the walls and over 400 baseball caps hang from the rafters. Specialties include a Mexican combo, deep-fried calamari, lobster and shrimp in garlic butter. The bar is a favorite watering hole for US expatriates.

Restaurant La Bufadora, up the hill from Los Gordos, specializes in full lobster dinners, but also serves fish dinners and lobster burritos.

Getting There & Away Transportes Brisa (☎ 8-38-88), at Calle 4a No 771 in Ensenada, offers regular bus service as far as Maneadero; supposedly another bus runs from the Ensenada depot to Punta Banda every Sunday. Several Ensenada travel agencies offer package tours by van or bus.

GUADALUPE

Settled by turn-of-the-century Russian immigrants, the village of Guadalupe, at Km 78 of México 3 about 18 miles (30 km)

northeast of the junction with México 1, contains ruins of the Dominican **Misión Nuestra Señora de Guadalupe**, the last mission built in the Californias (founded 1834 and destroyed by Indians only six years later). In a fertile zone for grain farming and grazing, during its brief existence it was a powerful and important mission. Almost nothing remains of the mission, but you can reach this site by turning left at the end of the paved lateral off the main highway. There are Indian pictographs on a huge granite boulder known as **Ojá Cuñúrr**, where the canyon of the Río Guadalupe narrows.

Only about 10 families of demonstrably Russian descent remain in the area (the oldest living colonist turned 107 years old in 1993!), but INAH's **Museo Comunitario de Guadalupe** documents the community's history with photographs and Russian artifacts like samovars and traditional clothing. The immigrants themselves, pacifist refugees from the area of present-day Turkey, first arrived in Los Angeles but found the lands not to their liking and chose to head south across the border in 1905. They first lived in Indian dwellings known by their Kumiai name of *wa*, but soon built adobe houses that the Kumiai later emulated.

To reach the museum, follow the dirt road at the end of the paved lateral off México 3. In addition to the interior exhibits, antique farming machinery decorates the museum grounds. Across from the site of the former Dominican mission (see above) are the arches of the former Russian school, which unfortunately was demolished a few years ago. The nearby Russian cemetery still contains headstones with Cyrillic inscriptions.

The surrounding valley is now one of Mexico's major vineyard regions, but grapes arrive at Domecq (the huge winery at the edge of town) from vineyards throughout the peninsula. Domecq is now open for public visits, as is nearby Vinícola L A Cetto, and their products are available at most liquor stores throughout the peninsula. In August, the **Fiesta de La**

Vendimia (wine harvest festival) takes place at several of the valley's wineries.

OJOS NEGROS

Southeast of Ensenada, at Km 39 on México 3 to San Felipe, a paved lateral reaches the village of Ojos Negros, whose decent *Restaurant Oasis* may soon add accommodation; the owner speaks English and is happy to provide tourist information. Twice-daily buses from Ensenada to San Felipe stop here briefly, and Magna Sin is available at the Pemex station.

PARQUE NACIONAL CONSTITUCIÓN DE 1857

From Ojos Negros, a 27-mile (43-km) dirt road climbs eastward onto a striking plateau of ponderosa pines in the Sierra de Juárez, part of which comprises Parque Nacional Constitución de 1857. The highlight of the 12,000-acre (5000-hectare) park is pine-sheltered **Laguna Hanson**, a shallow, marshy but pleasant and solitary lake which abounds with migratory birds –

ducks, coots, grebes and many others – in the autumn. Check the dying pines for woodpeckers. Hunting is prohibited, but birdwatchers will find the park an exceptional destination at this time of the year. Anglers may catch catfish, bluegills and large-mouth bass.

Camping along the lake, at about 4000 feet (1200 meters) elevation, is ideal except in winter. Because of the numerous livestock, the water is only suitable for dousing your campfire; bring your own. Fuel wood is scarce in the shoreline campgrounds, more abundant in the surrounding hills, but dry and not-so-dry cow patties are an easily acquired addition in a pinch. Only pit toilets are available. Camp robbers like gray squirrels and even coyotes will abscond with any food left in the open, but the coyotes' howling at least seems to quiet the cattle.

The low granite outcrops north and west of Laguna Hanson offer stupendous views but require very difficult ascents through dense brush and over and beneath massive

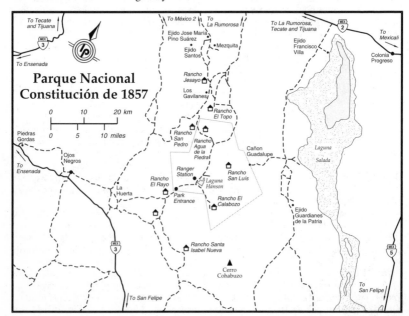

rockfalls – watch for ticks and rattlesnakes. The easiest view route is to take the abandoned road northwest from near the ruined cabins and pit toilets to the first dry watercourse, and then follow it toward the peaks; expect dead ends which are too steep to climb, but follow tunnels through the rockfalls before emerging on a saddle below the two main peaks. This very short climb, which should take only about an hour or so, is nevertheless very tiring.

For technical climbers, there are many challenging routes up the open granite despite the limited relief – most pitches do not exceed 200 to 300 foot in terrain resembling that of Joshua Tree National Monument in mainland California.

On the east side of Parque Nacional Constitución de 1857, at the base of the Sierra de Juárez, are several beautiful desert palm canyons, the most accessible of which is **Cañón Guadalupe**; for more information, see the Around Mexicali entry in the Mexicali & the Northern Gulf chapter.

Getting There & Away
In addition to the road from Ojos Negros, which is passable for almost any passenger car despite its frequent washboard surface, Parque Nacional Constitución de 1857 is also accessible from México 3 by a steeper road just east of Km 55, about 10 miles (16 km) southeast of the Ojos Negros junction, and by dirt roads leading south from México 2 (the Tijuana-Tecate-Mexicali highway). Drivers with low-clearance vehicles will undoubtedly prefer the Ojos Negros road, although the road from Km 55 should be passable for most, especially after the first 4.4 miles (7 km); the total distance is about 20 miles (32 km). There is no public transport.

EL ALAMO & VALLE DE TRINIDAD
From Ojos Negros, México 3 continues south to a marked junction with a dirt road leading west to the once-bustling mining town of El Alamo. After the discovery of gold in 1888, El Alamo boomed with thousands of goldseekers, but the ore ran out quickly and it is now almost deserted.

From the junction, the highway leads south into the verdant Valle de Trinidad – a prosperous agricultural development and, in the late 19th century, a mining zone – before crossing the San Matías Pass toward San Felipe. Just south of the junction, but 5 miles (8 km) east of the highway, is the site of the former **Misión Santa Catalina**, one of two Dominican missions in the peninsula's northern interior.

Founded in 1798, with a population over 600 at its peak in 1824, Santa Catalina de los Paipais was the largest of the Dominican missions, but also one of the most precarious. Because of the area's high altitude (about 3500 feet) and cool climate, the mission was not agriculturally self-sufficient and the Indians continued to collect wild foods, like piñon nuts, in the surrounding countryside. Indian hostility was widespread; an uprising of several groups in 1840 destroyed the mission. Unfortunately, parts of the adobe walls are the only remaining ruins, which lie on a hillock above the present village cemetery. An easily identifiable circular mound marks the remains of the mission watchtower.

Now known officially as Santa Catalina, the village is a sprawling hodgepodge of wrecked automobiles, a few adobe houses and trailers, and abandoned greenhouses – remnants of a federal government scheme to raise jojoba. Competing Catholic and Pentecostal churches, both of which emphasize the term *indígena* in their formal titles, vie for the souls of the remaining Paipai, who still speak their native language in addition to Spanish and continue to collect piñon nuts in the fall.

MANEADERO
The small farm town of Maneadero, about 10 miles (16 km) south of central Ensenada, contains little of note except an immigration checkpoint, only sporadically open (as of late 1993, it had apparently been vaporized). If it reopens, validate your tourist card by showing proof of citizenship. A current passport, official birth certificate or voter registration card (for US citizens) are all acceptable, but regulations

can change – check with a Mexican consulate or immigration at the border (see the Visas and Documents entries in the Facts for the Visitor chapter). Some travelers without proper ID have used the mordida to get past the authorities, but it's simpler and cheaper to follow established procedures.

EJIDO URUAPÁN

On the eastern side of the Transpeninsular, 10 miles (16 km) south of Maneadero, Ejido Uruapán (population 1000) is known for sea urchins, strawberries and quail – which draw hunters from north of the border. Hunters stay at luxurious lodges (US$130 per day) with guides, transport and, of course, meals featuring the day's bag of quail as well as lobster, shrimp and abalone.

Uruapán's sea-urchin processing plant, established with Japanese aid, exports countless *erizos* across the Pacific. The Japanese have also built greenhouses for cultivating strawberries, mostly for export to California. The well-shaded and well-maintained campground, at the junction with the Transpeninsular, has brick barbecue pits and is a fine place for camping or picnicking.

SANTO TOMÁS

The Dominican mission village of Santo Tomás, 6½ miles (10.5 km) south of Uruapán, takes its name from the surrounding Valle de Santo Tomás, one of Baja's key wine-producing areas. Founded in 1791 as the last link in the chain connecting Alta and Baja California, **Misión Santo Tomás de Aquino** soon moved upstream from its original site to escape infestations of gnats and mosquitoes which made it both uncomfortable and unhealthy. Winter rains bring forth hordes of harmless toads, who stage Darwinian sprint contests across the Transpeninsular, in reckless defiance of the thundering 18-wheelers passing north and south.

The wine industry is a legacy of the Dominicans, who planted thousands of grapevines and other fruit crops, most notably olives. At its peak, in 1824, the neophyte population may have exceeded 400. Abandoned in 1849, it was the last Dominican mission to maintain a priest. A few crumbling ruins remain of the original mission, on an alluvial fan where the river canyon narrows west of the Transpeninsular, but only a few faint foundations denote the upstream site, just north of El Palomar's campground/RV park (see below).

For modern visitors, Santo Tomás' key institution is venerable *El Palomar* (☎ 6-18-94), a restaurant, motel, general store, campground and picnic area at Km 51. Owner Enrique Villareal, before devoting most of his time to the family business, was Ensenada district attorney and then attorney-general for the state of Baja California.

Restaurant portions are huge and prices fairly high, so some visitors may wish to share a platter. The specialty is lobster tacos, accompanied by small but potent margaritas, but other specials include breaded shrimp, rib steak, abalone cream chowder, beef tacos and cheese enchiladas. On the slope behind the restaurant, *Motel El Palomar* offers clean, simple singles/doubles with hot water and heating for US$35/45.

Across the highway is a trailer park/campground in a grove of olive trees and bamboo; the olives are harvested, bottled and sold in the general store. In summer, the park's two tennis courts, volleyball court, children's playground, swimming pool and 100 barbecue pits attract up to 2000 visitors daily, sometimes including rowdy and unpleasant groups of middle-aged off-roaders from southern mainland California. There are only 30 spaces with full RV hookups, at US$10 for two people.

For more basic but cheaper meals, try the *Mi Refugio* truckstop about ½ mile (1 km) down the road, where passing truckers hang their personal coffee mugs on the wall.

EJIDO ERÉNDIRA & PUERTO SAN ISIDRO

Ejido Eréndira is a small farm community

where you can stock up on bread, milk, gasoline and other basic supplies for a beach outing at Puerto San Isidro, a beautiful fishing cove which is home to *Castro's Fishing Place*, where Fernando Castro Ríos rents several rustic *cabañas* (cabins) next to his home, facing the ocean, for US$25 per night; camping is free. Toilets are outside; refrigerator, sink, stove and six bunks are inside. Jorge Arballo leads all-day (7 am to 2 pm) fishing trips for US$25 per person. For more information, contact Fernando Castro Ríos (☎ 6-28-97), Apartado Postal 974, Ensenada.

South of Puerto San Isidro via a dirt road, *Malibu Beach Sur* has an RV park which offers camping, fishing and surfing; there are plans for an airstrip and a marina with boat launching facilities.

To reach Ejido Eréndira and Puerto San Isidro, take the paved lateral off the Transpeninsular, about 10 miles (16 km) south of Santo Tomás (look for the 'Ejido Eréndira' sign) for about 6½ miles (10.5 km). The local Pemex station has only Nova, so fill the tank with Magna Sin at El Palomar.

SAN VICENTE

The bustling agricultural community of San Vicente, on its namesake arroyo 7 miles (11 km) south of the Ejido Eréndira junction, was the site of **Misión San Vicente Ferrer** (founded 1780), one of the few Dominican missions which never moved from its original site. In some ways, it was the most important of them both for its centrality – it was convenient to the other Pacific coast missions – and its strategic location, exposed to Indian attacks from the east. The largest and most heavily fortified of the Dominican missions, it never enjoyed the protection of more than 31 soldiers, but controlled over 300 Indian neophytes.

These neophytes cultivated maize, wheat and beans, and tended the mission's livestock, which numbered up to 750 cattle and 1150 sheep, plus horses, burros and goats. After Yuman Indians destroyed most of the

mission, it closed in 1833, but for another 16 years the Mexican army maintained its garrison here. Substantial foundations and some walls of the fort and mission are still visible northwest of town, as is the stone-lined acequia; follow the dirt road west across from the llantera 1 km north of town, near the northbound sign which says 'Santo Tomás 37, Ensenada 80'.

Information

English-speaking Henriqueta McFarland runs a state-sponsored tourist information post, very conspicuously signed and with a decent selection of maps and brochures, from her house at Km 89 on the east side of the Transpeninsular – ring the bell at any reasonable hour.

San Vicente has a post office and Telnor long-distance service at the bus terminal. Buses between Ensenada and points south stop here.

Places to Stay & Eat

La Estrella del Sur, at Km 90 on the east side of the Transpeninsular, has good, reasonably priced meals and rooms with hot showers for US$10 per person. Very basic *Motel El Camino*, at Km 91 at the southern edge of town, has spartan, unheated but fairly clean rooms, most with private bath (about US$15 to US$17) and a few doubles with shared bath (about US$10 to US$12).

The town's best restaurant is probably *Valentina*, just south of La Estrella del Sur, which is also reasonably priced.

COLONET

Colonet, a major farming community 23 miles (37 km) south of San Vicente, is a good place to replenish supplies and fill your gas tank or backpack if heading to the beach at San Antonio del Mar or inland to the Meling Ranch and Parque Nacional Sierra San Pedro Mártir. There's no accommodation in town itself, but north of town, at Km 121, *Nuevo Hotel Sonora* has singles/doubles for US$10. The beach at San Antonio, four miles (6.5 km) northwest, has good camping and clamming.

SAN TELMO & MELING RANCH

The village of San Telmo is 4 miles (6.5 km) east of the Transpeninsular on the graded dirt road to Meling Ranch, Parque Nacional Sierra San Pedro Mártir, Picacho del Diablo and the observatory. A clinic operated by the Flying Samaritans (a team of volunteer doctors and nurses from California) operates in the village, which is subdivided into San Telmo de Abajo (lower San Telmo) and San Telmo de Arriba (upper San Telmo).

San Telmo's most notable cultural feature is the very faint remains of a Dominican chapel, built between 1798 and 1800; this was part of an *asistencia* (way station) under the jurisdiction of the mission at Santo Domingo near present-day Colonia Vicente Guerrero to the south. Look for its foundations behind a small, much newer chapel at the entrance to San Telmo de Arriba.

The *San José Meling Ranch*, some 27 miles (44 km) southeast of San Telmo, is a Baja institution. After arriving from Norway in the early 1900s, Soren Meling and his family established the 10,000-acre ranch still run by their descendants, who also offer accommodation, meals, horseback riding and pack trips into Parque

Nacional Sierra San Pedro Mártir. For latest information and rates, write or phone the Meling Hunting Service (☎ 6-98-85, 7-62-23) at Apartado Postal 1326, Ensenada, or c/o Dal Potter, PO Box 189003, No 73, Coronado, California 92178.

PARQUE NACIONAL SIERRA SAN PEDRO MÁRTIR

Baja California's most notable national park comprises 151,000 acres (63,000 hectares) of coniferous forests and granitic peaks reaching above 10,000 feet (3000 meters), plus deep canyons leading down into their steep eastern scarp. Major native tree types include several species of pines, plus incense cedar, Douglas fir and quaking aspen, while the most conspicuous fauna include raccoons, foxes, coyotes and mule deer. The rare desert bighorn sheep inhabits some remote canyon areas.

Unlike Parque Nacional Constitución de 1857, the park has no major bodies of water. Westward-flowing streams like the Río San Rafael, Arroyo Los Pinos and Arroyo San Antonio support the odd trout, but wildfowl no longer breed here, as they did a century ago, because of a history of grazing and timber cutting. Among the

Parque Nacional
Sierra San Pedro Mártir

typical breeding land birds are the mountain quail, pinyon jay, mountain chickadee, pygmy nuthatch, western bluebird, Cassin's finch, pine siskin, red crossbill and dark-eyed junco.

Climate

The Sierra San Pedro Mártir has a temperate climate similar to the mountains of southern mainland California; most precipitation falls in winter, when the snow depth at higher altitudes can be 3 feet (1 meter) or more, but the area also gets summer rainfall in the form of thunderstorms. The average annual temperature is around 59°F (16°C), with maxima approaching 68°F (22°C), but winter temperatures can drop well below freezing. At higher elevations, even in summer, changeable weather is a potential hazard.

Things to See & Do

The Sierra San Pedro Mártir is an underappreciated area for hiking, camping and backpacking, in part because access is awkward and it's a little far for weekend trips from mainland California. Still, for anyone seeking relief from overcrowded recreational areas north of the border, it's well worth exploring, especially in the spring when more northerly areas are inaccessible because of snow.

Within the park are many suitable car camping areas and hiking trails, though trail maintenance is limited and hikers should carry a compass along with the usual cold and wet weather supplies, canteens and water purification tablets. Below about 6000 feet (1800 meters) or even a bit higher, beware of rattlesnakes. A detailed topographic map (see Picacho del Diablo, below) is essential.

The **Observatorio Astronómico Nacional**, Mexico's national observatory, is 1¼ miles (2 km) from the locked gate at the parking area at the end of the public road from San Telmo. It's open to the public Saturdays only, from 11 am to 1 pm.

Picacho del Diablo

The 10,154-foot (3095-meter) peak of Picacho del Diablo, also known as Cerro Providencia, draws climbers from throughout the Californias, but only a handful actually reach the summit because finding routes is so difficult. Determined climbers should obtain the 2nd edition of Walt Peterson's *The Baja Adventure Book* (Wilderness Press, Berkeley, 1992), which also includes a good map and describes several routes up the peak.

An even better choice to carry is *Parque Nacional San Pedro Mártir*, with an area map at a scale of 1:100,000 (⅝ inch=1 mile or 1 cm=1 km), with details at a scale of 1:31,680 (1 inch=½ mile or 1 km=3.2 cm). This detailed topographic map is available from Centra Publications, 4705 Laurel St, San Diego, California 92105.

Norman Clyde, perhaps the most famous mountaineer ever in mainland California's Sierra Nevada, wrote *El Picacho del Diablo, the Conquest of Lower California's Highest Peak, 1932 & 1937* (Dawson's Book Shop, Los Angeles, 1975).

Getting There & Away

There is no public transport to Sierra San Pedro Mártir. Visitors will have to drive their own vehicle; high clearance and a short wheelbase are advisable.

From San Telmo From San Telmo de Abajo, south of Km 140 on the Transpeninsular, a graded dirt road climbs eastward through San Telmo de Arriba past Rancho Meling (Rancho San José) to the park entrance, about 50 miles (80 km) from the highway. Abounding with quail, rabbits, chipmunks and roadrunners, the road is passable to most passenger vehicles despite two major fords of the Río San Telmo. Spring runoff may cause problems for cars with low clearance, and drivers should probably avoid the road immediately after a snowfall in the high country, when the warm sun can melt the snow very quickly.

From San Felipe From late October to early March, the snowbound summit of Picacho del Diablo is visible from the desert floor. The rest of the year, its barren peak is a difficult climb that begins in Cañón del Diablo (Devil's Canyon), reached by a sandy road northwest of San Felipe. The road is reportedly safe and the surface mostly hard and dry, but ask for up-to-date information in San Felipe before attempting it.

Northwest of San Felipe, the road leads to Laguna Diablo, a usually dry salt lake, and Rancho Santa Clara, which marks the eastern approach to the park. From Rancho Santa Clara, follow tracks west of the dry lake bed, keeping Cañón del Diablo in sight. An alternative route to Rancho Santa Clara is a good graded road that leaves México 3, the Ensenada-San Felipe highway, just east of Km 164; rather than going down the middle of Laguna Diablo, the newly relocated road keeps to high ground along its eastern shoreline. A conspicuous roadside tire marks the turnoff to Rancho Santa Clara, which itself is marked by a similar tire.

About 1¼ miles (2 km) up the canyon, there's a striking waterfall. At about the 8-mile (13-km) point, you reach Campo Noche, a good camping site before starting an ascent the next day. For more details, consult *The Baja Adventure Book* (see above), the Mexican government topographic maps San Rafael H11B45 and Santa Cruz H11B55, and/or the Centra Publications map.

Mike's Sky Rancho

Thirty-seven miles (60 km) west along México 3 from the junction with Highway 5 is a 22-mile (35-km) road to *Mike's Sky Rancho*, situated in a small valley surrounded by the pine-covered foothills of the Sierra San Pedro Mártir. The graded dirt road makes it accessible to most passenger vehicles, but those seeking quiet and solitude should know that it's popular with fossil-fuel fanatics on motorcycles. At a few points, the road is steep and tricky for ordinary passenger cars.

The rancho itself offers basic, motel-style rooms, meals and wilderness treks, as well as an Olympic-size swimming pool. Rooms cost around US$45 per night,

breakfast and lunch are US$6 and dinner is US$12. For more information, contact Mike's Sky Rancho, PO Box 5376, San Ysidro, California 92073.

Misión San Pedro Mártir

Founded in 1794 in the mountains east of San Quintín, San Pedro Mártir de Verona was the most isolated of the Dominican missions. The initial site at Casilepe proved inadequate, wrote founder Fray Cayetano Pallás, when the crops froze. Even the new site of Ajantequedo, at an altitude of 5500 feet (1675 meters), was marginal but adequate for a neophyte population that never exceeded about 100.

The mission was established as a possible link to Indian rancherías on the Gulf and on the Río Colorado delta, but lasted only until 1824 because of its insecure location and the relatively small numbers of Indians in the area. On its demise, San Pedro's neophytes relocated to Misión Santo Domingo. Ruins still exist and may be reached either from Rancho Santa Cruz or from La Grulla, in Parque Nacional San Pedro Mártir, to the north.

COLONIA VICENTE GUERRERO

Colonia Vicente Guerrero is a booming agricultural center straddling the Trans-peninsular, which is the town's main street. It now has a single traffic light, a bank and a casa de cambio, but little else of interest to most tourists except its shady plaza, Parque General Vicente Guerrero, and nearby Misión Santo Domingo. The bus depot is in the center of town, on the Pacific side of the highway. The telephone area code is 616.

Misión Santo Domingo

Founded in 1775 by Manuel García and Miguel Hidalgo, at the mouth of the canyon of the Río Santo Domingo, Misión Santo Domingo de la Frontera was the second of nine Dominican missions in Baja California; it soon moved to a verdant upstream confluence about 5 miles (8 km) east of the present-day Transpeninsular. At first the mission was chaotic and undisciplined,

Hawksbill Turtle (BN)

Leatherback Turtle (CT)

Leatherback Turtle (CT)

Elephant seals, Isla San Benito Oeste

Elephant seal pup, Isla San Benito Oeste

with many Indians deserting, but by 1796 more than 350 Indian neophytes tended livestock and harvested grain here. By 1839 measles and smallpox had wiped out most of them, and the mission was abandoned.

To reach the ruins, the best preserved of any Dominican frontier mission, take the dirt road east on the north side of the Río Santo Domingo, at the northern entrance to town. Note the massive landmark **Peñón Colorado**, the reddish bluff that rises out of the sediments at the entrance to the canyon.

Though many walls are standing, the ruins are truly ruins; Peveril Meigs remarked in 1939 that the mission church then served as a pigpen. Parts of the system of acequias from mission times are still in use, though, and the ruins are now fenced off from animals.

Every year in the first week of August at the site of the ruins, the **Fiesta de Santo Domingo** features horse racing, charreadas, dancing and food stalls. A short distance west of the ruins is a pleasant private park with a swimming pool and a café – a good spot for a picnic accessible for a very modest admission.

Places to Stay & Eat

Colonia Vicente Guerrero has only two motels, but there are two RV parks/campgrounds at the southwest end of town. *Motel Sánchez* (☎ 6-22-01), conspicuously signed at Km 174 on the west side of the Transpeninsular, has large, fairly clean rooms for US$13/20 single/double. Señor Sánchez, the owner, speaks some English. Also on the west side, at Km 170, *Motel Ortiz* has rooms with double beds and hot water for US$13; rooms with two beds cost US$20.

The turn-off for both campgrounds is at Km 176 on the west side of the highway, just before the butane-gas station. *Mesón de Don Pepe RV Park & Restaurant* (☎ 6-22-16), which suffers from the noise of passing trucks on the highway, charges US$6 per night for sites with full hookups for two people, plus US$1 for each extra

person. Tent sites, on a pleasant grassy area, cost only US$4. Hot showers are available and the restaurant serves reasonably priced seafood and typical Mexican meals. Barbecued lamb is a weekend special.

Follow the dirt road on the south side of Mesón de Don Pepe west to the second campground, *Posada Don Diego RV Park* (☎ 6-21-81; note that crafty Don Pepe has built a conspicuous entrance road to ensnare potential Don Diego customers). Owned by José and Irene Martínez, who claim it is 'one of the finest RV parks in Baja', Don Diego has full hookups for US$6.50 per night for one person, US$8.50 for two, but only a few sites command shade. There are also hot showers, a laundry room, a restaurant and a bar. The restaurant deserves a visit even for travelers with no intention of staying in town – it has outstanding antojitos and seafood, gigantic margaritas at moderate prices (perhaps a sneaky method of inducing diners to spend the night) and world-class flan for dessert.

Posada Don Diego is closer to the beach, but the muddy road can be difficult for ordinary passenger vehicles. Hiking to the beach, which offers great clamming (respect size limits), takes 30 to 45 minutes.

The new *El Vaquero* steakhouse, at the north end of town, is easy to miss at 50 mph because of its inconspicuous rustic decor. There are also numerous taco stands and a few groceries, such as Conasupo, selling fruit, vegetables, bread and other staples.

SAN QUINTÍN

On a sheltered harbor 116 miles (190 km) south of Ensenada, San Quintín (population about 3000) is the center of an increasingly important agricultural region on the Llano de San Quintín (San Quintín Plain), but attractive Pacific beaches at the foot of a group of cinder cones also make it an ideal area for camping, clamming, beachcombing and fishing. Offshore Isla San Martín is part of the volcanic cordon which shelters the llano from the ocean's erosive power.

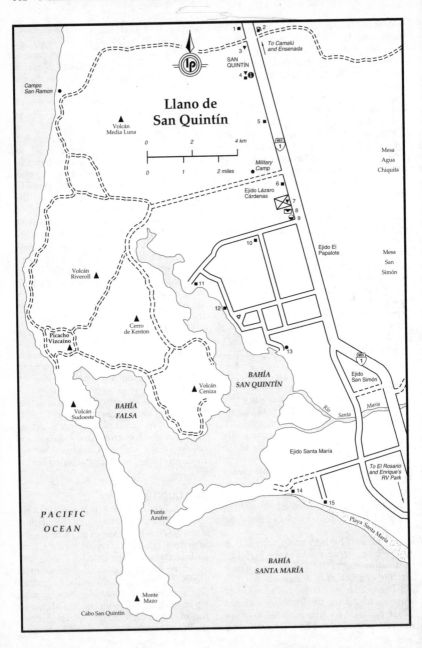

Llano de San Quintín

Campo San Ramon

Volcán Media Luna

To Camalú and Ensenada

SAN QUINTÍN

Mesa Agua Chiquita

Military Camp

Ejido Lázaro Cárdenas

Ejido El Papalote

Mesa San Simón

Volcán Riveroll

Picacho Vizcaíno

Cerro de Kenton

Ejido San Simón

Volcán Sudoeste

BAHÍA FALSA

Volcán Ceniza

BAHÍA SAN QUINTÍN

Río Santa Maria

Ejido Santa María

To El Rosario and Enrique's RV Park

PACIFIC OCEAN

Punta Azufre

Playa Santa María

BAHÍA SANTA MARÍA

Monte Mazo

Cabo San Quintín

■ PLACES TO STAY
1 Motel Uruapán
4 Motel Chávez
5 Motel Las Hadas
6 Hotel Romo
10 Rancho Sereno (B&B)
11 Motel Molino Viejo
12 Motel Muelle Viejo
14 Motel Cielito Lindo
15 Hotel La Pinta

▼ PLACES TO EAT
3 El Alteño
4 Bar San Quintín
7 Tacos La Pasadita

OTHER
2 Pemex Station
4 Bar San Quintín (tourist office)
8 Post Office
9 Bus Terminal
13 English Cemetery

History

Several briny coastal lagoons near San Quintín provided salt for the nearby Dominican missions in colonial times; 19th-century Russian settlements north of San Francisco Bay also acquired their salt here. The Russians and Americans hunted sea otters nearly to extinction, bringing Northwest Indians and their canoes along for the venture.

In the late 19th century, San Quintín was the focus of settlement schemes of the English-based Mexican Land & Colonization Company, which bought the concession of the International Company of Mexico – a US-based corporation that had obtained land rights to most of northern Baja for a massive colonization effort during the Porfiriato. The International Company attracted few settlers, but the Land & Colonization Company introduced English colonists and established a steam-powered flour mill, a customs house, a pier, schoolhouses, fertilizer plants and, after a few years, a cemetery.

The company also laid about 19 miles (32 km) of track, hoping to link up with the Southern Pacific Railroad in San Diego, but insufficient rainfall prevented the sustained cultivation of wheat they had hoped to market north of the border. Today, only the Motel Molino Viejo (Old Mill Motel), the Motel Muelle Viejo (Old Pier Motel) and the cemetery testify to the English presence. Only pilings remain of the pier itself, and the single identifiably English headstone is a recent construction memorializing Francis Barthemelon Henslowe of Wermigley, Norfolk and Santa María, who died 24 July 1896.

High-tech irrigation has at least temporarily overcome some of the problems encountered by early colonists, but fields west of the Transpeninsular are now suffering because growers have extracted so much fresh water that brackish sea water has contaminated the aquifers on which they rely. Cultivation has largely moved east of the highway, but some observers believe that this strategy may only provide a short reprieve for an unsustainable system.

Recent years have seen an influx of Mixtec Indians from impoverished rural Oaxaca, many of whom had previously worked for Sinaloa growers and labor contractors who have expanded operations into the San Quintín area. Unscrupulous contractors sometimes pay these Indians, poorly educated and with large families, US$4 or less per day for harvesting tomatoes and other off-season crops for the US market. The 1990 census recorded 8000 Mixtec speakers in the state of Baja California, but this figure may rise as high as 20,000 or more during the spring harvest.

In addition to these low wages, which are barely sufficient to buy a plate of tacos for lunch (let alone feed a family), farm laborers suffer serious health problems because local agriculture relies heavily on chemical fertilizers and pesticides, with almost no protective equipment or instruction for those who apply them; for an account of their plight, see Angus Wright's *The Death of Ramón González* (University of Texas Press, 1990).

Groups from north of the border occasionally offer health clinics in the area, but their efforts are largely ineffectual because itinerant workers following the harvest north do not receive regular medical attention for their ailments.

Orientation

The name San Quintín usually refers to an area that includes not only San Quintín proper, but also ejidos to the south – Lázaro Cárdenas, San Simón and Santa María. San Quintín and Lázaro Cárdenas stretch out along the Transpeninsular for about 3 miles (5 km), while the hamlet of San Simón is about 4 miles (6.5 km) south of Lázaro Cárdenas and adjacent to the highway. Santa María, a farming area west of the Transpeninsular, surrounds the Hotel La Pinta and Motel Cielito Lindo. The best beaches are near Santa María.

Information

At Km 192, Bar San Quintín (☎ 5-20-05; see Places to Eat, below) is the de facto tourist office, offering a good selection of local brochures, plus some good historical and contemporary photos of the area. There is a post office in San Quintín, as well as pharmacies, gasoline stations and groceries in both Lázaro Cárdenas and San Quintín. San Quintín's Banco Internacional cashes travelers' checks with no commission and gives cash advances on Visa and Master-Card.

Telephone Check the pharmacies along the Transpeninsular for telephone services; San Quintín's area code is 616.

Beaches

Activities in the region center around the beach and the ocean; the best beaches are near Hotel La Pinta in the Santa María area. Some motorists drive onto the beach at low tide, a very bad idea not just because it tears up the beach and disturbs other people, but also because the tide rises very quickly and can strand unsuspecting drivers, at least temporarily.

Activities

Clamming Clamming is superb on nearby beaches, but do not take undersized clams (those smaller than your hand) at risk of a hefty fine from the police or military.

Fishing Surf fishing is also good, but everyone over 16 years of age must have a fishing license; try to arrange this before traveling down the peninsula. George's Bait & Tackle in Ejido El Papalote, south of Lázaro Cárdenas, can provide additional information, but see also the Documents section in the Facts for the Visitor chapter.

The following list indicates which fish are most common each month in the vicinity of San Quintín:

January
    cabrilla, corvina, white sea bass
February
    corvina, white sea bass
March
    cabrilla, corvina, white sea bass
April
    cabrilla, corvina, sea trout, white sea bass
May
    cabrilla, corvina, sea trout, sierra
June
    cabrilla, corvina, grouper, sea trout, sierra
July
    cabrilla, corvina, grouper, sea trout, sierra
August
    cabrilla, corvina, grouper, sea trout, sierra
September
    cabrilla, corvina, grouper, sea trout, sierra
October
    cabrilla, grouper, sea trout
November
    white sea bass
December
    white sea bass

Places to Stay

Camping Free camping is possible at the beach near Hotel La Pinta, but stay well above the water line. You can distinguish the tide mark in the sand by finding the easternmost line of the flotsam left by the last high tide. 'Official' camping with some facilities is available just north of Motel Cielito Lindo. *Motel Muelle Viejo* (see below) has eight modest but shady campsites with fireplaces, hot showers and toilets for US$4 per night. *Motel Molino*

Viejo (see also below) has a new RV park for US$10 per site, but it's barren, windy and lacks electricity as yet.

About 10 miles (16 km) south of San Quintín and half a mile (1 km) west of the Transpeninsular, beachfront *Enrique's RV Park* and adjacent *El Pabellón* both have basic facilities for tents and RVs for US$5 per night. Backpackers without vehicles have complained about the shortage of nearby supplies, but a grocery which is only about a 20-minute walk away has just opened, and clamming and surf fishing are superb.

Hotels & Motels *Motel Las Hadas* (☎ 5-25-70) is San Quintín's cheapest accommodation, with 19 spartan singles/doubles for US$13/17 with private bath. The bugler from the nearby 67th Batallón de Infantería wakes all but the soundest sleepers at sunrise. Several travelers have applauded *Hotel Romo* (☎ 5-23-98) on the Transpeninsular just south of the 67th, which has singles/doubles for US$18/23 and good meals.

Basic *Motel Uruapán* (☎ 5-20-58), at Km 190, is fine for a bed and a roof over your head, with hot water and overhead fans; singles/doubles cost US$11/15. Rooms at the well-maintained *Motel Chávez* (☎ 5-20-05), at Km 194 just before the bridge, have tiled showers with hot water, filtered drinking water and, in some units, full kitchens with utensils and cookware; singles/doubles for US$21 are excellent value. Owner Marcos Chávez, born in Mexicali but a longtime local resident, speaks perfect English.

Southwest of town, in Ejido El Papalote, a wooden sign on the Transpeninsular points to a dirt road that crosses a field for about 1¼ miles (2 km) to *Motel Muelle Viejo* (no phone) on Bahía San Quintín, just north of the English cemetery. Simple rooms, each with bathroom, hot shower and bay views, cost US$25/30 single/double. Its restaurant offers lunch and dinner at moderate to expensive prices; all meals include soup, salad, rice and dessert. Its mailing address is Apartado Postal 111,

Bahía San Quintín, Baja California, México.

Signs on the Transpeninsular also point to the recently upgraded *Motel Molino Viejo* (no phone), on the site of the former flour mill, 4 miles (6.5 km) west of the highway and about 1¼ miles (2 km) northwest of Motel Muelle Viejo. Some of the old mill machinery still remains, while the motel has several attractive rooms, a few with kitchenettes, from about US$30 single/double, and comfortable suites from US$32. The attached restaurant has both good seafood and pleasant atmosphere, at moderate to high prices. Its US contact is ☎ (800) 479-7962 toll free or (619) 428-2779.

Hotel La Pinta San Quintín is the region's best hotel, suitable for beach lounging, clam digging and surf fishing, all of which can be done right in front of the hotel. Each room has two double beds and a shower/bath, plus balconies facing a wide, sandy beach. Rates are about US$55/60 single/double. In the USA, contact the Tijuana Baja Information Center (☎ (800) 522-1516 toll free, (619) 299-8518) for information and reservations.

Motel Cielito Lindo, south of town near Hotel La Pinta, once featured clean, large rooms with two queen-size beds each and a shower/bath for US$35 single/double, but now it's a bit rundown and the seafood at the attached restaurant is overrated for the price.

Perhaps the best choice is *Rancho Sereno* (no phone), an American-run B&B between the Transpeninsular and Bahía San Quintín; take the signed turnoff at Km 196. Reservations are essential for any of the three available rooms, on 11 wooded acres (4½ hectares), which cost from US$45 to US$55 for doubles; the king bedroom has a fireplace. The US contact is Marcía Beltrán, (☎ (909) 982-7087) 1442 Hildita Ct, Upland, California 91786.

Places to Eat
Tacos La Pasadita, a popular stand at the northeastern corner of the plaza, on the

west side of the Transpeninsular, has exceptional fish tacos.

Besides the hotels and motels listed above, *El Alteño* is a well-known establishment with moderate to high prices for specialties like shrimp, abalone and a fish combination plate. The restaurant at *Hotel Romo* has been recommended for breakfast, along with the *Misión Santa Isabel*. *Bar San Quintín*, the best source of tourist information, has good breakfasts but the service moves at a glacial pace. *Tuco's* offers pizza.

Getting There & Away
The bus terminal is in Lázaro Cárdenas, on the west side of the Transpeninsular, ½ mile (1 km) south of the plaza. Autotransportes de Baja California has a somewhat erratic schedule but runs direct buses from San Quintín to the following locations:

El Rosario
   (1 hour, US$2.50) at least three times daily
Ensenada
   (2 hours, US$8) hourly from 6 am to 7 pm
Tijuana
   (3½ hours, US$14) hourly from 6 am to 7 pm
Mexicali
   (6 hours, US$20) at least twice daily
Guerrero Negro
   (6 hours, US$15) at least twice daily
San Ignacio
   (7½ hours, US$20) at least twice daily
Santa Rosalía
   (9 hours, US$22) at least twice daily
Mulegé
   (10 hours, US$26) at least twice daily
Loreto
   (12 hours, US$32) at least twice daily
Ciudad Constitución
   (15 hours, US$38) at least twice daily
La Paz
   (18 hours, US$45) at least twice daily at 1 pm

Autotransportes Aragón has recently begun services between Tijuana, Ensenada and San Quintín. Other north- and south-bound buses stop here, but will not necessarily have empty seats.

Getting Around
Transportes Ejidales vans regularly shuttle between San Quintín and Camalú to the north and between San Quintín and Santa María to the south; you can flag down the vans anywhere en route. An average trip costs about US$0.50.

EL SOCORRO
El Socorro is a small colony of retired Americans nestled near an arroyo, 16 miles (26 km) south of San Quintín. Capitán Francisco (Pancho) Aguilar, one of few Mexicans here, leads fishing trips from his house next to the airstrip.

EL ROSARIO
About 36 miles (62 km) south of San Quintín, El Rosario marks the southern border of the Dominican mission frontier; known in pre-Spanish times as the Cochimí Indian ranchería of Viñadaco, it was officially founded in 1774 as Misión Nuestra Señora del Rosario Viñadaco. An abundant water supply permitted cultivation of wheat, corn and deciduous fruits, including almonds and peaches, while missionaries also directed the harvesting of lobster, abalone and clams. After relocating once when the major spring dried up, the mission closed in 1832 because epidemics had so ravaged the Cochimí population that no laborers remained for the mission fields.

After the mission closed, El Rosario was the seat of military government for northern Baja, but remained thinly populated until the late 1840s, when retired soldier Carlos Espinosa received a grant of 4000 acres (1600 hectares) from Governor José Castro. The Espinosa family is still prominent in the area.

Orientation & Information
El Rosario consists of two parts: Rosario de Arriba along the Transpeninsular, north of the Arroyo de Rosario, and Rosario de Abajo, 1½ miles (2.5 km) downstream. The few tourist services are in Rosario de Arriba, except for Rosario de Abajo's large billiard hall, which is about the only entertainment in town.

Museo

Rosario's nameless museum, on the south side of the highway, is a disorganized collection of objects of little antiquity and even less interest. If it's not open and you really want to see it, ask for the key at Espinosa's restaurant (see below).

Misión Nuestra Señora del Rosario

Only limited remains of the two missions are still standing. The initial mission site is at the end of a short dirt road above the highway, about 150 yards (135 meters) west of Motel Sinai, but only the outlines of the foundations are still visible. At Rosario de Abajo, across the Río del Rosario, several standing walls make up the ruins of the later mission.

Places to Stay & Eat

Next to the Pemex station at the north end of town, *Motel Rosario* is a low building with a satellite dish in front. Rooms with double beds, costing about US$17/20, are clean to the point of sterility. At Km 56.5 at the east end of town, the newer *Motel Sinai* has singles/doubles for US$22, as well as an RV park that charges US$10 for full-size RVs and US$5 for smaller vehicles. Electricity and water are available, and campers may use the shower in the motel office, but only a rustic pit toilet is available. There is a convenient new laundromat next door.

With the completion of the Transpeninsular in late 1973, *Casa Espinosa* became a favorite stop for a variety of travelers; in the early days of Baja road races, celebrities like Steve McQueen, James Garner and Parnelli Jones sampled Doña Anita Espinosa's lobster burritos here. Elderly Doña Anita no longer actively participates in its daily operations, and the restaurant is less consistent than it once was.

Yiyo's, at the east end of town beyond Motel Sinai, has palatable breakfasts. *El Pueblo Viejo* serves lobster dishes, while *El Grullense*, at the bus terminal, serves basic cheap antojitos. Near the local market, a taco stand offers excellent carnitas; the market itself has a variety of canned goods and produce.

AROUND EL ROSARIO
Punta Baja

At the end of a good but sometimes rough road leading west 10½ miles (16 km) from El Rosario, the fish camp of Punta Baja also attracts surfers and sea kayakers to a good right point break in the winter months, but no services are available.

From the hill overlooking the camp, arriving tourists and local goatherds can see the five volcanoes of the San Quintín area to the north, as well as the camp's satellite dish and school basketball courts.

Punta San Carlos

Some 46 miles (74 km) south of El Rosario by a series of decent graded and not-so-decent dirt roads, Punta San Carlos is one of the best windsurfing spots on the Pacific side of the peninsula.

Mexicali & the Northern Gulf

At the foot of the Sierra de Juárez and the Sierra de San Pedro Mártir, the lowlands of the Río Colorado delta and the region south to the Gulf port of San Felipe are, at least in summer, a roaring furnace where temperatures often exceed 110°F (45°C). Initially slow to be settled by Europeans, the agricultural Valle de Mexicali area grew rapidly in the 20th century as irrigation made it possible for farmers to take advantage of a long and productive growing season.

San Felipe's beaches and sport fishing draw more tourists than any other attraction in the entire region, but the eastern canyons of the sierras attract increasing numbers of campers and hikers. South of San Felipe, the village of Puertecitos is the starting point for a rugged but rewarding, alternative southbound connection to the Transpeninsular for motorists, motorcyclists and even bicyclists.

MEXICALI

Bustling Mexicali (population about 800,000) is the capital of the state of Baja California and also the northwestern terminus of Mexico's passenger rail system. Its prosperity as a regional agricultural and industrial center depends on irrigation water which enables farmers to grow wheat and cotton in the surrounding countryside's silt-laden soil.

Of all Mexico's northern border cities, Mexicali most impressively dwarfs its US counterpart, with a population at least 10 times that of neighboring Calexico and the Imperial Valley; while seven million foreigners crossed the border here in 1990, over 21 million Mexicans did. Many visitors from the north pass through Mexicali on their way south to San Felipe or east to Sonora and mainland Mexico, but only a handful stop for more than gasoline, cheap liquor, brief shopping sprees or visits to tawdry bars.

However, Mexicali, like Tijuana, is shedding its stereotypical border-town image; in the southern part of the city, the new Centro Cívico-Comercial (Civic & Commercial Center) includes local, state and federal government offices, a medical school, a bull ring, cinemas, a bus station, hospitals and restaurants. Unlike San Felipe or Cabo San Lucas, the city is made all the more interesting by its reluctance to pander to tourists.

History

In pre-Columbian times, relatively dense populations of sedentary Yuman farmers inhabited the Río Colorado delta, an area that the early Spanish failed to colonize because of its remoteness, hostile climate and determined peoples who resented missionary intrusions. Conditions changed in the early 20th century, when entrepreneurs from north of the border realized the agricultural potential of the deep river-borne sediments, if only they could be irrigated.

Events north of the border both contributed to and detracted from Mexicali's development. Since the mid-19th century, ambitious speculators and their engineers had sought to convey water from the Colorado to the Imperial Valley in California, but the sprawling Algodones Dunes were an insuperable obstacle with the available technology. Charles Rockwood's California Development Company circumvented this problem by diverting water from the Colorado's main channel into its westward-flowing Alamo channel, south of the border, and hence to the Imperial Valley. In return for permission to cross Mexican territory, Rockwood promised Mexico half the diverted water.

With completion of the Alamo Canal in 1902, the site known as Laguna del Alamo began to prosper and, the following year, was formally founded as the city of Mexicali. In succeeding years, however, flood waters silted up the canal's Hanlon Headgate and several bypasses near Andrade in mainland California, so that the company excavated a newer, more direct channel between the river and the canal without building a headgate that could accommodate the major floods of 1905. These floods poured water into the dry channel of the Río Nuevo for months, obliterating parts of the fledgling settlement of Mexicali as it swept north into mainland California's Salton Sink – which soon became the Salton Sea. Not until early 1907 did massive efforts by the Southern Pacific Railroad, which acquired the California Development Company shortly after the 1905 fiasco, succeed in returning the Colorado to its main channel.

After this reprieve Mexicali rebounded, only to falter and then benefit from the Revolution of 1910; when it was briefly occupied by anarchist Magonistas, the Mexican government grew alarmed at the Magonistas' internationalist membership and at agricultural developments north of the border – especially since Mexico had lost so much territory by the Treaty of Guadalupe Hidalgo in 1849. In 1915, these concerns led Colonel Estéban Cantú, a military political appointee, to relocate the territorial capital from Ensenada, though he governed more or less independently of either the revolutionaries or the established government. In 1952, Mexicali became capital of the new state of Baja California.

In Mexicali's early decades, nearly all the land was under control of the Colorado River Land Company, a US concern that engaged in large-scale cotton cultivation with imported Chinese laborers, who were later replaced by Mexicans from the mainland states. In the 1920s, US Prohibition fostered drinking, gambling and prostitution south of the border.

In 1937, after the famous 'Asalto a las Tierras' (Assault on the Lands) by laborers in the Mexicali valley, the government of President Lázaro Cárdenas forced the Colorado River Land Company to sell most of its land to Mexican farmers and ejidos. Around the same time, however, the Colorado River Compact among the US states in the great river's watershed led to the construction of the All-American Canal, north of the border, which bypassed Mexico and reduced the amount of water available to Mexican growers.

The Company's imprint on the cityscape is still apparent – its historic headquarters is now an office building, while the open spaces along the railway line, though now giving way to shopping malls, are a reminder of the numerous cotton mills that employed many city residents.

In 1947, the Ferrocarril Sonora-Baja California linked Mexicali to mainland Mexico via the rail junction of Benjamín Hill, Sonora; highways, airlines and telecommunications followed in short order. The city enjoys excellent cultural and educational facilities, thanks largely to institutions of higher education like the Universidad Autónoma de Baja California, the Universidad Pedagógica Nacional, the Instituto Tecnológico Regional and the Centro de Enseñanza Técnica y Superior.

Orientation

On the east bank of the intermittent Río Nuevo, most of Mexicali's main streets run east-west, paralleling the border. From Mexican customs and immigration, Avenida Francisco Madero begins soon on your left and heads past Parque Niños Héroes de Chapultepec, running through Mexicali's central business district of modest restaurants and shops, bars and bottom-end hotels.

The other streets that run parallel to Avenida Madero are also key shopping areas; better hotels and restaurants begin to appear a few blocks east of the border crossing. The largely residential area west of the Río Nuevo is known as Pueblo Nuevo.

Unfortunately, much of Mexicali is no longer pedestrian-friendly because local, state and federal authorities have consciously shifted government services to the new Centro Cívico and encouraged commercial development away from the border zone. From the border, the broad diagonal Calzada López Mateos heads southeast through Mexicali's relatively new industrial

Rails Across the Border

There is no better metaphor for the artificiality of the US-Mexico border than the rail lines which once ran from Tucson to San Diego, in part through Mexican territory. The San Diego & Arizona Eastern Railway, a subsidiary of the powerful Southern Pacific, consisted of several quasi-independent lines which crossed and re-crossed the border en route from the desert to the ocean.

At one time, San Diego expected to be the terminus of a trans-continental railway, but SP's decision to make Los Angeles the end of its Sunset Route passenger line from New Orleans left the border city with only limited service via a spur of the Atchison, Topeka & Santa Fe. Shortly after the turn of the century, however, SP had built a spur from Niland, California, on its transcontinental route, south into the Imperial Valley, crossing the border at Mexicali, then heading east to Algodones before re-entering the USA and then re-joining the Sunset Route near Yuma, Arizona. By passing through Mexican territory, it avoided the physical obstacle of the Algodones Dunes, which also impeded early irrigation projects on the US side of the Colorado River.

This Inter-California Railway line was the first link in the border chain. About the same time, SP planned a similar line from San Diego to El Centro on the Inter-California line, but company intrigues and disagreements with outside partners delayed its completion until 1919. The line actually began in Lakeside, a northeastern suburb of San Diego, linked up just south of Chula Vista with a spur from Coronado, and entered Mexico at Tijuana. From Tijuana to Tecate, it was known as the Ferrocarril Tijuana-Tecate (Tijuana & Tecate Railway).

At Tecate, the line re-entered the USA as the San Diego & Arizona line before descending the rugged eastern scarp of the Jacumba Mountains, including the difficult Carrizo Gorge, via a series of switchbacks and tunnels. At El Centro, it joined the Inter-California line, re-crossed the border at Mexicali and re-entered the USA just beyond Algodones.

The San Diego & Arizona line operated as such until 1970, carrying freight in its latter years, when SP sold the Tijuana & Tecate segment to the Mexican government's Ferrocarril Sonora-Baja California. A few years later, in 1976, Hurricane Kathleen demolished several trestles on the route, ending operations between San Diego and El Centro. SP's former Inter-California line continued to link Niland with Calexico, Mexicali and the Sonora-Baja California line, but the segment between Mexicali and Algodones, acquired by Mexico in 1964, soon ceased operations.

Recent years, though, have seen a resurrection of service, with promise or speculation of more to come. San Diego Metropolitan Transit's popular trolley covers the old SD&AE route from El Cajón to the border. The city of Calexico has recently approved a measure to build a new train station, which may lead to passenger service on the old Inter-California to El Centro, Niland and Los Angeles. An eastbound tourist service on the scenic portion of the SD&AE route from the mainland California town of Campo is unlikely because of the prohibitive expense of restoring bridges and tunnels.

More likely is the resurrection of the segment from San Diego and Tijuana to Tecate and back across the border to Campo in eastern San Diego County. A tourist service is a possibility, though the line is in considerable disrepair east of Tijuana, but the real impetus behind the project is the massive, controversial landfill at the Campo Indian Reservation. Should San Diego decide to dump its trash at Campo, the Tijuana & Tecate line could once again flourish, though the Mexican government has serious reservations about hauling US waste through its territory. Still, the remaining track on this historic line is a continuing symbol of the interdependence of the two Californias. ■

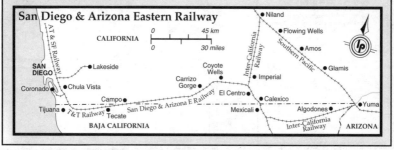

(SEE CENTRAL MEXICALI MAP)

Calexico

CALIFORNIA (USA)

Calle México
Calle Bravo
Calle del Comercio
Calle Morelos
Calle A
Calle B
Calle C
Calle D
Calle E
Calle Ulises Irigoyen (F)
Calle G
Calle H
Calle I
Calle J
Calle K
Calle L

Avenida Sebastián Lardo de Tejada
Avenida Ignacio Zaragoza
Avenida Mariano Arista
Avenida José Larroque

Avenida Baja California

Río Nuevo

Calle Valparaíso

Calle San Marcos

Calle Victoria

Calle Camelias

Calle Ciudad

BAJA CALIFORNIA

Compresora

Avenida Tapiceros

Cemetery

Calzada Independencia

9
10
Calle de la Industria
13
14
15   16
21
23
22   24
25

Avenida de la Patria

Zona Rosa

Calzada López Mateos

Calle Francisco Sarabia

Calzada

Calzada López Mateos

To Tijuana and Tecate

Blvd Lázaro Cárdenas

Calzada Anáhuac

Río Nuevo

To México 2

PLACES TO STAY
5   La Siesta Inn
7   Hotel Calafia
9   Holiday Inn Crowne Plaza
10 Motel Azteca de Oro
14 Hotel Colonial
15 Motel Las Fuentes
19 Holiday Inn Mexicali
26 Hotel Lucerna

PLACES TO EAT
3   La Placita
6   Mariscos Veracruz
17 El Dragón
21 Los Arcos
28 Sakura
29 La Misión Dragón

OTHER
1   Museo Regional de la Universidad Autónoma
2   Central Rent de Mexicali (Car Rental)
4   Estado de Be'isbol 'Nido de las Aguilas' (baseball stadium)
8   Galería de la Mora (Los Pinos mall)
11 Monumento Benito Juárez
12 El Armario (Plaza Azteca mall)
13 Hospital Civil
16 Ferrocarril Sonora-Baja California (train station)
18 Dollar Rent-A-Car
20 National Rent-A-Car
22 Centro Cívico-Comercial
23 Plaza de Toros Calafia
24 SECTUR (tourist office)
25 Central de Autobuses
27 Librería Universitaria
30 Monumento Lázaro Cárdenas

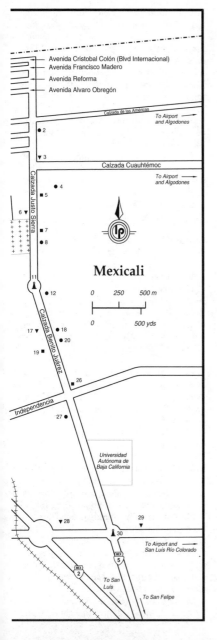

Avenida Cristobal Colón (Blvd Internacional)
Avenida Francisco Madero
Avenida Reforma
Avenida Alvaro Obregón

Calzada de las Américas

To Airport
and Algodones

● 2

▼ 3

Calzada Cuauhtémoc

To Airport
and Algodones

● 4

■ 5

6 ▼

■ 7

● 8

Calzada Justo Sierra

11

● 12

0   250   500 m

0   500 yds

17 ▼

● 18

● 20

19 ■

Calzada Benito Juárez

■ 26

Independencia

27 ●

Universidad
Autónoma de
Baja California

▼ 28

29 ▼

30

To Airport and
San Luís Río Colorado

MEX 5

MEX 2

To San
Luís

To San Felipe

Mexicali

and commercial section, where cotton and flour mills once lined the rail route. For pedestrians this new decentralization isn't so bad when the weather is cool, but the lack of trees or any other shade is almost lethal in summer's heat. Drivers are mostly courteous, but the busy boulevards have their own momentum – even Olympic sprinters may find crossing them difficult.

The Zona Rosa, an area of posh lodgings and restaurants just beyond the Centro Cívico, is about 2¼ miles (3½ km) south-east of the border post. López Mateos continues south another 3 miles (5 km) before dividing into México 5 (to San Felipe) and México 2 (to Sonora).

Information
Border Crossings The Mexicali-Calexico border is open 24 hours. If traveling east to mainland Mexico, obtain a tourist card; if driving to the mainland, get a combined car permit and tourist card. Both can be obtained from Mexican Customs (on the left as you pass through the border). Tourist cards and car permits are no longer necessary for travel south to San Felipe, at least for trips of 72 hours or less, but beyond this area a tourist card is essential.

In 1991, over seven million foreigners entered the country at this very congested border crossing. Motorists should avoid the northbound afternoon rush hour in particular. US Customs officials at Calexico sometimes X-ray the luggage of pedestrians crossing the border, so it is wise to remove photographic film from bags and back-packs.

US and Mexican authorities intend to open a new border complex in the industrial park area east of downtown, at the junction of Avenida República Argentina and Calzada Luis Echeverría. This would relieve the heavy congestion of the present crossing, much like Mesa de Otay has done in Tijuana. Hours would probably be similar to Mesa de Otay's daily schedule of 6 am to 10 pm.

Tourist Office The Comité de Turismo y Convenciones (COTUCO, City Tourism &

Convention Bureau, ☎ 57-23-76, 57-25-61, 52-43-91) is at the corner of López Mateos and Calle Camelias, about 1¾ miles (3 km) southeast of the border post. The helpful, knowledgeable staff usually includes someone who speaks English, and their city map is very useful. Hours are 8 am to 7 pm weekdays. Its US postal address is Mexicali Tourism & Convention Bureau, PO Box 7901, Calexico, California 92231.

SECTUR, the Secretaría de Turismo del Estado (☎ 56-10-72, fax 56-12-82) is in the Plaza Baja California mall on Avenida Calafia, opposite the Plaza de Toros. It's open weekdays from 8 am to 7 pm, Saturday 9 am to 3 pm, and Sunday 9 am to 1 pm.

Calexico's Chamber of Commerce (☎ (619) 357-1166), 1100 Imperial Ave (Hwy 111), is also a good source of information; it's open weekdays 8 am to 5 pm. The US-Mexico Visitor Information Center (☎ (619) 357-4883), 747 Imperial Ave in Calexico, is really the Oscar Padilla Automobile Insurance Agency, but the staff is helpful. Hours are 6 am to 9 pm weekdays, 6 am Friday to 9 pm Saturday and 7 am to 6 pm Sunday. Look for discount coupon books for Mexicali's better restaurants.

Sullivan Publications, 2904 Robidoux Blvd, Riverside, California 92509, publishes a map of the Imperial Valley that includes a very good, though not definitive, street map of Mexicali. Imperial Valley realtors distribute this map free of charge at several locations, the most convenient of which is the lobby of the Hotel De Anza, 233 4th St in Calexico.

Money Cambios are so abundant, especially in the immediate border area, that it's hardly worth visiting banks, which offer exchange services only on weekdays, 9 am to 1:30 pm. Downtown banks include Bancomer at Calle Azueta and Avenida Madero, and Banca Serfin directly across the street, but there are many others throughout the city. Several banks in both Mexicali and Calexico have 24-hour ATMs.

If passing through Calexico, you can change money and buy auto insurance along Imperial Ave, which leads straight to the border. Cambios in Calexico usually offer slightly better rates than their Mexicali competitors. There are also several money changers just across the border in Mexicali, none of which charges a commission.

Post & Telecommunications Mexicali's central post office is on Avenida Madero, at the corner of Calle Morelos.

Telephone cabinas are common in pharmacies and similar businesses, but public telephones are numerous, and most of them work, surprisingly enough. Local numbers now have six digits and begin with either a five or a six. Mexicali's area code is 65.

Cultural Centers The Instituto de Cultura de Baja California (☎ 54-64-18) presents film series at the Teatro del Estado's Café Literario, on Calzada López Mateos.

The main campus of the Universidad Autónoma de Baja California, on Calzada Benito Juárez just south of Avenida Independencia, has a theater which hosts numerous cultural events, including live drama and lectures.

Travel Agencies Mexicali has many downtown travel agencies, among them Aerolímpico Tours (☎ 52-50-25) at Avenida Madero 641, Támez Tours (☎ 54-24-68) at Reforma 907, and Ana Sol Tours (☎ 53-47-87) at Madero 1324-A near the university.

Bookshops Librería Universitaria, across from the Universidad Autónoma on Calzada Benito Juárez just south of Avenida Independencia, has a good selection of books mostly in Spanish on Mexican history, archaeology, anthropology and literature. It also carries the excellent Guías Urbanas series of city maps, which includes Mexicali, Tijuana, Tecate, Ensenada, San Felipe and La Paz, as well as others of mainland Mexico.

Closer to the border, on Avenida Madero between Calle Altamirano and Calle

Morelos, Librería Madero has a smaller but still respectable selection of books on similar subjects.

Medical Services The Hospital Civil (☎ 57-37-00) is at the corner of Calle del Hospital and Avenida Libertad, near the Centro Cívico. In the grid of streets near the border are many clinics, laboratories and hospitals, such as the Hospital México-Americano at Avenida Reforma 1000, corner of Calle B.

The area along Avenida Reforma and parallel streets, east of the border, includes many hospitals, clinics, laboratories, pharmacies and dental clinics catering to visitors from north of the border. Dentists trained at the Mexicali campus of the Universidad Autónoma offer quality work at a fraction of the cost north of the border.

Emergencies For the Cruz Roja, dial ☎ 132. The main police station (☎ 134) is on Calle Sur, just south of Calzada López Mateos.

La Chinesca
Mexicali's Chinatown, the largest in the country, is concentrated along an axis formed by Avenida Juárez and Calle Altamirano, south of Calzada López Mateos.

Galería de la Ciudad
At this private gallery (☎ 53-50-44, X23) at Calle Obregón 1209, just east of Calle D (Salazar), local artists display their paintings, sculptures and photographs, which are for sale at reasonable prices. It's open weekdays 9 am to 8 pm, Saturdays 9 am to 1 pm.

Historic Buildings
The **Catedral de la Virgen de Guadalupe**, at the corner of Avenida Reforma and Calle Morelos, is Mexicali's major religious landmark.

Now housing the rectory of the Universidad Autónoma, the grounds of the former **Palacio de Gobierno** (Government Palace, built between 1919 and 1922) interrupt Avenida Obregón just east of Calle E.

Just north of this imposing building, at the intersection of Avenida Reforma and Calle F, the former headquarters of the **Colorado River Land Company** is now used for offices, but its attractive patio fountain and restored balcony murals merit a visit. It dates from 1924.

At the corner of Avenida Zaragoza and Calle E, two blocks southwest of the rectory, the former **Cervecería Mexicali** (brewery) sits vacant but in a good state of preservation despite fire damage in 1986. Opened in 1923 under a German master brewer, for half a century it satisfied local demand and even managed to export some of its inventory.

City Monuments
Mexicali's monuments, which appear on its *glorietas* (traffic circles), are dedicated to past presidents, peasants, the fishermen of San Felipe and various other luminaries. Some notable figures honored in stone and steel are Benito Juárez (on Calzada Justo Sierra), Lázaro Cárdenas (at the intersection of Blvd Lázaro Cárdenas and Calzada Benito Juárez), Vicente Guerrero (on Calzada López Mateos) and Rodolof Sánchez Taboada (also on Calzada López Mateos).

Centro Cívico-Comercial
The highlight of Mexicali's modern civic center, located along Avenida Independencia just north of the Zona Rosa, is the state government's **Poder Ejecutivo** (Governor's Office), **Cámara de Diputados** (Legislature) and **Poder Judicial** (Supreme Court). The plaque on the monument between them describes Mexicali as 'La Ciudad Cuyo Cielo Capturó Al Sol' (the city whose sky captured the sun).

Museo Regional de la Universidad Autónoma de Baja California
This modest eight-room museum (☎ 2-57-15), at the corner of Avenida Reforma and Calle L, is also called El Museo Hombre, Naturaleza y Cultura (Museum of Man, Nature & Culture). Exhibits cover topics like geology, paleontology, human evolution, colonial history and photography. It's

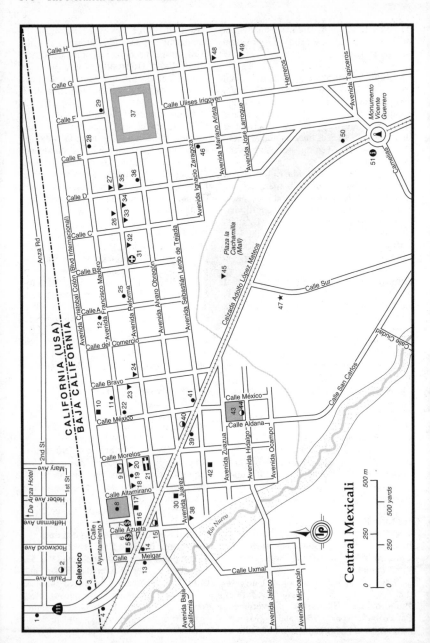

Central Mexicali

■ PLACES TO STAY	49	El Rincón del Sabor	28	Ana Sol Tours
			29	Ex-Colorado River Land
5 Hotel del Norte		OTHER		Company
10 Hotel Casa Grande			31	Hospital
16 Hotel Imperial	1	Golden State Lines		Mexico-Americano
17 Hotel Plaza		(Church's Fried Chicken,	36	Galería de la Ciudad
30 Hotel Nuevo Pacífico		Calexico)	37	Rectory of the Universidad
42 Hotel México	2	Greyhound (Calexico)		Autónoma (ex-Palacio de
	3	US Customs, Calexico		Gobierno)
▼ PLACES TO EAT	4	Mexican Customs,	39	Los Cristales
		Mexicali	40	Tebacsa (Buses to San
5 Restaurant del Norte	6	Bancomer		Felipe, San Luis Río
18 Petunia No 2	7	Banca Serfin		Colorado)
20 La Fábula Pizza	8	Parque Niños Héroes de	41	Central Rent de Mexicali
23 El Sarape		Chapultepec		(Car Rental)
24 China Town	9	Post Office	43	Plaza del Mariachi
26 Del Mar	11	Aerolímpico Tours		(Parque Constitución)
27 La Villa del Seri	12	Mexicana	44	Buses to Algodones
32 Mandolino	13	LF Caliente Foreign Book	46	Ex-Cervecería Mexicali
33 Rinconcito Gaucho	14	Transportes Golden State		(brewery)
34 La Fábula Pizza	15	City bus terminal	47	Police
35 La Parroquia/LF Caliente	19	Librería Madero	50	Teatro del Estado (state
Sports Book	21	Catedral de la Virgen de		theatre)
38 Alley 19		Guadalupe	51	COTUCO (tourist office)
45 Los Buffalos; Mar y Mar	22	Berlin 77		
48 Cenaduría Selecta	25	Támez Tours		

open 9 am to 6 pm Tuesday to Friday, 10 am to 4 pm Saturday.

Teatro del Estado

The state theater (☎ 52-92-29, 54-07-57) is an ultramodern building, seating 1100 spectators and equipped with the 'latest acoustical technology'. A variety of theatrical and musical performances, like the La Tropicana dance troupe of Cuba, appear throughout the year; the Casa de Cultura de Baja California also presents retrospective film series in the Café Literario. The theater is on the east side of Calzada López Mateos, just north of Avenida Tapiceros, opposite the COTUCO tourist office.

Plaza de Toros Calafia

On alternate Sundays from October to May, bullfights take place in the Plaza de Toros (☎ 57-06-81) at the corner of Avenida Calafia and Calzada Independencia, next to the Centro Cívico-Comercial. Tickets are available at the gate for US$6 to US$19.

LF Caliente Foreign Book

At Calle Melgar 166, less than a block from the border, Caliente Foreign Book (☎ 2-60-50) accepts bets for almost every major horse and greyhound racetrack, as well as other sporting events, in the USA. A second location is inside the restaurant La Parroquia, at the corner of Avenida Reforma and Calle D, opposite the Villa del Seri restaurant.

Festivals & Events

Mexicali hosts a number of annual festivals and events, most of which are less gringo-oriented than those in other parts of the peninsula. For detailed information on these and other festivals, contact the Comité Ferias y Exposiciones (Fairs & Expositions Committee, ☎ 54-55-81, 54-55-63).

6 September
   Biatlón de Mexicali (Biathlon of Mexicali)
17 October
   Triatlón de Baja (Baja Triathlon)

Mid-October to early November
   Fiesta del Sol (Festival of Sun) – Commemorating the city's founding in 1903, Fiesta del Sol events include pop music concerts, cockfights, art exhibits, theatrical performances and parades. A crafts exposition, local industrial products and agriculture are also featured.
November
   Baja 1000 – In 1993, the legendary Baja 1000 off-road race relocated from Ensenada to a course south of Mexicali.
November
   Feria de Muestra Gastronómica (Gastronomic Fair) – a cooking competition between Mexicali chefs

Places to Stay – bottom end

In and around the Chinesca are several places like *Hotel Nuevo Pacífico*, Avenida Juárez 95 near the corner of Calle Altamirano, which offer cheap but noisy accommodation in a questionable setting, from about US$8 double. Central Mexicali's best bargain may be the family-oriented *Hotel México* (☎ 54-06-09), Avenida Lerdo de Tejada 476 between Altamirano and Calle Morelos, with some rooms costing as little as US$10 single, though those with amenities like air-conditioning, TV, private bath and parking are a bit dearer. *Hotel Plaza* (☎ 52-97-57), Madero 366, charges US$17/20 single/double, a reasonable price for a respectable downtown hotel.

Closer to the border, *Hotel Imperial* (☎ 53-61-16), Avenida Madero 222 (with an additional entrance on López Mateos), is fairly clean, but the plaster is chipping and the bedspreads are worn; for US$24/31, there are much better values. Near the railroad station, the one-star, 37-room *Motel Las Fuentes* (☎ 57-15-25), Calzada López Mateos 1655, has single/doubles with TV for US$19/27 weekdays, US$23/31 weekends.

Motel Azteca de Oro (☎ 57-14-33), at Calle de la Industria 600 across from the railroad station, falls short of its advertised 'elegancia', but each room has telephone, TV and air-conditioning for about US$23 single or double.

Places to Stay – middle

La Siesta Inn (☎ 68-20-01), Calzada Justo Sierra 899, has carpeted singles/doubles from about US$25/29, but better rooms cost only a few dollars more. There's a coffee shop next to the lobby. *Hotel Casa Grande* (☎ 53-66-51), formerly Hotel Fortín de las Flores, faces the border fence from its location at Avenida Cristóbal Colón 612. Greatly improved in recent years, it now has air-conditioning, TV and a swimming pool for US$33/40 singles/doubles.

The landmark *Hotel del Norte* (☎ 52-81-01), very central at Calle Melgar 205 (corner of Avenida Francisco Madero), has 52 rooms, some with color TV and air-conditioning. Its downstairs restaurant serves moderately priced Mexican dishes, lunch and dinner specials, and huge margaritas. Conveniently located near the border crossing, it charges US$39/42 for singles/doubles, with breakfast included.

Ordinary accommodation is better and no more expensive in Calexico, just across the border. Most motels on East 4th St are in the US$20 to US$30 per night range. The *De Anza Hotel* (☎ (619) 357-1112), 233 Fourth St, is a noteworthy Spanish-style building with terracotta floors, a wrought-iron staircase and colorful tiled walls. It opened in 1931 to cater to wealthy Americans who crossed the border to drink and gamble during Prohibition. Some of its amenities show early signs of deterioration, but it's still good value at the discount rate of US$29.50 singles/doubles (with AAA membership card). Their coffee shop reputedly serves the best food in Calexico, especially during the lunch buffet, and the restaurant is a popular dinner choice.

Places to Stay – top end

The newest place in town is highly regarded *Hotel Colonial* (☎ 56-53-12, fax 56-11-41), López Mateos 1048, for US$60 double.

The 173-room *Hotel Calafia* (☎ 68-33-11 in Mexicali; ☎ (619) 452-2639, (800) 262-2656 toll free in the USA) is at Calzada Justo Sierra 1495, about 1½ miles

(2½ km) southeast of central Mexicali. Rooms are simple, comfortable and air-conditioned, most have color TV, and secure parking is available. Singles/doubles are about US$61 per night. Its US mailing address is PO Box 85458, San Diego, California 92138.

Hotel Lucerna (☎ 66-10-00, fax 66-47-06), about 3 miles (5 km) from downtown at Calzada Benito Juárez 2151, is known among Mexicali's yuppies and business community for its discos and nightclubs. In an idyllic setting of fountains and pseudo-colonial courtyards, its 192 rooms have color TV and air-conditioning; those overlooking the pool usually have balconies. Rates for singles/doubles are US$67/70. Its US postal address is PO Box 2300, Calexico, California 92231.

The *Holiday Inn Mexicali* (☎ 66-13-00, (800) 238-8000 toll free in the USA) is 2 miles (3½ km) southeast of central Mexicali at Calzada Benito Juárez 2220. It has all the usual Holiday Inn amenities for about US$73/80 singles/doubles. Its sister, the *Holiday Inn Crowne Plaza* (☎ 57-36-00, fax 57-05-55) at the junction of López Mateos and Los Héroes, is the most expensive in town at US$103 single or double.

Places to Eat

Mexicali has an outstanding variety of quality restaurants in a number of districts throughout the city. Buses are available from the city center.

Mexican Family-run *Cenaduría Selecta* (☎ 52-40-47), a Mexicali institution at the corner of Avenida Arista 1510 and Calle G, traditionally specializes in antojitos like beef tacos and burritos. However, recent improvements have driven prices up, so that it's no longer cheap. It's open 8 am to 11 pm. *El Rincón del Sabor* (☎ 54-08-88), nearby at Avenida Larroque 1500 and Calle G, is another good choice for Mexican food.

Part of Hotel del Norte (see Places to Stay, above), *Restaurant del Norte* is a US-style coffee shop that offers large, inexpensive but rather ordinary specials for breakfast, lunch and dinner. Another good and very inexpensive breakfast place is *Petunia 2*, on Avenida Madero between Calle Altamirano and Calle Morelos. *Rinconcito Gaucho*, a taquería on Avenida Reforma between Calle C and Calle D, is what remains of a much larger Argentine restaurant that formerly graced the site.

La Placita (☎ 68-10-51), Calzada Justo Sierra 377 at the corner of Honduras offers Mexican and international dishes in a pleasant atmosphere at moderate prices (especially with discount coupons). *Las Campanas de la Placita*, under the same management and almost next door on Justo Sierra, is very comparable.

El Sarape (☎ 54-22-87), Calle Bravo 140 between Madero and Reforma, is a popular, even raucous spot with live music; the food is good, but it's not the place for a quiet, romantic dinner.

La Villa del Seri (☎ 53-55-03), at the corner of Avenida Reforma and Calle D, specializes in Sonoran beef, but also has excellent seafood and antojitos. Prices are on the high side, but portions are large, so it's a good value. Across the street is *La Parroquia* (☎ 54-23-13), Reforma 1200, which doubles as a sports book. *Los Buffalos* (☎ 66-31-16), in the Plaza La Cachanilla mall on López Mateos, also specializes in beef and seafood.

Chinese Mexicali's 150-plus Chinese restaurants still offer the opportunity to dine well and relatively cheaply – less than US$10 for two in some cases. Opened in 1928, *Alley 19*, at Avenida Benito Juárez 8 in the Chinesca, near the corner of Calle Azueta, is Mexicali's oldest continuously operating Chinese restaurant; it's well worth a visit for budget travelers. Another downtown choice is *China Town* at Reforma 701, corner of Calle Bravo.

The pricier but highly regarded *El Dragón* (☎ 66-20-20) occupies a huge pagoda at Calzada Benito Juárez 1830; it's open from 11 am to 11:30 pm. The same proprietors operate *La Misión Dragón* (☎ 66-44-00), a quarter mile east of Calzada Benito Juárez at Blvd Lázaro Cárdenas 555, the decor of which includes beautiful gardens, fountains and pools; this scenic location is also known for its appealing food.

Italian Like every other Italian restaurant in Mexico, *Mandolino* (☎ 52-95-44), Avenida Reforma 1070 between Calle B and Calle C, features the obligatory *Godfather* photograph of Marlon Brando, but its food is excellent and the ambience is otherwise congenial. *La Fábula*, a pizza chain, has several Mexicali branches, the largest of which is at Reforma 1150, between Calle C and Calle D. Closer to the border is the branch at the corner of Avenida Madero and Calle Morelos.

Japanese *Sakura* (☎ 66-48-48), Blvd Lázaro Cárdenas 200 at the corner of López Mateos, serves sushi and other Japanese dishes.

Seafood Perhaps the most popular seafood restaurant in Mexicali is *Los Arcos* (☎ 56-09-03), Avenida Calafia 454 near the Plaza de Toros in the Centro Cívico-Comercial. *Mariscos Veracruz* (☎ 54-46-90) is at Carroceros Sur 2014, near Calzada Justo Sierra.

Another possibility is *Mar y Mar* (☎ 52-67-62), in the Plaza La Cachanilla mall. *Del Mar*, Reforma 1151, is down the block from Rinconcito Gaucho.

Entertainment
Baseball Mexicali's professional baseball team, Las Aguilas (the Eagles) plays in the Liga Mexicana del Pacífico, which begins its official season in October, shortly after the World Series in North America; the regular season ends in early January, when a series of play-offs determines the league's representative to the Caribbean Series, which takes place in Venezuela.

Mexicali's stadium, nicknamed 'El Nido de las Aguilas' (Eagles' Nest), is on Calzada Cuauhtémoc (also known as Avenida Cuauhtémoc), about 3 miles (5 km) east of the border post. During the week, games begin under the lights at 7

pm; on Sunday starting time is 1 pm in the sunshine. Ticket prices range from US$1 (in the remote bleachers) to US$6 (front row, behind home plate).

Most US players stay at Calexico's De Anza Hotel, which can be a good place for serious fans to meet them and talk baseball during the doldrums between the end of the World Series and the start of spring training.

Cinemas Mexicali has two major cinema complexes that show first-run films: the Multicinemas (☎ 57-19-85) in the Centro Cívico and the Cinemas Gemelos (☎ 66-07-48) in the Centro Comercial Gigante.

Nightclubs *Guaycura*, open 8 pm to 2 am at the Holiday Inn Mexicali on Calzada Benito Juárez, has a dance floor, live music and various floor shows. *La Capilla* at Hotel Lucerna, Calzada Benito Juárez 2151, is a music and dance club that is especially popular with local university students; hours are 8 pm to 2 am. *Los Cristales*, Calzada López Mateos 570, is renowned for performances by nationally known musicians; hours are 6 pm to 3 am. Another possibility is *Rock en Español*, Madero 360.

Calle México, north of López Mateos, has many of Mexicali's remaining seedy strip joints; the rest are mostly scattered throughout the Chinesca. *Berlin 77* (☎ 2-53-33), at the corner of Calle México and Avenida Francisco Madero, is a step above most of these. It's open from 11 am to 3 am.

Things to Buy
Curio shops selling cheap leather goods and kitschy souvenirs are concentrated on Calle Melgar and Avenida Reforma, within easy walking distance of the border. For a more sophisticated selection, try El Armario, Calzada Justo Sierra 1700 Suite 1-A, in the Plaza Azteca shopping center, or Galería de la Mora, Calzada Justo Sierra 1515-2, in the Centro Comercial Los Pinos.

Mexican beer and hard liquors are cheaper than in the USA, but remember that US Customs regulations allow each adult to bring only one liter of liquor into the USA if arriving on foot or by car. Travelers on common carriers, like buses or taxis, can carry any amount as long as it's for personal use, but duty is payable on anything above one liter.

Pharmaceuticals and medical services, including dentistry and optometry, are much cheaper on the Mexican side of the border. Many clinics and hospitals are located in the streets that parallel the US border, including Avenida Reforma and Avenida Obregón.

Getting There & Away

Air Aeropuerto Internacional General Rodolfo Sánchez Taboada (☎ 53-67-42) is about 7 miles (12 km) east of town via BCN 8. Mexicana (☎ 53-54-01, 52-93-91 at the airport), Avenida Madero 832 just west of Calle A, flies daily to Acapulco and to Tapachula, on the border with Guatemala. Aero California (☎ 56-04-56, 53-49-00 at the airport), in the Centro Cívico-Comercial at Avenida Calafia 672, flies daily to Aguascalientes, Puebla, Guadalajara and Mexico City.

AirLA (☎ (800) 010-0413 in Mexico, (800) 933-5952 in the USA, both toll free) provides international service to Los Angeles, weekdays at 9:15 am and 5:45 pm, Sunday at 1:20 pm. Round-trip fares are US$138.

Bus Major inter-city bus companies have offices at the Central de Autobuses (bus depot) on Avenida Independencia near Calzada López Mateos. Long-distance services now commonly feature services like video and on-board meals.

The main companies and their telephone numbers are:

Autotransportes del Pacífico (☎ 57-24-61)
Autotransportes Tres Estrellas de Oro
    (☎ 57-24-10)
Autotransportes Norte de Sonora (☎ 57-24-22)
Autotransportes de la Baja California
    (☎ 57-24-40)

Typical fares to mainland Mexican destinations include Hermosillo US$23, Ciudad Obregón US$33, Culiacán US$41, Mazatlán US$57, Guadalajara US$74 and Mexico City US$93.

Tres Estrellas and ABC fares to destinations within Baja California are:

Destination	Fare
Tecate	US$5
Tijuana	US$7.50
Ensenada	US$12
San Quintín	US$19
El Rosario	US$21
Guerrero Negro	US$35
Vizcaíno	US$37
San Ignacio	US$40
Santa Rosalía	US$44
Mulegé	US$46
Loreto	US$51
Ciudad Constitución	US$57
La Paz	US$64

ABC Buses to San Felipe (about US$7) depart at 8 am, noon, and 4 and 8 pm. The daily bus to La Paz (a trip of about 24 hours) leaves at 4:30 pm. ABC offers almost hourly service to San Luis Río Colorado, on the Sonora/Arizona border, and three buses daily to Sonora's Gulfside resort of Puerto Peñasco. Tebacsa, on López Mateos between Calle Morelos and Calle México, has one bus daily to San Felipe, at 6 am, and many to San Luis Río Colorado.

Buses to Algodones, in the northeastern corner of Baja California across from Andrade, California (only 8 miles from Yuma, Arizona), leave 11 times daily from the south end of Parque Constitución (Plaza del Mariachi), on Avenida Hidalgo between Calle Aldana and Calle Morelos.

In Calexico, on the US side of the border, Greyhound (☎ (619) 357-1895) is at 121 East 1st St, directly across from the pedestrian border crossing entrance. The approximate schedules from the Los Angeles terminal (☎ (213) 629-8400) to Calexico (US$18/35 one way/return) are:

Depart	Arrive
Los Angeles	Calexico
5:30 am	1:20 pm
10:45 am	6:00 pm
1:30 pm	7:50 pm
3:40 pm	10:00 pm
7:00 pm	1:30 am

Approximate schedules from Calexico to Los Angeles are:

Depart	Arrive
Calexico	Los Angeles
midnight	6:00 am
6:15 am	1:30 pm
9:15 am	2:50 pm
noon	5:00 pm
2:20 pm	7:10 pm
5:20 pm	11:00 pm
6:45 pm	12:25 am

There are frequent daily buses between Calexico and El Centro, Indio, El Cajon, San Diego, Riverside, San Bernardino and a few other cities. Schedules and fares change monthly, so call a local Greyhound office in the USA for the latest information.

From a stop on the south side of Calzada López Mateos at the corner of Calle Melgar near the border, Transportes Golden State (☎ 53-61-59) has services to the mainland California destinations of Indio and Mecca (US$20), Palm Springs (US$22) and El Monte and Los Angeles (US$27) at 8 am, and at 2:30 and 8 pm. It also maintains offices at the Central de Autobuses and, on the Calexico side, at Church's Fried Chicken, 344 Imperial Ave.

Train The Ferrocarril Sonora-Baja California (train station, ☎ 57-23-86 or 57-21-01, X 213, 222/3; phone between 6:30 am and 1 pm daily for information and reservations) is at Calle Ulíses Irigoyen (Calle F) near López Mateos. Passenger services go from Mexicali to Mexico City via Hermosillo, Guaymas (Empalme), Sufragio/Los Mochis (the Barranca del Cobre (Copper Canyon) rail junction), Mazatlán and Guadalajara. For mail reservations, write the Jefe de Estación, Estación de Ferrocarril, Box 3-182, Mexicali, Baja California, México (or PO Box 231, Calexico, California 92231).

The 'express' train departs daily at 8:20 am and the 'local' at 8:50 pm. One-way Pullman fares all the way to Mexico City are about US$50 per person. Express-train tickets are available at the station from 5 to 8 am daily, while local-train tickets are sold from 4:30 to 8:40 pm daily. Dining facilities are available on the express train, and a snack-bar service is available on the local train.

Southbound trains No 2 and 4 stop at Empalme (10:35 pm and 2:50 pm), 6 miles (10 km) east of Guaymas, and at Sufragio (3:03 am and 8:35 pm), 30 miles (52 km) northeast of Los Mochis. The eastbound Chihuahua al Pacífico, popularly known to travelers as the Copper Canyon train, arrives at Sufragio from Los Mochis at 7:46 am (tourist-oriented 'vista' train) and 9:11 am (local 'mixto' train).

The accompanying table illustrates current fares (in US$) from Mexicali; roomette sleepers are also available for about double the Servicio Estrella price.

Km from Mexicali	Destination	2nd	1st	Servicio Estrella
250	Pto Peñasco	3.50	5.50	10
410	Caborca	5.50	9	16
534	Benjamín Hill	7	12	21
660	Hermosillo	9	14	26
801	Empalme (Guaymas)	10	17	32
919	Ciudad Obregón	12	20	36
987	Navajoa	13	22	39
1340	Culiacán	17	29	53
1559	Mazatlán	20	34	62
1875	Tepic	25	41	75
2149	Guadalajara	28	47	85

The city of Calexico, north of the border, recently approved a bond issue to build a new train station, and a passenger rail service from Los Angeles may soon follow.

Car Rental Central Rent de Mexicali has branches at Calzada López Mateos 655 (☎ 52-22-06) and at Calzada Justo Sierra 515 (☎ 68-34-44), corner of Calzada de las Américas.

Most of the standard agencies are on

Calzada Benito Juárez, including: Dollar (☎ 65-62-62) at Juárez 1000; National (☎ 68-39-63) at Juárez 1004 or at the Hotel Colonial (☎ 56-13-12) at López Mateos and Calafia; Hertz (☎ 68-19-73) at Juárez 1223; and Budget (☎ 66-48-40) at the Holiday Inn Mexicali, Juárez 2220.

Getting Around

To/From the Airport Cabs are the only alternative to the airport, and they're expensive at US$20, though they may be shared.

Bus Most city buses start from Avenida Reforma, just west of Calzada López Mateos, two blocks from the border crossing. The 'Justo Sierra' bus goes to the museum. Any 'Centro Cívico' bus goes to the tourist offices, the Plaza de Toros and the train station. The 'Central Camionera' bus goes to the Centro Cívico-Comercial and the bus station. Local bus fares are about US$0.35.

Taxi A taxi from the border to the ballpark, train station or civic center averages from about US$6 to US$7; try bargaining, but agree on the fare before accepting the ride.

AROUND MEXICALI

South of Mexicali, México 5 passes through a prosperous farming region en route to the Gulf resort of San Felipe, 120 miles (200 km) south. Most of the area between Mexicali and the border with the state of Sonora became irrigated farmland at the turn of the century thanks to Río Colorado irrigation projects and the intrigues of *Los Angeles Times* publisher Harrison Chandler, the Southern Pacific Railroad and the Colorado River Land Company. Later, in the 1930s, Mexican President Lázaro Cárdenas' land reform measures gave land to laborers and peasants through the creation of many ejidos.

Seventeen miles (29 km) south of Mexicali and 2 miles (3½ km) east of the highway, rising clouds of steam mark the **Cerro Prieto** geothermal electrical plant, whose 620-megawatt capacity makes it the largest of its kind in North America. It is not open to the public.

At Km 56, 35 miles south of Mexicali, **Cucapá El Mayor** is an Indian village whose **Museo Comunitario** has exhibits of indigenous artifacts and subsistence; outside are examples of traditional Cucapá nomadic dwellings. A small shop within sells a selection of crafts, including very attractive bead necklaces. Both museum and shop are open daily except Sunday, but the hours can be erratic, depending on the availability of clerks.

Another 23 miles (39 km) south along México 5 (around Km 79) is the edge of the vast, desolate **Laguna Salada** – 500 sq miles (1400 sq km) of salt flats when dry (as is usual). Although these flats were part of the Gulf of California four centuries ago, today it is one of Baja's most arid regions. Unusually heavy rains in the mid-1980s, however, swelled the nearby Colorado and Bravo rivers, turning the landscape into an ephemeral marsh. Southeast of the laguna is the Río Colorado delta, a 60-mile (100-km) expanse of alluvium.

A hill just east of México 5 and north of the junction with México 3 is named *Cerro El Chinero* (Chinese Hill), memorializing a group of Chinese immigrants who died of thirst in the area.

Cañón Guadalupe

About 22 miles (35 km) west of Mexicali, a graded road that is passable for passenger vehicles in dry weather leads 27 miles (44 km) south to a junction which leads another 8 miles (13 km) west to palm-studded Cañón Guadalupe, on the eastern edge of Parque Nacional Constitución de 1857 (see the Tijuana & the Northern Pacific Coast chapter). Guadalupe, which has a dependable water supply, is an excellent area for hiking or even more sedentary camping. *Guadalupe Canyon Hot Springs* (☎ (714) 673-2670 in mainland California) has comfortable facilities, including hot tubs and a restaurant, for US$10 to US$15 per night. For reservations mail inquiries to its US address: PO Box 4003, Balboa, California 92661.

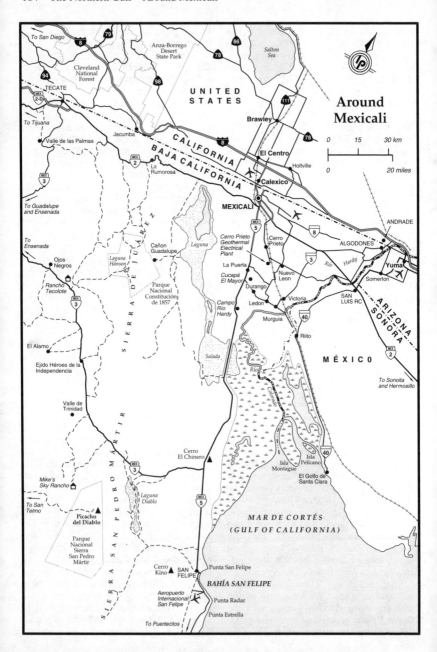

Around
Mexicali

ALGODONES

First settled by ranchers from Sonora in the mid-19th century, the border town of Algodones (estimated population 12,000), next to Andrade, California, was once a stagecoach stop on the route from Yuma, Arizona, to San Diego, in the days when the Río Colorado was navigable. Taking its name from the surrounding cotton fields, it is about 40 miles (65 km) east of Mexicali, but only about 8 miles (13 km) west of Yuma across the Río Colorado.

Nearly deserted in the brutally hot summer, Algodones bustles in winter; in 1991, over 1.4 million foreigners crossed the border here, many of them retirees from Yuma who find prescription drugs, eyeglasses and dental work much cheaper than in the US. So many 'snowbirds' frequent the town that Mexican professionals organize bus charters from Yuma for their benefit.

Besides its pharmacies, dentists and opticians, Algodones is virtually a wall-to-wall assemblage of kitschy souvenirs, but resolute shoppers may find attractive textiles from mainland Mexico. The border is open daily from 6 am to 8 pm, but Mexican authorities will only process auto permits from 8 am to 3 pm. There are many casas de cambio, but changing money is unnecessary unless you're continuing much farther into Mexico. There's a tourist information office (☎ 7-77-06) at Avenida B No 261. The telephone area code is 653.

Things to See

Just north of the border, the **Hanlon Headgate** was part of the Alamo Canal, which carried Colorado River water through Mexican territory en route to mainland California's Imperial Valley. In the wet winter of 1905, the headgate burst and the water flowed west through Mexico and then north, creating mainland California's Salton Sea and obliterating whatever benefits Mexican farmers had gained from water development. It was two years before the Southern Pacific Railroad, which acquired the stock of the California Development Company, halted the flow to the north.

Places to Stay & Eat

Misnamed *Motel Olímpico*, really· a hotel in the middle of the block opposite the Delegación Municipal, charges US$10 single or double and, perhaps as a public service, offers condoms for US$1 at the front desk. In Andrade, on the US side of the border, the Quechan Indians of Fort Yuma Reservation operate a spacious but hardly luxurious RV park/campground.

Algodones' most popular eateries are *Carlota's Bakery*, mobbed by snowbirds for breakfast, and the adjacent courtyard restaurant in the Real Plaza del Sol. The new *Restaurant Tucán*, just off the main street, has more elaborate meals at reasonable prices, with live music at lunchtime.

Getting There & Away

There is hourly public transport from Algodones to Mexicali, but none from Andrade to Yuma. California State Route 186 is now paved to Interstate 8, which leads east to Yuma.

Mexicali's Comité de Turismo y Convenciones offers full-day tours of Mexicali from Algodones, leaving at 9 am Monday through Saturday, for US$10.

SAN FELIPE

Once a tranquil fishing community on Bahía San Felipe, an inlet of the Gulf of California 120 miles (200 km) south of Mexicali, San Felipe has become 'Noise City', northern Baja's low-life retort to Cabo San Lucas. A particularly crass form of tourism has transformed it into a haven for roaring ATVs, firecrackers, property speculators and aggressive restaurateurs who almost yank potential patrons off the sidewalk. The population is about 20,000 but may seem many times that during US holidays and especially during spring break for university students from north of the border.

San Felipe does, however, lack Cabo San Lucas's insufferable pretentiousness. Local real estate speculators and time-share sellers may be less devious than those in the Cape Region, if only because their clients expect to be bamboozled into buying cactus-covered shoreline tracts whose only source of water is the briny Gulf and appear to relish it. San Felipe's US sister city is the equally undistinguished San Francisco Bay Area suburb of Hayward, California. Visit between November and April – after April, temperatures soar as high as 120°F (49°C).

History
In 1721, Jesuit missionary Juan de Ugarte landed at the port of San Felipe de Jesús, which appears in Fernando Consag's map of 1746. In 1797, Fray Felipe Neri, a Dominican priest from Misión San Pedro Mártir, established a small supply depot and settlement here, in the hope of replenishing his struggling mission, located in an isolated, mile-high valley about 45 miles (75 km) to the west. Both the depot and the mission failed in the early 1800s, in part because of water shortages. Mission ruins can still be seen but access is difficult; see the Tijuana & the Northern Pacific Coast chapter for more information.

Bahía San Felipe remained almost undeveloped until 1876, when Mexican speculator Guillermo Andrade decided to exploit a grant of approximately 75,000 acres (30,000 hectares) from the Mexican government. Andrade, who had obtained the concession almost two decades earlier, built a road to the gold mines at Real del Castillo, 120 miles (200 km) to the northwest, but his attempt to attract business from the mines was largely unsuccessful because well-established Ensenada was much closer to them.

After establishing control over Mexicali in 1915, Colonel Estéban Cantú opened a rough road south to San Felipe and even planned a railroad, but it was shrimpers from Guaymas, Loreto and Santa Rosalía who really turned San Felipe into a town. In 1925 its population was only about 100, but by 1948, when the improved highway made travel from Mexicali much easier, it reached nearly 1000.

Half a dozen fishing cooperatives operate out of San Felipe, exporting quantities of shrimp and various fish species to the USA,

Canada and elsewhere. The San Felipe fleet has 41 boats, several of which can remain at sea for as long as 40 days.

Sport fishing and warm winters have attracted hundreds of North American retirees, while large hotels and sprawling trailer parks have sprung up to accommodate the growing number of visitors. Many houses, subdivisions and condominiums are under construction. The international airport south of town now receives commercial flights from Los Angeles, Tijuana and Mexicali.

Orientation
San Felipe hugs the shoreline of its namesake bay, a curving inlet of the northern Gulf of California. North-south avenidas bear the names of seas around the world, while east-west calles bear the names of Mexican ports. Avenida Mar de Cortés is the main north-south drag, while Calzada Chetumal leads west to a junction with México 5, the highway north to Mexicali. Downtown, along the beach, is San Felipe's attractive *malecón* (waterfront promenade).

Information
Tourist Office SECTUR, the Secretaría de Turismo del Estado (☎ 7-11-55) is at the corner of Avenida Mar de Cortés and Calle Manzanillo, across from Motel El Capitán. It's open weekdays 8 am to 7 pm, Saturday 9 am to 3 pm and Sunday 10 am to 1 pm; the staff is helpful and someone there usually speaks English. The People's Gallery, on Avenida Mar de Cortés just north of Motel El Cortez, welcomes tourist inquiries as well.

Another source of information is the English-language monthly *San Felipe Newsletter*, available free around town. Although its main audience is US residents, it contains some useful travel information. The local postal address is Apartado Postal 105, San Felipe, Baja California, México; the US mailing address is PO Box 5259, Heber, California 92249.

Money Bancomer, San Felipe's only remaining bank, is on Avenida Mar de

Cortés, just north of Calzada Chetumal. It
changes US cash and travelers' checks
weekdays from 9 am to 1:30 pm, but nearly
all merchants accept dollars as readily as
pesos. Curios Mitla, at Chetumal and Mar
de Cortés, operates a casa de cambio.

Post & Telecommunications San Felipe's post office is on Avenida Mar Blanco,
between Calzada Chetumal and Calle
Ensenada. It's open 8 am to 1 pm and 4 to
6 pm weekdays.

A public long-distance telephone is
available from 7 am to 10 pm daily in the
Panificadora Singapur on Avenida Mar de
Cortés, just south of Chetumal; the public
phone outside the Singapur usually works
at all hours, but the one outside the Telnor
office, on Avenida Mar Bermejo just north
of Calle Puerto Peñasco, is quieter and less
crowded. San Felipe's area code is 657.

Medical Services San Felipe's Centro de
Salud (☎ 7-15-21) is on Avenida Mar
Bermejo, between Calzada Chetumal and
Calle Ensenada; for 24-hour emergency
service, however, the Cruz Roja (☎ 7-15-
44) is at the corner of Mar Bermejo and
Calle Puerto Peñasco.

Laundry Lavamática Burbujas is at Mar
Bermejo 212, between Calle Ensenada and
Calle Topolobampo; detergent is available
and English is spoken. Hours are 8 am to 8
pm weekdays and 10 am to 2 pm Sunday.

Capilla de la Virgen de Guadalupe
The local shrine of the Virgen de Guadalupe, Mexico's great national symbol, is a
small monument atop a hill north of town.
The climb to the top offers panoramic
views of the town and bay.

Off-Road Racing
Long a preferred destination for fossil-fuel
fanatics, San Felipe now boasts Mexico's
only racing stadium, which serves as both
the start and finish of annual off-road races.
The stadium is about 5 miles (8 km) south
of town, at the intersection of the Nuevo
Puertecito and airport roads.

Activities
Fishing For many people, fishing is the
main reason to visit San Felipe, and Bahía
San Felipe has become a parking lot of
pangas (skiffs), shrimpers, trawlers and
tuna clippers. Fishing licenses are obligatory for any type of fishing, including surf
fishing. The Oficina de Pesca has recently
moved, so contact the tourist office for its
present location.

A six-hour excursion on local boats costs
US$60 per person for up to four people.
Bait is usually provided. Most fishermen
use wood or fiberglass pangas ranging in
length from about 18 to 22 feet (5 to 7
meters). Travelers with their own boats will
find several launching ramps, including a
convenient one at Motel El Cortez, where
San Felipe Sport Fishing (☎ 7-10-55) is
located.

Enchanted Island Excursions (☎ 7-14-
31), on Avenida Mar de Cortés just south of
the tourist office, runs expensive excursions
on the 37-foot *Viento Loco* for about
US$100 per person per day, but also has
somewhat cheaper tours to Roca Consag
for US$240 (maximum of eight persons) as
well as other Gulf destinations. Its Mexican
mailing address is Apartado Postal 50, San
Felipe, while its US contact (☎ (619) 342-
4193) is 233 Paulin 8512, Calexico, California 92232. Flota Pelícanos (☎ 7-11-88),
Avenida Mar de Cortez 122, has similar
offerings.

The following list indicates which fish
are most common each month in the vicinity of San Felipe:

January
    cabrilla, halibut, rockfish
February
    cabrilla, halibut, rockfish
March
    cabrilla, halibut, rockfish, yellowtail
April
    cabrilla, halibut, rockfish
May
    barracuda, cabrilla, sea bass, yellowtail
June
    barracuda, bonefish, cabrilla, corvina,
    marlin, rockfish, sea trout, yellowtail
July
    albacore, barracuda, bonefish, cabrilla,

■ PLACES TO STAY	9 Bearded Clam	6 Cruz Roja (Red Cross)
1 Playa Bonita Trailer Park	10 Fish Taco Stands	7 Capilla de la Virgen de
2 Rubén's Trailer Park	11 Rosita Patio & Grill	Guadalupe
4 Vista del Mar RV Park	13 Petunia's	12 Plaza Club
18 Hotel La Hacienda de la	15 Rockodile	14 Bancomer
Langosta Roja	16 Cachanilla's	19 Curios Mitla
28 Motel El Pescador	17 Fish Taco Stands	21 Pemex (gasoline)
30 Motel Chapala	20 Beachcomber	22 Centro de Salud/Parque
33 Hotel Costa Azul	24 John's Restaurant	Hayward
34 Motel El Capitán	25 Los Mandiles	23 Post Office
35 La Jolla Trailer Park	26 Fish Taco Stands	31 Lavamática Burbujas
37 Campo San Felipe Trailer	27 Panificadora Singapur	32 AirLA
Park	29 Green House	36 SECTUR (tourist office)
40 Playa de Laura Trailer	39 Puerto Padre	38 Enchanted Island
Park	41 George's	Excursions
45 Las Palmas Hotel	42 El Nido	43 Caliente Foreign Book
46 Motel El Cortez	45 Restaurante Alfredo	44 The People's Gallery
47 Hotel Riviera		48 Terminal ABC (Buses to
	OTHER	Mexicali, Ensenada,
▼ PLACES TO EAT	3 Baseball Field	Tijuana)
8 Corona	5 Telnor (public telephone)	

corvina, marlin, rockfish, sea trout, yellowtail

August
albacore, bonefish, cabrilla, corvina, marlin, rockfish, sea trout, yellowtail

September
barracuda, cabrilla, corvina, marlin, rockfish, sea trout, yellowtail

October
barracuda, cabrilla, corvina, rockfish, sea trout, yellowtail

November
cabrilla, corvina, rockfish, yellowtail

December
cabrilla, rockfish

The popular totuava, which weighs up to 200 pounds (90 kg) and once attracted countless sportfishermen to the area, was over-fished in the 1980s and fishing for it is now prohibited.

Clamming Clamming is also popular, particularly when very low tides leave wide expanses of firm, wet sand. The best beaches for clamming are south of town beyond Playa El Faro and north of town beyond Campo Los Amigos. Small, tasty butter clams can be found around rocks while the larger, meatier white clams are just beneath the wet sand. Check with locals about minimum acceptable sizes –

clammers caught with specimens that are too small are subject to a hefty fine.

Water Sports Sailboat Charters, in the Motel El Capitán, also rents paddleboats, kayaks, sailboards and Hobie cats.

Organized Tours
Mexico Resorts International and Astro Tours Charters offer a three-day, two-night travel package that includes accommodation at the Hotel Las Misiones and return transport between San Diego/Chula Vista in the USA and San Felipe for US$110 per person (double occupancy). Departures from San Diego/Chula Vista are Sunday and Wednesday, returning Tuesday and Friday. For reservations in the USA, phone ☎ (619) 422-6900 or toll free nationwide (800) 336-5454.

Festivals & Events
On holidays like Thanksgiving, Christmas and New Year's, San Felipe becomes a mechanical zoo of ear-splitting motorcycles, dune buggies and other ATVs that could easily prod otherwise nonviolent pedestrians into carrying a bucket of nails or a spool of piano wire in self-defense.

Día de la Marina Nacional (National

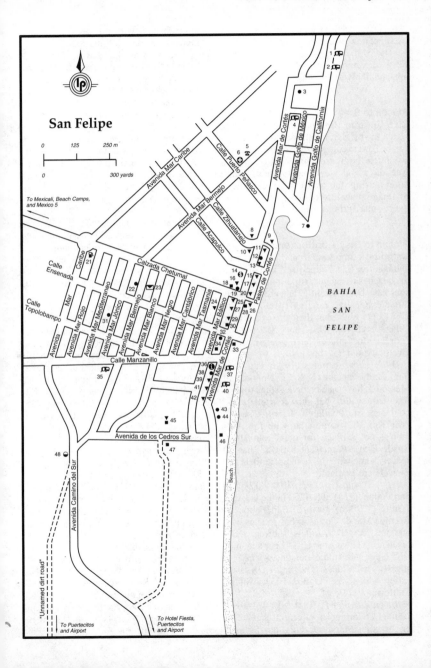

San Felipe

BAHÍA
SAN
FELIPE

Navy Day), celebrated on 1 June, is marked by street dances and a carnival. In November 1993, the town's first annual Shrimp Festival was successful enough that it appears likely to continue.

Places to Stay

Like Rosarito, Ensenada and other Baja beach towns, San Felipe's accommodation can be hard to categorize because rates vary so much both seasonally and between weekdays and weekends. A bottom-end hotel during the week may well be a midrange place on the weekend or during the popular spring vacation.

Places to Stay – bottom end

Camping Campgrounds and RV parks are abundant in San Felipe itself and also dot the beaches to the north and south. In-town sites have better facilities and are generally more expensive, ranging from US$5 to US$15 per night, but there are exceptions. Others cost from US$2 to US$5 for two people. Most places have potable water, electricity and hot showers.

Pete's Camp 6 miles (10 km) north of San Felipe at the Km 177 marker of México 5, has basic camping spots (only a few with shade), but showers, toilets and cold beer are available. *Campo Peewee*, near Km 182, is popular with the ATV mob – not a place for quiet relaxation. Rustic *Playa Blanca*, at Km 183, has 70 spaces, some with full hookups; toilets and showers are available.

Playa Bonita Trailer Park (☎ 7-12-15 in San Felipe, (714) 595-4250 in the USA) is 1 mile (1.6 km) north of San Felipe on Avenida Mar de Cortés. It has 35 sites with hookups as well as toilets, showers and a restaurant. The cost is US$15 per site, plus US$2 per additional person; prices rise slightly on holidays. The park's US reservation address is PO Box 1451, Walnut, California 91788.

Rubén's Trailer Park (☎ 7-14-42), about 1 mile (1.6 km) north of central San Felipe on Avenida Mar de Cortés, has 54 sites

(some shaded) with full hookups. A boat launch, a restaurant, toilets, showers and a patio are also available. Rates are US$20 per night for two people and US$2 for each additional person. The local postal address is Apartado Postal 196, San Felipe, Baja California, México.

Misnamed *Vista del Mar RV Trailer Park*, at Avenida Mar de Cortés 631 at the south end of San Felipe's baseball park, has better views of a vacant lot than of the sea, but it's quiet, immaculately maintained, and easy walking distance to central San Felipe. Rates are US$10 per site without electricity, US$12 with electricity.

La Jolla Trailer Park (☎ 7-12-22), near the center of town at the corner of Avenida Mar Bermejo and Calle Manzanillo, offers 50 fully equipped sites, toilets, showers and laundry facilities. A site costs US$12 per night for two people and US$2 for each additional person. Write PO Box 978, El Centro, California 92243 for more information.

Playa de Laura Trailer Park (☎ 7-11-28), in San Felipe between Avenida Mar de Cortés and the beach just south of Calle Manzanillo, has 50 sites, half with full hookups and the rest with water and electricity only. Hot showers and rental boats are also available. Costs are US$11 to US$16 per night for two people and US$2 for each additional person. Its US postal address is PO Box 130, Calexico, California 92231.

Also in town and on the beach is the *Campo San Felipe Trailer Park* (☎ 7-10-12), with showers, toilets and 34 fully equipped sites for US$11 to US$16 for two people (rates depend on beach proximity), plus US$2 for each additional person (children under age six are free). The registration office keeps a selection of trashy novels in English.

San Felipe's cushiest trailer park is *RV Park Mar del Sol* (☎ 7-10-88, (619) 422-6900 in the USA), in the south end of town at Misión de Loreto 149, next to Hotel Las Misiones. It offers 85 RV sites with full hookups and 17 tent sites at US$20 per night for two people and US$3 each additional person. Amenities include access to hotel facilities, showers, toilets, a small grocery, a laundry room, a boat ramp and a restaurant.

El Faro Beach Trailer Park (☎ 7-11-06), 12 miles (20 km) south of Bahía San Felipe at Punta Estrella, charges US$25 per night for sites with full hookups, plus showers, a tennis court and a swimming pool. Follow the airport road south and watch for signs. Go along another road eastward and continue to follow the signs.

Hotels & Motels One-star *Motel El Pescador* (☎ 7-10-44), at the corner of Calzada Chetumal and Avenida Mar de Cortés, has 24 rooms with air-conditioning for US$25 single/double weeknights, US$27 weekends. *Hotel la Hacienda de la Langosta Roja* (☎ 7-15-71), at Calzada Chetumal 125, adjoins a record shop with a deafening sound system aimed toward the street for the pleasure of everyone from Mexicali to Puertecitos and maybe even Puerto Peñasco across the Gulf. Rates are US$30/45 single/double weeknights, US$40/50 weekends.

Overlooking the town from Cedros Sur near Avenida Mar Báltico, *Hotel Riviera* (☎ 7-11-85) has air conditioned rooms with private bath and shower and a powerful odor of disinfectant; its two bars and the murky swimming pool are shelters from the summer heat. Rooms cost about US$32 double (including breakfast) during the week, US$42 weekends. The postal address is Apartado Postal 102, San Felipe, Baja California, México.

Places to Stay – middle
Friendly *Motel Chapala* (☎ 7-12-40), Avenida Mar de Cortés 142, offers clean, decent singles/doubles for US$35; most rooms have air-conditioning and others have kitchenettes. Its US postal address is PO Box 8082, Calexico, California 92231. The two-star, 36-room *Motel El Capitán* (☎ 7-13-03), Avenida Mar de Cortés 298 across from the state tourism office, has 40

basic rooms with air-conditioning, satellite TV and swimming pool for US$36 single or double weeknights, US$45 weekends. Its US postal address is PO Box 1916, Calexico, California 92231.

Across from the Riviera on Avenida Mar Báltico, three-star *Las Palmas Hotel*, (formerly La Trucha Vagabunda) (☎ 7-13-33, fax 7-13-82) has 45 clean, air-conditioned rooms for about US$40 weeknights, US$50 weekends. It has a pleasant pool area with plenty of lounge chairs, a poolside bar and a view of the Gulf of California. San Felipe's only Italian-Mexican restaurant and pizzeria, Restaurante Alfredo, is part of the hotel.

Places to Stay – top end
Motel El Cortez (☎ 7-10-55 in San Felipe) is a 90-room beachfront place on Avenida Mar de Cortés near the center of town. Singles/doubles with sea views, air-conditioning, TV and private bath with shower cost from about US$56 single or double, with discounts for AAA members; a few smaller rooms have beachfront patios. Amenities include a restaurant/bar (with satellite TV dish), a swimming pool and a boat ramp. The US postal address is PO Box 1227, Calexico, California 92232.

Two miles (3½ km) south of town at Avenida Misión de Loreto 148, the 190-room *Hotel Las Misiones* (☎ 7-12-80 in San Felipe, (800) 336-5454 toll free or (619) 422-6900 in California), has extensive facilities including a trailer park, two tennis courts, restaurants, bars, cafeterias and swim-up bars in two of the three swimming pools. Rooms cost about US$65 single or double; all have air-conditioning, color TV, telephone and shower bath. The hotel's US reservations agent is Mexico Resorts International, Suite G, 664 Broadway, Chula Vista, California 92010.

A new entry, dwarfing every other place in town in both size and, in all probability, price, is the extravagantly landscaped *Hotel Costa Azul* (☎ 7-15-48, 7-15-49). Not yet open when this book went to the press, it should be in business by late 1994.

Places to Eat

As a popular tourist destination, San Felipe has a good selection of restaurants serving the usual antojitos as well as outstanding seafood specialties. For inexpensive tacos of exceptional quality, try the numerous stands along the malecón, most of which specialize in fish and shrimp. *Tony's Fish Taco*, at the corner of Calzada Chetumal, is a dependable and inexpensive choice, but others nearby are also worth a try.

Despite its coffee-shop appearance, the *Corona* at Avenida Mar de Cortés 300 serves a good variety of seafood and Mexican dishes at modest prices. It's open 9 am to 3 pm. *Petunia's*, nearby at Avenida Mar de Cortés 241, specializes in pizza. *Cachanilla's*, on Avenida Mar de Cortés just north of Calzada Chetumal, serves good seafood. The *Green House*, at Avenida Mar de Cortés 132 just north of Motel Chapala, serves breakfasts and typical antojitos at very low prices by current Mexican standards.

El Nido, at Avenida Mar de Cortés Sur 348, serves various seafood and charbroiled steaks cooked over mesquite charcoal for about US$6 to US$10 for a full meal; hours are 2 to 9 pm (closed Wednesday). El Nido also serves breakfast on Friday, Saturday and Sunday.

Restaurante Alfredo, attached to Hotel Las Palmas, advertises 'Italian Hospitality in Mexico' and serves its best dishes in the evenings, including pizzas (delivery available), some with seafood toppings, pasta, veal scaloppini in wine sauce and 'Syracusian snails'. Entrees cost from about US$4.50 to US$10. See the *San Felipe Newsletter* for occasional discount coupons. This restaurant closes at unexpected times.

George's, a coffee shop at Avenida Mar de Cortés 336, is a breakfast favorite among local expatriates; hours are 6 am to 9 pm. Also on Avenida Mar de Cortés, *Puerto Padre* is open from 6 am to 9 pm for seafood and antojitos. *John's Restaurant*, on Avenida Mar Báltico just south of Calzada Chetumal, serves steak and seafood at upscale prices.

Los Mandiles, at the corner of Calzada Chetumal and Avenida Mar de Cortés, serves seafood and steak, with free appetizers. It's open 6 am to 9 pm. *El Gringo Loco*, near the arches on the highway to Mexicali, is more a watering hole with a variety of food and nightly entertainment ranging from televised US football to dancing.

Also on the malecón, the *Rockodile* patio and grill caters to a mostly younger crowd; a fenced-in sand lot with a volleyball net segregates the 'grill' side from the bar. Specialties include 'tacodile' (a big, meaty taco) and 'rockodile' (an alcoholic concoction based on tequila). Just south of the Rockodile, at the corner of Calzada Chetumal, the *Beachcomber* is a combination sports bar and grill. On the street side at the north end of the malecón, *Rosita Patio & Grill* has a large and varied menu, which stresses seafood, at moderate prices. *The Bearded Clam*, across the street on the beach side, is a new seafood restaurant.

For freshly squeezed juice, paletas, aguas, ice cream, milk shakes and similar treats, try *La Michoacana* with several locations on and around Avenida Mar de Cortés. *Panadería El Buen Gusto* offers a good selection of typically sweet Mexican pastries, as does the *Panificadora Singapur* on Mar de Cortés, just south of Calzada Chetumal.

Entertainment

Several of San Felipe's restaurants, like the Rockodile, Beachcomber and El Gringo Loco, are also prime night spots for drinking and dancing. Another is the *Plaza Club*, on Mar de Cortés just north of Calle Acapulco.

For bettors, *Caliente Foreign Book* has a convenient venue on Avenida Mar de Cortés, just north of Motel El Cortez.

Things to Buy

San Felipe's biggest source for souvenirs from around Mexico is Curios Mitla, at the corner of Avenida Mar de Cortés and Calzada Chetumal, but the entire street is lined with shops. For arts and crafts by

Boat yard, San Felipe

Malecón de San Felipe

Coastal Agave (*Agave shawii*), Desierto Central

Cemetary, Santa Catarina

Pitahaya dulce, organ pipe cactus (*Lemaireocereus thurberi*)

local and expatriate artists, as well as crafts classes, visit the People's Gallery, on Avenida Mar de Cortés just north of Motel El Cortez. Open seven days a week, it also serves as an informal tourist information service; the mailing address is Apartado Postal 154, 21850 San Felipe, Baja California, México.

Getting There & Away

Air Aeropuerto Internacional San Felipe (☎ 7-13-68) is 8 miles (13 km) south of town. AirLA (☎ (800) 010-0413 in Mexico, (800) 933-5952 in the USA, both toll free) now provides international service to Los Angeles Wednesday, Thursday, Friday and Sunday. It has a downtown office (☎ 7-17-27) in San Felipe at Avenida Mar de Cortés 238, opposite Hotel Costa Azul. Round-trip fares to/from Los Angeles are US$149 midweek, US$174 for a weekend-midweek combination, and US$199 weekends. The one-way fare is US$129.

Bus Terminal ABC (☎ 7-15-16) is on Avenida Mar Caribe, just south of Los Cedros Sur. Buses to Mexicali (about US$7, two hours) leave at 7:30 am, noon and 4 and 8 pm.

Buses (some air-conditioned) leave for Ensenada (US$10, four hours) at 8 am and 6 pm daily. Service to Puertecitos, south of San Felipe, has been discontinued.

Getting Around

To/From the Airport Only taxis serve the international airport, which is 8 miles (13 km) south of town. Fares should be around US$10.

AROUND SAN FELIPE
Parque Nacional
Sierra San Pedro Mártir

The eastern approach to the Sierra San Pedro Mártir and the famous peak of Picacho del Diablo is easiest via a turnoff from México 3, northwest of San Felipe. For more details, see the entry for Parque Nacional Sierra San Pedro Mártir in the Tijuana & the Northern Pacific Coast chapter.

PUERTECITOS

As paved México 5 gradually extends southward, access to the once-isolated string of communities stretching to Puertecitos and beyond is becoming easier; the road to Puertecitos is very good despite numerous *vados* (fords), which require slowing down, and potholes the last few miles. The fishing settlement of **Puertecitos** (population around 1000), 52 miles (85 km) south of San Felipe, is increasingly popular for its sport fishing opportunities; *Campo Los Chinos*, at the north end of town, has camping for US$5 at a pleasant bayside site with *palapas* (palm-leaf shelters), and also runs fishing excursions. Several warm, spring-fed pools near the point just south of town make for good bathing. The Pemex station lacks Magna Sin, but at least the town recently obtained public telephone service.

Fishing

The following list indicates which fish are most common each month near Puertecitos:

January
  cabrilla, corvina, grouper, white sea bass
February
  cabrilla, corvina, grouper, white sea bass
March
  cabrilla, corvina, grouper, white sea bass
April
  cabrilla, corvina, grouper
May
  cabrilla, corvina, grouper, sierra, yellowtail
June
  corvina, grouper, marlin, rockfish, sierra, yellowtail
July
  corvina, grouper, marlin, roosterfish, sierra, yellowtail
August
  corvina, grouper, marlin, roosterfish, sierra, yellowtail
September
  grouper, marlin, rockfish, sierra, yellowtail
October
  cabrilla, grouper, sierra, yellowtail
November
  cabrilla, grouper, white sea bass
December
  cabrilla, grouper, white sea bass

SOUTH OF PUERTECITOS

Ask about conditions before heading south of Puertecitos, because much of the road is very rough and subject to washouts as far as Bahía San Luis Gonzaga, about 50 miles (80 km) south. While vehicles with high clearance and short wheelbase are desirable, 4WD is not necessary; one Argentine family in an overloaded Volvo station wagon has gone the distance in two successive years, and a Yukon couple with an aged Datsun burdened with two kayaks also managed the route. Allow at least four to five hours to Bahía San Luis Gonzaga, and drive slowly to avoid punctures of both tires and oil pan.

Trailers and large RVs, with luck and skill, can go as far as **La Costilla**, about 5 miles (8 km) south of Puertecitos. About 25 miles (40 km) south of Puertecitos, *Campo Turístico Las Paredes* is typical of the many fish camps that dot the mountainous coastline and wait patiently and optimistically for construction of a better road. Camping costs US$3 per night.

Eighteen miles (30 km) south of Las Paredes, the fishing camp at *Punta Bufeo* has basic but tidy stone rooms for US$10 per person (cold showers only), but its restaurant has been closed for lack of a cook. Beyond Punta Bufeo, the road becomes easier, but still requires caution as far as Rancho Grande. For further details on the highway, see the Bahía San Luis Gonzaga section in the Desierto Central chapter.

The Desierto Central & the Llano de Magdalena

One of the least visited parts of the peninsula, Baja's Desierto Central (Central Desert) extends roughly from El Rosario, where the Transpeninsular turns inland, to Loreto, at the north end of the Sierra de la Giganta. In pre-Columbian times, this extensive territory belonged to Cochimí Indians, who foraged in its vast deserts and fished its extensive coastline. It is still more rural than other parts of the peninsula, with few resort-style hotels and restaurants with English-language menus. Many of its small farming towns, fishing villages and century-old ranchos are accessible only by dirt and gravel roads.

Most visitors come to central Baja to fish its hidden coves or explore isolated beaches – ideal for camping, clamming and lounging in the sun. Verdant valleys of grapes and tomatoes, extinct volcanoes and massive granite boulders on high plateaus are all accessible to well-outfitted travelers, but Baja's colonial and later historical heritage is more palpable here than it is farther north. Well-preserved or restored mission churches and modest plazas in San Ignacio, Loreto and elsewhere reveal close links to mainland Mexican life and culture. In Santa Rosalía, French colonial clapboard buildings and a prefabricated Eiffel church recall a 19th-century copper boom that drew miners from around the world.

The terrain in this region is diverse and alluring. The sinuous 76-mile (125-km) stretch of the Transpeninsular between El Rosario and Cataviña traverses a surrealistic desert landscape of massive granite boulders among stands of the cardón cactus (resembling the saguaro of the southwestern USA) and the twisted cirio (nicknamed 'boojum' for its supposed resemblance to an imaginary creature in Lewis Carroll's *The Hunting of the Snark*). The cirio grows only here and in parts of the mainland state of Sonora.

Beyond Guerrero Negro, the Desierto de Vizcaíno is a harsh, desolate expanse, but the unexpected oasis of San Ignacio augurs the semitropical environment of the Gulf Coast between Mulegé and Cabo San Lucas. The Sierra de la Giganta parallels the Gulf, dividing the region into an eastern semitropical zone and a western region of arid lowlands and high plateaus. South of Loreto, the Transpeninsular turns west to the Llano de Magdalena (Magdalena Plain), a major agricultural zone that offers tourists opportunities for activities like whale-watching, fishing, surfing, and windsurfing.

MISIÓN SAN FERNANDO

About 35 miles (61 km) southeast of El Rosario, near the site of the Franciscan mission of San Fernando, the roadside **Rancho El Progreso** offers some food and cold drinks. *La Misión RV Park*, across the highway, is out of service, but campers and RVs can still spend the night there. From Km 114, just west of the rancho, a dirt spur leads west about 3 miles (5 km) to the mission ruins. Despite a couple of sandy spots, the road is passable for anything but a low rider.

The famous Franciscan Fray Junípero Serra founded the mission of **San Fernando Velicatá** in 1769, but the Dominicans assumed control four years later when Serra decided to concentrate his efforts in Alta California. Epidemics a few years later nearly obliterated the native population, and the mission closed in 1818.

Some of the mission church's adobe walls are still standing, but of greater interest are the petroglyphs on a conspicuous granite outcrop a few hundred yards down the arroyo. Dating from about 1000 AD to 1500 AD, these include both abstract (curvilinear and geometric) and representational (human and animal) designs. Some of the latter appear to be shaman figures. Rather than the Cochimí designs to the south, these more closely resemble sites in mainland California's Imperial, Inyo,

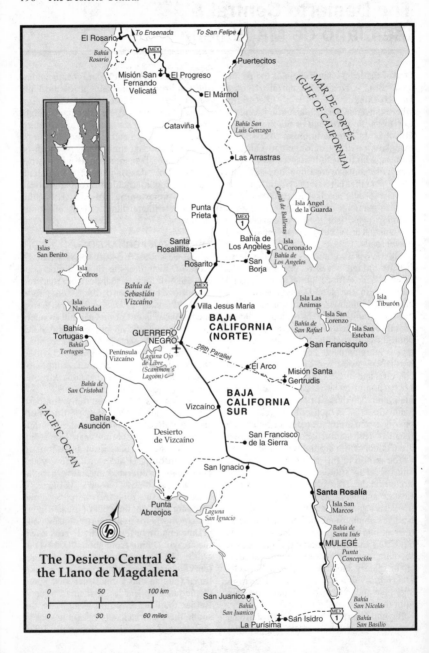

The Desierto Central &
the Llano de Magdalena

Mono and San Bernardino counties. Unfortunately, vandals have damaged some paintings and others have weathered poorly, but together with the mission they make the trip worthwhile.

EL MÁRMOL

At Km 143, an excellent graded lateral off the Transpeninsular leads to a major onyx quarry now being worked by nearby Ejido Revolución. Once trucked to the Pacific and shipped north to San Diego, the decorative stone now takes the modern highway north to Tijuana, where it's turned into table tops and similar items; some still reaches the USA, as it did at the turn of the century.

Well worth seeing are the ruins of the onyx schoolhouse, which sheltered the children of the quarry workers when North Americans still ran the operation. The school closed around 1967, but its huge buttresses and unpolished, yard-thick walls are still imposing.

At Km 144 of the Transpeninsular, just beyond the El Mármol turnoff, *Rancho Sonora* has basic tourist facilities, including RV parking and a restaurant.

CATAVIÑA

Cataviña, an isolated wind-blown rest stop, is a good place to fill the tank and stock up on groceries. Fatigued travelers can stay at *Hotel La Pinta* (☎ 6-26-01), a pseudo-colonial place set around a small courtyard, but at US$55/60 single/double, it's not for the budget traveler.

Next to the hotel is the barren *Parque Natural RV Park*, with hot showers but no electricity, for about US$5 per site. Across the highway, next to the Pemex station, *Café La Enramada* has fine and reasonably priced meals, including specialties like quail and traditional Mexican chocolate (ask for 'chocolate Ibarra' or you may get instant Quik, however), in a remarkably pleasant atmosphere.

Rancho Santa Inés, at the end of a paved spur half a mile (1 km) south of Cataviña, permits camping, offering toilets but no hot showers, for US$2 per site. It also has very

clean dormitory accommodation, also without hot showers, for US$8 per person; a restaurant provides good meals, and its proprietors can arrange excursions to the isolated ruins of Misión Santa María ('Mission Impossible', according to Walt Peterson's *The Baja Adventure Book*). Misión Santa María is 17 miles (29 km) east by a road difficult even for 4WD vehicles, though ace Baja hiker Graham Macintosh recently walked the trail.

For great free camping, drive off into the desert north of the arroyo to the north of Cataviña and west of the Transpeninsular; hearty travelers will find gigantic granite boulders and towering cardones. Firewood is plentiful (keep it small, though), but bring food and water.

BAHÍA SAN LUIS GONZAGA

About 32 miles (52 km) south of Cataviña, across from *Lonchería Los Cirios* (a basic restaurant) between Km 229 and Km 230 of the Transpeninsular, a graded but rough road, passable even for large RVs, cuts northeast to Bahía San Luis Gonzaga and San Felipe. Beyond San Luis Gonzaga, storms have destroyed sections of the roadway to Puertecitos and the popular Gulf resort of San Felipe. For more details on this route, which is now very difficult for vehicles with low clearance and impossible for those without a short wheelbase, see also the Puertecitos section in the Mexicali & the Northern Gulf chapter.

Bahía San Luis Gonzaga is a quiet, beautiful area which is experiencing increased but not overwhelming tourist development, primarily attracting fishing enthusiasts. Except for a few large but not extravagant vacation homes, accommodation is fairly basic, though good food is available.

Before taking the road to San Luis Gonzaga and Puertecitos, ask about current conditions at the llantera next to Lonchería Los Cirios and deflate your tires – the sharp rocks on the road east can shred even heavy duty tires that are fully inflated. Speeds higher than 15 mph (25 kph) are not advisable.

About 13 miles (21 km) east of the junction is **Coco's Corner**, a wild assemblage of ready-made' *objets d'art*, including beer can ornaments, a cactus garden, ocotillo 'street trees', hubcaps, fanbelts and other odds and ends. Radiator water, motor oil and automatic transmission fluid are available here as are cold drinks and modest meals. Camping is encouraged (free of charge, with pit toilets).

From Coco's Corner, another dirt road leads east to little visited **Bahía de Calamajué**. The main road continues about four miles south to **Rancho Las Arrastras de Arriola**, which has water, a mechanic, a llantera and cold drinks. The sandy parallel tracks sometimes offer better driving than the main roadway on the 20-mile (32-km) stretch to **Rancho Grande**, on Bahía San Luis Gonzaga itself. The entire stretch from the Transpeninsular to Rancho Grande, where Magna Sin is available for US$3 per gallon, takes about three hours.

North of Bahía San Luis Gonzaga, the San Felipe road deteriorates and, while 4WD is not necessary, it is impossible for any vehicle larger than a camper van. For information on the road from Puertecitos south, see the Mexicali & the Northern Gulf chapter.

Fishing

The following list indicates which fish are most common each month in and around Bahía San Luis Gonzaga:

January
    white sea bass
February
    white sea bass
March
    corvina, white sea bass
April
    bass, corvina, grouper
May
    bass, corvina, grouper, yellowtail
June
    bass, corvina, grouper, yellowtail
July
    cabrilla, corvina, grouper, sierra, yellowtail
August
    corvina, grouper, sierra, yellowtail

September
    corvina, grouper, sierra, yellowtail
October
    grouper, yellowtail
November
    white sea bass
December
    white sea bass

Places to Stay & Eat

RV Park Rancho Grande rents beachfront campsites for US$5 per car plus US$5 per *palapa* (palm-leaf shelter); facilities are still limited, but it may soon have hot showers. Just to its north, *Alfonsina's* has its own airstrip, basic rooms for US$10 per person (cold showers only) and a good restaurant (make reservations for meals). Two and a half miles (4 km) north is the turnoff for *Papá Fernández*, a popular fish camp with basic accommodation.

BAHÍA DE LOS ANGELES

In colonial times, Bahía de Los Angeles (population about 450) was a supply port for the interior mission of San Borja. About 107 miles (175 km) southeast of Cataviña via a paved spur off the Transpeninsular, it is now a popular fishing village on the shore of its sparkling namesake bay, an inlet of the Gulf of California. The surface of the 42-mile (70-km) road, which meets the Transpeninsular at a junction 65 miles (105 km) south of Cataviña, resembles the grooved shell of a leatherback turtle.

Most people come here to fish the offshore islands and nearby isolated beaches, rather than to see Bahía de Los Angeles itself. Some have complained that the inshore waters have been fished out, but there is still a yellowtail season from May to October (also one of the hottest periods of the year).

After millennia of telephonic isolation, Bahía de Los Angeles now has a Telnor long-distance office which has the *only* phone in town. Unfortunately, this office does not permit collect calls.

Museo de la Naturaleza y de la Cultura

Bahía de Los Angeles's self-supporting

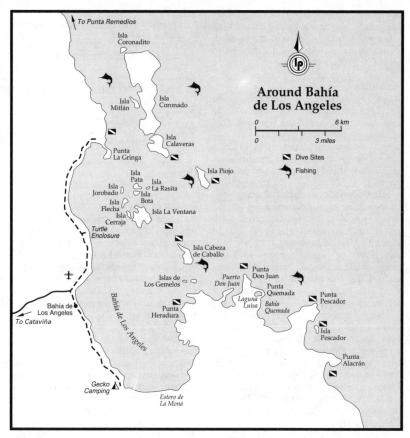

Around Bahía de Los Angeles

To Punta Remedios

Isla Coronadito

Isla Mitlán

Isla Coronado

Punta La Gringa

Isla Calaveras

Isla Pata

Isla Jorobado

Isla La Rasita

Isla Bota

Isla Flecha

Isla Cerraja

Turtle Enclosure

Isla La Ventana

Isla Piojo

Isla Cabeza de Caballo

Islas de Los Gemelos

Puerto Don Juan

Punta Don Juan

Punta Quemada

Laguna Luisa

Bahía Quemada

Punta Pescador

Isla Pescador

Punta Alacrán

Bahía de Los Angeles

To Cataviña

Bahía de Los Ángeles

Punta Heradura

Gecko Camping

Estero de La Mona

0   6 km

0   3 miles

Dive Sites

Fishing

museum of nature and culture features well-organized displays of shells, sea turtles, whale skeletons and other local marine life, native cultures (including Cochimí artifacts and rock art displays), mining, and horsegear and vaquero culture. Also on the grounds are a desert botanical garden and a good reconstruction of a mining site.

Admission is free, but the museum enjoys volunteer labor and depends on donations and sale of books and T-shirts for support. The volunteers, mostly gringo residents of the area, are a good source of information. Just uphill from the central plaza, it's open daily 9 am to noon, and 2 to 4 pm.

Programa Tortuga Marina (Sea Turtle Program)

In a modest facility at the now unused Brisa Marina RV Park, the Secretaría de Pesca's Programa Tortuga Marina (Sea Turtle Program) conducts research on sea turtle biology, ecology, morphometry and conservation. While it's not a major effort, its tanks offer the opportunity to see endangered sea turtle species such as the *caguama* (leatherback, *Dermochelys* spp), *tortuga prieta* (green turtle, *Chelonia mydas agasizii*) and *carey* (hawksbill, *Eretomochelys imbricata*). Parents should keep close watch on their children – the smallish hawksbill will quickly (but not painlessly) amputate a dangling finger.

Activities
Kayaking According to San Diego-based kayaker Ed Gillet, kayaking from Bahía de Los Angeles is one of the best and most challenging adventures in the Gulf of California. Northeasterly winds up to 35 knots can suddenly appear and churn the water into a nasty mess, so expect some exciting paddling.

Isla Coronado, northeast of town, is the most popular local destination for kayakers. To get there, follow the dirt road north out of town for about 5 miles (8 km) to Punta La Gringa; in winter, there are usually plenty of campers around to watch your vehicle while you paddle. On Coronado, Gillet recommends camping on the west side (near the islet of **Mitlán**) and fishing on the east side.

Many kayakers continue north from Punta La Gringa to Punta Remedios and **Isla Angel de la Guarda**. Gillet has written extensively about kayaking in this area, most notably in the fall (autumn) 1989 edition of *Baja Traveler*, and he publishes a quarterly newsletter on the activity; contact Southwest Kayaks (☎ (619) 222-3616) at 1310 Rosecrans St, San Diego, California 92106.

Fishing Casa Díaz arranges full-day (6 am to 1 pm) panga excursions for US$75. The following list indicates which fish are seasonally abundant in the vicinity of Bahía de Los Angeles:

January
    cabrilla, grouper, roosterfish, yellowtail
February
    corvina, grouper, roosterfish, yellowtail
March
    corvina, sierra, yellowtail
April
    cabrilla, corvina, grouper, halibut, roosterfish
May
    cabrilla, corvina, dolphin, grouper, sailfish, yellowtail

June
    cabrilla, corvina, dolphin, grouper, marlin, sailfish, yellowtail
July
    cabrilla, grouper, marlin, roosterfish, sailfish, yellowtail
August
    cabrilla, grouper, marlin, roosterfish, sailfish, yellowtail
September
    cabrilla, grouper, sailfish, yellowtail
October
    cabrilla, grouper, yellowtail
November
    cabrilla, grouper, roosterfish, yellowtail
December
    cabrilla, grouper, roosterfish, yellowtail

Places to Stay & Eat
Bahía de Los Angeles has several hotels, trailer parks and other campsites north and south of town, plus a handful of decent restaurants. Punta La Gringa, a beautiful beach area to the north, has several rugged camp sites with choice views of offshore islands, but the road is a bit hard to follow, the trash cans are overflowing and toilet facilities are nil.

Gecko Camping, in a quiet shoreline location 3½ miles (6 km) south of town, has rustic, ramshackle cabins for US$10 double with shared flush toilets, cold hand-pumped showers (hot showers are said to be in the works), firewood, garbage service and furnishings that appear to have been liberated from a Salvation Army warehouse sealed up since the 1950s. It also offers camping for US$5 per night with access to the same limited amenities.

Hotel Villa Vitta (☎ (619) 298-4958 in the USA for information & reservations) offers very clean, comfortable and air-conditioned rooms ranging from US$20 to US$60, depending on the number and size of beds. Its restaurant, specializing in seafood, serves moderately priced meals. Across the road, *Villa Vitta Trailer Park* is a shadeless RV site with toilets, showers and a few beachfront spaces with full hookups for about US$5 per vehicle, plus US$2 for hot showers (US$3 for non-guests). The nearby boat ramp is available 24 hours for about US$6 a day, regardless of tides.

Next door, separated from the beach by an unsightly row of trailers and fishing shanties, *Guillermo's Trailer Park & Restaurant* has about 40 spaces for tents and RVs, some with shade and a few with full hookups, for about US$4 per night; the baths are less than immaculate, but the hot water supply is good. Its new motel annex has singles/doubles with private bath for US$38, while meals at the restaurant cost about US$7 to US$10.

Family-run *Casa Díaz* is a combined restaurant, trailer park, campground, grocery and motel. The motel, consisting of 15 cozy stone cabins with hot showers, charges about US$25/30 for singles/doubles. Camping is possible on the motel grounds for about US$5 for two or three people, including hot showers. The restaurant specializes in shrimp, scallops and lobster.

Hotel La Hamacas (☎ 6-87-15 in Ensenada) has new, clean and spacious doubles for US$30, plus US$10 each additional person. Its restaurant is a good choice, and a bit cheaper than others in town.

Getting There & Away
Getting to Bahía de Los Angeles without private transport is easier than it once was, since a weekly bus now leaves Tijuana at 6 am Saturdays, returning the following day (confirm the return, however).

SANTA ROSALILLITA
Santa Rosalillita is an overgrown fishing camp about 10 miles (16 km) west from a junction with the Transpeninsular via a graded but unrelentingly washboarded road (signed southbound but not northbound) which resembles nothing so much as an eternal progression of speed bumps. The exit off the Transpeninsular is 24 miles (40 km) south of the Bahía de Los Angeles junction. Across the Bahía de Vizcaíno, the twin peaks of Isla Cedros are visible in the distance.

The waters north of Punta Santa Rosalillita, reachable by a difficult 7½-mile (12-km) dirt road that requires high clearance, is renowned among surfers for exceptional breaks, while Punta Rosarito to the south, known among surfers as 'The Wall', may be the most consistent break on the entire peninsula.

ROSARITO
Rosarito is a small truck stop, 8½ miles (14 km) south of the Santa Rosalillita junction and 32 miles (51 km) south of the Bahía de Los Angeles junction. For surprisingly good food, try *Restaurant Mauricio*, in which the onyx counter comes not from the massive quarry at El Mármol (see above) but from a smaller local quarry known as El Marmolito. Rosarito (impossible to mistake for its namesake resort between Tijuana and Ensenada) offers the most convenient approach to Misión San Borja, one of the most significant and best preserved on the peninsula.

MISIÓN SAN BORJA
At Rosarito, a lateral off the Transpeninsular leads 21 miles (35 km) east to the extensive ruins of Misión San Borja de Adac, founded in 1758 by Jesuit Fray Jorge Retz because of its abundant water supply – the few remaining nearby families still cultivate grapes, olives and other crops. Of all the adobe ruins in Baja California, these are the best preserved.

Dominicans built the now-restored landmark church, hewn of locally quarried volcanic stone with many outstanding details, well after expulsion of the Jesuits; see the custodian to climb the spiral staircase to the chorus, and leave a small (or large) donation. Other notable remains include the old mill and wine vats. On 10 October, the local saint's day, devotees from throughout the region converge on the tiny ranchería to pray and party.

The well-signed road from Rosarito is rough in spots, but any vehicle with a short wheelbase and the clearance of a small pickup can handle it. The route passes through a spectacular wild-west valley landscape of cirio, cardón, torote (elephant tree), *datilillo* (yucca) and cholla beneath broad volcanic mesas. About 2 miles (3 km) before San Borja the road forks; a sign indicates that both forks go to the mission, but the left (south) fork is much easier on both car and driver.

An alternative route to San Borja leaves the paved road to Bahía Los Angeles at Km 44. By reputation, this is a 4WD route, but local residents profess to have taken ordinary passenger vehicles on the road.

PARALELO 28

Marked by a 140-foot (43-meter) steel monument ostensibly resembling an eagle (but more accurately described by veteran travel writer Joe Cummings as 'the world's largest tuning fork'), the 28th parallel marks the border between the states of Baja California Norte (northern Baja) and Baja California Sur (southern Baja). It also symbolizes the completion of the Transpeninsular: during celebrations of the completion of the highway, thousands jammed the amphitheater at the foot of the monument, but the facilities are now trashed almost beyond salvation. The time zone changes here: 'Pacific' time (to the north) is one hour behind 'Mountain' time (to the south).

Hotel La Pinta Guerrero Negro, one of several La Pinta hotels in Baja, is precisely on the 28th parallel. It has a restaurant, a bar and 28 comfortable singles/doubles for US$55/60, but some of its details show wear and tear. *Trailer Park Benito Juárez*, next to La Pinta, has a few palapas and spacious pull-through sites but no electricity or hot water, for US$3 per night.

GUERRERO NEGRO

Guerrero Negro (population 7900), the first settlement south of Paralelo 28 in Baja California Sur, is a company town that boasts the world's largest evaporative salt works and the famous Laguna Ojo de Liebre (better known in English as Scammon's Lagoon), the mating and breeding ground of California gray whales. The Exportadora de Sal (ESSA) dominates the economy, but the tourist trade is an important supplement, especially in the winter whale-watching season.

Orientation

Guerrero Negro comprises two very distinct sectors: a disorderly strip development along Blvd Emiliano Zapata, just west of the Transpeninsular, and ESSA's very orderly company town, with a standard grid pattern which begins shortly after Blvd Zapata curves southwest near the airport. Nearly all the town's accommodation and restaurants are in the former area, lining both sides of Blvd Zapata.

Information

Money Banamex, on Blvd Zapata at the entrance to the ESSA sector, changes US cash and travelers' checks at reasonable rates with a minimum of bureaucracy, weekdays from 8:30 to 11 am. Supermercado La Ballena will change cash or travelers' checks, but expects a substantial purchase in the latter case.

Telephone Guerrero Negro's public telephones are few and poorly maintained; only the one outside the bus terminal works consistently, but long-distance connections are poor and it's nearly impossible to hear when diesel buses are revving their engines. Several pharmacies have long-distance cabinas, but they do not permit collect calls. Guerrero Negro's area code is 115.

Medical Services Guerrero Negro's Clínica Hospital IMSS (☎ 7-04-33) is on the south side of Blvd Zapata, at the point where the road curves to the southwest.

Water Campers and RVs can obtain purified drinking water at reasonable cost at Fresk-Pura on the south side of Blvd Zapata.

Laundry Two blocks north of Supermercado La Ballena is a laundromat which is quick, efficient and reasonable.

Salt Works

ESSA's Guerrero Negro salt works consists of thousands of evaporative ponds, each about 110 sq yards (100 sq meters) in size

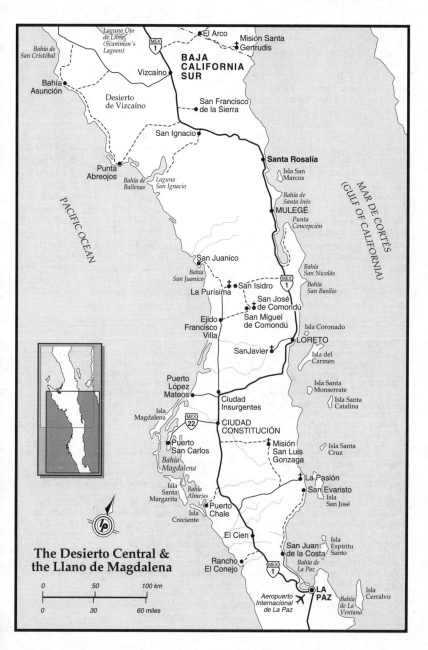

The Desierto Central & the Llano de Magdalena

0		50		100 km

0		30		60 miles

and about a yard deep, just south of Guerrero Negro. In the intense sunlight and high winds of the Desierto Vizcaíno, water evaporates quickly, leaving a saline residue, which is then dredged from the pools and hauled to nearby quays. From there it is barged to Isla Cedros for transshipment by freighter. The works produces over five million tons of salt annually.

To visit the salt works, contact Señor Leonardo Villavicencio (☎ 7-00-13), Exportadora de Sal, Guerrero Negro, Baja California Sur, México.

Places to Stay

Guerrero Negro has fairly abundant and reasonably priced accommodation, but the winter whale-watching season can put a strain on these resources. For this reason, reservations are advisable from January through March.

Camping Camping is free at most beaches outside town. In town, the rather barren

Malarrimo Trailer Park (☎ 7-02-50) charges from US$5 per night and also permits tent camping; not all the electrical outlets work, so check before setting up. Hot water is plentiful and the toilets are clean, but one of the shower heads emits a stream thinner than a pencil lead. The largest RVs, especially those with trailers, may have trouble maneuvering into a site.

Hotels & Motels *Motel Gamez* (☎ 7-03-70), on the north side of Blvd Zapata toward the airfield, has slightly shabby but adequate rooms for US$12 double; nonguests may use the hot showers for US$2. About 200 yards south, across Blvd Zapata, family-run *Mini Hotel Asunción* is simple but very clean and friendly, with hot showers and TV for US$12 single or double. At *Motel California*, next to the Pemex station on the south side of Blvd Zapata, very basic rooms with shared toilets and hot showers cost US$9 to US$11 single; doubles cost US$18.

Scammon & the Whales

The main breeding grounds for the California gray whale *(Eschrichtius robustus)* are in Laguna Ojo de Liebre (Scammon's Lagoon), south of the Guerrero Negro salt works and about 15 miles (24 km) from the junction with the Transpeninsular, an area now designated as Parque Natural de la Ballena Gris (Gray Whale Natural Park) and part of the Reserva Biosfera Vizcaíno. Other major breeding areas are farther south at Laguna San Ignacio and Bahía Magdalena.

Each year, the whales migrate 6000 miles (10,000 km) from the Bering Sea to the warm waters of Baja California, where they stay from late January to early March. The lagoons offer an ideal, protected place for the whales to give birth and nurture their offspring. By late March, they begin the long journey back to the Arctic.

Laguna Ojo de Liebre takes its English name from Captain Charles Melville Scammon, an American whaler who frequented the area in the 1850s. Born in Maine, Scammon yearned to captain a trading ship but had to settle for command of less lucrative whalers like the *Boston* out of San Francisco. In 1857, he learned from some Mexicans of an estuary near the Bahía de Sebastián Vizcaíno which he learned was the breeding grounds of the gray whale and soon headed there.

Scammon dispatched his men in small whaleboats, but their first attempts were disastrous because of the whales' enormous size and strength – two boats were crushed and half the crew was seriously injured. Resorting to 'bomb lances' – bombs fired into a whale from a hand-held gun – instead of harpoons, Scammon and his crew managed to fill virtually every container on board with 740 barrels of oil, later sold in San Francisco as a lubricant.

Other whalers learned of Scammon's discovery, and by the end of 1859 they had nearly eliminated the gray. It took nearly a century for the population to recover. Today, the US and Mexican governments have their own laws, in addition to international agreements, to protect the gray whale and its habitat.

For a more detailed account of the interactions of humans and cetaceans in the area, see David Henderson's *Men and Whales at Scammon's Lagoon* (Dawson's Book Shop, Los Angeles, 1972). ■

Las Dunas Motel, at Blvd Zapata and División del Norte, has 28 rooms with showers, firm beds and a powerful odor of disinfectant. Singles cost US$13, plus a refundable key deposit of US$3. *Motel Brisa Salina*, on the north side of Blvd Zapata, is comparably priced. Probably the best value in town is five-room *Motel Las Ballenas*, just north of Hotel El Morro (see below), which is new, clean and tidy, with hot water and color TV in every room, for US$17 single or double.

The *Motel San José*, opposite the bus terminal, is upstairs from a small shopping center with fairly heavy auto traffic. It has singles/doubles with TV and hot showers for US$20/23. Improved *Motel San Ignacio*, on the north side of Blvd Zapata, has clean, spacious singles/doubles with TV for US$22. *Cabañas Don Miguelito*, part of the Malarrimo restaurant-RV park complex, has pleasant detached singles/doubles for US$22/25. Recently upgraded *Hotel El Morro* (☎ 7-04-14), on the north side of Blvd Zapata, has clean, pleasant singles/doubles for US$25/28. All rooms have cable TV and hot showers.

Places to Eat

Guerrero Negro's best bargains are its numerous taco stands, which keep erratic hours but maintain very high standards. *El Taco Feliz*, in a palapa on the south side of Blvd Zapata, has superb fish and shrimp tacos with excellent condiments, but many others specialize in carne asada, *birria* (goat), and other fillings. *Supermercado La Ballena* (whose landmark sign depicts a sperm whale rather than the gray whale which draws tourists to the area) has reasonably priced take-out food and a wide selection of groceries and produce for campers who plan to go into the backcountry.

Cocina Económica Letty, on the south side of Blvd Zapata, has very good antojitos and seafood at prices a fraction of those at Malarrimo (see below), and it also serves a good breakfast. *Mario's*, next door to Motel El Morro on the north side of Blvd Zapata, serves excellent, moderately priced seafood dishes.

Malarrimo, on the north side of Blvd Zapata as you enter Guerrero Negro, is the town's best restaurant, specializing in seafood dishes ranging from fish and shrimp to clams and abalone, both as traditional antojitos and in more sophisticated international dishes. While it's no longer cheap, portions are abundant and it's a good value.

Getting There & Away

Air Aerolíneas California Pacífico (☎ 7-00-55, 7-00-57, the same as Supermercado La Ballena) flies rickety DC-3s (bring your own seat belt – seriously!) to nearby Isla Cedros for US$25 one way. While these flights are the quickest option to the island, they fail to inspire confidence in their safety. Flights are often booked early, so it's best to reserve at least a day in advance and arrive at 8 am for the 10 am (Mountain time) flights, daily except Sunday. Three days a week, these flights continue from Cedros to Bahía Tortugas (US$20). Return flights from Cedros ostensibly leave at 1 pm (Pacific time), but arrive at least an hour ahead of time in case of early departure.

The airline's offices are on the west side of the airfield, in a yellow shed with blue trim and doors. It's better to make reservations and purchase a return ticket in Guerrero Negro than to do so on Cedros itself, unless you're planning to fly north to Ensenada with the Sociedad Cooperativa de Producción Pesquera (tickets available only on Cedros or in Ensenada; see Isla Cedros section for information).

Aerovizcaíno (☎/fax 7-10-00), on Blvd Zapata, is an air-taxi service which offers charter flights.

Bus From Guerrero Negro's bus terminal, on the south side of Blvd Zapata, Autotransportes de Baja California offers services throughout the peninsula, while Autotransportes Aguila operates in Baja California Sur only. Northbound buses depart at 3 am (to Mexicali), 6 am, and 7:30, 8:30 and 10 pm; southbound buses as far as La Paz depart at 4:30, 5, 6:30, and 7 am, and at 4, 8 and 11 pm. Approximate fares from Guerrero Negro are:

Northbound	Fare
Rosarito	US$3.50
Punta Prieta	US$5.50
Cataviña	US$10
El Rosario	US$13
San Quintín	US$17
Colonia Vicente Guerrero	US$18
San Vicente Ferrer	US$20
Ensenada	US$22
Tijuana	US$27
Mexicali	US$35

Southbound	Fare
Vizcaíno	US$3.50
San Ignacio	US$6
Santa Rosalía	US$9
Mulegé	US$11
Loreto	US$16
Ciudad Constitución	US$22
La Paz	US$29

AROUND GUERRERO NEGRO
Reserva Biósfera El Vizcaíno

Also known in part as Parque Natural de la Ballena Gris (Gray Whale Natural Park), the six million acre (2½ million hectare) Vizcaíno Biosphere Reserve sprawls from Laguna San Ignacio, Guerrero Negro, Isla Natividad and Isla Cedros and even across to the Gulf of California, taking in part of the Sierra de San Francisco. It is the joint responsibility of Mexico's Servicio de Desarollo Urbano y de Ecología (SEDUE) and Ejido Benito Juárez, whose lands the reserve occupies.

Local pangueros (fishermen with skiffs) take visitors for two to three-hour excursions in the shallow waters of Laguna Ojo de Liebre (Scammon's Lagoon), while several travel agencies in Guerrero Negro, including the Malarrimo Restaurant/RV Park, arrange trips for about US$30. Without a minimum number of passengers (around 10), trips may not take place.

Five miles (8 km) south of the Guerrero Negro junction, a graded road leads 15 miles (25 km) west to Ojo de Liebre. While low-cost camping is available at the lagoon, the road may be closed in the weeks

leading up to the start of whale-watching season, which officially begins 1 January. Day-trippers pay a parking fee of US$3.

Misión Santa Gertrudis

About 17 miles (27 km) south of Guerrero Negro, a once-paved but now truly dismal 26-mile (42-km) lateral leads to **El Arco**, a 19th-century gold-mining town that now serves as a supply center for surrounding ranchos; anyone fortunate enough to survive this spine-shattering route at the posted 80 kph speed limit will, at the very least, need both a chiropractor and an orthodontist.

From El Arco, which is of little interest to anyone not planning a surprise attack on the Mexican army's 67th Batallón de Infantería, a dirt road leads west to **Bahía San Francisquito**, on the Gulf of California; just west of Bahía San Francisquito, another graded road leads north to Bahía de Los Angeles.

About 23 miles (37 km) southeast of El Arco, isolated **Misión Santa Gertrudis La Magna**, was the focus of the Jesuits' northward missionary efforts. Initially founded by the famous Jesuit Fernando Consag in 1751, its original church, of adobe with a stone foundation, was built under the direction of Fray Sebastián Sisteaga and an extraordinary blind Cochimí Indian named Andrés Comanjí. Padre Jorge Retz took charge of the 600 Cochimí here, digging a well, building acequias and planting wheat, maize, olives, grapes, dates, pomegranates and figs. The mission also maintained livestock such as cattle, horses, mules, goats and sheep.

After the Spanish government expelled the Jesuits in 1768, the Dominicans took over and finished the small stone church, now in the process of restoration, which bears a ceiling date of 1796. Labor and water shortages forced the mission's abandonment in 1822.

The church museum contains a selection of Guaycura, Cora and Cochimí artifacts, as well as ofrendas (offerings) left by pilgrims whose wishes have been granted by Santa Gertrudis – common among the

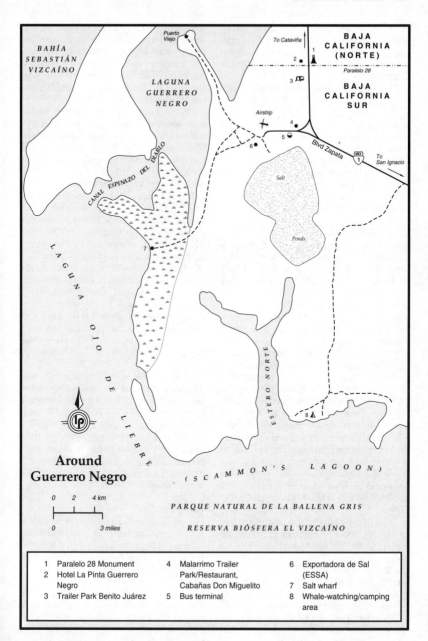

Around Guerrero Negro

0 2 4 km

0 3 miles

1 Paralelo 28 Monument
2 Hotel La Pinta Guerrero Negro
3 Trailer Park Benito Juárez
4 Malarrimo Trailer Park/Restaurant, Cabañas Don Miguelito
5 Bus terminal
6 Exportadora de Sal (ESSA)
7 Salt wharf
8 Whale-watching/camping area

ofrendas are the lengthy tresses of young women who visit this popular pilgrimage site. Every 16 November, pilgrims jam the village for the **Fiesta de Santa Gertrudis**.

Another landmark is **El Camino Real**, the royal road (really a trail), which still leads 29 leagues (100 miles or 161 km) from San Ignacio to San Borja via Santa Gertrudis. Most travelers will prefer the recently improved road from El Arco, passable for any passenger vehicle and even small RVs (though one van with California plates now stands on blocks behind the church). The entire trip takes 2½ to 3 hours from Guerrero Negro.

ISLA CEDROS

Isla Cedros is a mountainous northward extension of the Península de Vizcaíno, separated from the mainland by the Canal de Kellet, the much smaller Isla Natividad and the Canal de Dewey. Reaching altitudes of nearly 4000 feet (1200 meters) above sea level, this desert island is a rewarding, off-the-beaten track destination for adventurous travelers.

Early Spanish explorers found surprisingly large numbers of Cochimí Indians on the island, who were so intransigent that the Jesuits forcibly relocated them to the mainland mission of San Ignacio. Manila galleons later used Cedros as a port of refuge on their return across the Pacific. The island supports an unusual vegetation, including endemic tree species, and coastal wildlife such as elephant seals and sea lions; the Cedros mule deer (*Odocoileus hemionus cedronsensis*, an endangered subspecies) still inhabits the rugged back-country.

Most of the island's 2696 inhabitants live in the tiny port of Cedros on the sheltered eastern shore, but many also live at ESSA's company town at Punta Morro Redondo, at the southern tip of the island, which is the site of the airfield and the transshipment point for salt barged over from Guerrero Negro. The Sociedad Cooperativa de Producción Pesquera, the local fishing cooperative, is the other main employer, but commercial pressure has reduced the offshore abalone, just as earlier hunters had vastly depleted the numbers of fur seals and sea otters (otters may have returned to the area). The first abalone divers were Japanese, but the Mexican cooperative took over the business after WW II.

Cedros's commercial abalone season runs from December to June at three different locations: Cabo San Agustín, Cabo Norte and Islas San Benito. Divers work in groups of three and gather up to 100 abalone per day; there is also a lobster season from October to April.

The village of Cedros, facing the Bahía de Sebastián Vizcaíno, is a ramshackle locale on the slopes beneath towering Cerro Vargas (or Cenizo) (3950 feet or 1204 meters), whose summit is usually hidden by clouds. Your initial impression of dilapidation will soon fade as you discover its good points, but it's definitely not a stereotypical tourist destination; Cedros has no bank or any other place to change money, no phone service (this situation may soon change), and you can't even get a margarita. It does have a Capitanía del Puerto and an IMSS hospital/clinic, however.

Several two-story buildings, with porches or balconies facing the bay, add a touch of vernacular architectural interest. Electricity is only available from 6 am to noon and 5 to 11 pm; running water is available mornings only, though most houses have storage tanks. Prices are high, because nearly everything is imported – including, astonishingly, salt! – despite the mountains of it at Punta Morro Redondo.

Things to See

In Cedros's tidy hillside church, murals in the curious **Capilla de la Reconciliación** (Chapel of Reconciliation) depict events in Mexican and Baja Californian history, such as the expulsion of the Jesuits, in a comic book style. According to local residents, the hilltop **Panteón** (cemetery) harbors the remains of early Japanese divers, but only a single headstone bears a conspicuous Japanese inscription.

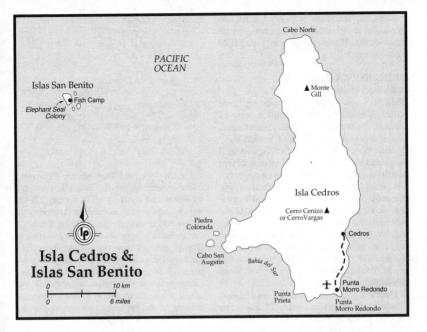

Isla Cedros & Islas San Benito

Places to Stay & Eat

Accommodation in Cedros is very basic. *Casa de Huéspedes Elsa García*, up the hill from the dusty triangular plaza, is the best in town, with clean singles/doubles for US$12. Its only competition is shabby, overpriced *Casa de Huésped Aguilar* on the waterfront, which charges US$13 for gloomy singles/doubles with shared bath (no hot water) or US$17 with private bath. To find the unsigned building, walk straight downhill from the church; before entering the grounds of the fishing cooperative, look for the two-story house on your left. If no one is on duty, you'll have to hike up the hill to Manuel Aguilar's house, a brown stucco next to the elementary school and the power plant, to check in.

Cedros has only a few places to eat and, surprisingly enough, prices for abalone are double or triple those on the mainland – few locals or visitors will wish to pay US$40 to sample this delicacy at *Restaurant El Marino*, whose antojitos, fish and

shrimp are good and much more reasonably priced. *La Pacenita* is a bit cheaper, but heavily fried foods are the rule. A friendly taco stand up the main drag from El Marino serves only carne asada.

Getting There & Away

Cedros' airfield is at Punta Morro Redondo, about 5 miles (8 km) south of the village. Taxis charge about US$6 per person. Often the locals will offer you a ride there.

Purchase tickets for Aerolíneas California Pacífico at Licores La Panga, up the hill from the northern point of Cedros' triangular plaza. Return flights from Cedros to Guerrero Negro (US$25) ostensibly leave at 1 pm (Pacific time), but travelers should arrive at least an hour ahead of time to avoid being left at the airstrip. Three days a week, these flights return to Guerrero Negro via Bahía Tortugas (US$20), near the tip of Península Vizcaíno.

Flights from Ensenada arrive regularly.

Tickets for Ensenada from Isla Cedros are available at the Sociedad Cooperativa de Producción Pesquera in the village of Cedros.

AROUND ISLA CEDROS
Islas San Benito

This tiny archipelago consists of three small islands, 30 nautical miles west of Cedros; the westernmost island, the largest of the three, supports a large winter camp of abalone divers and their families, as well as a substantial breeding colony of northern elephant seals *(Mirounga angustirostis)*. The seals begin to arrive in December, but are most numerous in January and February. Another notable animal is the black storm-petrel *(Oceanodroma melania)*, locally known as the *nocturno* because it leaves its nesting burrows only at night. Sea turtles and occasional whales are visible offshore (the islands are just off the main whale migration route).

Unless you bring camping equipment, food and water to stay overnight, expect to be able to spend no more than an hour on shore. Avoid getting too close to the elephant seals, especially the enormous bulls; not only are they potentially dangerous, but frightened bulls may accidentally crush or injure newborn pups, which cannot get out of their way.

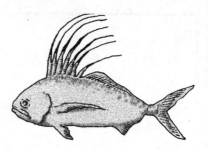

Passing yachts often anchor here and come ashore to see the seals, but budget travelers can catch a lift with the *Tito I*, which carries daily supplies to the abalone divers and returns to Cedros with the day's catch. For a passage on the *Tito I*, which is free of charge, visit the Sociedad de Producción Pesquera in the village of Cedros before 1 pm, when it closes to the public. On request, with routine approval of the chief, the secretary will issue a letter to present to the captain that evening for the following day's voyage.

The crew of the *Tito I* is exceptionally friendly and will probably offer breakfast to passengers, but travelers prone to seasickness should refrain from eating too heavily. The four-hour voyage to the San Benitos, against the wind and the northwest swell, is generally rougher than the voyage back.

Isla Natividad

Most surfers will only be able to stare with longing as the plane from Cedros to Guerrero Negro passes above what, by acclamation, is Baja California's prime surf spot and one of the best in the world. The season runs from April to October, but the southern swells are at their best in June, July and August.

If demand is sufficient, Bill Eastman at Baja Surf Adventures (☎ (800) 428-7873 in the USA) runs day excursions by launch from the tip of Península Vizcaíno to Isla Natividad in conjunction with more extensive surfing holidays in the area. Week-long trips cost about US$740 per person.

PENÍNSULA VIZCAÍNO

Península Vizcaíno, one of the most thinly populated parts of Baja California, is a sparsely vegetated, mountainous extension of the Desierto Vizcaíno. For detailed information about driving and road conditions, consult the guidebook published by the Automobile Club of Southern California. While you may not need a rugged 4WD vehicle everywhere – roads are generally passable – conditions are terrible in certain areas.

About 40 miles (65 km) south of Guerrero Negro, the crossroads town of **Vizcaíno** is the gateway to the peninsula; accommodation is available at *Motel Kadakamán* for US$17/20 single/double; its rather barren RV park charges US$3 per person, but lacks hot showers.

From Vizcaíno there are three buses weekly to **Bahía Tortugas**, near the western tip of the peninsula, a five to six-hour drive on a partly paved but mostly graded surface which is negotiable for any vehicle. Passing yachts often stop at Bahía Tortugas, making it a good spot for lifts south despite its remoteness; hang out on the pier near the tuna cannery. Anglers cruise the offshore kelp beds for bass, mackerel and barracuda, while farther offshore they find bonito and yellowtail.

Bahía Asunción, reached by a graded road at the south end of the Sierra Santa María (no public transport), is a prime site for barracuda, bonito, dorado, yellowfin and yellowtail, but the area is very windy and offshore waters are rough.

Both Bahía Tortugas and Bahía Asunción have Pemex stations, but are unlikely to have Magna Sin except perhaps in drums, so carry extra fuel.

SAN IGNACIO

After the scrub and cacti forests of the Desierto de Vizcaíno, the oasis of San Ignacio is a soothing scene. In 1728 the Mexican Jesuit Juan Luyando located Misión San Ignacio de Kadakaamán here, planting dense groves of date palms and citrus in the Arroyo El Carrizal surrounding the town. After the Jesuits' expulsion,

Dominican missionaries supervised construction of the striking lava-block church (finished 1786) that still dominates San Ignacio's laurel-shaded plaza.

Surrounding ranchos and fish camps rely on the town for supplies – San Ignacio has several groceries, a couple of restaurants, a hotel and a motel, and a several modest trailer parks. With its lingering colonial atmosphere, San Ignacio offers a pleasant respite from the bustling development of many other Baja towns.

Orientation

San Ignacio proper is about 1 mile (1.6 km) south of the Transpeninsular – a paved lateral leads from the highway junction (known as San Lino) past a small lagoon and through groves of date palms into the town. Parking is easy, and the town invites walking.

Information

Most basic services are found around the plaza. International collect calls are quick and easy from the public telephones on the plaza – much easier, in fact, than from some larger Baja towns. San Ignacio's area

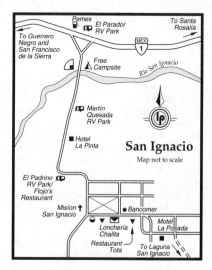

code is 115. Bancomer, at the southeast corner of the plaza, is open for foreign exchange weekdays from 8:30 am to noon.

Cave Paintings
Oscar Fischer, at Motel La Posada, arranges mule trips to see Cochimí rock art near San Ignacio, most of which depict figures of humans and animals, giving some indication of life in the area before the missions, but some are more abstract. Fischer charges about US$20 per person for the tour to Cueva del Ratón for visitors without vehicles, but mule trips can be arranged more cheaply at San Francisco de la Sierra (see below).

Misión San Ignacio
With lava-block walls nearly 4 feet (1.2 meters) thick, the one-time Jesuit Misión San Ignacio de Kadakaamán is one of Baja's most beautiful churches, and it is still in use since its founding in 1728. Opposite the plaza, occupying the site of a former Cochimí ranchería and initiated by the famous Jesuit Fernando Consag, it was completed in 1786 under the direction of Dominican Juan Crisóstomo Gómez. Epidemics reduced the Cochimí population from about 5000 at contact to only 120 by the late 18th century, but the mission lasted until 1840.

Places to Stay
Camping At the San Lino junction and behind the Pemex station, dilapidated *El Parador RV Park* has full RV hookups, but these do not always work and there is no shade. Toilets are in bad shape, and tents are difficult to erect because the ground is too hard for stakes. If someone is around to collect charges, a site is about US$5. On the east side of the lateral into San Ignacio is the very basic *Martín Quesada RV Park*; sites go for US$2.

Just south of Hotel La Pinta, on the west side of the road, *El Padrino RV Park* (☎ 4-00-89) is rather shabby (though not dirty). It is well shaded with aging date palms (some of which may not live much longer), but it has only a single toilet/shower for the

entire 25-plus sites, only a few of which have full hookups. Fees are US$5 for camping, a bit more for larger RVs.

Hotels & Motels Oscar Fischer's *Motel La Posada* (☎ 4-03-13), the closest thing to budget accommodation, has comfortable but spartan doubles with hot showers for about US$20. It's conspicuously located at Calle Venustiano Carranza 22 on a rise southwest of the plaza.

Hotel La Pinta San Ignacio (☎/fax 4-03-00) is on the main road just north of San Ignacio. For about US$55 single/double, its pseudo-colonial architecture, tiled courtyard, swimming pool and groves of date palms and citrus cater more to affluent holiday-makers than to shoestring travelers. In the USA, contact the Tijuana Baja Information Center (☎ (800) 522-1516 toll free) for information and reservations.

Places to Eat
On the plaza, near the Conasupo Market, *Lonchería Chalita* serves the usual antojitos at very low prices in a family atmosphere – literally, their living room – but service is painfully slow and the food is not especially appetizing.

The restaurant at Hotel La Pinta also serves typical Mexican food but at much higher prices, specializing in beef from nearby ranches. *Restaurant Tota*, up the block from the plaza, serves very good, reasonably priced antojitos and seafood dishes, and claims to be open 24 hours a day. *Flojo's*, at El Padrino RV Park, serves good, fresh seafood; its lobster is considerably cheaper than Tota's. On the Transpeninsular, west of the San Lino junction, *Restaurant Quichuley* serves good antojitos at moderate prices.

Getting There & Away
Transpeninsular buses now enter the town and pick up passengers on the south side of the plaza; drivers may or may not pick up passengers at the old terminal at San Lino (the junction with the short road to San Ignacio). Supposedly, there are at least five northbound buses between 6 am and 3 pm

The Rock Art of the Desierto Central

When Jesuit missionaries inquired who created the giant rock paintings of the Sierra de San Francisco and about the meaning of those paintings, the Cochimí Indians responded with a bewilderment that was, in all likelihood, utterly feigned. The Cochimí claimed ignorance of both symbols and techniques, but it was not unusual, when missionaries came calling, to deny knowledge of the profound religious beliefs which those missionaries wanted to change.

At sites like Cueva Pintada, Cochimí painters and their predecessors decorated high rock overhangs with vivid red and black representations of monos, borregos, pumas and deer, as well as more abstract designs. It is speculated that the painters built scaffolds of palm logs to reach the ceilings. Post-contact motifs do include Christian crosses, but these are few and small in contrast to the dazzling pre-Columbian figures surrounding them.

Cueva de las Flechas, across Cañón San Pablo, has similar paintings, but the uncommon feature of arrows through some of the figures is the subject of serious speculation. One interpretation is that these depict a period of warfare. Similar opinions suggest that they record a raid or an instance of trespass of tribal territory, or perhaps constitute a warning against such trespass. One researcher, however, has hypothesized that the arrows represent a shaman's metaphor for death in the course of a vision quest; if this is the case, it is no wonder that the Cochimí would claim ignorance of the paintings and their significance in the face of a missionary presence unrelentingly hostile to such beliefs.

Such speculation is impossible to prove, since the Cochimí no longer exist, but over the past two years the Instituto Nacional de Historia y Antropología has undertaken the largest systematic archaeological survey of a hunter-gatherer people yet attempted in Mexico. Results soon to be published reveal that, besides well-known features such as rock art sites and grinding stones, the Cochimí left evidence of permanent dwellings and even pottery. In recognition of its cultural importance, the Sierra de San Francisco will soon be declared a UNESCO World Heritage Site. It is already part of the Reserva Biósfera El Vizcaíno, which includes the major gray whale calving areas of Laguna San Ignacio and Laguna Ojo de Liebre.

Unfortunately this means more publicity than protection. The Sierra will remain an INAH-protected archaeological zone, which means that foreigners will need entry permits to conduct research – not everyone has been scrupulous in this regard. However, Mexican government funding may soon dry up. The INAH will probably need to impose a modest tourist admission fee to guarantee basic infrastructure and provide such services as an interpretive guidebook to the paintings. It will also be challenged to provide area residents with a stake in management of the sites, without which the project is unlikely to be successful. ■

and as many southbound between 6 am and 10:30 pm.

AROUND SAN IGNACIO
Sierra de San Francisco

From a conspicuously signed junction 28 miles (43 km) north of San Ignacio, at Km 118, a graded road climbs eastward to the village of San Francisco de la Sierra, gateway to the Desierto Central's most spectacular examples of pre-Columbian rock art. To date, researchers have located about 500 different sites in an area of roughly 4300 sq

miles (12,000 sq km). About 1½ miles (2½ km) before San Francisco, **Cueva del Ratón** is the most accessible site, but independent visitors must obtain a guide at San Francisco in order to see the paintings, which are protected by a chain link fence and locked gate.

Cueva del Ratón, which features typical representations of *monos* (human figures), *borregos* (desert bighorn sheep) and deer, is well worth seeing for day visitors, but they are not as well preserved as paintings elsewhere in the area. The most rewarding excursion is a descent into the dramatic Cañón San Pablo to see its famous **Cueva Pintada**, **Cueva de las Flechas** and other magnificent sites.

Cueva Pintada, really an extensive rock overhang rather than a cave, is the single most imposing site. Among English speakers, it is popularly known as Gardner's Cave after the popular American novelist Earle Stanley Gardner, who wrote several popular books about his own adventures in the area, but Mexicans intensely resent the identification with Gardner and strongly prefer the Spanish term.

Exploring Cañón San Pablo requires a minimum of two days and preferably three; visitors must contract guides through Enrique Arce, the INAH representative at San Francisco (just ask around for him), and agree to a series of guidelines that include refraining from touching the paintings, from smoking at the site and from employing flash photography (400 ASA film easily suffices even in dim light), and to other similar restrictions in the interest of preserving the paintings. By the time this book appears, INAH expects to introduce a new management plan, based on similar rock art zones in Australia's Kakadu National Park, which will restrict but not eliminate access to most areas; only Cueva del Ratón is likely to remain accessible on demand.

Local guides to Cueva del Ratón require only a modest tip, around US$1, but excursions to Cañón San Pablo involve hiring a guide and his mule for US$20 per day, a mule for each individual in the party for US$9 per day, and additional pack animals, either mules or burros for US$9, to carry supplies such as tents and food. Visitors must also provide food for the guide; San Francisco has a Conasupo and another small market, but it's better to bring food from Guerrero Negro or San Ignacio.

Backpacking is permitted, but backpackers must still hire a guide and his mule; most visitors will find the precipitous volcanic terrain much easier to manage on muleback, which leaves more time to explore the canyon and enjoy the scenery.

The precipitous descent into the canyon takes about five or six hours, the ascent slightly less; in winter, this means almost an entire day devoted to transport alone. Perhaps the best time of the year is early spring, in late March or April, when days are fairly long but temperatures have not become unpleasantly hot.

The residents of San Francisco de la Sierra are descendants of the early *vaqueros* (cowboys) who settled the peninsula along with the missionaries. They still maintain a distinctive pastoralist culture, herding mostly goats in the surrounding countryside. They retain a unique vocabulary with many terms surviving from the 18th century, and they produce some remarkable crafts – look at the guides' *polainas* (leather leggings) for riding in the bush, for instance. Such items are generally made to order, but occasionally villagers will have a pair of men's *teguas* (leather shoes) or women's open-toed *huaraches* (sandals) for about US$25.

INAH expects to post a conspicuous sign at the turnoff to San Francisco de la Sierra. The road from the Transpeninsular is regularly graded but, because parts of its surface are poorly consolidated at times, there are spots which are difficult for vehicles with poor traction and low clearance (4WD is not necessary, however). It can be very difficult after a rain.

Cuesta Palmarito

At a signed junction at Km 59 of the Transpeninsular, about 9 miles (15 km) east of San Ignacio, a decent road leads 24 miles (40 km) to Rancho Santa Martha, the starting point for excursions to rock art sites at Cuesta Palmarito. The local INAH representative will arrange guides and mules and prices comparable to those at San Francisco de la Sierra.

Punta Abreojos

Reached by a 45-mile (70-km) graded road that leaves the Transpeninsular about 16 miles (26 km) west of San Ignacio, Punta Abreojos is one of the prime fishing spots on the west coast of the peninsula.

Laguna San Ignacio

Along with Laguna Ojo de Liebre and Bahía Magdalena, Laguna San Ignacio is one of the major winter whale-watching sites on Baja's Pacific Coast. At the La Laguna and La Fridera fish camps on the south shore of the Laguna, excursions of about three hours cost around US$25 per person with José María Aguilar (known by his nickname 'El Chema'), Francisco Mayoral (nickname 'Pachico') and Antonio Aguilar Osuña.

Antonio Aguilar has a house which he rents for about US$20 to tourists who go out in his boat, but otherwise camping is the only alternative; knowledgeable visitors claim his wife cooks the best meals in Baja. Maldo Fischer, at La Base, is another possibility for whale trips; his wife will also prepare meals. Ejido Luís Echeverría, in the village of San Ignacio, will also arrange excursions.

Whale-watching excursions take place only in January, February and March, but at other seasons the area is still an outstanding site for bird-watching in the stunted mangroves and at the offshore **Isla Pelícanos**, where about 150 ospreys and as many as 5000 cormorants nest (landing on the island is prohibited, but pangas may approach it). This is not Baja's best fishing area, but cabrilla, corvina, grouper, halibut, and sierra are found here, and boats can be hired for fishing. Sea kayaking is prohibited when whales are present in the lagoon.

The recently improved road from the village of San Ignacio is a dubious blessing – most passenger cars can now make the 38 miles (61 km) to La Fridera in about 1½ hours if no rain has fallen recently, but the road may also assist the Exportadora de Sal in developing the area for an even larger salt works than its Guerrero Negro operation.

San Juanico

About 60 miles (100 km) south of La Fridera, the village of San Juanico is well known among surfers for nearby **Punta Pequeña**, at the north end of Bahía San Juanico, whose right point breaks, some believe, provide the highest quality surf on the peninsula in a south swell between April and October. Other possible activities in the area include windsurfing, sea kayaking, diving and sportfishing for halibut, corvina and, especially, roosterfish.

Unfortunately, despite its depiction as a graded surface on the AAA map, the high road south from Laguna San Ignacio is potentially hazardous, according to Serge Dedina and Emily Young, who have spent several months in the area:

The high road is the worst of all of them, only recommended for high-clearance vehicles (or sturdy little trucks). I wouldn't recommend it to anyone. Locals avoid it always – so there is little traffic to help out if you break down.

The lower road veers off from the graded road approximately 8 miles south of Laguna San Ignacio. This is the Baja 1000 road – and passable by most trucks – granted drivers know how to drive dirt roads. The road passes through a few sand dunes between La Laguna and El Dátil. It is also easy to get lost and very stuck there. In short, avoid the route unless you have a great vehicle and lots of experience driving unmarked roads (with lots of detours), and unless you speak good enough Spanish to understand directions. Given the general lack of topographic features to fix on (only endless dunes and salt flats), I would say this is the easiest place to get lost in the entire peninsula.

Camping costs US$3 per person per day at a well-run site operated by an American in cooperation with the local ejido, and there's an excellent palapa restaurant. San Juanico is also accessible by a good graded dirt road north from the village of La Purísima, which can be reached by an excellent paved highway from Ciudad Insurgentes (see below).

SANTA ROSALÍA
History

Despite the nearby discovery of copper as early as the 1860s, Santa Rosalía (population 10,650) really dates from the 1880s, when the French-owned Compañía del Boleo (one of the Rothschild family's many worldwide ventures) built it as a company town for its mine workers.

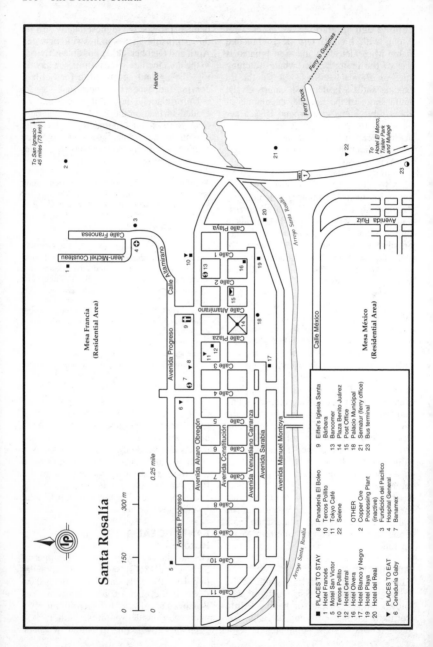

Santa Rosalía

0.25 mile

| 0 | 150 | 300 m |

Mesa Francia
(Residential Area)

Mesa México
(Residential Area)

To San Ignacio
45 miles (73 km)

Harbor

Ferry Dock

Ferry to Guaymas

To
Hotel El Morro,
Trailer Park
and Mulegé

MEX 1

Arroyo Santa Rosalía

PLACES TO STAY
1 Hotel Frances
5 Motel San Victor
10 Tercos Pollito
12 Hotel Central
16 Hotel Olvera
17 Hotel Blanco y Negro
19 Hotel Playa
20 Hotel del Real

PLACES TO EAT
6 Cenaduría Gaby

8 Panadería El Boleo
10 Tercos Pollito
11 Tokyo Café
22 Selene

OTHER
2 Copper Ore
   Processing Plant
   (inactive)
3 Fundición del Pacífico
4 Hospital General
7 Banamex

9 Eiffel's Iglesia Santa
   Bárbara
13 Bancomer
14 Plaza Benito Juárez
15 Post Office
18 Palacio Municipal
21 Sematur (ferry office)
23 Bus terminal

Imported timber from Oregon and British Columbia frames the clapboard houses and French-style colonial homes that still stand along the main streets. The French also assembled a prefabricated, galvanized-iron church designed by Alexandre Gustave Eiffel (the same!) for the 1889 World Fair in Paris. The church is still in use, while balconies and porches along the tree-lined streets encourage a spirited street life contrasting with the residential segregation of the mining era.

The French left by 1954, but their legacy is still palpable in features such as the town's atypical architecture and a bakery that sells the best baguettes in Baja California. Most of the original ore-processing plant is still intact; the Transpeninsular passes beneath the plant's old conveyor belt, north of the turnoff into town.

After the mines closed, the federal government took charge of the facilities in order to preserve jobs, but the Compañía Minera de Santa Rosalía closed in 1985 on the eve of the town's centenary, because of a high incidence of arsenic poisoning among the miners and their families. This was not the only adverse environmental impact of mining: from the turn of the century, commercial egg collectors raided the gull colonies of the islands of the Midriff to supply the miners and their families.

Orientation

Most of central Santa Rosalía nestles in its namesake arroyo, west of the Transpeninsular, while residential areas occupy plateaus north and south of the canyon. French administrators built their houses on the northern Mesa Francia, now home to municipal authorities and the historic Hotel Francés, while Mexican officials occupied the southern Mesa México.

Santa Rosalía's narrow avenidas run east to west, while its short calles run north-south; one-way traffic is the rule. Large RVs will find it very difficult to turn around in town, and should park along or near the Transpeninsular.

Plaza Benito Juárez, about four blocks

west of the highway, is the focus of the town. The new **Andador Costero**, south of downtown overlooking the harbor, is an attractive malecón with good views of offshore Isla Tortuga.

Information

Tourist Office In late 1993, the tourist office on the waterfront, south of downtown, closed.

Money Travelers bound for Mulegé, which has no banks, should change US cash or travelers' checks here. Bancomer is at Avenida Obregón and Calle 2, while Banamex is at Obregón and Calle 4.

Post & Telecommunications The post office is at the corner of Avenida Constitución and Calle 2.

The Telmex office at the west end of Avenida Obregón is only a business office, but has a working public phone outside for collect overseas calls. Hotel del Real, on the exit road from town, also has long-distance services. Santa Rosalía's area code is 115.

Medical Services Santa Rosalía's new Hospital General (☎ 2-07-89) overlooks the town from a hilltop site on Mesa Francia, opposite the historic Fundición del Pacífico which once housed the mining headquarters.

Iglesia Santa Bárbara

Designed and erected in Paris, disassembled and stored in Brussels, intended for West Africa and finally shipped to Mexico when a director of the Compañía del Boleo stumbled upon it by chance, Gustave Eiffel's prefabricated church reached Santa Rosalía in 1895 and was reassembled by 1897. It has attractive stained glass windows. The church is located on the corner of Avenida Obregón and Calle Altamirano.

Places to Stay

Camping Just south of town at Km 4 on the Transpeninsular, *Las Palmas RV Park* (☎ 2-01-09) has grassy but shadeless campsites, with hot showers and clean toilets, right on Bahía de San Lucas. A space costs about US$5 to US$10. There is also a small seafood restaurant under a large palapa that serves standard antojitos.

A bit farther south, about ½ mile (1 km) west of the Transpeninsular between Km 181 and Km 182, spacious *San Lucas RV Park* has a good beach and boat launch sites, but no amenities except for hot showers. Rates are US$6 per night.

Hotels & Motels *Hotel Olvera* (☎ 2-00-57), near the corner of Avenida Venustiano Carranza and Calle 1, is one of the best deals in town for budget travelers. Spotless wood-paneled singles/doubles, most with carpets and fans, cost US$13. About a block west of the Olvera, the shabby *Hotel Playa* has rooms with private bath for US$8. The rooms tend to be noisy and it's not recommended for women traveling on their own.

Travelers have recommended the 'very quaint' *Hotel Blanco y Negro* (☎ 2-00-80), at the top of a spiral staircase on the 2nd floor of a small building at Avenida Sarabia 1, which has 12 clean, basic singles/doubles with hot water for about US$10/12. North of Plaza Juárez, *Hotel Central* looks all of its 108 years, but it's not bad for US$10 single with shared bath, despite creaky wooden floors, peeling wallpaper and bare light bulbs hanging from the ceiling. Its ample 2nd-floor balconies offer good views of Santa Rosalía's lively (but noisy) Avenida Obregón.

Tidy *Motel San Victor* (☎ 2-01-16), Avenida Progreso 36 at Calle 10, is a pleasant, family-run operation on a shady, quiet street. Its 12 rooms, all with overhead fans, air-conditioning and tiled bathrooms, cost US$20 single or double. *Hotel del Real* (☎ 2-00-68) on Avenida Venustiano Carranza has clean but small singles/doubles with air-conditioning for US$17/20. A nameless hotel adjacent to Restaurant Tercos Pollito, at the entrance to town, has clean but dark singles/doubles for US$18/22.

Partly restored and recently reopened *Hotel Francés* (☎ 2-08-29), on Calle Jean-Michel Cousteau on Mesa Francia, once catered to French idiosyncrasies but now offers an atmospheric bar, wonderful views of the rusting copper smelter and air-conditioned singles/doubles for US$25/29. Santa Rosalía's best accommodation is the cliffside *Hotel El Morro* (☎ 2-04-14), just off the Transpeninsular about 1 mile (1.6 km) south of town. Along with sea views and a relaxed atmosphere, it has a swim-

---

Eiffel beyond the Tower

Few know that French engineer Alexandre Gustave Eiffel, so renowned for his controversial tower in Paris, also played a significant role in the New World. New York's Statue of Liberty is his most prominent trans-Atlantic landmark, but his constructions also dot the Latin American landscape from Mexico to Chile. Santa Rosalía's Iglesia Santa Bárbara is only one of many examples.

In 1868, in partnership with another engineer, Théophile Seyrig, Eiffel had formed G Eiffel et Compagnie, which later became the Compagnie des Etablissements Eiffel. While the bulk of its metal construction work took place in France and its colonies, an aggressive agent in Buenos Aires obtained many contracts for public buildings in South America. Among his notable creations were the Aduana de Arica (customs house, in 1872 part of Peru, now part of Chile), Arica's Iglesia San Marcos, the gasworks of La Paz (Bolivia) and the railroad bridges of Oroya (Peru). Most of these were designed and built in Eiffel's workshops in the Parisian suburb of Levallois-Perret and then shipped abroad for assembly.

What might have been his greatest Latin American monument effectively ended his career. In the late 19th century, he had argued strongly in favor of building a trans-oceanic canal across Nicaragua, but a few years later he obtained a contract to build the locks for Ferdinand de Lesseps's corruption-plagued French canal across Panama. Implicated in irregular contracts, Eiffel was sentenced to two years in prison and fined a substantial amount; though his conviction was overturned on appeal, he never returned to his career as a builder. ■

ming pool, restaurant and bar for US$26/31 single/double.

Places to Eat

The *Tokyo Cafe*, on Avenida Obregón, is a popular local hangout for its inexpensive Mexican food and beer. Despite the name, only the calligraphy on the windows is Japanese. *Cenaduría Gaby* (de Pedro García) on Calle 4 just north of Obregón, serves standard antojitos at reasonable prices. Taco stands are numerous along Avenida Obregón.

South of downtown, the oceanfront *Restaurant Selene* serves sumptuous seafood dishes at upscale prices. *Tercos Pollito*, on Avenida Obregón near Calle 1, specializes in chicken but also serves meat and lobster lunches or dinners.

Started by the French when mining operations were in full swing at the turn of the century, *Panadería El Boleo* is on Avenida Obregón between Calle 3 and Calle 4. For many travelers, it's an obligatory stop for its delicious Mexican and French-style breads and pastries. Baking begins at 4 am daily, but baguettes usually sell out by 10 am.

Getting There & Away

Bus All buses between Tijuana and La Paz stop at Santa Rosalía's bus station, on the west side of the Transpeninsular, opposite the Andador Costero. Northbound buses pass at 2 am (Guerrero Negro), 4 am (Tijuana), 5 am (Guerrero Negro), 5 pm (Tijuana), 7 pm (Guerrero Negro), and midnight (Mexicali). Sample fares include San Ignacio US$3, Vizcaíno US$7, Guerrero Negro US$9, Punta Prieta US$14, El Rosario US$20, San Quintín US$21, Colonia Vicente Guerrero US$25, Ensenada US$29, Tijuana US$34 and Mexicali US$42.

Southbound buses pass at 2 am (La Paz), 8 am (Loreto) and 9, 10:30, and 11 am (all to La Paz), and 8, 9:30 and 11 pm (all to La Paz). Sample fares include Mulegé US$3, Loreto US$7, Ciudad Insurgentes US$11, Ciudad Constitución US$12 and La Paz US$22.

Ferry The ferry terminal (☎ 2-00-13) is just south of the Arroyo Santa Rosalía, right along the Transpeninsular. Sematur ferries sail to Guaymas (an eight-hour journey when there are no delays) Wednesday and Sunday at 8 am; in winter, strong winds can cause long delays. Ticket windows are open Tuesday and Friday, 8 am to 1 pm and 3 to 6 pm; Sunday and Wednesday 6 am to 7:30 am; and Thursday and Saturday, 8 am to 3 pm. Drunks and pregnant women are not allowed; draw your own conclusions.

Passenger fares are US$13 in *salón* (reclining seats) class, US$27 in *turista* (bunks in three-person roomettes), US$40 in a more comfortable *cabina* and US$53 in *especial*. Vehicle rates start at US$102 for those up to 16 feet, 5 inches (5 meters); obtain your permit at the US border beforehand if possible, but it should now be possible to do so on the spot. Vehicles up to 21 feet, 4 inches (6½ meters) cost US$133; to 29 feet, 6 inches (9 meters) US$184; and to 55 feet, 9 inches (17 meters) US$336. Motorcycles pay US$15. For more information about permits, see the Documents and Insurance section in the Facts for the Visitor chapter.

Make reservations at least three days in advance and, even if you have reservations, arrive early at the ticket office. It is essential to show your tourist card; if you have a vehicle, the car permit and tourist card will be the same.

Yacht Santa Rosalía's small marina offers some possibilities for catching a ride south along the Gulf or to mainland Mexico.

AROUND SANTA ROSALÍA
Isla San Marcos

Every Friday at 6 am, a free boat carries the residents of the mining settlement on this offshore island to their weekly shopping spree in Santa Rosalía. Travelers interested in hiking the island are welcome to hop aboard the return voyage at 10:30 am (ask around the harbor for the exact docking site), but they will either have to wait a week or contract a launch to return to the mainland. It's also possible to hire a boat in the tiny fish camp of San Bruno, about midway between Santa Rosalía and Mulegé, and visit an offshore sea lion colony.

MULEGÉ
South of Santa Rosalía, the Transpeninsular tracks the base of the eastern scarp of the northern edge of the Sierra de la Giganta, passing the peninsula of Punta Chivato, before winding through the Sierra Azteca and dropping into the subtropical oasis of Mulegé. Beaches to the south, along Bahía Concepción, attract more conventional holiday-makers than areas to the north, but the Mulegé area is especially popular with divers.

The *ejidatarios* (ejido members) of Mulegé have a running feud with local landowners over property rights to some of the town's most highly developed tourist areas, but nothing is likely to change despite suits and counter-suits, and accusations and counter-accusations.

Orientation
Mulegé (population 3350) straddles the verdant Arroyo de Santa Rosalía (sometimes known as Río Mulegé) about 2 miles (3 km) inland from the Gulf of California; the bulk of tourist services are on the north side of the arroyo, on or near Jardín Corona, the town plaza. Mangroves extend along the lower reaches of the river's estuary, frequented by large numbers of birds, while farther inland date palms line its banks. Avoid swimming at the mouth of the estuary, which is badly polluted.

Information
Money Mulegé's only bank recently closed, but local merchants will usually change cash dollars or accept them in payment. Travelers needing to change travelers' checks or obtain cash advances on credit cards should do so in Santa Rosalía or Loreto, the closest towns with banks, before arriving in Mulegé.

Post & Telecommunications Mulegé's post office is on the north side of Jardín Corona, the main plaza.

Long-distance telephone and fax services are available at the corner grocery on Calle Zaragoza at Avenida Martínez, but you can also dial an international operator (☎ 09) from one of the pay telephones on the plaza. Mulegé's area code is 115.

Approximate long-distance rates per minute are US$0.90 within Baja California, US$1.15 elsewhere in Mexico, US$2.30 to the USA and US$4.50 to Europe. Faxes cost US$1.75 per page within Mexico, US$2.30 to the USA; there is no charge for receiving a fax.

Medical Services Mulegé's Centro de Salud is on Calle Madero, opposite the Canett Casa de Huéspedes.

Water Jorge's RV Park beneath the Mulegé bridge no longer takes overnighters, but it still sells purified water and ice at reasonable prices.

Laundry Efficient Lavamática Claudia, at the corner of Calle Zaragoza and Calle Moctezuma, is open 8 am to 6 pm daily except Sunday. A full load costs about US$4, washed, dried and folded.

Misión Santa Rosalía
Across the Transpeninsular near the south bank of the arroyo, the recently restored Misión Santa Rosalía de Mulegé stands on a hill above the village. Founded in 1705 and completed in 1766, the mission functioned until 1828, when the declining Indian population led to its abandonment. Remodeled several times, the church is less distinguished in architectural terms – imposing but utilitarian, with fewer enticing details – than its counterparts at San Ignacio and San Borja. The exterior is still faithful to the original, but the succeeding centuries have altered the interior greatly.

Behind the church a short footpath climbs a volcanic outcrop to an overlook with soothing views of the palm-lined Río Mulegé and its surroundings. This is one of the visual highlights of the area, well worth

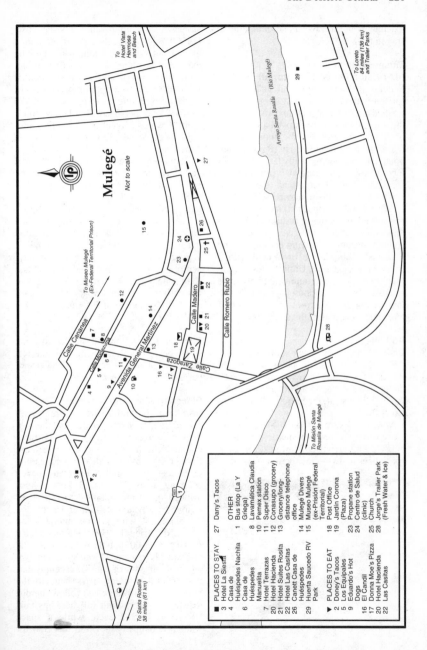

Mulegé

Not to scale

To Hotel Vista Hermosa and Beach

To Museo Mulegé (Ex-Federal Territorial Prison)

Arroyo Santa Rosalía (Río Mulegé)

To Loreto 84 miles (136 km) and Trailer Parks

Calle Cañanea

Calle Madero

Avenida General Martínez

Calle Romero Rubio

Calle Zaragoza

To Misión Santa Rosalía de Mulegé

To Santa Rosalía 38 miles (61 km)

PLACES TO STAY
3 Hotel La Siesta
4 Casa de Huéspedes Nachita
6 Casa de Huéspedes Manuelita
7 Hotel Terrazas
20 Hotel Hacienda
22 Hotel Suites Rosita
26 Hotel Las Casitas de Huéspedes
29 Huerta Saucedo RV Park

PLACES TO EAT
2 Doney's Tacos
5 Los Equipales
9 Eduardo's Hot Dogs
16 El Candil
17 Donna Moe's Pizza
20 Hotel Hacienda
22 Las Casitas

27 Dany's Tacos

OTHER
1 Bus stop (La Y Griega)
8 Lavamática Claudia
10 Pemex station
11 Super Disco
12 Conasupo (grocery)
13 Grocery/long-distance telephone office
14 Mulegé Divers
15 Museo Mulegé (ex-Prisión Federal Territorial)
18 Post Office
19 Jardín Corona (Plaza)
23 Propane station
24 Centro de Salud (clinic)
25 Church
28 Jorge's Trailer Park (Fresh Water & Ice)

a detour even for travelers not intending to stay in town.

Museo Mulegé
(ex-Prisión Federal Territorial)

Federal inmates from Mulegé's former 'prison without doors', a strikingly white-washed neocolonial building overlooking the town, traditionally enjoyed a great deal of liberty. Except for the most serious felons, who were confined in its inner compound, the prisoners usually left at 6 am for jobs in town, returning at 6 pm; in some cases they could even attend town dances and a number of them married locally.

After decades of neglect, the building is due to undergo a major restoration and its interesting but eclectic museum artifacts – cotton gins, antique diving equipment and firearms – should be organized into a coherent presentation. Until the restoration is complete, museum hours are likely to be irregular, but it's supposedly open mornings except Sunday, from about 9 am to 1 pm, and sometimes in the afternoon.

Activities

Diving Mulegé's best dive spots are around the Santa Inés islands and just north of Punta Concepción. There is excellent beach diving and snorkeling at Punta Prieta, near the lighthouse at the mouth of the Río Santa Rosalía.

Mulegé Divers (☎ 3-00-59) recently moved to spacious new quarters on Avenida General Francisco Martínez. The shop specializes in diving instruction and excursions: A four-hour scuba course costs US$60, including all equipment and a guided underwater dive tour, while a diving excursion involving a boat, a dive-master guide, two tanks and a weight belt is US$40; there is a minimum charge of US$70. Snorkeling excursions cost US$20 to US$25 per person, with a US$60 minimum. Owners Miguel and Claudia Quintana both speak English (Claudia is American).

Rental equipment is also available on a daily basis, including items such as a buoyancy compensator (US$8), weight belt (US$3), tanks with air (US$6 each), regulator (US$8) and wet-suit jacket (US$5).

The shop also sells snorkeling fins and masks, fishing equipment, such as lures and lines, T-shirts and miscellaneous supplies, a good selection of books on the Baja peninsula, and the AAA road map of Baja California. Open 9 am to 1 pm and 3 to 6 pm daily except Sunday, it's also a good and friendly source of information on the Mulegé area.

Fishing The yellowtail, similar to tuna, could be Mulegé's mascot, as it attracts thousands of anglers here between December and May each year.

Places to Stay – bottom end

Camping The Mulegé area has numerous campgrounds and trailer parks, but many of them no longer accept overnighters. Eastbound Calle Madero and Calle Romero Rubio merge into a single dirt road leading to *Mulegé No 2* and *Sombrerito*, beach camping areas 2 miles (3 km) east of Mulegé. Both are open all year free of charge. Nearby are a cantina and a grocery.

Abounding with palms, mangos and citrus, the friendly *Huerta Saucedo RV Park* (☎ 3-03-00, popularly known as 'the Orchard') is ½ a mile (1 km) south of town, on the Gulf side of the Transpeninsular; from central Mulegé, pass beneath the Transpeninsular bridge and follow the dirt road east. Spaces with full hookups cost US$10 to US$12 each, while a space without hookups costs US$5 to US$6 for

two people, plus US$1.50 for each additional person. Hot (sometimes lukewarm) showers, clean toilets and a boat ramp are available. Members of AAA and some other travel clubs get a 10% discount. The park also offers frequent Mexican buffets and other special meals at bargain prices.

Casas de Huéspedes Cheapest of Mulegés several guest houses is the eight-room *Canett Casa de Huéspedes* on Calle Madero. It's not a bad place, but late sleepers should know that across the street the church bells chime loudly every quarter hour from 6 am; singles with private bath cost US$8.

Casa de Huéspedes Manuelita (☎ 3-01-75), kitty-corner from Lavamática Claudia on Calle Moctezuma, and *Casa de Huéspedes Nachita*, half a block to the northwest, are comparable. Nachita offers hot showers for non-guests for US$2.

Hotels & Motels *Hotel Suites Rosita* (☎ 3-02-70), on Calle Madero just a short walk from the plaza, is a pleasant, family-oriented, budget-style hotel. Each room has air-conditioning, a kitchenette and a sitting room with a table. Rates are US$20 single or double. *Hotel Terrazas* (☎ 3-00-09), on Calle Zaragoza just north of Lavamática Claudia, has several fine view rooms, but its hot water and electricity are erratic. At US$20 single or double with fan, US$25 with air-conditioning, it's a bit overpriced.

Places to Stay – middle
Sharing a courtyard with its namesake restaurant, *Hotel Las Casitas* (☎ 3-00-19) on Calle Madero near the junction with Avenida General Martínez, was once home to poet Alán Gorosave. All rooms have hot showers, air-conditioning and plenty of shade trees in front. Singles/doubles are US$21/28.

Built around a small patio and a swimming pool, remodeled *Hotel Hacienda* (☎ 3-00-21), Calle Madero 3 at the southeast corner of the plaza, is much improved from previous years despite occasional spots of peeling paint. It's also more expensive than it was – rooms with twin beds, refrigerator, air-conditioning and hot showers cost US$25 single/double. Every Sunday evening, its restaurant offers a special Sunday evening pig luau for US$9, while the bar is renowned for its 'Mulegé milk shake' – a potent concoction of tequila, rum, Kahlúa, milk and ice.

The new and appealing *Hotel La Siesta*, near the Y-intersection at the entrance to town, has singles/doubles for US$25, triples for US$28 and quadruples for US$31.

Places to Stay – top end
Hotel Serenidad (☎ 3-01-11), 2½ miles (4 km) south of town on the Transpeninsular, features clean, comfortable doubles with air-conditioning which cost US$38/50 single/double – it's a nice touch that all the rooms have names instead of numbers. The hotel also has a swimming pool, restaurant and bar. Wednesday's feature is a big Mexican dinner with a mariachi band, while the Saturday night special is roast pork. There's a small trailer park next door (US$6 per night).

About 2 miles (3 km) west of town, *Hotel Vista Hermosa* (☎ 3-02-22) is suffering from neglect; the swimming pool is in full algal bloom and, after any kind of rain, the entrance road may be impassable without 4WD. Its 20 rooms are still clean and comfortable, but it attracts few guests willing to pay US$53 single/double for an obviously declining hostelry. To get there, drive east on Calle Madero and follow the 'Vista Hermosa' signs on the Camino al Puerto.

Places to Eat
At the west end of Mulegé, just before the Transpeninsular, *Doney's Tacos* serves some of the region's best tacos. *Restaurant La Almeja*, near the Sombrerito campground, serves low-priced beer and fish tacos.

At the intersection of Calle Romero Rubio and Calle Madero, the chain restaurant *El Nido* has closed, but its former chef now operates next-door *Dany's*, the closest the humble taco will ever get to *haute cuisine*. With a variety of fillings, from carne asada to carnitas to chicken to shrimp, and a cornucopia of tasty condiments, this may be the best taco stand on the entire peninsula. Prices are more than reasonable.

Local expats suggest *Eduardo's Hot Dogs*, across from the Pemex station on Avenida Martínez, for fast food such as quality hot dogs, burgers, fish tacos and the like. *Donna Moe's Pizza*, at the northwest corner of the plaza, draws steady crowds as well.

Try *Las Casitas*, one of Mulegé's more upscale places, for typical antojitos (daily specials) and a few seafood dishes, plus unusual drinks like a mango daiquiri. A good value for breakfast is the generous combination fruit plate. *Los Equipales*, on Avenida Moctezuma just west of Calle Zaragoza, serves outstanding meals which, if dearer than most in Mulegé, are well worth the money. *El Candil*, on Calle Zaragoza near the plaza, has filling meat and seafood dishes at moderate prices. Its bar is a popular meeting place for gringos, but later in the evening it draws a more strictly Mexican crowd.

Other recommendations include the restaurant at *Hotel Vista Hermosa* for lobster and shrimp; the restaurant at *Hotel Serenidad* for Saturday night pig roasts and weekly Mexican feasts; and *La Jungla Bambú*, next to the Oasis Río Baja Trailer Park south of town, for breakfast fruit crepes, omelets and home-baked desserts.

Entertainment
Fridays, Saturdays and Sundays, Super Disco, at the corner of Calle Zaragoza and Avenida Martínez offers live, and sometimes canned, music for dancing. Hotel Hacienda also offers dancing on weekends.

Getting There & Away
Mulegé has no proper bus terminal, but buses from Tijuana to La Paz stop daily at the Y-junction (known locally as 'La Y Griega') on the Transpeninsular, at the western edge of town. Northbound buses stop at approximately 4, 5, 8 and 10 pm, and 1 and 4 am. Southbound buses stop at noon, 4, 8 and 11 pm, and 1, 2 and 4 am.

It's a pleasant half hour walk to the beaches and trailer parks south of Mulegé.

Getting Around
Hotel Hacienda rents mountain bikes for a very reasonable US$10 per day.

AROUND MULEGÉ
Misión Guadalupe
From Mulegé a rough dirt road (ask locals for help finding it) leads west into the mountains to San Estanislao, where a marked branch leads to the ruins of remote Misión Nuestra Señora de Guadalupe de Huasinapi (established in 1720), of which only foundations remain.

Trinidad (Cave Paintings)
Kerry Otterstrom, bartender at El Candil and a longtime resident of the area, leads day excursions to Cochimí rock art sites at Trinidad for US$33 per person, or overnight trips for US$50. Contact him at El Candil or through the Hotel Hacienda. Visitors intending to spend quite a bit of time in the area might consider acquiring his self-published guidebook, *Mulegé*.

BAHÍA CONCEPCIÓN
Along Bahía Concepción, south of Mulegé, are more than 50 miles (80 km) of beaches; the most accessible (and most crowded) run along the western edge of the bay, but few people travel the dirt road to Punta Concepción at the peninsula's northern tip. Camping is possible on almost every beach in the area, but most of the best sites charge for the privilege.

Kayaking
Baja Tropicales (☎ 3-00-19, fax 3-03-40 in Mulegé), operated by Roy Mahoff and Becky Aparicio, offers local kayak trips from Playa Santispac (see Places to Stay & Eat, below) for US$35 per person, including meals and beverages; they require a minimum of four people.

In addition, they offer five and six-day

Misíon Nuestra Señora de Loreto

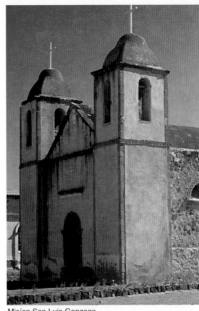

Misíon San Luis Gonzaga

Misión San Ignacio

Misión San Ignacio

Misión San Ignacio

Misión San Javier

Interior of Misión San Javier

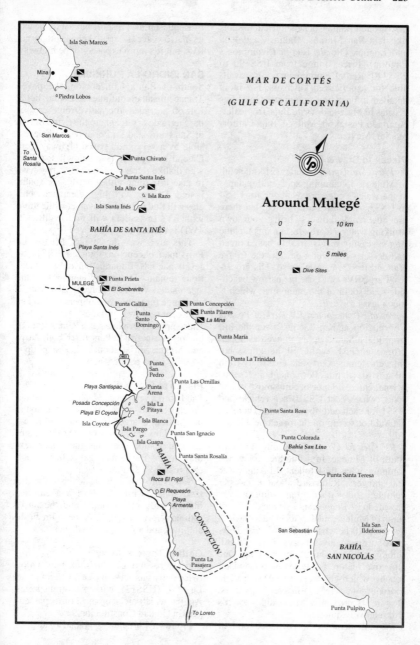

Isla San Marcos

Mina

Piedra Lobos

MAR DE CORTÉS

(GULF OF CALIFORNIA)

San Marcos

To Santa Rosalía

Punta Chivato

Punta Santa Inés

Isla Alto

Isla Razo

Isla Santa Inés

Around Mulegé

BAHÍA DE SANTA INÉS

0   5   10 km

0   5 miles

Playa Santa Inés

Dive Sites

MULEGÉ   Punta Prieta

El Sombrerito

Punta Gallita

Punta Concepción

Punta Santo Domingo

Punta Pilares

La Mina

Punta María

Punta La Trinidad

Punta San Pedro

Punta Las Ornillas

Playa Santispac

Punta Arena

Posada Concepción

Isla La Pitaya

Playa El Coyote

Isla Blanca

Isla Coyote

Punta Santa Rosa

Isla Pargo

Punta San Ignacio

Isla Guapa

Punta Colorada

Bahía San Lino

BAHÍA

Punta Santa Rosalía

Roca El Frijól

Punta Santa Teresa

El Requesón

Playa Armenta

CONCEPCIÓN

Isla San Ildefonso

San Sebastián

BAHÍA SAN NICOLÁS

Punta La Pasajera

To Loreto

Punta Pulpito

trips around Bahía Concepción and to spots like Isla San Marcos, Bahía Magdalena and Laguna Ojo de Liebre (Scammon's Lagoon). Prices range from US$290 to US$340. Rental equipment is also available for experienced kayakers. For more detailed information, inquire at Hotel Las Casitas in Mulegé or write Baja Tropicales, Apartado Postal 60, Mulegé, Baja California Sur, México.

Places to Stay & Eat

At *Playa Santispac*, 13 miles (21 km) south of Mulegé, 35 camping spots with palapas at the water's edge are available for US$4 to US$5. Amenities are limited, but there are now cold showers; bring your own drinking water. Nearby restaurants include *Ana's*, serving meals, freshly baked bread and desserts for over a decade, the *Coffee Hut* and the *Café*. Ana's also sells groceries. Large RVs can't use the narrow beachside road south of the main area, which is much less crowded.

Posada Concepción RV Park at Posada Concepción at Km 23, just over the hill from Playa Santispac, is an overdeveloped gringo enclave with full hookups, hot showers, tennis courts and electricity from 10 am to 10 pm. Permanent and semi-permanent residents occupy most of the spots, which cost US$10 per vehicle and US$1 for each additional person. There's a natural hot spring on the beach behind the mill.

RV Park El Coyote is 18 miles (30 km) south of Mulegé, in a fine area for beach camping; it has flush toilets, drinking water and showers. Rates are about US$4 per vehicle, but it's often unpleasantly crowded. *El Requesón*, 28 miles (45 km) south of Mulegé, made a recent list of Mexico's top 10 beaches in *Condé Nast Traveler*, but its scanty services mean it's still suitable only for short-term camping. One attractive feature is the tombolo (sandspit beach), which connects it to offshore Isla El Requesón, except during very high tides. Despite its proximity to the highway, it's still relatively quiet.

Playa Armenta, a short distance south of El Requesón, has a short but sandy beach; its narrow access road keeps out larger RVs, but it's more exposed to the highway.

SAN ISIDRO-LA PURÍSIMA

South of Bahía Concepción, the paved Transpeninsular continues to Loreto, but at Km 60 a graded alternative route crosses the Sierra de la Giganta to the twin villages of San Isidro and La Purísima, both accessible by a very good paved highway from Ciudad Insurgentes (see below). Travelers who dislike retracing their steps may wish to take this route either north – or southbound. Drivers with high clearance vehicles will find it more enjoyable, while those with RVs or trailers will find it difficult; 4WD is unnecessary, however.

This area was the site of Misión La Purísima Concepción, founded in 1717 by Jesuit Nicolás Tamaral, but only foundations remain. The major landmark is the steep-sided volcanic plug of **El Pilón**, a challenge for technical climbers, which lies between the two villages. Neither San Isidro nor La Purísima has a Pemex station, but private petrol sellers offer both Nova and Magna Sin at about a 25% markup – look for hand-painted signs.

Places to Stay & Eat

San Isidro's very basic *Motel Nelva*, behind the church and conveniently adjacent to the bus station, charges US$5 per person; the shared baths have hot water. The only other accommodation is an unsigned place next door to La Purísima's gas seller, which charges US$8 single.

San Isidro has a basic lonchería and a taco stand, while La Purísima eateries include only a taco stand and the fairly ordinary *Restaurant Claudia*, with basic antojitos and a few seafood dishes.

Getting There & Away

San Isidro and La Purísima now enjoy twice daily bus service (7 am and 3 pm) to La Paz (US$13) with Autotransportes Aguila, which picks up most of its passengers in Ciudad Constitución.

From La Purísima, a graded road goes

northwest to San Juanico, one of the Pacific Coast's prime surf spots, and to Laguna San Ignacio, a major whale-watching area. For more information, see the Around San Ignacio section, above.

AROUND SAN ISIDRO-LA PURÍSIMA
Paso Hondo
Paso Hondo, 19 miles (30 km) north of San Isidro by a dirt road (inquire as to condition), features Cochimí rock art sites.

Comondú
South of San Isidro, a bumpy, rocky, undulating but never really difficult (at least for high clearance vehicles) road crosses a volcanic upland before dropping steeply into San José Comondú, site of the Jesuit **Templo Misional de San José de Comondú**, dating from the 1750s.

Comondú was a propitious site for a mission because of its location near a perennial spring where several groups of Indians lived, roughly midway between the Pacific Ocean and the Gulf of California. Jesuit Franz Inama, an Austrian, oversaw the construction of the church, abandoned in 1827 and demolished, in part, at the turn of this century. Only part of the mission temple remains intact, but there are extensive walls surrounding it.

Restoration is lagging, but the building contains good examples of traditional religious art, though the canvases are deteriorating badly. Note the historic photos (dated 1901), when a major *recova* (colonnade) and two short *campanarios* (bell towers) still existed. Ask for the key to the temple at the bright-green house 30 yards to the east.

West of San José is its almost equally picturesque twin, San Miguel de Comondú. Most inhabitants of the area are fair-skinned descendants of early Spanish pioneers, in contrast to later mestizo arrivals from mainland Mexico.

For vehicles without high clearance, access to Comondú is easier by a graded lateral from Ejido Francisco Villa, which leaves the paved highway about 40 miles (65 km) north of Ciudad Insurgentes. One tricky stream ford may present problems for vehicles with low clearance.

Driving north from San José to San Isidro, the steep climb over loose rock may cause some problems. At the crest of the hill, take the left fork to San Isidro.

LORETO
A spectacularly restored mission accentuates the key role of Loreto (population 7850) in the history of the Californias. Some 210 miles (340 km) north of La Paz and 84 miles (135 km) south of Mulegé, it is still a modest fishing port with cobblestone streets, but aggressive tourist development in nearby Nopoló threatens either to kill Loreto by dehydration by siphoning off its water or to turn it into a 'Cabo San Lucas Norte'.

History
In 1697 Jesuit priest and explorer Juan María Salvatierra established Misión Nuestra Señora de Loreto as the first permanent European settlement in the Californias. In concentrating local Indians at mission settlements instead of dispersed rancherías and converting them to Catholicism, the Jesuits directly extended the influence and control of the Spanish crown in one of New Spain's most remote areas.

The first capital of the Californias, Loreto served that role until its near-destruction by a hurricane in 1829. It was a convenient staging point for missionary expansion even after the official expulsion of the Jesuits in 1767 – in 1769, Franciscan Junípero Serra trekked northward to found the now-famous chain of missions in mainland California.

Orientation
Between the Transpeninsular and the shores of the Gulf of California, Loreto has an irregular street plan, but the colonial mission church on Calle Salvatierra is a major landmark; most hotels and services are within walking distance of it. The Plaza Cívica, as the zócalo is known here, is just north of Calle Salvatierra, between Calle Madero and Calle Davis. Salvatierra itself

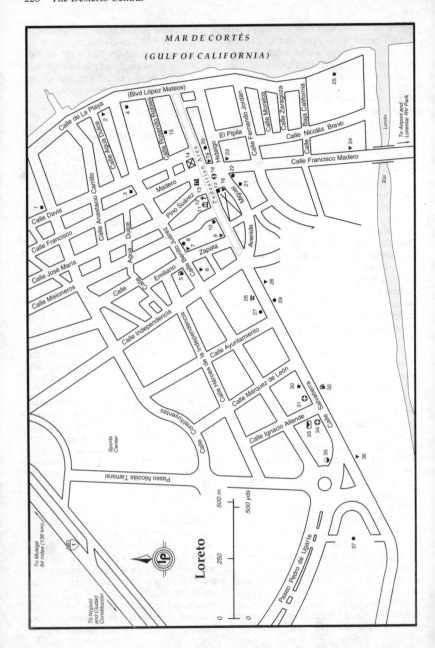

MAR DE CORTÉS

(GULF OF CALIFORNIA)

Loreto

is a de facto pedestrian mall (automobile access is limited and inconvenient), lined with topiary laurels from Calle Independencia to the beach, whose attractive malecón is ideal for sunset strolls along the Gulf.

Information

Tourist Office The former tourist office on the Plaza Cívica has closed and, as of this writing, a new building intended for the purpose on the Transpeninsular bypass stood empty and apparently abandoned. If you have a few million to invest in Nopoló (see below), the Infonatur office (☎ 3-03-03) at Km 111 will be happy to provide information, but they're not seriously interested in promoting Loreto itself.

Look around town for the monthly (more or less) newsletter *Loreto Avanza*, a good source of information on the town and its surrounding area.

Money Bancomer, at the corner of Salvatierra and Madero, changes US cash and travelers' checks from 8:30 to 11:30 am.

Post & Telecommunications Loreto's post office has moved to new quarters on Calle Ignacio Allende, just north of Calle Salvatierra.

Telmex is at Salvatierra 75, opposite the laundromat, but closes as early as 7 pm. Several other businesses along Salvatierra

have long-distance services, but add a surcharge of US$1 for domestic collect calls and US$2 for international collect calls. Loreto's area code is 113.

Loreto telephone numbers which formerly began with 3 now begin with 5; those at Nopoló, however, still begin with 3.

Customs & Immigration Loreto's Oficina de Migración y Aduana (☎ 5-04-54) is at the airport, south of town.

Travel Agencies Viajes Pedrín (☎ 5-02-04) is on the south side of Avenida Miguel Hidalgo, next to Hotel Plaza Loreto. Loretours (☎/fax 5-00-88), at the waterfront Hotel Misión, arranges fishing, diving, snorkeling and glass-bottom boat excursions, as well as car and motorbike rentals, plane tickets, hotels and tours.

Medical Services Loreto's Centro de Salud (☎ 5-00-39) is at Salvatierra 68, near the corner of Ignacio Allende. The Cruz Roja is also on Salvatierra, just west of Allende.

Laundry Lavandería El Remojón is on Calle Salvatierra, between Calle Independencia and Calle Ayuntamiento.

Misión Nuestra Señora de Loreto

Above the entrance to Misión Nuestra Señora de Loreto, the inscription 'Cabeza y

Madre de las Misiones de Baja y Alta California' (Head and Mother of the Missions of Upper & Lower California) aptly describes the role of the mission in the history of the Californias. Featuring a floor plan in the shape of a Greek cross, it suffered serious damage when the ceiling and bell tower collapsed during the 1829 hurricane; it has been restored only over the last two decades.

Museo de las Californias

Next to the mission church, INAH's mission museum (open weekdays 9 am to 12:30 pm and 1 to 5 pm) chronicles the conquest of Baja California in a rather conservative, chronological manner, extolling the missions and their accomplishments without mentioning the demographic collapse to which they contributed. While virtually ignoring the peninsula's native peoples, it does not refrain from a rather gratuitous and bombastic (if not completely inaccurate) critique of the USA in asserting that:

The missionaries not only created local agriculture and transplanted its fruits to feed man, but also introduced a technology then nonexistent in both Californias. North America, at the peak of its technology and power, breathing its own arrogance, should never forget the sacrifices and titanic efforts of the humble missionaries of Baja California, who made the Anglo-American colonization of the Far West possible; one might say that, when those pioneers arrived, the table was already set.

Nevertheless, the museum contains interesting artifacts like an early mission bell, a room of religious art, antique weapons like swords and cannon, a horse-powered *trapiche* (mill) in the interior courtyard and a kettle big enough to boil a Jesuit in oil. Of particular note is a 15th-century French astronomical globe. A set of intricate leather saddles and other horse gear used on 19th-century ranchos fills an entire room next to the museum bookstore, which sells many Spanish-language books about the archaeology, anthropology and history of Mexico and Baja California.

Museum admission costs about US$1.75.

Activities

Diving, Snorkeling & Kayaking Reefs around Isla del Carmen, Isla Coronado and other sites are superb locations for water sports. Diving and snorkeling trips can be arranged at the Loreto Inn in Nopoló, or at Deportes Blazer, on Calle Hidalgo just east of Madero, which also rents kayaks.

From April to November, the water temperature averages from 75°F to 85°F (24°C to 29°C) and visibility is about 60 to 80 feet (18 to 24 meters). From December to March, the water temperature averages from 60°F to 70°F (15°C to 21°C) and visibility is about 30 to 50 feet (9 to 15 meters).

Fishing Fishing is the main attraction for many visitors to Loreto, and many guides are available for all-day fishing trips. The fishing near Loreto, however, is poorer than it once was, as professional shrimpers' gill nets snag and kill up to 10 tons of fish for each ton of shrimp. In the late 1980s, the government of southern Baja began to consider measures to curtail the depletion of fisheries in the Gulf of California.

Dorado swarm offshore in the summer months from June through September, but marlin, sailfish and yellow tuna also inhabit these waters, along with bottomfish like cabrilla, grouper and red snapper. In the winter season, from October to April, yellowtail are the main attraction.

Loretours (see Travel Agencies, above) arranges all-day fishing trips for US$105 for up to three people, as does Alfredo's (☎ 5-01-65), on Blvd Adolfo López Mateos between Benito Juárez and Callejón Agua Dulce. Hotel Oasis (see Places to Stay, below) offers similar excursions.

Places to Stay – bottom end

Camping At Rosendo Robles 8, only half a block from the beach and a couple blocks from the mission, *RV Park El Moro* has about 20 sites with full hookups for US$6 to US$10, depending on the size of the vehicle. It's very friendly and tidy, with clean baths and hot showers, but little shade. It also 'enjoys' a cacophony of roosters and barking dogs for much of the night.

Spacious *Loremar RV Park* (☎ 5-07-11), on the beach across the Río Loreto, has full hookups, clean bathrooms, hot showers and a laundry room, but very little shade. Office hours are 8 am to 1 pm and 2 to 9 pm. Rates are US$6/8 single/double without hookups, US$11 with hookups; non-guests can use the showers for US$1. Unofficial free camping is possible at the small cove just south of the nearly vacant streets of Nopoló.

Hotels & Motels Very basic *Hotel San Martín* (☎ 5-00-42), at Calle Benito Juárez 4, is the cheapest in town for US$12 single or double. *Motel Salvatierra* (☎ 5-00-21), at Calle Salvatierra 123 between Ignacio Allende and Márquez de León, has clean but worn rooms with air-conditioning and hot showers for US$27 double.

Places to Stay – middle
Loreto generally lacks mid-range accommodation, but a new entry, very central and attractive, is the *Hotel Plaza Loreto* (☎ 5-02-80, fax 5-08-55). At Avenida Hidalgo 2 across from the mission, it has singles/doubles for US$30/35. Its mailing address is Apartado Postal 150, Loreto.

Try also the 32-room waterfront *Hotel Misión de Loreto* (☎ 5-00-48) at Calle de la Playa 1 (also known as Blvd López Mateos), which has air-conditioned singles/doubles for about US$35/40, plus a swimming pool and two restaurants on the premises.

Places to Stay – top end
On the beachfront, at the corner of Calle de la Playa and Calle Baja California, the 35-room *Hotel Oasis* (☎ 5-01-12, fax 5-07-95) offers subtropical gardens and rooms with private bath, hot water, air-conditioning and all meals for about US$75/100 single/double, including taxes. Its mailing address is Apartado Postal 17, Loreto, Baja California Sur, 23880 México.

Hotel La Pinta Loreto (☎ 5-00-25), on Calle Davis about a mile north of the plaza,

has a swimming pool, a restaurant and bar, and easy beach access. Its 48 air-conditioned rooms have private balconies facing the Sea of Cortés, showers and TVs, but some guests have complained that the lack of heating makes winter nights chilly. Singles/doubles cost around US$55/60, plus 10% tax. For more information, contact the Tijuana Baja Information Center (☎ (800) 522-1516 toll free), Suite 202, 7860 Mission Center Court, San Diego, California, USA 92108.

Places to Eat
César's (☎ 5-02-03), near the intersection of Calle Zapata and Calle Benito Juárez, comes highly recommended for both meat and seafood dishes at moderate to high prices. At Loremar RV Park (see Places to Stay, above), *George's American Style Sports Bar & Grill* has good seafood and huge, reasonably priced drinks; it will prepare to order anything caught on offshore fishing excursions.

Café Olé at Madero 14 just south of the Plaza Cívica, serves good, inexpensive breakfasts and antojitos. *Rancho Viejo*, on Juárez west of Caesar's, specializes in steak and lobster. *Asadero Las Brasas*, on the cobblestone pedestrian street near the mission, is supposedly Loreto's best taco stand.

Anthony's Casa de La Pizza, on Calle Madero south of Avenida Hidalgo near the Río Loreto, boasts 'the world's worst pizza'. American-owned *Tiffany's Pisa Parlor*, at the corner of Avenida Hidalgo and Calle Pino Suárez, appeals to an exclusively gringo clientele, in part because of its high prices – the cheapest item on the menu is a small cheese pizza for US$9 – but quality is also high. Smoking is prohibited.

El Nido (☎ 5-02-84), across from the bus station on Calle Salvatierra, is the local representative of the widespread Baja steakhouse chain. *El Buey de la Barranca*, on Calle Salvatierra between Calle Independencia and Calle Ayuntamiento, is a very popular grill with outstanding tacos as well as more elaborate dishes. *El Embarcadero*

(☎ 5-01-65), on the malecón just south of Calle Agua Dulce, specializes in seafood, as does *Playa Blanca*, on Avenida Hidalgo at the corner of Calle Madero.

La Michoacana, on Calle Salvatierra near the corner of Zapata, has decent ice cream, but excellent paletas and aguas. The bakery on Benito Juárez, one block east of Rancho Viejo, sells several kinds of pan dulce (sweet rolls) and breads.

Things to Buy

For a variety of handicrafts, try El Alacrán at the corner of Calle Salvatierra and Calle Misioneros. Conchita's, at the corner of Salvatierra and Pino Suárez, has a nice selection of jewelry, a decent selection of Baja books, high prices (even postage stamps get a substantial markup) and products made from endangered species like sea turtles which may not be imported into the USA. For hand-crafted jewelry, try El Risito de Oro on Calle Salvatierra next to the Telmex office, which also unfortunately deals in suspect items like tortoiseshell and black coral.

Getting There & Away

Air Aeropuerto Internacional de Loreto (☎ 5-04-54) is reached by a lateral off the Transpeninsular, just across the Río Loreto.

Aero California (☎ 5-05-00), on Juárez between Misioneros and Zapata, is open daily 8:30 am to 6 pm, including holidays but not Sundays. It flies daily from Los Angeles to Loreto, continuing to La Paz, and vice versa; make connections to mainland México in La Paz. Some promotional fares allow holders of tickets to La Paz to continue to Loreto for only N$1.

Bus Loreto's new bus station (☎ 5-07-67), near the traffic circle where Calle Salvatierra, Paseo Pedro de Ugarte and Paseo Nicolás Tamaral converge, is open from 6:30 am to 11 pm. Northbound buses leave at 2 pm (for Santa Rosalía), 3 pm (Tijuana), 5 pm (Santa Rosalía), Mexicali (9 pm) and Guerrero Negro (11 pm). Southbound

buses for La Paz and intermediates stop at 12:30, 7, 9, and 11 am, and 12:30, 2 and 10:30 pm; on request, buses will usually stop at Nopoló and Puerto Escondido.

Getting Around
To/From the Airport Taxis from town to Aeropuerto Internacional de Loreto cost US$7 for one person, plus US$2 for each additional person.

Car Rental Thrifty Car Rental (☎ 3-07-00, X430), in the Loreto Inn at Nopoló, is the only nearby place to rent cars.

AROUND LORETO
Nopoló

French interests have reportedly reached an agreement to take over Nopoló from Fonatur (the federal tourist development agency, also responsible for mainland Mexican debacles like Cancún and Ixtapa), which dropped this extravagant, incongruous resort complex onto an erstwhile goat ranch, 4 miles (6½ km) south of Loreto. Despite construction of an international airport and an elaborate street plan off a single palm-lined avenue, it remains largely vacant and weedy except for its single upscale hotel, lighted tennis courts and the sprawling 18-hole golf course. Nopoló also has its own clinic and fire department.

The Campo de Golf Loreto (☎ 3-04-08), which probably uses more water than the entire town of Loreto, features a cart bridge which many isolated rural communities might start a revolution for. Greens fees are US$20, while cart rentals cost US$20 and club rentals US$15.

The 250-room *Loreto Inn Hotel* (☎ 3-07-00 in Loreto; (310) 943-6233 or (800) 472-3394 toll free in the USA, fax (310) 943-4078), Nopoló's only hotel, is the best and, of course, the dearest hotel in the area. It has two swimming pools (sometimes heated), tennis courts (sometimes with nets) with a stadium for competitive matches, a disco, a bar and two restaurants. Since its recent sale, rates are more reasonable, and it also offers more reasonably priced four-day, three-night hotel-activity packages from Los Angeles, including diving (US$235 per person), fishing (US$218), golf (US$129) or just plain sun (US$89). Its US mailing address is 16211 E Whittier Blvd, Whittier, California 90603.

Misión San Francisco Javier

Built from blocks of volcanic stone in the Sierra de la Giganta, west of Loreto, San Francisco Javier de Viggé-Biaundó is one of the best preserved mission churches in the Californias. Founded in 1699 at nearby Rancho Viejo by the famous Jesuit Francisco María Piccolo, the Californias' second mission moved to its present site in 1720 but was not completed until 1758.

The church itself is in very fine condition, with its original walls, floors and venerable religious artworks, but visitors may no longer climb the spiral staircase to the chorus. Acequias of Jesuit vintage, the first on the peninsula, still irrigate the village fields. Every 3 December, hundreds of pilgrims celebrate the saint's fiesta here.

Just over 1 mile south of Loreto is the junction for the spectacular 22-mile (35-km) mountain road to the village, which takes about 1½ hours not counting photo opportunities. The dirt surface is graded only to Rancho Viejo, but is passable for most passenger cars despite a few bumpy spots and arroyo crossings. At **Rancho Las Parras**, in a verdant canyon halfway to San Javier, there are figs, dates, olives and citrus for sale, but livestock have contaminated most of the water along the route – do not drink without treating it. A spring just before Km 20, westbound, should be potable, and there are a couple of potential swimming holes.

With an early start, this would be a good day trip on a mountain bike, but parts of the road are steep enough that even the strongest biker will probably have to walk for short stretches. The village's only tourist facility is *Restaurant Palapa San Javier* near the mission church, which serves simple meals and cold sodas (no beer) under a shady palapa.

PUERTO ESCONDIDO

Puerto Escondido, a well-protected port/marina 16 miles (26 km) south of Loreto, is the site of a major joint venture between Fonatur and a French investment company to build a Mediterranean-style deep-water port and resort complex with five-star hotels, luxurious private homes, condominiums, shops and a fitness center, and moorings for 300 yachts.

Near the lateral to Puerto Escondido is the *Tripui Resort RV Park* (☎ 3-08-18), an antiseptic RV park/campground/fortress in a noisy location along the highway and remote from the bay. Full hookups, a swimming pool, lighted tennis courts, a laundry room, a restaurant and a grocery store are available. Rates are US$14 for a vehicle and US$10 for a tent. Members of RV clubs should ask for discounts.

Budget travelers can try catching a lift with a yacht at the marina here; there's a radio net on channel 68 between 8 and 8:30 am. Ask at the yacht dock near the seawall

for permission to use a radio and state your business.

BAHÍA MAGDALENA &
THE LLANO DE MAGDALENA

Beyond Puerto Escondido, the road climbs and twists through the Sierra de la Giganta before turning westward into the Llano de Magdalena (Magdalena Plain). See map on page 203. **Ciudad Insurgentes**, a major highway junction, has restaurants, several groceries and two Pemex stations, but no accommodation; if planning to continue west to Puerto López Mateos or north to Comondú, stock up on supplies here.

Bahía Magdalena, one of the key whale-breeding sites on the entire coast, is popularly known as 'Mag Bay' among English speakers. The area has had a colorful history despite (or perhaps because of) its thinly populated coastline. In colonial times, Sebastián Vizcaíno anchored nearby but, finding no surface water, soon departed; some years later missionary Clemente Guillén found no suitable harbor and, though the Jesuits built a lowland chapel under the control of Misión San Luis Gonzaga, they never really colonized the area.

Both before and after Mexican independence, Bahía Magdalena attracted smugglers; foreign whalers worked the area from 1836 to 1846, assisted by laborers from Comondú. During the Mexican-American War, the US Navy promised local residents US citizenship in return for their support. After the failure of secret negotiations that would have kept Baja California under US control in exchange for a cash indemnity and after the signing of the Treaty of Guadalupe Hidalgo, these residents were forced to leave.

There have been several other US attempts to acquire the Baja peninsula. Though the government of Benito Juárez was willing to sell, it set too high a price but still encouraged foreign projects like Jacob Leese's Lower California Colonization & Mining Company, later known as the Lower California Company. In 1866, this company gained title to all Baja lands between 24°20' N and 31° N (roughly from La Paz to San Quintín) in a transparently fraudulent colonization attempt.

The San Francisco-based company went so far as to issue bogus paper money under the name of 'The Bank of Lower California Trust and Loan Association' for the proposed city of Cortez. After an exploration in 1867, one disillusioned member warned that 'To send a party of colonists here, without previous preparation of the land at great expense, would be criminal', but the company responded with a barrage of propaganda in its favor.

As an agricultural colonization project, the company failed scandalously, but its concession to collect orchilla, a valuable dye plant, employed about 500 gatherers in the Llano de Magdalena. This spurred the opening of a customs house and a brief boom until the development of alternative aniline dyes reduced the market. Another attempt at agricultural colonization, under the successor Chartered Company of California, also failed.

In the late 19th century, the government of Porfirio Díaz had allowed the US Navy to establish a coaling station in Bahía Magdalena and, after the turn of the century, to hold target practice and maneuvers in the area. In the latter years of the Díaz dictatorship, however, a request by the US State Department to extend these agreements aroused nationalist sentiments; one newspaper editor in Mazatlán even thundered that 'the history of Texas and California will be repeated'.

Despite displays of force and fears of Baja's annexation by the US, the Navy departed when the agreements expired. The subsequent sale of the Chartered Company, the spread of the Mexican Revolution and a Mexican fishing agreement with Japan served as pretexts for annexationists in the US Congress and the press (most notably the Hearst newspapers) to urge a US takeover, but President Woodrow Wilson resisted the pressure.

Accelerating agricultural development in the latter half of the 20th century finally consolidated Mexican control of the area, and today the area around Ciudad Constitución, in particular, is booming. Its main lure for travelers, however, is whale-watching.

PUERTO LÓPEZ MATEOS

Protected by the offshore barrier of Isla Magdalena, Puerto Adolfo López Mateos (population 2414) is one of the best sites for whale-watching on the entire Pacific Coast. Boca de Soledad, only a short distance north of the port, boasts the highest density of whales anywhere along the peninsula.

Servicios Turísticos El Faro operates a whale-watching camp 3 km from town (bring your own equipment), but it's also possible to see the whales from the shore at **Playa El Faro**, just beyond the lighthouse. Pangueros like Sergio García Tapía (☎ (113) 1-01-39) and Ramiro Castro González charge US$30 per hour for up to eight persons, though they generally prefer to take only five or six on three-hour whale-watching excursions.

Before agreeing to a whale-watching trip here, check to see the guide's permit; pirate guides from elsewhere know little about local conditions, their boats and equipment may be unsafe and they lack commitment to the local community.

Places to Stay & Eat

Free camping is possible among the scrubby mangroves at Playa El Faro, but watch for high tides, which can strand vehicles. María del Rosario González offers clean but basic accommodation for US$10 per person, and was planning to add hot water; her inconspicuous, unsigned place is two short blocks north of the IMSS (Seguridad Social) clinic, on the right as you enter town on the paved highway.

Restaurant El Faro is open all year, but *Restaurant Ballena Gris* is open only during the whale-watching season. López Mateos also has a couple of taco stands.

Getting There & Away

Puerto López Mateos is 20 miles (32 km) west of Ciudad Insurgentes by an excellent paved road; Autotransportes Aguila provides twice-daily bus service from Ciudad Constitución, at 11:30 am and 7 pm; return service to Constitución leaves at 7 am and 12:30 pm.

CIUDAD CONSTITUCIÓN

Ciudad Constitución (population 37,480), a major agricultural center 134 miles (215 km) northwest of La Paz and 36 miles (58 km) east of Puerto San Carlos on Bahía Magdalena, has grown dramatically with the Llano de Magdalena's rapid expansion of commercial agriculture. It bears all the marks of a 'progressive' city: clean, broad paved streets (at least in the center), several banks and even high culture – the Baja California symphony of La Paz made the local Teatro de la Ciudad (City Theater) a major stop on its national tour.

At the north entrance to town, at the turnoff to Puerto San Carlos, is a monument to General Agustín Olachea Avilés, a native of Todos Santos who was a striker at the famous Cananea copper mine in Sonora; he then joined the revolutionary forces in 1913, became a general in 1920 at the age of only 28 and put down a Yaqui Indian rebellion in Sonora in 1926. Later, as governor of Baja California's Territorio Sur, he promoted agricultural development in Ciudad Constitución.

Fresh water for cultivation was a serious problem before the exploitation of huge aquifers beneath the plain; Israeli technicians have since advised farmers on water conservation and crop substitution to take advantage of newly perforated wells. Water-efficient crops like garbanzos (chickpeas) and citrus are superseding thirsty cotton.

Because Ciudad Constitución is primarily a farming town in recent times, most travelers find little of interest here, but it's very convenient to the major whale-watching centers of Puerto San Carlos and Puerto López Mateos, which have only limited accommodation.

Orientation

The north-south Transpeninsular, known

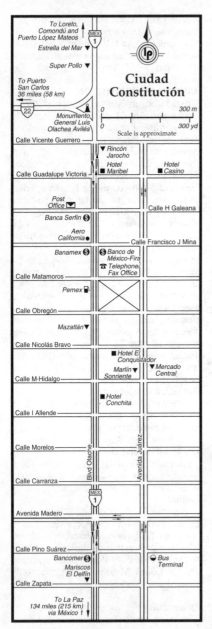

To Loreto,
Comondú and
Puerto López Mateos

Estrella del Mar ▼

Super Pollo ▼

To Puerto
San Carlos
36 miles (58 km)

Monumento
General Luis
Olachea Avilés

Ciudad
Constitución

0   300 m

0   300 yd

Scale is approximate

Calle Vicente Guerrero

▼ Rincón
Jarocho

Hotel
■ Maribel

Hotel
■ Casino

Calle Guadalupe Victoria

Post
Office ▼

Calle H Galeana

Banca Serfin §

Aero
California ●

Calle Francisco J Mina

Banamex §

§ Banco de
México-Fira
☎ Telephone/
Fax Office

Calle Matamoros

Pemex ⛽

Calle Obregón

Mazatlán ▼

Calle Nicolás Bravo

■ Hotel El
Conquistador

Marlín ▼
Sonriente

▼ Mercado
Central

Calle M-Hidalgo

■ Hotel
Conchita

Calle I Allende

Calle Morelos

Calle Carranza

Blvd Olachea

Avenida Juárez

Avenida Madero

Calle Pino Suárez

Bancomer §

Mariscos
El Delfín

● Bus
Terminal

Calle Zapata

To La Paz
134 miles (215 km)
via México 1 ▼

formally as Blvd General Agustín Olachea Avilés and more commonly as Blvd Olachea, is Ciudad Constitución's main street, but the city has outgrown the strip development phase (unlike northern Baja towns like San Quintín). Still, most important services are within a block or two of Blvd Olachea, where passing delivery trucks have clipped, bent and turned the city's once shiny Banamex street signs so that through traffic seems to cross Olachea at every corner. The other main street is the parallel Avenida Juárez, one block to the east.

Information

Money Constitución's has no cambios, but several banks on Blvd Olachea will change cash dollars or travelers' checks: Banca Serfin at the corner of Galeana, Banamex at the southwest corner of Francisco J Mina, Banco de México-Fira at its southeast corner and Bancomer on Pino Suárez, just west of Blvd Olachea.

Post & Telecommunications The post office is on Calle Galeana, just west of Blvd Olachea. Nearly all of Constitución's many public phones seem to be out of order, so try the cabinas on the east side of Blvd Olachea, between Matamoros and Francisco J Mina. Constitución's area code is 113.

Places to Stay

Camping *Campestre La Pila* (☎ 2-05-62) is an RV park at the end of a dirt road just south of town, which leads west for about half a mile (1 km); follow the signs. There is no hot water but showers, electrical outlets, toilets and a swimming pool are available. The park, also a popular picnic ground for locals on the weekend, is a pleasant, grassy area surrounded by a farm (with accompanying animal sounds) and a few shade trees. At harvest times, freshly picked vegetables are available from the farm. Rates for two people are about US$8; an extra person is US$2.

Hotels *Hotel Casino* (☎ 2-04-55), on

Guadalupe Victoria about one block east of Hotel Maribel, has very spartan rooms for about US$20 single or double; the go-cart track across the street can play hell with your afternoon siesta. *Hotel Conchita* (☎ 2-02-66), Blvd Olachea 180, charges US$20 double (US$22 with TV).

Three-star *Hotel El Conquistador* (☎ 2-17-31) at Calle Nicolás Bravo 161, charges US$37 double; it's a bit dark and formal, but the restaurant has cheap meals. *Hotel Maribel* (☎ 2-01-55), at Calle Guadalupe Victoria 156 near Blvd Olachea (the Transpeninsular), has rooms comfortable enough for a night – each with telephone and TV – which cost about US$39/46 single/double. The attached restaurant offers basic Mexican dishes from about US$5 to US$7.

Other choices include *Hotel Reforma* (☎ 2-09-88) at Calle Obregón 125 and *Hotel Julia* (☎ 2-23-69) at Calle Galeana 219 (both rated 'economical'), plus *Hotel Lizajú* (☎ 2-05-32) at Calle Guerrero 521 and *Auto Hotel Villa Park* (☎ 2-20-82) at Calle Allende 24 (both rated three-stars).

Places to Eat

For Constitución's cheapest eats, try the many taco stands (less appealing than their counterparts in many other Baja locations) or the *Mercado Central* on Blvd Juárez, between Calle Hidalgo and Calle Bravo.

Super Pollo, just north of the Olachea monument, specializes in grilled chicken, Sinaloa-style. Next door *Estrella del Mar* is a seafood restaurant, as is *Rincón Jarocho*, on the east side of Olachea just south of the monument. Other seafood choices include *Mariscos El Delfín* at Blvd Olachea and Calle Zapata, and the more upscale *Marlín Sonriente*, on Avenida Juárez between Hidalgo and Bravo. Try also *Restaurant Mazatlán*, on Blvd Olachea between Bravo and Obregón.

Getting There & Away

Air Constitución has no commercial air services, but Aero California has an office on Blvd Olachea, at the corner of Francisco J Mina, where it's possible to make or reconfirm reservations for flights from Loreto or La Paz.

Bus The bus terminal is at the corner of Avenida Juárez and Calle Pino Suárez, one block east of Blvd Olachea. North-south buses on the Transpeninsular stop here, and there are also buses to Puerto San Carlos, Puerto López Mateos and points north on the paved coastal highway as far as La Purísima and San Isidro.

PUERTO SAN CARLOS

On Bahía Magdalena, about 36 miles (58 km) west of Ciudad Constitución by an

excellent paved road (watch for livestock, including cattle and even pigs), Puerto San Carlos (population 3571) is a dusty, windy but friendly deep-water port that ships cotton and alfalfa from the fields of the Llano de Magdalena. All the streets are named for Mexican port cities.

Nearby beaches are fine for free camping, clam-digging and fishing, while from January to March, whale-watching is a major attraction. Gasoline, including Magna Sin and diesel, are available at the Pemex station.

In the late 19th century, a US Navy coaling station in the area became a major political controversy in mainland México. More recently, a Japanese company has obtained a concession of 5000 acres (2000 hectares) for a tourist development south of Puerto San Carlos, but offshore Isla Magdalena, a barrier island, is under control of the Mexican navy and off-limits to this enterprise.

Whale-Watching

In season, for US$20 per hour, local pangueros will take up to five or six passengers to view whales in Bahía Magdalena. Many people come for the day from Loreto (only 1½ hours away) or La Paz in rental cars.

Places to Stay & Eat

Puerto San Carlos has no RV parks, but it's possible to camp on the fairly clean public beach north of town without charge. Some installations exist, but they're falling into disrepair. South of town, among the mangroves, it's a bit messier, but there's a good selection of bird life – proving that aesthetics are more important to humans than to birds.

Hotel accommodation is more abundant than in the past, but the whale-watching season puts a strain on local capacity. *Motel Las Brisas* (☎ 6-01-52), on Calle Madero, has basic but clean rooms from US$12 to US$18, depending on the number of beds. The newer *Hotel Palmar* (☎ 6-00-35) charges US$17/20 single/double, while the very new and friendly *Hotel Alcatraz* (☎ 6-

00-17) has singles/doubles with TV for US$20/23; its attractive *Restaurant Bar El Patio* is unquestionably the best in town.

A nameless but newly landscaped taco stand at Calle Puerto La Paz and Calle Puerto Madero, around the corner from Motel Las Brisas, has tremendous shrimp tacos at very low prices.

Getting There & Away

Autotransportes Aguilar has two buses daily, at 7:30 am and 1:45 pm, to Ciudad Constitución (US$3) and La Paz (US$10). This is the town's only public transportation.

AROUND THE LLANO DE MAGDALENA

Misión San Luis Gonzaga

At Km 195, about 9 miles (15 km) south of Ciudad Constitución on the Transpeninsular, a graded lateral good enough even for low riders or mammoth RVs leads 25 miles (40 km) east to the edge of the Sierra de la Giganta and the date palm oasis of San Luis Gonzaga. Look for the sign reading 'Presa Iguajil'.

Founded in 1737, the mission of San Luis Gonzaga closed with the departure of the Jesuits in 1768 – after an original Indian population of 2000 had fallen to only 300. Its well-preserved church, dating from the 1750s, is not one of the gems of the mission system, lacking the embellishments of San Borja or San Javier, but its twin bell towers are unusual. Besides the church, there are several notable ruins of more recent vintage, with elaborate neoclassical columns.

The only facilities in the village are a school and a Conasupo. Just east of the arroyo, a road suitable for high-clearance, short-wheelbase vehicles only (4WD is not essential) leads 16 miles (27 km) south past Ranchos Iraquí, La Palmilla (Conasupo and cold drinks), El Caporal and Pozo de Iritú to Las Tinajitas, where it meets another lateral from Santa Rita (see below), which climbs east into the sierra as far as the extensive but poorly preserved ruins of Misión La Pasión. This route is more difficult but much more interesting than the corresponding segment of the Transpeninsular.

Puerto Chale
About 36 miles (58 km) south of Ciudad Constitución is the village of Santa Rita, where a 15-mile (24-km) graded dirt road leads west to the tiny fishing camp of Puerto Chale, popular with windsurfers.

Misión La Pasión
From Km 128, on the Transpeninsular, a graded dirt road climbs east to Rancho Las Tinajitas (see the entry for Misión San Luis Gonzaga, above) and Rancho Los Ciruelos, beyond which the ungraded surface to the Jesuit Misión La Pasión becomes difficult for vehicles without high clearance. The ruins themselves are just west of Santa María Toris, a friendly rancho beyond which a 4WD route continues toward **Misión Dolores del Sur**, but stops just short of those ruins – an hour's hike or five minutes by panga from the end of the route. Toris itself has a Conasupo market and an *internado* (boarding school), but no other facilities. There are cave paintings in the canyon below Toris, among its numerous volcanic plugs and mesas, but these are difficult to locate without a guide.

Only foundations remain of La Pasión, which lasted from 1737 until expulsion of the Jesuits in 1768, when its Indians were transferred to Todos Santos. Those foundations are very extensive, however; about 10 years ago, according to local residents, the last standing wall fell. Note that the usually reliable AAA road map places the ruins on the wrong (north) side of the road and has several other inaccuracies. At the junction 3 miles (5 km) west of Toris (not shown on the AAA map), the right fork leads to Rancho Soledad and the Gulf fish camp of San Evaristo, where another rather difficult

road leads south to La Paz (see the La Paz chapter for details of this road). Unless more detailed information is available, only 4WD vehicles should attempt this route.

EL CIEN
El Cien, so called because it lies exactly 100 km northwest of La Paz on the Transpeninsular, is 35 miles (56 km) south of Santa Rita. It has a Pemex station and a decent restaurant. Thirteen miles (21 km) farther south, at Km 80 just beyond a microwave station, is a junction with a 12-mile (20-km) dirt road to **Punta Conejo** (some smaller RVs have successfully navigated this route, but not without cosmetic damage).

Countless tiny crabs scurry over Punta Conejo's firm, sandy beach to the safety of their burrows, wary of the gulls overhead, while apparent bicycle tracks disappear under a rock overhang, where hermit crabs hide from their pursuers. The area attracts many surfers to its right break, mostly in southerly swells, but it is far from crowded; surf fishing is also popular.

At the southeast end of the beach, a jutting headland consists of a marine conglomerate composed almost entirely of fossils – follow the informal trail at the base of the cliff to a number of smaller, more secluded beaches, but be prepared to scramble over the rocks. Remember that Mexican law prohibits fossil hunting; in any event, all these fossils are comparatively recent.

There are oyster beds about 5 miles (8 km) south of Punta Conejo, but drifting sand makes the road difficult beyond that point even for 4WD vehicles. Surfers headed for **Punta Márquez** might find it easier to approach via the graded road from the Transpeninsular to Ejido Conquista, between Km 55 and 54.

La Paz & the Cape Region

This chapter covers the modern, southern city of La Paz and surrounding areas, including the popular resorts of Los Cabos (San José del Cabo and Cabo San Lucas). This is the costliest and most self-consciously tourist-oriented part of the peninsula, but it still offers unconventional opportunities for determined travelers.

The La Paz Region

LA PAZ
History
At the south end of Bahía de La Paz, the sheltered port of La Paz (population 149,360) is capital of the state of Baja California Sur. In 1535 on nearby Península Pichilingue, Hernán Cortés himself established the first European settlement in Baja California; despite the discovery of pearls in the Gulf of California, it was soon abandoned due to Indian hostility and food and water shortages.

By the late 16th century, England and Holland were disputing Spain's maritime hegemony, raiding Spanish ships throughout the world; the treasure-laden galleons that sailed from Manila to Acapulco were especially popular targets.

In 1596, the Viceroy of New Spain granted Sebastián Vizcaíno a license to exploit the pearl fisheries of the Cape Region and establish settlements to discourage the activities of Northern European privateers.

Though Vizcaíno renamed the former Bahía de la Santa Cruz aş Bahía de La Paz (Bay of Peace), he abandoned the idea of a settlement because of the shortage of supplies and the area's limited agricultural potential. In 1720, the Jesuits established a mission, but epidemics and Indian uprisings led to its abandonment only 29 years later.

La Paz became a permanent settlement in 1811, after most of the Indians had succumbed to European diseases, thanks in part to a grant of mineral rights to Juan José Espinoza at nearby San Antonio. In 1830, after a hurricane destroyed Loreto and inland San Antonio proved unsuitable, La Paz became the capital of California. American troops occupied the town during the Mexican-American War (1846 to 1848) but left after the governments of Mexico and the USA signed the Treaty of Guadalupe Hidalgo.

A few years later, in November 1853, renegade US filibuster William Walker occupied La Paz with a group of armed mercenaries and 'cabinet officers' who imprisoned Mexican government officials and proclaimed a 'Republic of Lower California'. Finding little support, Walker and his partisans retreated from Baja a few months later as Mexican forces advanced. After the Walker fiasco, La Paz became a more settled trading port, with a thriving pearl and pearl shell industry that nearly disappeared when the Revolution of 1910 broke out.

La Paz is still a significant port, but it has also become a resort. Spectacular sunsets over the bay, a palm-lined malecón, neocolonial buildings and nearby Península Pichilingue's beautiful beaches are its main attractions. It is also the terminus for ferries to the mainland Mexican ports of Topolobampo and Mazatlán.

Orientation
As the Transpeninsular approaches the city, it runs parallel to Bahía de La Paz and becomes Calzada (Calle) Abasolo; to continue straight to Cabo San Lucas, turn right on Calle 5 de Febrero and follow signs to 'Carretera al Sur' and 'Cabo San Lucas'. Four blocks east of 5 de Febrero, Abasolo becomes Paseo Alvaro Obregón, which runs along the palm-lined waterfront

---

The Dutch in the Pacific

New World piracy was largely the province of the English, but other Northern European countries also eagerly joined in the battle against Spanish wealth and hegemony in the Americas. The French and especially the Dutch were most active in the Caribbean and on the coast of Brazil, but the Dutch had ambitions in the Pacific as well.

Since the late 16th-century voyage of Sir Francis Drake, British buccaneers had frequented the Pacific Coast of North and South America, despite logistical difficulties arising from the distance between their home and convenient, well-watered island bases in the Caribbean. In New Spain and Baja California, the British lay in wait for treasure-laden galleons returning from Manila and sometimes took major prizes. Thomas Cavendish's capture of the *Santa Ana* off Cabo San Lucas in 1587 attracted interest to New Spain.

The Netherlands, having rebelled against Spanish domination in 1566, was eager to make its mark on the seas. The Dutch became rivals to the Spaniards in the Caribbean, and to the Portuguese in Brazil, and they soon rounded the Horn to the Pacific. Though they lurked at Cabo San Lucas in anticipation of emulating Cavendish's windfall, their earliest voyages had limited success. Profit was not the only motive that spurred the Dutch; a religious element also lay behind their actions. The Dutch were fanatical Protestants who resented the reactionary Catholicism the Spaniards had imposed on them in Europe.

In 1615, the surprisingly genteel occupation of Acapulco by the Dutch privateer Joris van Speilbergen induced the Spaniards to build the famous port's landmark castle, the Fuerte de San Diego. For decades, though, the menace of Dutch privateers forced the Spaniards to send patrols from the mainland to the Cape Region. Península Pichilingue, north of La Paz, even takes its name from the Dutch privateers whom the Spaniards called 'Flexelingas', after their home port of Vlissingen, just north of the modern Belgian border. ■

---

malecón and eventually leads to Península Pichilingue.

Most of La Paz has a regular grid pattern that makes orientation easy, but the city center's crooked streets and alleys change their names almost every block. Four blocks south of the pier, on Avenida Independencia, Plaza Constitución is the heart of the city.

Both Plaza Constitución, now known officially as the Jardín Velasco, and the tourist pier on the malecón have attractive bandshells. Many tourist activities take place on the tourist pier on weekends.

Information

Tourist Office The Secretaría de Turismo del Estado (SECTUR) maintains an Oficina de Información Turística (☎ 2-59-39) on the waterfront, at the corner of Paseo Alvaro Obregón and Calle 16 de Septiembre. The helpful, English-speaking staff distribute a variety of leaflets and also help tourists find hotel space. Its open from 8 am to 8 pm daily, and 9 am to 1 pm weekends.

SECTUR also has offices (☎ 2-11-90) at Km 5 of the Transpeninsular, west of down-

town, open 8 am to 8 pm weekdays; and at Aeropuerto Internacional La Paz, open Monday, Thursday and Friday 8 am to 8 pm, Tuesday and Wednesday 3 pm to 8 pm.

The Baja Californian, a bimonthly English-language newspaper published in La Paz, usually contains a few informative articles and lists of current events and festivities.

Money Most banks and cambios are on or around Calle 16 de Septiembre; Bancomer and Banoro are both across from the intersection of Calle Esquerro. Bank hours for changing money are 8:30 to 11 am weekdays.

Banco Mexicano and Banamex (which is probably the most efficient of all the banks in town) are across the street from each other, at the junction of Calle Agustín Arreola and Calle Esquerro. Banco Internacional, is at the corner of Calle 5 de Mayo and Revolución.

Shopping centers like the Centro Comercial Californiano, across from the Palacio de Gobierno, and the Centro Comercial Colima, near the corner of Abasolo and

Colima, will change travelers' checks if the holders make purchases of at least 10% of the face value of the checks.

Immigration Servicios Migratorios (☎ 5-34-93), on the 2nd floor of the Edificio Milhe at Paseo Obregón 2140, between Calle Allende and Calle Juárez, is open 8 am to 8 pm weekdays. Travelers planning to go to mainland Mexico must have their tourist cards stamped (validated) before purchasing a ticket; bring a passport or birth certificate. On weekends, immigration officials staff the ferry terminal at Pichilingue and the airport (☎ 2-18-29).

Post & Telecommunications The post and telegraph office is at the corner of Constitución and Revolución, one block east of Jardín Velazco.

Seemingly placed at the noisiest intersections in town, La Paz's public telephones are nearly all out of order, so it's difficult to make a collect call without paying a surcharge of up to US$2 at private phone offices in pharmacies and boutiques along Obregón and elsewhere. Newer public telephones are being installed in several locations, so this deplorable situation may improve.

Verify charges before calling, as rates can vary up to 50% between offices. One reasonable place is Jazahel, a small boutique at the corner of Calle 16 de Septiembre and Calle Belisario Domínguez.

La Paz's area code is 112.

Travel Agencies Turismo La Paz (☎ 2-83-00, 2-76-76), at Calle Esquerro 1679 near Calle La Paz, is the local American Express representative.

Viajes Palmira (☎ 2-40-30), on the malecón across from Hotel Los Arcos, offers all the usual travel services and also rents cars and bicycles; one reader recommends not paying for snorkel trips and similar excursions until the day of departure.

Viajes Lybsa (☎ 2-60-01), next to Thrifty Rent-a-Car on Paseo Obregón, near the corner of Lerdo de Tejada, runs full-day excursions to Isla Espíritu Santo (US$40)

from Pichilingue, but these usually require at least seven or eight persons total. Viajes Baja (☎ 2-36-60, 2-41-30) is at Paseo Obregón 2110, corner of Allende.

Turipaz (☎ 5-74-77), at the El Cardón Trailer Park at Km 4 of the Transpeninsular, arranges city tours, beach tours, whale-watching (US$85) and all-day diving trips to Cabo San Lucas (US$100).

Bookshops Librería Contiempo, Agustín Arreola 25-A near Obregón, keeps a selection of more or less outdated US newspapers and magazines, but usually carries the most recent issue of the English-language Mexico City *News*.

The Museo Regional de Antropología e Historia (☎ 2-01-62), at the corner of Calle 5 de Mayo and Calle Ignacio Altamirano, has a good selection of Spanish-language books on Baja California and mainland Mexico; next-door Librería Ágora de La Paz (☎ 2-62-04) is even better, offering many of the same items for more reasonable prices.

Medical Services La Paz's Hospital Salvatierra (☎ 2-14-96, 2-15-96) is on Calle Bravo between Licenciado Verdad and Ortiz de Domínguez. For the Cruz Roja, dial ☎ 2-11-11 or 2-12-22.

Laundry Lavandería Yoly is on Calle 5 de Mayo, between Licenciado Verdad and Conde de Revillagigedo, opposite the baseball park.

Museo Regional de Antropología e Historia

La Paz's exceptional anthropological & historical museum (☎ 2-01-62), at the corner of Calle 5 de Mayo and Calle Ignacio Altamirano, chronicles the peninsula's past from prehistory to the Revolution of 1910. Exhibits cover pre-Columbian rock art, native peoples, the mission era, various mining booms, the arrival of independence and William Walker's invasion (note the replica of Walker's flag).

Open weekdays 8 am to 6 pm, Saturdays 9 am to 1 pm, the museum also has a good

To Aquamarina RV Park and Hotel Gran Baja La Paz

To Hotel La Posada de Engelbert

See Inset

53

Calle Rangel

Calle Topete

Calle Abasolo

To Airport, RV Parks and Ciudad Constitución

Calle Belisario Domínguez

56

60

57 58 61

55

54

59 62

63

Calle Francisco Madero

Calle Revolución

Calle Aquiles Serdán

Calle Guillermo Prieto

Calle Ignacio Ramírez

Calle Ignacio Altamirano

Calle Valentín Gómez Farías

Calle Sonora

Calle Cuauhtémoc

Calle 5 de Febrero

Calle Navarro

Calle Encinas

Calle Legaspi

Calle Márquez de León

Calle Pineda

Calle Juárez

Calle Allende

Calle Rosales

Calle Bravo

70

71

Calle Héroes de la Independencia

Calle Josefa Ortiz de Domínguez

72

Calle Jalisco

Calle Oaxaca

Calle Nayarit

Calle Puebla

Calle Sinaloa

Calle Veracruz

Calle Lic Verdad

Calle Conde de Revillagigedo

School

Camino A Las Garzas

Calle General Felix Ortega

Calle Isabel La Católica

Calle Isabel La Católica

76

75

Calle Melitón Albañez

Calle Melitón Albañez

77

Calle México

Calle México

Calle Durango

Calle Durango

Calle Chiapas

Calle Chiapas

Calle Yucatán

Calle Yucatán

Calle Padre Kino

To Cabo San Lucas
138 mi (221 km)

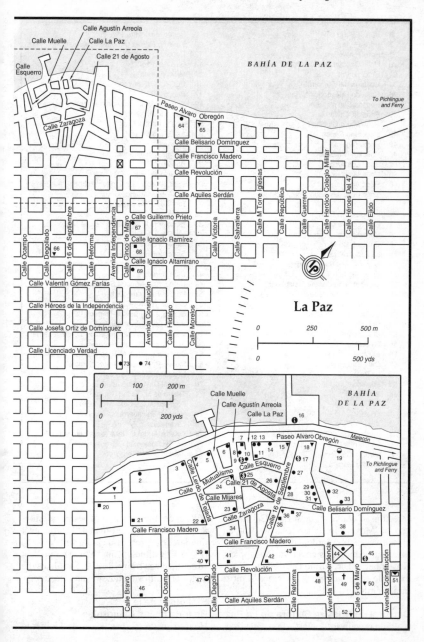

Calle Muelle
Calle Agustín Arreola
Calle La Paz
Calle 21 de Agosto
Calle Esquerro

BAHÍA DE LA PAZ

To Pichlingue
and Ferry

Paseo Alvaro Obregón

Calle Zaragoza

64
65

Calle Belisario Domínguez
Calle Francisco Madero
Calle Revolución
Calle Aquiles Serdán

Calle Ocampo
Calle Degollado
Calle 16 de Septiembre
Calle Reforma
Calle Cinco de Mayo
Avenida Independencia

Calle Guillermo Prieto
67
Calle Ignacio Ramírez
68
Calle Ignacio Altamirano
69

Calle M Torre Iglesias
Calle Victoria
Calle Salvatierra
Calle República
Calle Guerrero
Calle Heroico Colegio Militar
Calle Héroes Del 47
Calle Ejido

66

Calle Valentín Gómez Farías
Calle Héroes de la Independencia
Calle Josefa Ortiz de Domínguez

Avenida Constitución
Calle Hidalgo
Calle Morelos

La Paz

0   250   500 m

0   500 yds

Calle Licenciado Verdad
73   74

0   100   200 m

0   200 yds

BAHÍA
DE LA PAZ

Calle Muelle
Calle Agustín Arreola
Calle La Paz
16

Malecón

Paseo Alvaro Obregón
7 12 13
8   15   18
5   6   10 14   19
9   11   17
4   Calle Esquerro
3   Mutualismo
Calle Leandro de Tejeda
24   Calle 21 de Agosto
25
2
26   27
29
30   32
1   28   31
33
20   Calle Belisario Domínguez
21
22   23   Calle Zaragoza
34   35 36 37
38
Calle Francisco Madero
39   41
40   Calle Francisco Madero   42   43   44   45
Calle Revolución
46   47   48   49   50   51
Calle Aquiles Serdán
52

Calle Bravo
Calle Ocampo
Calle Degollado
Calle Reforma
Calle 16 de Septiembre
Avenida Independencia
Calle 5 de Mayo
Avenida Constitución

To Pichlingue
and Ferry

selection of books on both Baja California and on Mexico in general, as well as an attractive cactus garden on the grounds. Seasonal exhibitions cover various topics; November's 'Day of the Dead' display, for example, commemorates Mexico's most famous informal holiday.

Catedral de Nuestra Señora de La Paz

Nothing remains of La Paz's first cathedral, built under the direction of Jesuit missionaries Jaime Bravo and Juan de Ugarte, near the site of present-day Jardín Velazco (Plaza Constitución) in 1720. The present structure dates from 1861 but simulates the styles of California mission architecture.

Biblioteca de la Historia de las Californias

Housed in the former Casa de Gobierno

(Government House) on the northwest side of Jardín Velasco, this library (☎ 5-37-67) features a small but valuable collection of books and newspapers about the Californias in Spanish and English. Its interior artwork ranges from ghastly (a kitschy representation of Calafia, the mythical Amazon whose name presumably survives in the word 'California') to mediocre (privateer Thomas Cavendish's crew boarding the Manila galleon *Santa Ana)* to respectable (a replica mural of Desierto Central rock art).

Teatro de la Ciudad
The city theater, a sprawling concrete edifice at the corner of Calle Gómez Farías and Calle Legaspi, is part of the Unidad Cultural Profesor Jesús Castro Agúndez (☎ 5-19-17), a cultural center that includes a library, an art studio and a children's arts-and-crafts workshop. The theater proper offers performances by musical and theatrical groups such as Guadalajara's Ballet Folklórico, as well as occasional film series.

At the theater entrance is the **Rotunda de los Hombres Ilustres** (Rotunda of Distinguished Men), a sculptural tribute to the men who fought against filibuster Walker's invasion of La Paz in 1853.

Street Market
On Saturdays and Sundays, countless baubles change hands at the flea market which turns downtown Calle Madero and Avenida Independencia, at right angles to each other, into pedestrian malls.

Activities
Most activities in the area are beach-oriented, but Mexican authorities admit that Bahía de La Paz is itself badly polluted; areas beyond the bay are cleaner.

Diving & Snorkeling For diving and snorkeling in Bahía de La Paz itself (beware contaminated water) or beyond in the Gulf, arrange equipment rentals and day trips with Baja Buceo y Servicio (☎ 2-18-26, 5-25-75), at Avenida Independencia 107-B.

Owner Fernando Aguilar offers a variety of diving and snorkeling trips:

Isla de las Focas – an island just north of Punta Coyote and Bahía de La Paz renowned for its beaches and sea-lion colony. The cost of US$40 per person includes transport, snorkeling gear, lunch and unlimited soft drinks and beer.

Scuba trips leave daily at 8 am for dives among various ship wrecks, underwater caves and reefs, and sea-lion colonies. The cost of US$70 per person includes transport, two tanks, a weight belt, a guide, lunch and unlimited soft drinks and beer. Full gear rentals are US$15, a basic lesson is US$15, a resort course costs US$45 and open-water certification costs US$360.

Deportiva La Paz (☎ 2-73-33), on Obregón at the corner of Calle La Paz, also rents diving equipment.

Fishing In the lobby of Hotel Los Arcos is an information desk for the Dorado Vélez Fleet (☎ 2-00-38, 2-27-44), which offers trips on boats ranging from 25 to 32 feet and provides all equipment, licenses and transport. Most of La Paz's other major hotels and travel agencies can also arrange trips.

Seasons for various fish in the La Paz area are as follows:

January
   Crevalle, grouper, rockfish, roosterfish, sea bass, sierra, yellowtail
February
   Grouper, rockfish, sea bass, sierra, yellowtail
March
   Grouper, rockfish, sea bass, sierra, yellowtail
April
   Crevalle, grouper, rockfish, roosterfish, sea bass, sierra, snapper, yellowtail
May
   Crevalle, grouper, marlin, needlefish, rockfish, roosterfish, sailfish, sea bass, sierra, snapper, tuna, wahoo, yellowfin tuna, yellowtail
June
   Crevalle, grouper, marlin, needlefish, rockfish, roosterfish, sailfish, sea bass, sierra, snapper, tuna, wahoo, yellowfin tuna, yellowtail

July
  Black marlin, crevalle, grouper, marlin, needlefish, rockfish, roosterfish, sailfish, sea bass, sierra, snapper, tuna, wahoo, yellowfin tuna

August
  Black marlin, crevalle, grouper, marlin, needlefish, rockfish, roosterfish, sailfish, sea bass, snapper, tuna, wahoo, yellowfin tuna

September
  Black marlin, crevalle, grouper, needlefish, rockfish, roosterfish, sailfish, sea bass, snapper, tuna, wahoo, yellowfin tuna

October
  Black marlin, crevalle, grouper, rockfish, roosterfish, sailfish, sea bass, sierra, snapper, tuna, wahoo, yellowfin tuna, yellowtail

November
  Black marlin, crevalle, rockfish, roosterfish, sailfish, sea bass, sierra, tuna, wahoo, yellowfin tuna, yellowtail

December
  Black marlin, crevalle, rockfish, roosterfish, sea bass, sierra, yellowtail

Language Courses

The Centro Cultural Hispano-Americano offers an intensive Spanish language program. For more information, contact Hotel Posada (☎ 2-40-11), PO Box 138B, La Paz, Baja California Sur, México.

Festivals

February or March (date varies)
  Carnaval – La Paz's pre-Lenten celebrations are probably the best on the peninsula and among the best in the country.

May 3
  Fundación de la Ciudad – Paceños take two weeks to celebrate the founding of La Paz in 1535. Events include a dramatization of the landing of Hernán Cortés, sports events like a half-marathon, and a commercial exhibition.

June 1
  Día de la Marina – Navy Day

Late November
  Festival de las Artes – Arts Festival

Places to Stay – bottom end

Camping Several trailer parks in and around La Paz charge about US$5 to US$10 per vehicle or tent; rates for tents may be negotiable. Camping (usually tents only) costs only a few dollars, or is some-times free, at beaches on Península Pichilingue (see the Beaches entry in the Around La Paz section below).·

About 9 miles (14.5 km) west of La Paz on the Transpeninsular, in the bayside community of El Centenario, is *Oasis Los Aripez Trailer Park*. Facilities include toilets, hot showers, a restaurant, a bar and a laundry room, but there is almost no shade and, at this point, the bay is a bit malodorous. All spaces face the water, have full hookups and cost about US$7 to US$12 per night for one or two people. No tent sites are available.

At Km 4 on the Transpeninsular, west of downtown in a partly shaded area distant from the beach, is the well-organized *El Cardón Trailer Park* (☎ 2-00-78). Each of its 90 spaces has full hookups, electric light and a small palapa, but maintenance has declined in recent years. Facilities and services include a laundry room, a swimming pool, hot showers, clean toilets, a small paperback exchange, a travel agency and international long-distance telephone service. Tent spaces cost US$6, while vehicle spaces cost about US$8 per night. The postal address is Apartado Postal 104, La Paz, Baja California Sur, México.

Just west of El Cardón, the shady, secure and well-maintained *RV Park Casa Blanca* (☎ 2-00-09) has a pool, a restaurant and full hookups from US$10 per night. *La Paz Trailer Park* (☎ 2-87-87) is a deluxe park about 1 mile (1.6 km) south of central La Paz. Facilities include very clean bathrooms and showers, a fine restaurant, a Jacuzzi, a swimming pool and a small book exchange. Rates are about US$12 for a vehicle and US$10 for a tent.

The new bayside fortress of *Aquamarina RV Park* (☎ 2-37-61), at the foot of Calle Nayarit, is highly regarded, but some may find its heavy-duty security intimidating. Sites cost about US$12.

Youth Hostel Open from 6 am to 11 pm, the youth hostel *(CREA* or *Casa de la Juventud,* ☎ 2-46-15), is about 20 blocks southwest of the city center, near the junction of Calle 5 de Febrero, Camino A Las

Garzas and the Carretera al Sur (the south-bound Transpeninsular). At US$6.50 per night, a bunk in one of the single-sex, dormitory-style rooms is a good value. From downtown, catch any 'Universidad' bus from the Mercado Francisco Madero, at the corner of Calle Degollado and Calle Revolución.

Pensiones, Hosterías & Casas de Huéspedes
Pensión California (☎ 2-28-96), Calle Degollado 209 between Madero and Revolución, is a longtime budget favorite; its patio is surrounded by tropical trees and vines, and its walls are lined with quirky artwork. For US$8/13 single/double, each room is basic, with ceiling fan, fluorescent light, jalousies and a shower.

Hostería del Convento (☎ 2-35-08), Calle Madero 85, resembles Pensión California, but families also reside here. Clean and basic, but dark and dilapidated, rooms with two to three beds cost US$8/13. The toilets are tolerable but less than spotless.

Casa de Huéspedes Miriam (☎ 2-11-04), Calle 16 de Septiembre 202, is a dive; singles/doubles with cell-like bathrooms cost about US$8/12. *Hotel San Carlos* (☎ 2-04-44), at the noisy corner of Calle Revolución and Calle 16 de Septiembre, charges US$11 single or double.

The 14-room *Posada San Miguel* (☎ 2-18-02), Calle Belisario Domínguez 1510, is a pleasant, pseudo-colonial place set around a central patio. Its dark but clean rooms have private bath, but hot water is available only after 6 pm. Rates are US$12/14 for singles/doubles. *Hotel María Cristina I* (☎ 2-67-26), Revolución 85 near Calle Degollado, has singles/doubles with air-conditioning and pool for US$13/18.

Hospedaje Mareli (☎ 2-10-17) is a small guesthouse at Calle Aquiles Serdán 283, between Calle Bravo and Calle Ocampo, a 10-minute walk from Plaza Constitución. Despite its location across from a noisy schoolyard, it has 10 clean, pleasant rooms with fans for about US$16 to US$18 double.

Expanded *Hotel Lorimar* (☎ 5-38-22, fax 5-63-87), with an attractive interior patio at Calle Bravo 110 near Madero, is becoming a 'real crossroads for travelers'. Singles/doubles cost US$18/22; most have air-conditioning (check to see whether it works) and tiled showers with hot water. There is also good laundry service. *Hotel Yeneka* (☎ 5-46-88), Calle Madero 1520, is a motel-style place with 20 rooms and a quasi-cafe with eclectic automotive decor, including countless bumpers, mud-splattered license plates and hub caps. Clean singles/doubles with firm beds (a mattress over concrete) are US$17/20. *Hotel Plaza Real* (☎ 2-93-33), at the corner of Calle La Paz and Calle Esquerro, charges US$22/31.

Places to Stay – middle
The recommended three-star, 60-room *Hotel Acuarios* (☎ 2-92-66), at Calle Ignacio Ramírez 1665 near Calle 5 de Mayo, has a restaurant and a swimming pool. Singles/doubles cost US$31/35; all have air-conditioning, full carpeting, TV and telephone. *Hotel El Mesón* (☎ 5-74-54), Calle General Félix Ortega 2330, has pleasant rooms with tiled floors, private bath, satellite TV, swimming pool privileges and other amenities for US$30/40 single/double. *Hotel Mediterrané* (☎ 5-11-95), at Allende 36-B, is in the same range.

Historic *Hotel Perla* (☎ 2-07-77), at Paseo Obregón 1570 right across from a short stretch of beach on the malecón, has a swimming pool, a restaurant, a bar and a nightclub. Some rooms offer bay views, while others overlook the pool; all have air-conditioning, TV and private bath. Rates run around US$42/48.

On Avenida Reforma, the Spanish-style *Hotel La Posada de Engelbert* (☎ 2-40-11), which is owned by crooner Engelbert Humperdinck, has 25 bungalow-type rooms with brick fireplaces; facilities include a swimming pool, tennis courts, a restaurant and a bar. Rates are US$44 single or double. Across the bay on the Mogote sandspit, 35-room *Hotel Misiones de la Paz* (☎ 4-40-11, ☎ 2-06-63) is accessible only by boat from here. Rooms and rates are similar.

Hotel Palmira (☎ 2-40-00), about 1½ miles (2½ km) from downtown on the road to Pichilingue, is a modern hotel which appeals to families on vacation and small conventions, with a swimming pool, a tennis court, a restaurant, a dance club and rates from about US$45 to US$50 for a double, plus 10% tax. In the USA, ☎ (800) 336-5454 toll free or (619) 422-6900 for reservations. The Palmira's US representatives are Mexico Resorts International, PO Box 85458, San Diego, California 92138.

Places to Stay – top end

Hotel Los Arcos (☎ 2-27-44), Paseo Alvaro Obregón 498 near Calle Rosales, has two swimming pools, a sauna, a restaurant and a coffee shop; ask for a bay view. All rooms have air-conditioning, telephones, color TV and showers. Rates are about US$75/77 single/double, excluding tax.

Prices are comparable at its nearby sister, the *Hotel Cabañas de los Arcos*, on Calle Mutualismo; its lush, tropical gardens feature cabaña-style rooms with fireplaces, thatched roofs, tiled floors, TV, air-conditioning and minibars. Its US agent is Baja Hotel Reservations (☎ (800) 347-2252 or (714) 476-5555 in mainland California), 18552 MacArthur Blvd, Suite 205, Irvine, California 92715.

One of La Paz's tallest buildings, 256-room *Hotel Gran Baja La Paz* (☎ 2-39-00), at the north end of Calle Nayarit, has singles/doubles for US$74/81 (plus 10% tax); all rooms have full carpeting, satellite TV and bay views. In the USA, contact Pan American Hotels International Inc (☎ (800) 678-7244 toll free, (619) 422-6918), PO Box 4406, Chula Vista, California 91909.

At Km 5 on the road to Pichilingue is the 107-room *La Concha Beach Resort* (☎ 2-65-44), a beachfront hotel with palm trees, a swimming pool, a water-sports center, a poolside bar and a fine Mexican restaurant. Its comfortable rooms are air-conditioned and all have balconies overlooking the bay. Single/double rates range from US$70 (1

August to 30 September) to US$85 (1 October to 31 July), plus 10% tax. Bargain packages are also available. In the USA, make reservations by phoning ☎ (800) 999-2252.

Places to Eat

Restaurant del Centro, one of downtown's most inexpensive eateries, is two doors south of Pensión California on Calle Degollado. Its basic menu includes soup, rice and a choice of chicken, fish or pork chops. Two blocks southeast of Plaza Constitución is *La Flor de Michoacán*, on Calle 5 de Mayo between Calle Guillermo Prieto and Calle Aquiles Serdán, which sells delicious aguas, paletas licuados, ice cream and sandwiches.

Super Tacos Baja California, a mobile stall at the corner of Agustín Arreola and Calle Mutualismo, thrives on both local and tourist trade; it's a bit dearer than most taco stands, but the quality of its fish and shrimp tacos, plus outstanding condiments, more than justifies the extra peso. *Mariscos*, at the corner of Obregón and Calle Morelos, is a palm-shaded stand with tables for taco lovers weary of standing while eating.

El Quinto Sol is a popular vegetarian restaurant and health-food market on the corner of Avenida Independencia and Calle Belisario Domínguez. Besides its bean specialties, it offers large servings of yoghurt, either plain, with fruit or with muesli. Licuados, fresh baked breads and pastries are other specialties. Another good, reasonably priced breakfast choice is *Café San Francisco*, on Allende just south of the malecón.

On Paseo Alvaro Obregón a block south of Hotel Los Arcos on a veranda overlooking the bay, *Restaurant/Bar El Cheff* offers filling portions of standard antojitos, seafood specialties like lobster and shrimp, and a Sunday brunch. Hours are 7 am to 10 pm daily and all major charge cards are accepted.

Restaurant Camarón Feliz (☎ 2-90-11), on Paseo Obregón near Calle Mutualismo, specializes in shrimp, but its expensive for a small restaurant, with prices in the US$8 to US$12 range. It's open 8 am to 10 pm daily and accepts all major credit cards. *La Caleta* (☎ 3-02-87), on the malecón at the corner of Calle Pineda, is a very popular place with reasonably priced meals and drinks. *Blackbeard's*, across the street at the corner of Calle Márquez de León, is a major gringo hangout for drinks and dining.

The *Quinto Patio*, at the corner of Calle Lerdo de Tejada and Paseo Alvaro Obregón, is a rowdy sort of place with a Mexican rock-and-roll band that sings in English. It bills itself as a party club, but also specializes in steaks and seafood. For pizza, try *La Fábula*, across from the malecón and tourist office; there's a branch on Calle 5 de Mayo between Revolución and Aquiles Serdán. It's open 1 to 11 pm daily.

Restaurant/Bar El Moro (☎ 2-70-10), near the Hotel Palmira on the road to Pichilingue, features Sonoran beef, salads, pasta dishes and a few Cantonese dishes. It's open 12:30 to 11 pm daily, except Monday, and accepts all major credit cards. La Paz also has a small Chinatown with a few restaurants, on or around Calle 21 de Agosto, near the Palacio Municipal and Dorian's department store.

La Pazta (☎ 5-11-95), at Allende 36-B just south of the malecón, has good Italian specials at reasonable prices, but the drinks are small, weak and relatively expensive. *Carlos 'n' Charlie's*, on Obregón near Calle 16 de Septiembre, is part of the extensive chain known more for drinking than dining.

The *Bismark II*, at the corner of Calle Degollado and Calle Ignacio Altamirano, is popular with local families for its generous helpings of excellent seafood, but recent correspondents indicate that prices have risen and quality has stagnated – one even observed that it 'seems to be the place where the yacht snobs dine these days'. *Samalú*, on Calle Rangel between Colima and Jalisco, advertises turtle steak, but all sea turtles are endangered species which travelers should not only avoid eating, but should make the reasons for such abstinence apparent to tourist-oriented businesses.

Entertainment

Cinemas *Cine Gemelos*, on Calle Revolución near the corner of Avenida Independencia, offers first-run international films. *Cine La Paz*, on Belisario Domínguez between Independencia and Calle 5 de Mayo, has occasional first-run films but more often shows Stallone-Schwarzenegger commando and martial-arts flicks.

Avoid the so-called *Cine Arte*, around the corner on Avenida Independencia, which deals exclusively in sordid sex and gratuitous violence.

Other Entertainment Las Varitas, at Independencia 111 near Belisario Domínguez, regularly offers live music and dancing; there's a US$3 cover charge.

Across the street is the Bar Video Internacional, which shows international sports events and big-screen music videos. Éxtasis, at the corner of Agustín Arreola and Calle Zaragoza, is very popular with younger Mexicans.

Things to Buy

Peter Gerhard, in his classic *Lower California Guidebook* of the 1960s, tells of a tourist who bought a 'black pearl' in La Paz only to discover that it was an exquisitely burnished ball bearing! Few visitors are so credulous, but there is plenty of junk as well as good stuff in La Paz.

La Carreta Curios at the corner of Paseo Alvaro Obregón and Calle Muelle, offers items from all over Mexico. Try also México Lindo, on Paseo Obregón opposite the tourist office, which has good mainland items in addition to postcards and T-shirts. Bazar del Sol, on Obregón near Calle La Paz, is loaded with kitsch.

México Mágico, on Agustín Arreola opposite Librería Contiempo, has especially good tapestries and serapes.

Getting There & Away

Air Aeroméxico (☎ 2-00-91), on Paseo

Alvaro Obregón between Calle Hidalgo and Calle Morelos, has daily flights between La Paz and Culiacán, Durango, Guadalajara, Guaymas, Los Angeles, Mazatlán, Mexico City and Tijuana.

Aero California (☎ 5-10-23 or (800) 258-3311 in the USA) has offices at the airport and at Alvaro Obregón 550, near the corner of Calle Bravo. Hours are 8 am to 6 pm daily. It operates daily flights between La Paz and Aguascalientes, Ciudad Juárez, Colima, Culiacán, Durango, Guadalajara, Loreto, Los Angeles, Los Mochis (for the Barranca del Cobre train), Mazatlán, Mexico City, Puebla, Tijuana and Torreón.

Bus Autotransportes de La Paz (☎ 2-21-57), Autotransportes Aguila (☎ 2-42-70) and ABC (☎ 2-30-63) operate inter-city buses. Aguila and ABC use the Central Camionera (central bus station) at the corner of Calle Jalisco and Calle Héroes de la Independencia. ABC buses go to:

Ciudad Constitución
(three hours, US$7.50) at least five times daily between 7 am and 9:30 pm

Puerto Escondido
(five hours, US$12) at least five times daily between 9 am and 10 pm
Loreto
(5½ hours, US$13) at least five times daily between 9 am and 10 pm
La Purísima-San Isidro
(six hours, US$12) twice daily, leaving at 7 am and 12:30 pm
Mulegé
(eight hours, US$7) at least three times daily between 9 am and 10 pm
Santa Rosalía
(nine hours, US$22) at least twice daily, usually morning and afternoon
San Ignacio
(10 hours, US$24) at least five times daily between 10 am and 10 pm
Guerrero Negro
(12 hours, US$29) at least five times daily between 10 am and 10 pm
San Quintín
(18 hours, US$40) at least five times daily between 10 am and 10 pm
Ensenada
(22 hours, US$51) at least five times daily between 10 am and 10 pm
Tijuana
(22 to 24 hours, US$56) at least five times daily between 10 am and 10 pm
Mexicali
(28 hours, US$64) once daily, departing at 4 pm

Southbound buses depart several times daily for:

El Triunfo
(30 minutes, US$2)
San Antonio
(40 minutes, US$2.50)
Buena Vista
(1½ hours, US$5)
Miraflores
fare costs US$6
San José del Cabo via the Transpeninsular
fare costs US$9

Autotransportes Aguila buses take México 19 from La Paz to Cabo San Lucas (US$9) at least five times daily between 7 am and 7 pm, and to Todos Santos (US$4) at least five times daily between 7 am and 7 pm.

Autotransportes de La Paz buses leave from in front of the Mercado Francisco

Madero at the corner of Calle Revolución and Calle Degollado for Todos Santos (US$4), Cabo San Lucas (US$9) and San José del Cabo (US$9), five times daily from 8:45 am to 5:45 pm.

There are also local buses to Península Pichilingue and the ferry port from the terminal at the corner of Paseo Alvaro Obregón and Calle 5 de Mayo. (See the Getting Around section for fares and times.)

Ferry Pichilingue, about 14 miles (23 km) north of central La Paz, is the major terminus for the recently privatized ferry system to the mainland, now operated by Sematur (☎ 5-38-33, 5-46-66), whose La Paz offices are at the corner of Calle Guillermo Prieto and Calle 5 de Mayo.

Before shipping your vehicle, ferry officials require a vehicle permit, for which you must show an ownership certificate (pink slip) or a valid vehicle-registration certificate and tourist card (Form FMT). You must then make a deposit of US$10 on Visa or MasterCard at the Banco del Ejército (Banjército) in Pichilingue as a bond against its eventual return to the USA; this is possible from 8 am to 3 pm weekdays, 9 am to 1 pm weekends. For more information, see the Documents & Insurance section in the Facts for the Visitor chapter.

To leave your vehicle in La Paz while returning to the USA or crossing to mainland Mexico, you theoretically need authorization from Mexican customs, which may require leaving the vehicle in a *Recinto Fiscal* (official garage).

Tickets must be confirmed by 2 pm the day before departure. At 3 pm, cabins that have not been confirmed are sold on a first-come, first-serve basis, which sometimes results in a shoving match to see who stays at the head of the line.

Weather permitting (high winds often delay winter sailings), the Mazatlán ferry departs at 3 pm, the Topolobampo ferry at 8 pm. Approximate passenger fares from La Paz are:

Class	To Mazatlán Los Mochis (Daily, 16 hours)	To Topolobampo (Daily, eight hours)
Salón	US$21	US$13
Turista	US$40	US$27
Cabina	US$60	US$40
Especial	US$80	US$53

Vehicle rates are as follows:

	To Mazatlán	To Topolobampo
Length up to 5 meters	US$153	US$102
5.01 to 6½ meters	US$200	US$133
With trailer up to 9 meters	US$276	US$184
9.01 to 17 meters	US$512	US$348
Motorcycle	US$23	US$15

Yacht According to one LP correspondent, between November and March, La Paz is a good place to catch a lift on a yacht to mainland Mexico:

The Marina de La Paz, which houses the Dock restaurant and the Club Cruceros, are the best places to hang out. There is a radio at Club Cruceros, and plenty of people to show you how to use it. Also ask Mort the owner of the Dock – he is always glad to help. The most frequent passage is La Paz to Puerto Vallarta with stops at Bahía de los Muertos, Los Frailes (great coral snorkeling), then Isla Isabél and Puerto Vallarta. Allow about one week, with two to three nights at sea.

Getting Around

To/From the Airport Aeropuerto General Manuel Márquez de León is just 10 minutes from downtown, but taxis charge an outrageous US$20 per trip (fares are officially set, but even then bargaining may be necessary). Fares are per car or group, but some taxi drivers try to charge per person. Shared cabs from the airport charge only US$10 per person

To/From the Ferry Terminal From the Terminal Malecón, at the corner of Paseo Alvaro Obregón and Avenida Independencia, Autotransportes Aguila goes to Pichilingue at 8, 10 and 11 am, noon, and 1, 1:30, 2:20, 4 and 6 pm. The fare is about US$1.10.

Bus Most local buses leave from the front of the Mercado Francisco Madero at the corner of Calle Degollado and Calle Revolución

Car Rental Several local agencies rent cars, including AMCA (☎ 3-03-35), Calle Madero 1715, and Servitur (☎ 2-14-48), Calle Abasolo 57 between Calle Cuauhtémoc and Calle 5 de Febrero. Rates start at about US$60 per day for a Volkswagen, with insurance and unlimited mileage.

Budget (☎ 2-10-97) is on Paseo Alvaro Obregón between Calle Morelos and Calle Hidalgo. Thrifty (☎ 5-96-96), on Obregón at Calle Lerdo de Tejada, charges US$80 per day (including tax, insurance and 300 km per day) for a Nissan Tsuru, Nissan Van, Jeep Wrangler or Jeep 4x4. Each additional km costs US$0.20. Additional Thrifty offices are at the airport (☎ 2-90-65), Hotel La Concha (☎ 2-65-44) and Hotel Palmira (☎ 2-40-00).

Motorcycle Restaurant Camarón Feliz (☎ 2-09-11), at the corner of Paseo Alvaro Obregón and Calle Bravo, rents mopeds and small motorcycles.

Bicycle Bicycles can be hired at Viajes Palmira (☎ 2-40-30), on Paseo Alvaro Obregón between Calle Rosales and Calle Allende, across from Hotel Los Arcos.

AROUND LA PAZ
Beaches
There are several small but pleasant beaches north and west of La Paz. To the west are the bayside **Playa El Comitán** and **Playa Las Hamacas** (see the Around La Paz map), but no public transport serves them. El Comitán has deteriorated in recent years, and swimming is no longer advisable.

On Península Pichilingue, to the north, the nearest beaches are **Playa Palmira**,

Playa Coromuel and **Playa Caimancito**. Playa Palmira has the *Hotel Palmira*, a marina, and a couple of condominium complexes with restaurant and bar, while the latter two have restaurants and bar, toilets and shady palapas. Playa Coromuel has a good seafood restaurant, toilets, shade and a big Plexiglas water slide. **Playa Tesoro**, the next beach north, also has a restaurant and shade.

Camping is possible at **Playa Pichilingue**, 110 yards (100 meters) north of the ferry terminal; it has a restaurant and bar, toilets and shade. The road north of Pichilingue is now paved to the exceptional beaches of **Playa Balandra** and **Playa Tecolote**; windsurfing rentals are available at Tecolote. Balandra is not very good for camping because of insects in the mangroves, but Tecolote, spectacularly located directly across from Isla Espíritu Santo, is ideal for camping; it lacks potable water and other amenities, but does have the nearby steak-and-seafood *Restaurant El Tecolote*. **Playa Coyote**, on the Gulf side of the peninsula, is more isolated.

Local expatriates warn that particularly stealthy and skillful thieves break into campers' automobiles at Tecolote and other isolated beaches – even while the campers are sleeping.

Punta Arena de la Ventana
Punta Arena is home to the *Hotel Las Arenas* (☎ 2-20-33 in La Paz), about 36 miles (58 km) southeast of La Paz via the farming town of San Juan de los Planes, which marks the end of paved Hwy 286. (At Rancho Los Tamales, about 13 miles (21 km) south of La Paz on the paved road, are samples of pre-Columbian rock art.)

Punta Arena's 12-mile (19-km) beach offers opportunities for snorkeling, diving, windsurfing and fishing (pangas can be hired). The hotel has a swimming pool, tennis courts and a restaurant. Rooms have two queen-size beds, tiled floors and French doors opening onto the ocean; rates start at US$75/115 single/double. For more information, ☎ (213) 921-0109/1309, (800) 423-4785 toll free or (800) 352-4334 toll

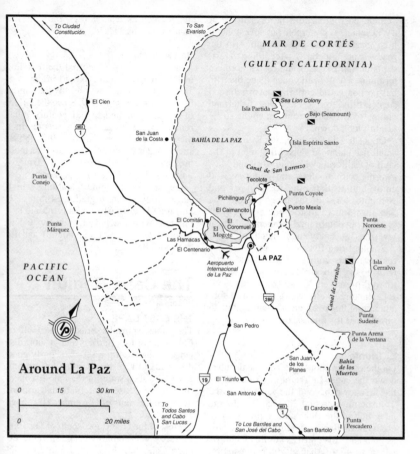

Around La Paz

| 0 | 15 | 30 km |

| 0 | 20 miles |

free in mainland California, or write to PO Box 3766, Santa Fe Springs, California, USA 90670.

San Evaristo

West of La Paz, just beyond the village of El Centenario, a paved but potholed spur off the Transpeninsular leads north along the western shore of Bahía de La Paz to **San Juan de la Costa**, a phosphate mining port with a passable restaurant and a detachment of Mexican marines.

North of San Juan, the graded coastal road skirts the eastern scarp of the Sierra de

la Giganta, a polychrome mountain range whose layered sediments resemble nothing so much as a cutaway of Arizona's Grand Canyon of the Colorado. Most impressive in the morning sun, which accentuates its vivid colors, the route is badly washboarded in spots but passable even for low clearance vehicles until a difficult climb at Punta El Mechudo.

The **Cuesta El Mechudo** consists of four separate crests, the first and last of which are fairly easy, but the second and third are abrupt climbs on narrow roadways with many loose rocks – meeting another vehicle en route could be disastrous. A 4WD vehicle is preferable but not essential; high clearance and close attention to the roadway are imperative. According to residents at San Evaristo, the road's northern terminus, a VW beetle once made the trip, but no one could confirm that it returned successfully to La Paz. One fisherman claims to drive the route at night so he needn't look down.

Opposite Isla San José, San Evaristo is a small fish camp on a sparkling inlet of the Gulf of California which, in April and May, swarms with boaters and campers who enjoy bountiful fishing for snapper and cochinito. Most of the beaches along the San Juan-San Evaristo route are rocky or gravely, but determined campers will find a few pleasant, sandy and isolated spots.

South of San Evaristo, an ungraded dirt road connects with La Soledad and other roads to the ruins of Misión La Pasión and to well-preserved Misión San Luis Gonzaga. Inquire locally as to conditions before attempting this road, and do not hesitate to turn back if it's impassable.

El Triunfo

On the eastern route (the Transpeninsular) down the cape, El Triunfo ('Triumph') is the first town beyond the junction of the Transpeninsular and México 19. In the latter half of the 19th century, this was one of southern Baja's most important towns, as gold and silver strikes swelled its population to more than 10,000, consisting mostly of mestizo miners plus Yaqui Indian laborers from the state of Sonora.

Today, it might be more accurately called El Fracaso (Failure). After the mines closed in 1926, the population dwindled to just a few hundred, and only a smokestack, an old mill and some vintage houses remain from its heyday. There is no accommodation, and *Restaurant Las Glorias* seems an ironic name for a virtual ghost town.

The Instituto Nacional de Historia y Antropología has recently proposed designating El Triunfo as a national historical site. Local artisans produce a few craft items, such as leather toys and colorful, hand-woven baskets.

San Antonio

Nearby silver strikes spurred the founding of the village of San Antonio in the mid-18th century, which was briefly the capital of the Californias in 1829. Since the failure of the mines in the late 19th century, it has remained a modest farming center in a picturesque canyon location. Its cobbled streets and restored buildings give it a more prosperous appearance than El Triunfo, only 4½ miles (7½ km) to the north.

Opposite the Pemex station, which carries Magna Sin, a graded 14-mile (22-km) road follows Arroyo San Antonio to a junction with the paved highway to San Juan de los Planes (southbound) and La Paz (northbound).

The Cape Region

THE EAST CAPE

The Transpeninsular brushes the Gulf of California at Los Barriles and, a short distance farther south, a series of fairly good dirt roads follow the coastline toward San José del Cabo. South of the Palo Escopeta road to San José's international airport, however, the rains of November 1993 have cut the road.

Most of the East Cape, south of Los Barriles, likely resembles what now overdeveloped Cabo San Lucas and San José del Cabo were decades ago. The region is still difficult to reach and likely to remain so for some time, as government money goes to rebuilding the San José-Cabo San Lucas highway; in a sense, the storms were a stroke of luck for those who wish to preserve the area in a relatively undeveloped state, with its numerous broad, sandy beaches open for placid camping.

LOS BARRILES

South of La Paz, the Transpeninsular skirts the northern edge of the Sierra de la Laguna before touching the coast at the

Playa de Amor, Cabo San Lucas

Cuesta El Mechudo, near San Evaristo, north of La Paz

San Javier Rd, near Loreto

Playa Cerritos, West Cape

Fishermen, West Cape

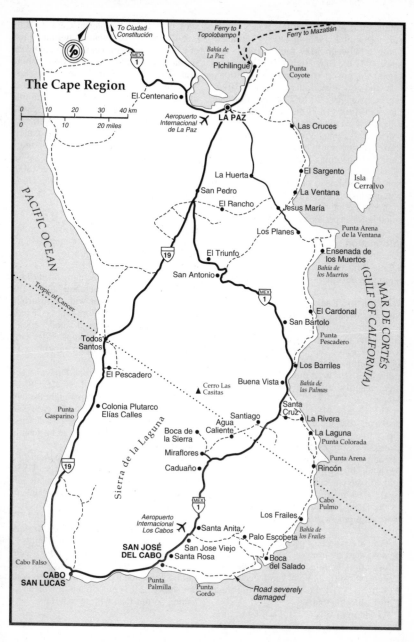

The Cape Region

To Ciudad Constitución

Ferry to Topolobampo

Ferry to Mazatlán

Bahía de La Paz

Pichilingue

Punta Coyote

El Centenario

LA PAZ

Aeropuerto Internacional de La Paz

Las Cruces

La Huerta

El Sargento

San Pedro

La Ventana

El Rancho

Jesús María

Los Planes

Punta Arena de la Ventana

El Triunfo

Ensenada de los Muertos

Bahía de los Muertos

San Antonio

El Cardonal

San Bartolo

Punta Pescadero

Todos Santos

Los Barriles

El Pescadero

Buena Vista

Bahía de las Palmas

Cerro Las Casitas

Colonia Plutarco Elías Calles

Santiago

Santa Cruz

La Rivera

Agua Caliente

Boca de la Sierra

La Laguna

Punta Colorada

Miraflores

Punta Arena

Caduaño

Rincón

Cabo Pulmo

Aeropuerto Internacional Los Cabos

Los Frailes

Santa Anita

SAN JOSÉ DEL CABO

San Jose Viejo

Palo Escopeta

Bahía de los Frailes

Santa Rosa

Boca del Salado

Cabo Falso

CABO SAN LUCAS

Punta Palmilla

Punta Gordo

Road severely damaged

PACIFIC OCEAN

Tropic of Cancer

Punta Gasparino

Sierra de la Laguna

MAR DE CORTÉS (GULF OF CALIFORNIA)

Isla Cerralvo

0   10   20   30   40 km
0   10   20 miles

small resort of Los Barriles, Baja's windsurfing capital. Fishing always attracted visitors between May and October, but since 1981 the Baja High Wind Center has organized group trips and competitions here and at nearby Bahía de Palmas. Brisk winds, averaging 20 to 25 knots, descend the 6000-foot (1800-meter) western cordillera toward the launching site in front of the Rancho Buena Vista Hotel, where the shoreline runs south and then east into the Gulf of California. Theoretically, because of the curved shoreline and the wind direction, it is possible to sail 20 miles out to sea without losing sight of the beach, but the high wind conditions make the area most suitable for experienced sailboarders.

Information
Fast growing Los Barriles has a post office, a Cruz Roja station and other services, but no tourist information office as such.

Windsurfing Packages
Vela Highwind Centers is based in the San Francisco Bay area, but every year from November to April, its headquarters move to Hotel Playa del Sol (formerly Hotel Playa Hermosa) in Los Barriles. The season's highlight is an annual championship race, usually held the second week of January.

The Center offers various week-long packages that include accommodation at either the Playa Hermosa or the Hotel Palmas de Cortez, all meals, unlimited use of equipment, daily instructional seminars, mountain-bike trips, snorkeling excursions and horseback riding. At the seminars, world-class instructors employ prototypes of the latest Mistral, Seatrend, Naish and North equipment direct from the manufacturers.

Typical seven-day packages (prices per person) start at around US$700. For more information, contact Vela's Highwind Center (☎ (800) 223-5443 toll free, (415) 525-2070), 351-C Foster City Blvd, Foster City, California 94404.

An alternative is Mr Bill's Boardsailing Adventures, which offers one-week packages with B&B lodging at Casa de Rafa (see Places to Stay, below), unlimited use of windsurfing equipment, mountain bikes, snorkeling equipment, sea kayaks, fishing gear and sailboats. Low season rates (early November to mid-December, mid-March to June) are US$425 per person double occupancy, US$525 single. High season rates (mid-December to mid-March) are US$525 per person double occupancy, US$625 single. For reservations or more details, contact Mr Bill's (☎ (503) 386-7639, fax (503) 386-4899 or toll free (800) 533-8452), 1635 Avalon Court, Hood River, Oregon 97031.

Places to Stay
Camping Free camping is possible on the beaches, but amenities are nonexistent. Most formal RV parks are just north of Rancho Buena Vista Hotel.

Many campers have recommended *Playa de Oro RV Resort*, perched above the ocean, which is popular with windsurfers for its access to the offshore zephyrs. Facilities include hot showers, a laundry room, clean toilets and full hookups. Sites cost from US$11, depending on proximity to the beach.

Martín Verdugo's Trailer Park charges US$8 per night for a small vehicle, US$10 for a larger one and US$5 per night for tent camping, but the park can be very crowded. Facilities include hot showers, electricity, full hookups, a laundry room and a sizable paperback exchange.

A recent entry is Chilean-run *Juanito's Garden* (☎ 1-00-24), which charges US$6 per night or US$180 per month with full hookups, and seems to be well organized. It's not on the beach, but it's not far either. Its mailing address is Apartado Postal 50, Los Barriles, Baja California Sur, México.

La Capilla Trailer Park, about 2 miles (3 km) south of town and right on the beach, charges US$7 per day. Facilities include full hookups and well-kept bathrooms with hot showers. It is more popular with sport fishing parties than with windsurfers.

Hotels Other than camping, no really economical accommodation exists in Los Barriles. *Casa de Rafa* (☎ 5-36-36), at Km 109 on the Carretera al Sur, is a new B&B that caters mostly to windsurfers but also arranges fishing excursions. Rates are US$35/45 single/double.

The 50-room *Rancho Buena Vista Hotel*, popular with anglers and their families, is southeast of Los Barriles and half a mile east of the Transpeninsular. Facilities and amenities include a swimming pool, a bar, a restaurant, tennis courts and 20 inboard cruisers for fishing trips. Family-style meals are 'all you can eat'; most of the cattle, poultry and vegetables are raised on the hotel's farm. Rooms with screened windows, tiled bathrooms, ceiling fans and/or air-conditioning cost US$75/130 for singles/doubles, including all meals but excluding 10% gratuity and 10% tax. The hotel closes yearly from mid-August to early October because of the heat, humidity and hurricane risk. For more information, phone ☎ (818) 303-1517 or (800) 258-8200 (toll free) in the USA or write PO Box 673, Monrovia, California 91017.

Hotel Playa del Sol, in Los Barriles, offers clean, comfortable singles/doubles for US$55/80, including meals. Make reservations in the USA by phoning (408) 375-2252, or write Baja Safaris, PO Box 1827, Monterey, California 93942.

At *Hotel Buenavista Beach Resort*, a quarter mile south of Rancho Buena Vista, single/double rooms are US$65/88, US$85/135 with full board; it also has a hot mineral spa, a swimming pool and tennis courts. Various accommodation/fishing packages are also available, ranging from US$285 per person double occupancy for five days and four nights (including meals, taxes and gratuities, airport transfers and sometimes fishing). For more information in the USA, phone ☎ (800) 752-3555 (toll free) or (310) 943-0869; alternatively, write Apartado Postal 574, La Paz, Baja California Sur, México, or 16211 E Whittier Blvd, Whittier, California 90603.

The 42-room *Hotel Palmas de Cortez* resembles other hotels in the area. Charges for singles/doubles are US$55/85, includ-

ing three meals a day; suites and condominiums cost from US$120 to US$150 for one to five people. Rates do not include 10% in gratuities and another 10% in taxes. For more details, phone ☎ (818) 222-7144 or (800) 368-4334 in the USA or write Baja Fishing Resorts, PO Box 9016, Calabasas, California 91372.

The Inn at Rancho Leonero is an isolated resort southeast of La Capilla Trailer Park; follow the dirt road leading south from La Capilla. The rancho consists of an airstrip, cozy rooms, a restaurant and a bar at a spectacular beachfront location. Having acquired a reputation for some of Baja's best food, the restaurant sometimes serves up to 120 guests.

Owner John Ireland has also expanded the inn's water-sports facilities, opening a dive center complete with the latest equipment and a scuba instructor from the USA. Rental equipment is available; dive trips like the 'Pulmo reef dive' cost US$100 per person for a minimum of two people, including boat rental, two tanks, all other necessary equipment, a guide and lunch. Boats are also available for fishing trips.

Spotless, spacious rooms have thatched roofs, stone walls, tiled floors and patios overlooking the sea. Singles/doubles with all meals included are US$100/125 from August to March, US$125/150 from April to August, plus 10% for service and taxes. For more details, phone ☎ (714) 375-3720 or ☎ (800) 696-2164 (toll free) or write Rancho Leonero, 8691 El Rancho, Fountain Valley, California 92708.

Places to Eat

Popular with gringos, *Tío Pablo* has a good pizza menu as well as massive portions of

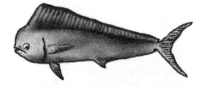

Mexican specialties like chicken fajitas – with rice, beans, salad and tortillas, one dish easily feeds two-plus persons. Despite a raucous decor and satellite TV connections for international sports, it seems fairly sedate, and the margaritas are a bit weak.

AROUND LOS BARRILES

North of Los Barriles, a mostly graded but rough and potentially dangerous road, not suitable for large RVs, hugs the coast to Punta Pescadero, El Cardonal, and even crosses the very difficult Cuesta de los Muertos (Crest of the Dead) en route to San Juan de los Planes and La Paz. Roadside doggerel, mimicking the Burma Shave signs of the 1950s in the USA, reminds drivers that:

Hardly a man
Is now alive
Who took this road
At 65

Hotel Punta Pescadero about 10 miles (16 km) from Los Barriles, is a small, elitist resort also accessible by air (on its private landing strip). Each room has ocean views from private tiled terraces and patios; several also have fireplaces. Singles/doubles cost US$90, while a one-bedroom villa is US$150; meals are extra. Make reservations in the USA by phoning ☎ (714) 863-1116 or ☎ (800) 426-0835 (toll free), or writing Punta Pescadero Reservations at 4695 MacArthur Court, Suite 150, Newport Beach, California 92660.

Sport fishing cruises at Punta Pescadero cost US$100 per day on an 18-foot skiff, US$150 on a panga, US$200 on a regular cruiser and US$250 on a luxury cruiser. Whale-watching flights (US$300 per hour), scuba rentals, shore fishing equipment and horses are also available. The resort's own air taxis carry passengers from the international airports at La Paz or Los Cabos for US$125 per trip for up to four passengers.

While most beaches north of Los Barriles are rocky or gravely, some are suitable for free camping. El Cardonal, to the north, is more hospitable than snobbish Punta

Pescadero in this regard, but *El Cardonal Resort* is also a good choice. Tent sites cost US$5, RV sites US$7, and a one-bedroom house goes for US$39 daily, US$199 per week. The Quebecois owners lead rock art trips at Rancho Boca del Alamo to the north. Their North American contact in Montreal is ☎ (514) 767-6036, fax (514) 767-7180.

LA RIVERA

At a junction about 12 miles (20 km) south of Los Barriles, a paved lateral off the Transpeninsular leads to the farming village of La Rivera, which lacks hotels but has one quiet gulfside campground, the shady *RV Park Correcaminos* (☎ 5-39-00), which charges US$6 with all hookups. Its English-speaking Chilean owner, Eduardo Baeza, also rents a palapa studio apartment for US$45 per night and a secluded three-bedroom house for $45 per night or US$250 per week.

American-owned *Las Tres Banderas* is a fine Italian restaurant that also serves Mexican antojitos, but its real forte is fabulous desserts like key lime pie and home-made ice cream.

PUNTA COLORADA

At Punta Colorada, about 4 miles from the end of the paved road and just over 11 miles (18 km) from the Transpeninsular, *Hotel Punta Colorada* is a favorite for anglers because of the abundant roosterfish offshore. Singles/doubles/triples/quadruples cost US$50/80/115/140, including three meals a day, while fishing trips cost from US$115 to US$240 per day. For more information in the USA, phone ☎ (818) 222-5066 or write PO Box 9016, Calabasas, California 91306.

CABO PULMO

Thanks in large part to a road that is still impassable for larger RVs, Cabo Pulmo enjoys a stunning coastline and an ecologically unique coral reef, which is exceptional for diving and snorkeling. This section of the East Cape is a legally protected area, featuring several hundred species of tropical fish, and no fishing is permitted. The reef's maximum depth of 70 feet (22 meters) is ideal for optimum air time.

Tourist development has arrived, but American-owned *Cabo Pulmo Resort* may be a model for what such development should be – decentralized but not sprawling, well landscaped but not water-hungry (thanks to a drip irrigation system). The self-contained units are even solar-powered. Unlike hotels on the southern Cape, its comforts, without extravagance, do not overwhelm its natural environment.

Bungalows with double beds cost US$45 nightly, 'casitas' (cottages) US$60 and full houses US$75; all have kitchens or kitchenettes and there's a 20% discount after the second night. Weekly rentals are US$240 for a bungalow, US$320 for a casita and US$400 for a house; monthly tenure is also available. The real bargain, for budget travelers, is the resort's only bed-and-bath unit, which goes for US$20. The resort's US contact is Jackie Vork (☎ (208) 726-9233 or fax (208) 726-5545), or write PO Box 774, Ketchum, Idaho 83340.

Pepe's Dive Center, Apartado Postal 532, Cabo San Lucas, organizes guided dives for US$35 (one tank) to US$55 (two tanks); rents dive equipment and fills air tanks; and also offers four-day PADI courses with full certification for US$350. Snorkeling and sightseeing tours (including trips to the Sierra de la Laguna) are possible for non-divers. Reservations are not essential but can be made with US contact Anita Kelley (☎ (619) 489-7001).

BAHÍA LOS FRAILES

Beyond Cabo Pulmo, the East Cape highway is impossible for RVs, and many of the diners at *Hotel Bahía Los Frailes* come from yachts anchored offshore. Despite its small size, the place employs both a Mexican and an Italian chef, plus additional kitchen staff. It will be adding more cabañas.

Room rates are US$90 per person, all meals included, for a single room with two queen-size beds; US$110 per person in a one-bedroom suite; and US$400 for up to four guests in a four-bedroom suite. Taxes and gratuities are extra, and there are additional charges for children under 13, but those under five are generally free of charge. Fishing pangas, with skipper but no tackle, cost from US$150 to US$175 per day. The local mailing address is Apartado Postal 230, San José del Cabo, Baja California Sur, México; the US contact (☎ (415) 956-3499) is 220 Montgomery St, Suite 1019, San Francisco, California 94104.

Beyond Bahía Los Frailes, the highway becomes increasingly rough but still passable for vehicles with good clearance and a short wheelbase. South of the junction with the road to the village of Palo Escopeta and San José del Cabo's international airport, however, the rains of November 1993 made the road impassable for everyone except pedestrians, burros, mules, mountain bikers and perhaps truly determined motorcyclists. For more information on this road, see the 'Around San José del Cabo' section, below.

At Rancho La Vinorama, near the junction of the Palo Escopeta road, some extravagant development has already occurred. Despite a climb through a sandy arroyo from the airport, the Palo Escopeta road is passable for almost any vehicle – an old VW squareback, with almost no clearance, made it easily to Rancho Vinorama.

THE CENTRAL CAPE & THE SIERRA DE LA LAGUNA

Even travelers who deplore the unrestrained development in the Cape Region's coastal areas will enjoy the scenic Sierra de la Laguna, an ecological treasure that should be a national park. Several foothill villages provide access to these unique mountains of the interior, which may also be reached from Todos Santos, on the Pacific slope of the range.

SANTIAGO

Tranquil Santiago, a charming village about 6 miles (10 km) south of La Rivera junction and 1½ miles (2½ km) west of the

Transpeninsular, was the site of one of the bloodiest episodes in Baja's history, when Pericú Indians revolted and murdered the Jesuit Lorenzo Carranco and several other Spaniards before being subdued by the Spanish army and European epidemics. No trace remains of the mission, which closed in 1795.

The tidy **Zoológico Santiago** contains a variety of animals, including a Bengal tiger, an African lion, a black bear, badgers, bobcats, coatimundi, deer, monkeys, native reptiles (mostly rattlesnakes), peccary and a collection of colorful macaws. Unfortunately, almost none of the animals are named, so most visitors have to guess at everything other than the big draws. There are swing sets, and many families have a barbecue here on Sundays.

Places to Stay

Modest *Hotel Palomar* (☎ 128), just down the hill from the plaza, is more notable for its restaurant, which serves very fine seafood at moderate prices, than for its accommodation. A single/double with hot shower, amidst spacious and pleasant grounds, costs about US$20/25 per night, and the English-speaking owner is a good source of information on the Sierra de la Laguna.

AROUND SANTIAGO
Tropic of Cancer

Precisely at latitude 23.5° N, just south of Santiago on the Transpeninsular, a concrete sphere marks the tropic of Cancer, which also passes through Hawaii, Taiwan, the middle of India, Saudi Arabia and the Sahara Desert.

Cañón San Dionisio

The hike up Cañón San Dionisio, in the Sierra de la Laguna about 15 miles (25 km) west of Santiago, is one of Baja California's real highlights, a scenic area with a unique ecology in which cacti, palms, oaks, aspens and pines grow virtually side by side. The deciduous *huerivo* (aspen, *Populus brandegeei glabra)*, whose main California counterpart is dormant for up to six

months, does not lose its leaves until December and sprouts out again by January.

The trail up Cañón San Dionisio is easy to follow, but in some cases requires scrambling over large granite boulders; if rainfall has been sufficient, there are many pools suitable for swimming. This is the northernmost of three major east-west routes across the Sierra de la Laguna; the other two are Cañón San Bernardo, west of Miraflores, and Cañón San Pedro, west of Caduaño. The best guide for hiking these routes is Walt Peterson's *The Baja Adventure Book* (see the Books section in the Facts for the Visitor chapter).

To reach San Dionisio from Santiago, take the dirt road off the plaza to the video store; then at the next junction, take the middle (uphill) fork where it divides into three; from this point, San Dionisio is a straight shot. Despite some damage from the rains of November 1993, the road is passable for any passenger vehicle driven with caution. Taxi drivers from Santiago will drop hikers at the trailhead for US$34, not an unreasonable price if two or three can share the expense.

Agua Caliente

Five miles (8 km) west of Santiago by a good dirt road, Agua Caliente is an otherwise nondescript village whose hot spring attracts campers and hikers to the canyon of the Arroyo de Agua Caliente. The spring itself, at the foot of the Sierra de la Laguna, is a further 2½ miles (4 km) west by another dirt road that requires fording a stream; alongside a dam at the end of the road, it is tepid rather than hot (old-timers claim it has cooled considerably in recent years). In theory, Ejido Agua Caliente charges US$5 for camping or day use, but rarely does anyone show up to collect.

MIRAFLORES

Miraflores is situated 5½ miles (8½ km) south of Agua Caliente by a dirt road but also accessible by a junction from the paved Transpeninsular at Km 71, 8½ miles (14 km) south of Santiago. The town has little of interest in its own right, but a good 4-mile (7-km) road leads to the village of Boca de la Sierra and **Cañón San Bernardo**, one of the major routes into the Sierra de la Laguna. Ask for guides to nearby rock art sites.

Only two minutes from the trailhead, at the point where the acequia enters the village, the route crosses the Arroyo Boca de la Sierra past an unfortunately trashy campsite. However, it soon ascends into a wonderland of native vegetation and wildlife, including hairy tarantulas and other spiders, peculiar insects that look like walking twigs, and colorful tree frogs, along a series of attractive granite pools. Many of these pools are suitable for swimming.

Note that the dirt road from Miraflores to Caduaño, which appears on both the AAA and ITM road maps, no longer exists. It is necessary to return to the Transpeninsular in order to travel between the two villages.

THE WESTERN CAPE
The Western Cape, from Todos Santos south along México 19, has so far been spared the grotesque overdevelopment of Cabo San Lucas, but subdivision signs are sprouting along its sandy Pacific beaches. The near absence of potable water may yet save the area.

TODOS SANTOS
Founded in 1724 as a Jesuit *visita* (outstation) dependent on La Paz, Misión Santa Rosa de Todos Los Santos became a full-fledged mission a decade later, but the two-year Pericú rebellion nearly destroyed it. When the La Paz mission was abandoned in 1749, it became Misión Nuestra Señora del Pilar de Todos Santos. Epidemics killed Indians relocated from San Luis Gonzaga and La Pasión, and Todos Santos then limped along until its abandonment in 1840.

In the late 19th century, the former colonial village became a prosperous cane-milling town with four red-brick *trapiches*

(mills), which produced the dark sugar known as *panocha*; the first mill was shipped from San Francisco to Cabo San Lucas and then overland to Todos Santos. Depleted aquifers eliminated most of the thirsty sugar industry, though mills still operate in nearby Pescadero and San Jacinto. Some farmers have instituted multi-cropping methods for their fruits and vegetables that rely much less on chemical fertilizers.

In recent years, Todos Santos has seen an influx of North Americans, including refugee artists for whom Santa Fe and Taos have grown too large and impersonal. Since the completion of México 19 in 1985, it has received many more visitors, as the straighter western highway is a much quicker route to Cabo San Lucas than the serpentine Transpeninsular. Nearby beaches, especially to the south, have begun to attract increasing numbers of visitors, but Todos Santos itself is a charming destination that is unlikely to follow the deplorable example of overdeveloped Cabo San Lucas.

Orientation & Information
Like many Mexican towns, Todos Santos has a fairly regular grid plan, but local residents rely more on landmarks than street names for directions (though street names do exist).

Todos Santos' de facto tourist office is El Tecolote, an English-language bookstore that distributes a very detailed (some might say cluttered) town map and a sketch map of nearby beach areas. It's in a cluster of shops at the corner of Benito Juárez and Hidalgo.

Money Bancomer, at the corner of Benito Juárez and Obregón, changes money weekday mornings.

Post & Telecommunications The post office is on Heróico Colegio Militar, between Hidalgo and Márquez de León.

Pilar's Tacos, at the corner of Heróico Colegio Militar and Zaragoza, is the de facto phone office, but a new phone, fax

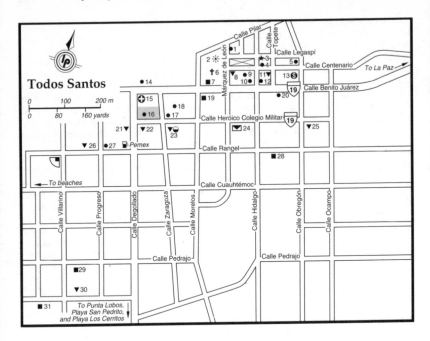

Todos Santos

0   100   200 m
0   80   160 yards

To La Paz

To beaches

To Punta Lobos,
Playa San Pedrito,
and Playa Los Cerritos

and message center is due to open in a complex at the corner of Juárez and Hidalgo.

All telephones in Todos Santos formerly began with 4, but now begin with 5. Todos Santos' area code is 114.

Bookshop El Tecolote (☎ 5-03-72, see also Information, above), at the corner of Juárez and Hidalgo, maintains a good selection of English-language books and magazines, specializing in books on Baja California; it also carries Lonely Planet guides. Its mailing address is Apartado Postal 42, Todos Santos.

Medical Services Todos Santos' hospital is at the corner of Benito Juárez and Degollado. There is a good private physician, Dr Morales, on Morelos between Benito Juárez and Heróico Colegio Militar, and a good dentist, Dr Guluarte, at the corner of Heróico Colegio Militar and Zaragoza.

Things to See

The restored **Teatro Cine General Manuel Márquez de León**, on the north side of the plaza, no longer shows films, but occasional live performances still take place.

Scattered around Todos Santos are the remains of former *trapiches* (mills), including **Molino El Progreso** at El Molino Trailer Park & Restaurant, and **Molino de los Santana**, on Juárez opposite the hospital. **Molino Cerro Verde** and **Molino Jesús Amador** are on the northern outskirts of town.

Centro Cultural Todosanteño (Escuela General Melitón Albañez)

Murals at Todos Santos' former schoolhouse and pending cultural center located on Calle Benito Lopez near Calle Topete, date from 1933; they contain nationalist and revolutionary motifs such as missionaries and Indians, the Spanish conquista-

■	PLACES TO STAY	2	Mirador (vista point)
7	Hotel California	3	Policía
19	Motel Guluarte	4	Municipalidad
27	El Molino Trailer Park	5	Stewart Gallery
28	Hostería Las Casitas	6	Iglesia Nuestra Señora del Pilar
29	Hotel Santa Rosa de las Palmas	9	Galería Santa Fe
31	Hotel Miramar	10	Casa Franco
		12	El Tecolote (bookstore & information)
▼	PLACES TO EAT	13	Bancomer
7	Las Tejitas	14	Ex-Molino de los Santana
8	Café Santa Fe	15	Hospital
11	Caffé Todos Santos	16	Parque de los Pinos\taxi stand
21	Santa Mónica	17	Doctor Guluarte (Dentist)
22	Las Fuentes	18	Doctor Morales
23	Pilar's Tacos	20	Centro Cultural Todosanteño (Escuela
25	La Langosta Loca		General Melitón Albañez)
26	El Molino	23	Bus/Long-distance telephone
30	Casa de Margarita	24	Post Office
		26	Ex-Molino El Progreso
	OTHER		
1	Teatro Cine General Manuel Márquez de León		

dores, Emiliano Zapata, cooperativism, rural laborers, industry, athletics ('vigor in mind and muscle') and 'emancipation of the rural spirit'. Scenes of the Revolution in the northern colonnade are badly faded, but attempts at restoration have slowed because the torrential rains at Los Cabos in November 1993 diverted state funds.

When in full swing, the center will hold classes in art, pottery, dance and other subjects for both locals and expatriates.

Beaches

Only about 1 mile (1.6 km) from Todos Santos, through the fields behind the Hotel California, lie pleasant but rarely visited beaches, which are also accessible via the dirt road that leads west from the Pemex station; passing the ballpark, it becomes steep, rutted and gullied. The shoreline lagoons are good spots for birding and camping is possible, but bring water (local expats report that Todos Santos' tap water is potable).

More accessible but more populous beaches are 6½ miles (10 km) northwest, and south of town; see the Around Todos Santos section, below.

Festivals & Events

Todos Santos' annual **Festival de Artes** (art festival), in late January, now lasts two days; in 1994, it had 110 exhibitors and drew over 2000 viewers. At other times, it is possible to visit local artists, such as Charles Stewart, in their homes/studios, where their works are for sale.

In late February, Todos Santos holds a tour of local historic homes.

Places to Stay

Camping *El Molino Trailer Park* (☎ 5-01-40), behind the Pemex station, has a laundry room, toilets, showers, a small book exchange and 21 RV spaces with full hookups for US$6 to $10 per site. Its spacious, immaculately clean bathrooms merit a citation for being perhaps the only ones on the entire peninsula with enough hooks for hanging clothes and towels as you shower; the doors even open and close properly. Its US reservations number is ☎ (818) 986-7420.

Hotels, Motels & B&Bs In recent years Todos Santos' accommodation has improved in quality and increased in quantity, but it is still limited in all categories. Rather misnamed *Hotel Miramar* (☎ 5-03-41), on a quiet side street in Barrio San Vicente south of Calle Degollado, has only limited ocean views from the 2nd-floor balconies, but it's clean and reasonably priced at US$15/18 single/double.

Remodeled *Motel Guluarte*, at the corner of Benito Juárez and Morelos, now has a swimming pool as well; if no one is on duty at the desk, check the grocery across the street. Rooms are about US$20 double.

Todos Santos' newest accommodation is *Hostería Las Casitas*, a Canadian-run B&B on Calle Rangel between Obregón and Hidalgo, which also offers moderately priced tent sites. Its rolled palapa roof edges, rarely seen nowadays, add authentic detail to the remodeled, five-room building. Prices are US$25/45 single/double; the restaurant is open to the public. Las Casitas' mailing address is Apartado Postal 73, Todos Santos, Baja California Sur, México.

The new *Hotel Santa Rosa de las Palmas* (☎ 5-00-31), on Calle Pedrajo between Villarino and Progreso, has 15 rooms with kitchenettes for US$33 single or double, among pleasant gardens with a swimming pool. *Hotel California* (☎ 5-00-02), a longtime favorite, is on Benito Juárez between Márquez de León and Morelos. Its original owner bought gold from campesinos in the Sierra de la Laguna and traded the gold for lumber from Mazatlán; its zigzag corridors and creaky floorboards give it a distinct personality. Clean singles/doubles, each with private bath, cost about US$35/42; there is no air-conditioning, but all rooms have ceiling fans. It also has a restaurant and a clean, well-maintained pool.

Places to Eat

For fine food at bargain prices, try any or all of the taco stands along Calle Heróico Colegio Militar between Márquez de León and Degollado; each has its own specialty, be it fish, chicken, shrimp or beef. Family-run *Casa de Margarita*, in Barrio San Vicente, has attracted a devoted following for fine, reasonably priced antojitos and

seafood, but it has no liquor license. It's on a street whose name is disputed – consult the map to locate it.

For breakfast, coffee-conscious tourists can down their cappuccinos at *Caffé Todos Santos*, at the corner of Centenario and Topete, among savory pastries and visually enticing fruit salads. Its American owner plans to offer regular foreign film programs with dessert in the evening. It's closed Mondays.

La Langosta Loca, on Heróico Colegio Militar at Alvaro Obregón, serves various seafood dishes such as tuna salad, shrimp salad and local grilled fish under a big, palm-thatched roof. With daily specials around US$6 and other dishes rather higher, it's about mid-range for current Mexican restaurants. Slightly cheaper *Las Tejitas* in the Hotel California offers a basic continental breakfast, a dearer French-toast breakfast and a Mexican breakfast of orange juice, coffee and chilaquiles (a scrambled concoction of eggs, chiles and bits of tortillas).

Expatriate North Americans also recommend gringo-run *El Molino*, on the grounds of the town's last sugar mill and next to its namesake trailer park, for its salad bar and Sunday brunches. *Santa Mónica*, on Calle Degollado at the corner of Heróico Colegio Militar, is also highly regarded. Across from the Santa Mónica, *Las Fuentes* has very fine antojitos (the chicken with mole sauce is exceptional) and seafood specialties served in a shady patio among colorful bougainvilleas and three refreshing fountains. Prices are moderate.

In a class by itself, *Café Santa Fe* attracts patrons from as far away as La Paz and Cabo San Lucas to its plaza location at the corner of Centenario and Márquez de León. The grub is Italian and prices are high, but it's worth a holiday splurge.

Things to Buy

As an artists' colony, Todos Santos has several shops and galleries open to the public, displaying samples of local work. Try Casa Franco, on Benito Juárez between Márquez de León and Hidalgo, the Santa

Fe Gallery alongside the Café Santa Fe, or the Stewart Gallery on Obregón between Legaspí and Centenario.

Entertainment
Proud of its tranquillity, Todos Santos is no party town, but La Langosta Loca (see Places to Eat, above) offers dancing some evenings. Most visitors will find walking around town entertaining enough.

Getting There & Away
The bus station, which doubles as the long-distance telephone office, is at the corner of Calle Heróico Colegio Militar and Calle Zaragoza. At least six buses a day go to La Paz (US$5) between 6 am and 6 pm, and to Cabo San Lucas (US$4) between 8 am and 7 pm.

Getting Around
Visitors not wishing to hike the roundabout route to the beaches west of Todos Santos can hire a cab at Parque de los Pinos, diagonal from the bus terminal.

AROUND TODOS SANTOS
Punta Lobos
At Punta Lobos, about 1½ miles (2½ km) south of Todos Santos, pangueros sell their catch from the beach in late afternoon, offering a cheaper, better selection than local markets. Shark fins bring nearly US$70 per kg in La Paz.

Campo Experimental Forestal Todos Santos
Four miles (6½ km) south of Todos Santos, around Km 56, Mexico's Servicio Agrícola y de Recursos Hidraúlicos (SARH) operates this desert botanical garden, which is a good place to become acquainted with the peninsula's native plants (there are also sections with non-natives). Separate areas emphasize food plants, medicinal plants and forage plants. The weekday staff will show visitors around, but on weekends there is only a watchman.

Playa San Pedrito
Across from the botanical garden, a 2½-mile (4-km) dirt road leads to this sandy crescent beach with surfable breaks. Spacious *San Pedrito RV Park* (☎ 4-01-47) charges US$3 for camping without hookups, US$12.50 for RV sites with all hookups, and US$33 double for modest cabañas. Amenities include a restaurant and a swimming pool.

Playa Los Cerritos
In a north swell, Los Cerritos' crescent beach has a good right break with only a few surfers. There is also good fishing from the rocky headland to the north.

At Km 64, *Los Cerritos RV Park* is operating on a shoestring budget, but the toilets flush and the cold showers work (water is expensive because it's trucked in – consider a 'sea shower' to conserve this precious commodity). There is some shade but no electricity. Ejido Pescadero keeps the area weed-free, charging US$3 to park outside the fence, US$4 to park inside; there have been reports of thefts, so secure your possessions at night.

Playa Las Cabrillas
South of Playa Los Cerritos, livestock are very common along México 19; drive with care. Beyond Km 81, Playa Las Cabrillas features a long but steep sandy beach not really suitable for surfing. However, there are many good rustic campsites just off the highway.

Playa Migriño
Between Km 97 and Km 98, a dirt road leads half a mile west among mangroves to **Estero Migriño**, a good site for birding that also has a good right break in the winter months. Cow patties and insects are both abundant, so watch your step and bring bug repellent.

THE SOUTHERN CAPE
The Southern Cape area, especially the luxury hotel corridor between San José del Cabo and Cabo San Lucas, is the most expensive, and in many ways the least appealing, part of the entire Baja peninsula. Only central San José del Cabo has

William Walker & the Cape

William Walker, the infamously quixotic American adventurer who spent and lost his life trying to build an Anglo empire in Mexico and Central America, was the first to try to bring the sleepy Cape Region into the modern world. In 1853, planning to establish a self-styled 'Republic of Sonora and Lower California', he sailed south from San Francisco, touching at Cabo San Lucas before anchoring at the territorial capital of La Paz.

Misrepresenting themselves as commercial voyagers to gain permission to land, Walker's forces arrested the governor, took possession of public buildings and raised the flag of the new republic under the legal code of Louisiana – which permitted slavery. Walker, a native of Tennessee, later made slavery a cornerstone of his proposed Central American empire in an apparent attempt to gain political support from the slave states.

Improvised Mexican resistance failed to dislodge Walker from La Paz, but the threat of a more organized force from Todos Santos and the failure of his own reinforcements to arrive drove him back to Cabo San Lucas. Concerned that a Mexican warship was trailing him, he gave up plans to establish a new capital at Bahía Magdalena to return to Ensenada, where he led a heroically foolish attempt to cross to Sonora. Eventually, he straggled across the US border to hatch the Central American schemes that led to his death in Honduras.

Despite Walker's failures in Baja California, some have argued that his adventures brought territorial gains to the United States – the Gadsden Purchase of southern Arizona and New Mexico brought the USA part of what Walker tried to obtain by force. Today, given the overwhelming Americanization of Cabo San Lucas, concerned Mexicans might well wonder if, in the long run, Walker triumphed in spite of his self-imposed disasters.■

retained any integrity in the face of aggressively vulgar tourist development.

History

Until about 20 years ago the southern tip of the Baja peninsula had been, in succession, a somnambulant haven for Pericú Indians, a sheltered hideaway for pirates and a string of sedate fishing communities. The Pericú inhabited the foothills of the Sierra de la Laguna to the north, never settling around Cabo itself because fresh water was scarce, but the majority soon died when arriving Europeans brought deadly pathogens.

When Europeans first saw the peninsula in the 16th century, water shortages still made the Southern Cape an unappealing place for permanent settlement, but its secluded anchorages offered privateers an ideal base from which to raid Spain's Manila galleons. One of the earliest English pirates in the area was Sir Francis Drake, who stopped briefly in 1578 or 1579 to take on water before continuing north to present-day San Francisco. In 1587 Thomas Cavendish commanded three ships that attacked and captured the treasure-laden *Santa Ana* – a galleon that weighed about 700 tons, more than twice the total weight of Cavendish's fleet. Cavendish could take only a fraction of the gold, silver and other booty, abandoning the rest.

By the early 17th century, the Spanish had lost enough gold and silver to prompt the establishment of a small *presidio* (military outpost) at Cabo San Lucas. Around 1730, the Jesuits established Misión San

José del Cabo, which became a more permanent settlement. The presidio deterred the pirates and, eventually, both towns became villages whose inhabitants primarily depended on fishing and fish-canning for their livelihood. During the Mexican-American War, US troops occupied the area, as did William Walker's forces a few years later.

After WW II, private pilots from north of the border returned to the USA with tales of the area's big game fish and magnificent beaches. As more North Americans arrived, upscale hotels and restaurants began to appear and the federal government built an international airport near San José del Cabo. Cruise ships soon included Cabo San Lucas in their itineraries, and a ferry service (since discontinued) began to operate to and from the mainland city of Puerto Vallarta. In recent years, hordes of North American tourists and retirees have frequented the area, central Cabo San Lucas has lost its village ambiance entirely, and the coastline between Cabo San Lucas and San José del Cabo has become grossly overdeveloped with multi-story luxury resort hotels.

SAN JOSÉ DEL CABO

On the southern coast of the peninsula, San José del Cabo (population 19,000) is still a quaint town of narrow streets, Spanish-style buildings and a tree-shaded plaza, 20 miles (32 km) east of Cabo San Lucas and 112 miles (180 km) south of La Paz. Because of its dependable fresh water supply, the San José area attracted both the Manila galleons that carried treasure across the Pacific to Acapulco and the buccaneers who preyed on them.

Established in 1730 as a mission village, San José suffered Indian rebellions, floods, military attacks (from Spanish loyalists in the Wars of Independence) and foreign occupation (by US Marines and, later, William Walker) before settling into a more placid existence since the mid-19th century. Ambitious developers have not totally succeeded in transforming San José

into a major tourist resort; grandiose plans for a yacht marina at the outlet of Arroyo San José, an ecologically sensitive area, recently fizzled because of local opposition. These plans have not completely died, but for now San José remains a much more pleasant destination than Cabo San Lucas.

Orientation

San José consists of two distinct parts: central San José, atop a hill about 1 mile (1.6 km) inland, plus a row of resort hotel complexes, condominiums and time-share complexes along a wide stretch of beach that are the fault of Fonatur, Mexico's quasi-governmental tourist agency. Manicured Blvd José Antonio Mijares, named for a Mexican naval officer who distinguished himself for bravery during San José's occupation by US Marines in 1847-48, links the two areas.

In town, the northernmost blocks of Blvd Mijares are a miniature gringoland of restaurants and souvenir shops, but compared to Cabo San Lucas it's tasteful and tranquil. Shady Plaza Mijares is a pleasant place for relaxing with an ice cream.

Calle Zaragoza and Calle Doblado, San José's other main streets, both cross Blvd Mijares and lead to the Transpeninsular. If walking toward town from the beach, turn left on either street to cross the heart of San José – small, red-tiled buildings, the colonial-style Iglesia San José and Plaza Mijares. The town's few budget hotels and restaurants are on or near these streets.

Across Arroyo San José, Pueblo La Playa is a tranquil fishing village with several good restaurants and limited accommodation. The heavy rains of November 1993 cut the East Cape road to Bahía Los Frailes and Los Barriles just beyond Rancho Las Destiladeras, about 12 miles (20 km) east of Pueblo La Playa. Only pedestrians, bicycles and perhaps motorcycles will be able to handle the route, which may not be completely restored for some years.

Information

Tourist Office The staff at the Dirección

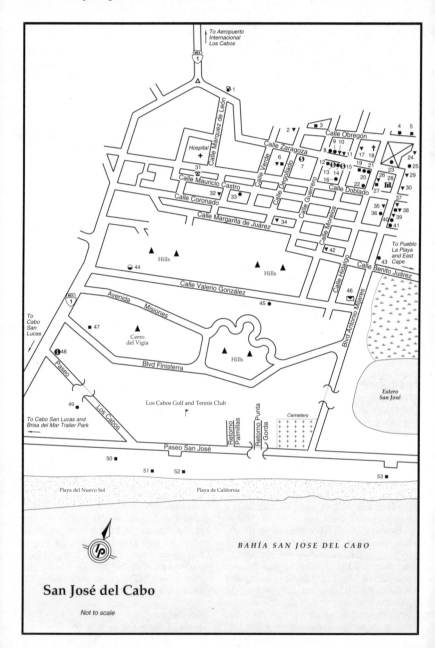

San José del Cabo

Not to scale

BAHÍA SAN JOSE DEL CABO

■	PLACES TO STAY	25	Café Fiesta	16	Real Turismo (travel
3	San José Inn	26	Cafetería Girasol		agency)
5	Posada Señor Mañana	29	Ivan's	18	Iglesia San José
6	Posada Terranova	30	Almacenes Goncanseco	20	El Copal (crafts)
12	Hotel Diana	32	Mercado Municipal	21	Antigua Los Cabos (crafts)
19	Hotel Ceci	34	Pizza Fiesta	22	Killer Hook Surf Shop
27	Hotel Colli	35	Iguana Bar	23	Plaza Mijares/Dirección
38	Hotel Tropicana	37	Helados Bing		General de Turismo
47	Howard Johnson Plaza	38	Tropicana Bar & Grill		Municipal (tourist office)
	Suite Resort	39	Marco's Kitchen	28	Palacio Municipal
50	Fiesta Inn	42	Le Bistrot	31	Public telephone office
51	Hotel Aguamarina Los			33	Deportiva Piscis
	Cabos		OTHER	36	La Botica (bookshop)
52	Hotel Posada Real	1	Pemex station	40	Calafia (dance club)
53	Stouffer Presidente Los	4	Casa de la Cultura	41	Eclipse (dance club)
	Cabos	7	Banca Serfin	43	Craft stalls
		8	Dollar Rent-A-Car	44	Bus station
▼	PLACES TO EAT	9	Señor Bacco (dance	45	Lavandería Vera
2	Asadero Los Candiles		club/comedy)	46	Post Office
6	Posada Terranova	13	Casa de Cambio (money	48	Infonatur (tourism
10	Pietro		exchange)		development office)
11	La Fogata	14	Fantasía del Cristal (blown	49	Mexicana
17	Restaurant Diana		glass)		
24	Damiana	15	Bancomer		

General de Turismo Municipal (☎ 2-04-46), on Plaza Mijares, are not overly helpful. Hours are weekdays 8 am to 3 pm.

During the same hours, the Infonatur office on Paseo Los Cabos, at the southern Transpeninsular approach to town, also regards requests for information as unwarranted intrusions. San José's best source of information may be the talkative, English-speaking owner of Hotel Señor Mañana (see Places to Stay, below).

Money The cambio at Aeropuerto Internacional Los Cabos offers very poor rates, so try to avoid changing money until you get to town. Banks are only open in the morning.

Bancomer is at the corner of Calle Zaragoza and Calle Morelos, while Banca Serfin is at the corner of Zaragoza and Degollado. The cambio on Zaragoza between Guerrero and Doblado offers poor rates (though better than at the airport), but keeps longer hours.

Post & Telecommunications The post office has moved from Plaza Mijares south to the intersection of Blvd Mijares and Valerio González.

Direct and collect calls to the USA are fairly simple from the public telephone office on Calle Doblado, but several other offices also have phones. San José's area code is 114.

Cultural Centers San José's Casa de la Cultura is more an educational resource for locals than a sightseeing attraction for tourists, but a few interesting historical photographs line the walls. It's on Calle Obregón, just north of Plaza Mijares.

Travel Agencies Real Turismo (☎ 2-00-37), Calle Morelos s/n between Doblado and Zaragoza, will deal with airline tickets and other tourist needs.

Bookshops La Botica, Blvd Mijares 33 near Calle Doblado, carries a modest selection of English-language magazines, pot-boiler novels, *USA Today* and the *Los Angeles Times*.

Medical Services San José's Hospital Municipal is ·on Calle Doblado at the corner of Márquez de León. The Cruz Roja (☎ 2-03-16) is on Blvd Mijares.

Emergencies San José's police and fire departments are both on Blvd Mijares, just north of Valerio González.

Laundry Lavandería Vera, on Valerio González about 2½ blocks west of Blvd Mijares, is efficient and reasonably priced.

Jardín del Arte

Every Sunday, from 10 am to 2 pm, San José's artists and artisans display their paintings, photographs, sculptures, jewelry and other crafts for sale in Plaza Mijares.

Beaches

San José's glittering beach areas, **Playa del Nuevo Sol/Playa de California** and **Pueblo La Playa** are its major attractions. Playa del Nuevo Sol and its eastward extension, Playa de California, are at the south end of Blvd Mijares, but Pueblo La Playa is really a small beachside fishing community about 1½ miles (2½ km) east of the junction of Calle Benito Juárez and Blvd Mijares.

The road to Pueblo La Playa passes the freshwater Arroyo San José, surrounded by palms and replenished by an underground spring, whose estuary has been declared a protected wildlife area. Eighteenth-century English pirates took refuge here between raids on Spanish galleons.

Activities

Fishing In San José itself, Deportiva Piscis (☎ 2-03-02), on Calle Mauricio Castro, arranges fishing excursions and also sells and rents tackle. Victor's Aquatics, reached through major hotels like the Stouffer Presidente, the Posada Real Cabo and the Fiesta Inn, organizes six-hour panga trips for US$150 (maximum three persons) and eight-hour cabin-cruiser trips from US$325 (maximum four) to US$395 (maximum six). Their US contact is Jig Stop Tours

(☎ (714) 496-3555, fax (714) 496-1384) in Dana Point, California.

Beyond the lagoon, the road leads to the popular fishing beach at Pueblo La Playa. Local fishermen will arrange fishing excursions at this beach; you can usually find them here in the late afternoon, cutting up their day's catch. La Playa Sport fishing (☎ 2-11-95 from 6 to 8 pm), in Pueblo La Playa, arranges excursions with the local cooperative to the offshore Gordo Banks for marlin, dorado, roosterfish, wahoo, tuna and sailfish. Trips last from 6 am to noon, and cost US$150 for one, two or three persons.

Seasons for various game fish in the Los Cabos area are as follows:

January
    Dorado, shark, striped marlin, tuna
February
    Dorado, shark, striped marlin, tuna
March
    Dorado, shark, striped marlin, tuna
April
    Shark, striped marlin, tuna
May
    Dorado, roosterfish, shark, striped marlin, tuna
June
    Dorado, roosterfish, sailfish, striped marlin, tuna, wahoo
July
    Black marlin, dorado, roosterfish, sailfish, striped marlin, tuna, wahoo
August
    Black marlin, blue marlin, dorado, roosterfish, sailfish, striped marlin, tuna, wahoo
September
    Black marlin, blue marlin, dorado, roosterfish, sailfish, striped marlin, tuna, wahoo
October
    Blue marlin, dorado, roosterfish, sailfish, striped marlin, tuna, wahoo
November
    Blue marlin, dorado, roosterfish, sailfish, striped marlin, tuna, wahoo
December
    Dorado, roosterfish, striped marlin

Golf & Tennis The nine-hole, par 35 course at the Los Cabos Golf & Tennis Club (☎ 2-09-05) costs around US$16 for nine holes, US$23 for 18 holes. Tennis courts rent for US$10 per hour in the day, US$20 per hour at night.

Surfing Run by Mexicans rather than gringos, Killer Hook Surf Shop (☎ 2-24-30), on Calle Hidalgo between Zaragoza and Doblado, is the best source of surfing information in the Los Cabos area. Boards rent for US$15 per day; other items for rent include boogie boards (US$8), surf videos (US$3), snorkeling gear (US$8), surf casting poles (US$10), beach umbrellas (US$5) and mountain bikes (US$11 to US$15). Its mailing address is Apartado Postal 346, San José del Cabo, Baja California Sur, México.

Brisa del Mar Trailer Park (see Places to Stay, below) also rents surfboards for US$10 per day.

Festivals
March 19 marks the *Fiesta de San José*, a celebration of the town's patron saint.

Places to Stay- bottom end & middle
San José's budget and mid-range accommodation are decent and reasonably priced, but there's not much of either. If possible, try to make reservations in high season.

Camping Free unofficial camping is possible on the beach at Pueblo La Playa, about 1½ (2½ km) miles northeast of town. The best site for a fee, also at Pueblo La Playa, is Swedish-run *El Delfín RV Park* (☎ 2-11-99), much too small for large RVs but close to the beach and excellent for tent campers. It also has beautifully decorated cabañas with twin beds for US$25 (an extraordinary value) and a discount agreement with the owner of Hotel Señor Mañana (see below) for extended stays for travelers who wish to alternate lodgings in town and at the beach.

About 2 miles (3 km) southwest of San José, at Km 28 on the Transpeninsular, *Brisa del Mar Trailer Park* has 50 RV spaces from about US$9 to US$15 for two people, plus US$2 for each additional person. Full hookups, hot showers, toilets, a restaurant/bar and a laundromat, plus a few motel-style rooms are available, but it's

very crowded with North Americans from mid-November to February.

Hotels *Hotel Ceci*, Calle Zaragoza 22, has 20 clean, basic rooms with private showers and fans. Singles/doubles are about US$15/17, but it can be very crowded in high season. Quirky but friendly *Posada Señor Mañana* (☎ 2-04-62), at Calle Obregón 1 just north of Plaza Mijares, is increasingly popular with travelers. With singles/doubles for US$20/25, it may be the best value in town. Its talkative manager Rogelio López, better known by his nickname 'Yuca', is fluent in English and a good source of information.

The very popular *Hotel Diana* (☎ 2-04-90), upstairs at Calle Zaragoza 30, has singles/doubles with private bath and TV for US$23.

The rather homely *San José Inn* (☎ 2-14-28), on Calle Obregón between Degollado and Guerrero, has 23 singles/doubles with private bathrooms for US$20/25, plus taxes. Recently expanded and upgraded *Hotel Colli* on Calle Hidalgo, half a block south of Zaragoza, has clean, carpeted rooms for about US$25 single or double.

Posada Terranova (☎ 2-05-34), on Degollado between Doblado and Zaragoza, is a modernized but inviting place with singles/doubles for US$44/50, and it also has a good restaurant.

Places to Stay – top end

Top-end hotels start around US$55 for an off-season single, from mid-April to mid-December. In high season, it's worth checking with airlines and travel agencies for special packages.

The new and surprisingly inconspicuous *Hotel Tropicana* (☎ 2-09-09, fax 2-15-90) on Blvd Mijares, reached by a passage through its namesake restaurant, has 40 double rooms with satellite TV for US$65. It's probably the best hotel in San José proper (as opposed to the luxury beach-front accommodations).

The four-star Best Western *Hotel Posada Real* (☎ 2-01-55, (800) 528-1234 toll free in the USA), located right on the beach, sometimes fails to meet the chain's standards; when guests are few, the Jacuzzi and swimming pool are not heated and hot water supplies can be sporadic. Singles/doubles are US$60 from mid-April to mid-December, but high season rates are US$80.

The 250-room *Stouffer Presidente Los Cabos* (☎ 2-00-38, fax 2-02-32; ☎ (800) 472-2427 toll free in the USA), on the beach near the lagoon, has stunning ocean views, high standards and even higher rates, from US$85 to US$125 for a single or double. Its mailing address is Apartado Postal 2, San José del Cabo, Baja California Sur, México.

The 99-room *Hotel Aguamarina Los Cabos* (☎ 2-00-77, fax 2-02-87; ☎ (800) 897-5700 toll free in the USA) is 1½ miles (2½ km) south of town right on the beach, with the standard amenities of the US-based Quality Inn chain: a swimming pool, air-conditioning and clean, comfortable, carpeted rooms. Singles/doubles normally cost US$55/US$85, but off-season specials, from 30 April to 15 December, cost as little as US$20 per person, double occupancy, with breakfast.

The beachfront *Fiesta Inn* (☎ 2-07-01), also on the shoreline's hotel row, has a restaurant, a bar, golf-club facilities, a swimming pool and around 160 air-conditioned rooms. Singles/doubles cost about US$60 from mid-April to Christmas but rise to US$85 thereafter.

San José's newest accommodation is the *Howard Johnson Plaza Suite Resort* (☎ 2-09-09, fax 2-08-06) at Paseo Finisterra 1, overlooking the Los Cabos Golf & Tennis Club (where guests get discount rates). All rooms have telephone, TV, air-conditioning and purified drinking water, and the hotel also has a mini-gym, a mini-market, a laundry, a travel agency, two restaurants and a bar. Rates start at US$90 single or double in the off-season, mid-April to mid-December, and rise slightly the rest of the year. The US contact is Delfin Hotels & Resorts (☎ (510) 652-6051 or (800) 524-5104 toll free), 3012 College Ave, Berkeley, California 94705.

Places to Eat

The *Mercado Municipal* (municipal market), a great place for cheap eats, has numerous restaurant stalls; try the juice stall for fresh fruit juices and licuados (milk shakes). The mercado is located on a short street between Calle Castro and Calle Coronado. *Helados Bing*, on Blvd Antonio Mijares, has tasty ice cream, paletas, milk shakes and various other cold concoctions. *Cafetería Girasol*, on Hidalgo between Zaragoza and Doblado, has simple, inexpensive antojitos. *Restaurant Diana* (not to be confused with Hotel Diana), on Morelos between Obregón and Zaragoza, is comparable.

The *Tropicana Bar & Grill*, the street-side face of Hotel Tropicana, is a noisy place with a big, open bar with satellite TV coverage of US sports; behind the bar is a restaurant serving a variety of Mexican-American fish and meat dishes, including baby-back ribs and a lobster-steak combination. A marimba band performs most nights at 9 pm. *Iguana Bar*, across the street, is a popular new gathering place for expatriates, with good, moderately priced meals and drinks.

In a restored 18th-century house facing the plaza, *Damiana* is a romantic seafood restaurant with wood-beam ceilings. Traditional weavings and painted clay vessels cover the walls, and cloth napkins, table-cloths and candles cover the tables for dinners that are mid to upper range. Abalone in garlic butter, charcoal-broiled lobster and chile relleno with lobster are among the specialties, but breakfast is also served. During high season around Christmas and New Year's Day, reservations are recommended. It's open 10:30 am to midnight.

Café Fiesta, just south of Damiana, has good breakfasts, light meals and desserts, with pleasant outdoor seating. Almost next door, directly opposite city hall, *Ivan's* features European specialties at mid-range to high prices; it's open for breakfast, lunch and dinner. Belgians Thierry Paquet and Veronique Thiriaux opened *Le Bistrot*, at Calle Morelos 4, in late 1989 after running an establishment of the same name in Todos Santos. Dishes include chicken in white-wine sauce, mushrooms on toast, quiche lorraine, fish in a special sauce and steak with green peppers, but prices are reasonable. The menu changes daily; it's open for lunch and dinner only.

A recent addition to San José's restaurant scene is *Asadero Los Candiles*, on Degollado near Obregón, which has outstanding beef but also prepares vegetarian brochettes; it also has attractive outdoor seating. *La Fogata*, across from Bancomer on Calle Zaragoza, caters primarily to North Americans with typical Mexican fare and seafood, including steak and lobster combinations, as well as a few pasta dishes. *Pietro*, on Calle Zaragoza, features Italian cuisine. For pizza, try *Pizza Fiesta*, at the corner of Degollado and Coronado, or *Marco's Kitchen*, on Blvd Mijares just south of the Tropicana.

Campers and travelers tired of restaurants can obtain staple food items – including North American junk food like Twinkies and M&Ms, at *Almacenes Goncanseco*, a sizable grocery on Blvd Mijares, just north of Calle Doblado.

Entertainment

Noisy nightlife doesn't dominate San José

the way it does Cabo San Lucas, but clubs like *Calafia* and *Eclipse*, both on Blvd Mijares north of Calle Coronado, should satisfy most partygoers. *Señor Bacco*, Calle Zaragoza 71 near the corner with Calle Guerrero, is a dance club that occasionally features live music and standup comedy. It has a happy hour from 7 to 9 pm.

Every Saturday night, local merchants sponsor a fiesta in the Plaza Mijares, from 6 am to midnight, with live music, food, drink, crafts, dances and other attractions.

Things to Buy

Antigua Los Cabos, in a mission-style building on Calle Zaragoza, offers a nicely displayed selection of hand-crafted household items such as sturdy glassware, plates, mugs and wall-hangings. Next door Copal has a very interesting selection of crafts, especially masks.

Fantasía del Cristal, on Calle Zaragoza alongside Bancomer, sells stained-glass artwork. On Blvd Mijares, south of Calle Coronado, a series of market stalls sells souvenirs of generally good quality from throughout Mexico; hammocks are an especially good choice.

Getting There & Away

Air Aeropuerto Internacional Los Cabos (☎ 2-03-99, 2-02-30), serving both San José del Cabo and Cabo San Lucas, is 6½ miles (10 km) north of San José. Mexicana, the only airline with the offices in town, is at the Plaza Los Cabos, on the beachfront Paseo San José.

Alaska Airlines (☎ 2-10-15/6) flies to San Diego, Los Angeles, San Francisco, Seattle and Anchorage. Mexicana and Aero California (☎ 2-09-42/3) have daily flights between Los Cabos and the USA. A four-day, advance-purchase return ticket between Los Angeles and Los Cabos costs as little as US$185.

Aero California flies at least daily to Los Angeles (twice daily Monday, Thursday, Saturday and Sunday), Phoenix and Denver. Mexicana flies daily to Mexico City; Aerolitoral, in the same office as Mexicana, flies daily to Culiacán.

Continental Airlines has recently proposed flights from Houston to Los Cabos, but as of this writing the service had not yet begun.

Bus From San José's new bus station (☎ 2-11-00), on Valerio González just east of the Transpeninsular, buses leave for Cabo San Lucas (30 minutes, US$2) at least once hourly between 6:45 am and 10 pm, and for La Paz (two hours, US$9) at least seven times daily between 6 am and 7 pm.

Getting Around
San José is small enough to be pedestrian-friendly; from the Stouffer Presidente and the other beachfront hotels, it takes only half an hour to walk into town. Outside town, buses, cabs or bicycles may be necessary. The largest cab stand is on Calle Hidalgo, between the church and Plaza Mijares.

To/From the Airport From San José, the official, government-run company Aeroterrestre runs bright yellow taxis and minibuses to Aeropuerto Internacional Los Cabos, about 7 miles (11 km) north, for about US$12. The officially set fare depends either on the number of passengers or on the size of the vehicle. Top-end hotels often provide transportation for their guests.

Other options for getting to and from the airport include walking 1½ miles (2½ km) from the terminal to the highway and then flagging down a bus, or taking a local bus from the San José bus station and getting off at the airport turnoff (the trip costs less than US$1).

Car Rental Dollar Rent-a-Car (☎ 2-01-00 in San José or 2-06-71 at the airport; (800) 421-6868 in the USA) offers daily rates from about US$59 and weekly rates from about US$366, both with unlimited mileage. The office is at Calle Zaragoza, corner of Calle Guerrero.

Thrifty (☎ 2-16-71), Paseo San José 2000-A in the Zona Fonatur, also has an office (☎ 2-01-55) in the lobby of the Hotel Posada Real. National (☎ 2-04-04), whose main office is at Km 238 on the Transpeninsular, also has a branch at Hotel Palmilla (see Playa Palmilla, below).

Local companies offer competitive rates. AMCA (☎ 2-13-14), at Km 33.5 on the Transpeninsular, probably has the best prices in Baja Sur and will arrange airport pickups.

Other Transport Bicycles, scooters and other vehicles are available from Vagabundos Rentals, next to the Stouffer Presidente Hotel, in the winter season. Brisa del Mar Trailer Park rents mountain bikes for US$15 per day.

AROUND SAN JOSÉ DEL CABO
East of Pueblo La Playa, a dirt road leads east-northeast toward Bahía Los Frailes and Los Barriles, but the rains of November 1993 cut the road southeast of the junction with the Palo Escopeta road from San José's international airport. Because several bridges and culverts are out, the temporary arroyo tracks may be impassable after any sort of rain.

At Km 90, 10 miles (16 km) east of San José, is **Santa Cruz de los Zacatitos**, site of the first developers' assaults on the East Cape area. Another 2 miles (3 km) west is the nearly identical **Playa Tortuga**, beyond which is **Shipwreck Beach**, a popular surf spot in summer swells. For more information on the East Cape road, see the East Cape section, above.

THE LOS CABOS CORRIDOR
West of San José is a succession of opulent high-rise, cookie-cutter resorts whose sandy beaches are now cluttered with debris after the torrential rains of November 1993, and are unlikely to be cleaned up very soon, except immediately in front of the luxury hotels. The four-lane, divided segment of the Transpeninsular between San José de Cabo and Cabo San Lucas, completed only in July 1993, may not be completely restored for several years. The bridge across Arroyo El Tule, built with culverts which clogged under the pressure

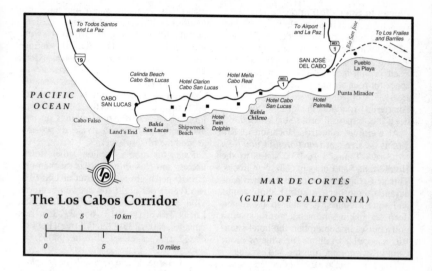

The Los Cabos Corridor

of flood debris rather than on pilings which would have let flood waters pass beneath it, formed a dam which ultimately burst as the water's weight behind it grew too great. It is scheduled to reopen by December 1994, but motor traffic must now use a temporary graded route through this and other arroyos whose bridges were also destroyed.

Playa Palmilla

At Km 27 of the Transpeninsular, 3 miles (5 km) southwest of San José, Playa Palmilla features a small diving and watersports shop that rents snorkels, masks, fins and other beach supplies, and also has an air compressor for filling air tanks. On a hillside just west of the Hotel Palmilla is the *Montañas de Palmilla RV Park* (☎ 2-01-91). On the hill above the beach, *Restaurant Playa Palmilla* has been recommended by several travelers.

Surfing Near Hotel Palmilla are exceptional surfing beaches at Punta Mirador and at Km 28 of the Transpeninsular. Experienced surfers claim that summer reef and point breaks at the latter beach,

popularly known as Zipper's, match the best in Hawaii. In June and July, championship events bring surfers from around the world.

Places to Stay & Eat – top end *Hotel Palmilla* (☎ 2-05-82), on the west side of the beach, caters to clientele such as royalty and movie celebrities, but its daily happy hour offers reasonably priced margaritas and appetizers. Its *La Paloma Restaurant* prepares grilled fish from the catch of the day; a full meal for two averages about US$60, including wine. Rates for rooms vary dramatically according to the season. High-season rates (1 November to 31 May) range from US$250 to US$340 for a double, all meals included (the only option available). Low-season rates for doubles are US$95 to US$135 without meals (meal packages are unavailable during this season). Make reservations by phoning toll free ☎ (800) 637-2226 in the USA.

The Italian restaurant *Da Giorgio*, west of Hotel Palmilla, offers various Italian-style seafood dishes, pizza and pasta at fairly high prices.

Places to Stay – top end

At Km 18, about midway between San José del Cabo and Cabo San Lucas, *El Salate* is a resort with deluxe palapas/bungalows on a more modest scale than Hotel Palmilla. Each palapa has two double rooms with space for four people; prices start at around US$125. Contact manager Eduardo López Abaroa at Apartado Postal 217, San José del Cabo, Baja California Sur, México.

At a prime waterfront location at Km 19.5 is the five-star *Hotel Meliá Cabo Real* (☎ 3-09-99, fax 3-10-03), sister to the Hotel Meliá San Lucas in Cabo San Lucas. This self-contained complex has two restaurants, three bars, a coffee shop, tennis and squash courts, a water-sports center, deep-sea fishing, horseback riding and a golf course. In September, the hotel sponsors a popular triathlon for athletes proficient in swimming, running and cycling.

There are 292 double rooms and seven suites; singles range from US$100 to US$195 and doubles from US$110 to US$205 (plus 10% tax and service charges), depending on the season. Meals average US$8 to US$11 for breakfast, US$22 for lunch and US$31 for dinner. For more information, contact the hotel's US office (☎ (800) 876-3542 toll free) at Suite 914, 6151 West Century Blvd, Los Angeles, California 90045.

Bahía Chileno *Hotel Cabo San Lucas*, at Km 14 (about 11 miles (18 km) from San José), claims to be Mexico's most elegant resort. It is certainly one of the most pretentious, with luxuriant tropical gardens, pseudo-Aztec fountains, tri-level swimming pools and an Oriental art boutique stuffed with museum-quality pieces. Along with a beachfront water-sports center (operated by Cabo Acuadeportes – see the Cabo San Lucas Activities section) and cliffside tennis courts, the hotel offers a long list of activities and outings on land and sea. Snorkeling and diving are possible around the offshore reef.

Rates for rooms, studios, suites, townhouses and 'luxurious' villas start around US$70 per night and top out at US$1410 (no typo!) per night for a seven-bedroom villa. For information, contact Cabo San Lucas Travel (☎ (213) 655-2323 in Los Angeles, (800) 733-2226 toll free), PO Box 48872, Los Angeles, California 90048.

Playa Santa María *Hotel Twin Dolphin*, on secluded Playa Santa María at Km 11.5 between San José del Cabo and Cabo San Lucas, has 44 luxurious rooms and suites overlooking the ocean; facilities include tennis courts, a swimming pool, a water-guzzling golf course, horseback riding and its own eight-boat fishing fleet (see the Cabo San Lucas Activities section). High season (1 November to 31 May) singles/doubles with all meals cost US$260/335 per day, plus 10% tax; off-season rates are about a third cheaper. Its US reservations office (☎ (800) 421-8925 toll free, (213) 386-3940 in Los Angeles) is at Suite 1005,

1625 West Olympic Blvd, Los Angeles, California 90015.

Beach access requires walking through the hotel, but as it's on federal land the hotel cannot exclude non-guests (who cannot use the hotel's parking lot, however). The Twin Dolphin also arranges fishing charters but encourages a catch-and-release policy in the interests of conservation.

Calinda Beach Cabo San Lucas At Km 4.5 of the Transpeninsular is the *Calinda Beach Cabo San Lucas* (☎ 3-00-44, fax 3-00-77 in Cabo San Lucas, (800) 228-5151 toll free in the USA), a cliffside hotel about 3 miles (5 km) east of Cabo San Lucas. It has 125 deluxe air-conditioned rooms, all of which overlook the ocean. There are also two tennis courts, a restaurant, three swimming pools and Jacuzzis perched on cliffs. Singles/doubles start at US$70/80 in the off-season, rising to US$100/110 in winter.

CABO SAN LUCAS

Cabo San Lucas is a resort of international stature, but for many visitors its quintessential experience might be to stagger out of a bar at 3 am, pass out on the beach, and be crushed or smothered at daybreak by a developer's rampaging bulldozer. Survivors, of course, could then call upon the handy therapist at the Hacienda Beach Resort 'to help you strengthen, empower and revitalize your life'.

Cabo's most sinister bottom feeders are not sharks offshore, but real estate agents and time-share sellers who have metamorphosed a placid, scenic coastal village into a depressing, hedonistic jumble of exorbitant five-star hotels, pretentious restaurants and rowdy bars, and tacky souvenir stands – an achievement comparable to turning Cinderella into her stepsisters. The once tiny fishing port's current status as a tourist enclave and retirement retreat for North Americans has engendered bitter resentment among many Mexicans.

Only a few blocks inland, away from the harbor, souvenir shops, restaurants and hotels, local people live in a different Cabo San Lucas, with dusty potholed streets where burros and swine roam through shanty town gardens, punctuated only by the occasional government-built prefab house. Even so, the standard of living is higher than in mainland Mexico, and unemployment is less of a problem than in most other Mexican cities.

Orientation

At the southernmost tip of the Baja peninsula, Cabo San Lucas is 1059 miles (1700 km) from Tijuana and 137 miles (220 km) from La Paz. After splitting south of La Paz, the paved routes of the Transpeninsular and México 19 rejoin at Cabo San Lucas, making a potentially fine bicycle circuit.

North of Calle Lázaro Cárdenas, which leads out of town to the highway junction, Cabo San Lucas has a fairly regular grid pattern. South of Lázaro Cárdenas, Blvd Marina curves along the west side of the harbor toward Land's End.

Very few hotels, restaurants or any place else have street addresses, and street names are primarily for the benefit of visiting gringos, so it's easiest to locate places by referring to the Cabo San Lucas map. The densely built-up center has almost no open space except for Parque Imelia Wilkes, a plaza honoring a longtime local schoolteacher, on Calle Hidalgo between Madero and Lázaro Cárdenas.

Information

Tourist Office Astonishingly, Cabo San Lucas has no formal tourist office, but the stubborn time-share sellers on almost every corner of Blvd Marina distribute town maps and will happily provide information. But once they have your attention, you'll have difficulty escaping their sales pitch – at least you may end up with some restaurant discount coupons. Try speaking limited English with a very heavy French or German accent.

Several local publications, wholly or partly in English and containing information useful to visitors, are available free in restaurants and hotel lobbies. They include:

■ PLACES TO STAY

3	Hotel Casablanca
18	Hotel Mar de Cortez
21	Giggling Marlin Inn
35	Hotel Dos Mares
36	Siesta Suites Hotel
37	Hotel Marina
43	El Faro Viejo Trailer Park
44	Medusa Suites
53	Hotel Meliá San Lucas
58	Hacienda Beach Resort
64	Hotel Finisterra
68	Hotel Solmar

▼ PLACES TO EAT

1	Mercado Castro
2	Super Tacos de Baja California
4	Jugos Tuti Fruti
7	Panadería San Angel
9	El Squid Roe Cabo Grill
13	Cabo Wabo Cantina
16	Mercado Aramburo
19	Cabo Gourmet
22	Giggling Marlin Restaurant & Bar
24	Salsitas
26	Mi Casa
31	Broken Surfboard
34	Chile Willie's
38	Shrimp Factory
39	Pancho's
40	El Coral
41	Señor Sushi's
43	El Faro Viejo
46	La Golondrina
49	Peacock's
50	El Rey Sol
51	Alfonso's
54	El Delfín
55	The Office
56	Mama's
59	Manuel's Carnitas
61	Mobeso's Bakery
63	Romeo y Julieta
65	El Galeón

OTHER

5	Main bus station
6	Los Delfines (travel agency)
8	Bus station (Autotransportes de La Paz)
10	Banca Serfin
11	Budget Rent-A-Car
12	Farmacia Aramburo
14	Long-distance telephone/fax
15	Faces of Mexico
17	Bancomer
20	Giggling Marlin Co Store
23	Books Books/Libros Libros
25	Marina Cabo San Lucas
26	Casas Mexicanas (crafts)
27	Parque Amelia Wilkes/Aero California
28	Banco Unión
29	Baja Business Center
30	Minerva's Baja Tackle
32	Baja Diving Explorers
33	Mercado Mexicano
40	Cabo Diving Services
42	Baja Money Exchange
45	Servicios Migratorios
47	Lukas (dance club)
48	Post Office
52	Club Cascadas de Baja (condominiums)
57	Cabo Acuadeportes (dive shop)
60	AMCA Rent-A-Car
62	US Consulate
66	Government Crafts Centre/Cruise Ship Landing
67	Amigos del Mar (dive shop)
69	Playa del Amor/ Land's End

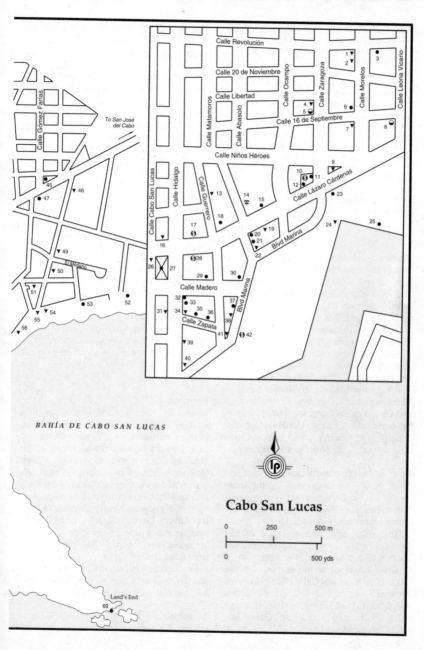

Cabo San Lucas

All About. . . Los Cabos-La Paz – a monthly tourist publication with a few area maps, brief information sections and lots of advertisements.

Noticias de los Cabos – a monthly newspaper in English and Spanish covering general and tourism-related news, including an occasional feature on some aspect of tourism in the Los Cabos region.

A Visitor's Guide to Cabo San Lucas & San José del Cabo – a seasonal English-language booklet published by Travel Arts of San Diego, with maps and information sections covering nightlife, shopping, restaurants, sports and condominium complexes.

Los Cabos Magazine – a fortnightly tabloid with plenty of real estate and restaurant propaganda, a few good stories and a decent map of Cabo San Lucas.

Money Baja Money Exchange, on the Plaza Naútica on Blvd Marina next to Café Europa, will change US cash or travelers' checks at poor rates, or give cash advances (with a usurious 10% commission) on Visa or MasterCard; hours are 9 am to 7 pm weekdays, 9 am to 5:30 pm Saturday. There's also a branch in the Baja Business Center, at the corner of Madero and Guerrero, whose opening hours are 8 am to 7 pm weekdays, 8:30 am to 5:30 pm Saturdays.

For regular banking, try Banca Serfín at Plaza Aramburo (corner of Calle Zaragoza and Calle Lázaro Cárdenas), Bancomer on the north side of Lázaro Cárdenas between Hidalgo and Guerrero, and Banco Unión directly across the street from Bancomer.

Post & Telecommunications The post office occupies new quarters on the south side of Lázaro Cárdenas, near the intersection with Calle 16 de Septiembre, on the eastern approach to downtown.

Numerous new long-distance offices have sprung up in shops and pharmacies. There's also a long-distance office in the Centro Comercial at the corner of Calle Lázaro Cárdenas and Calle Hidalgo, open 8 am to 10 pm, and there's a combination telephone/fax office on Matamoros, just north of Lázaro Cárdenas. Cabo San Lucas' area code is 114.

Foreign Consulate The US Consulate (☎ 3-35-36) is on the west side of Blvd Marina, just south of the Plaza Las Glorias.

Immigration Servicios Migratorios is on the corner of Lázaro Cárdenas and Gómez Farías.

Travel Agencies Real Turismo (☎ 3-16-96) is in the Plaza Aramburo mall, at the corner of Lázaro Cárdenas and Zaragoza. Los Delfines (☎ 3-13-96), at Morelos and 16 de Septiembre, publishes the current airline schedule from Los Cabos in the *Los Cabos Times*.

Bookshops Books Books (also known as Libros Libros), in the Plaza Bonita mall at the junction of Blvd Marina and Lázaro Cárdenas, carries a selection of coffee-table books on Baja California, potboiler novels and popular magazines in English, and the odd Lonely Planet guide.

Medical Services Cabo's IMSS hospital (☎ 3-14-44) is at Km 3 of México 19, the Western Cape highway to Todos Santos. A decent pharmacy, Farmacia Aramburo, is on Lázaro Cárdenas at Ocampo.

Beaches

There are several good beaches within walking distance of central Cabo, but the best are outside town. For sunbathing and calm waters **Playa Médano**, in front of the Hacienda Beach Resort, is ideal. **Playa Solmar**, on the Pacific side of the cape, has a reputation for unpredictable, dangerous breakers that drown several unsuspecting tourists every year. Nearly unspoiled **Playa de Amor** (Lover's Beach), near Land's End, is accessible by boat or a class 3 scramble over the rocks (at least at high tide) from Hotel Solmar.

For beaches between Cabo San Lucas and San José del Cabo, see the Around San José del Cabo section, above.

Activities

Diving Known for spectacular reefs and

outstanding diving, Cabo San Lucas has a wide choice of dive shops. Amigos del Mar (☎ 3-05-05, fax 3-08-07), Apartado Postal 43, Baja California Sur, is across from the sport fishing dock at the south end of Blvd Marina. Its US contact is ☎ (800) 447-8999. Cabo Diving Services (☎ 3-16-58), at Restaurant El Coral on Blvd Marina, is open daily 9 am to 7 pm.

Cabo Acuadeportes (☎ 3-01-17), next to the Hotel Cabo San Lucas on Playa Chileno and in front of the Hacienda Beach Resort, is open daily from 9 am to 5 pm. Its postal address is Cabo Acuadeportes, Apartado Postal 136, Cabo San Lucas. Pacific Coast Adventures (☎ 3-30-76) is in the Hotel Plaza Las Glorias. The newest entry is Baja Diving Explorers (☎ 3-36-01), on Calle Hidalgo at the corner of Calle Madero.

Among the best diving areas are Roca Pelícano, where Jacques Cousteau once did a documentary of the impressive underwater sand falls, the sea lion colony off the tip of Land's End, the reef off Playa Chileno, and the Gordo Banks.

The following rates for scuba equipment and activities are roughly comparable for all local diving services:

Equipment	Rates
Mask-fin-snorkel set	US$10 per day
Tank	US$12 per day
Air fill	US$5 each
Weight belt with weights	US$5 per day
Buoyancy compensator	US$8 per day
Depth gauge	US$5 per day
Regulator with pressure gauge & power inflator	US$8 per day
Wetsuit	US$5 per day

For boat divers, one-tank dive packages are available for US$35 per person, while two-dive packages cost US$66 and three-tank packages US$70. Packages include tanks, weights, certified dive guide and dive boat. Beach-diving packages include tanks, weights and unlimited air (free with same-day two-dive package). Rates are the sum

of equipment charges. Trips to distant diving sites, like the Gordo Banks, are correspondingly more expensive – US$70 for a single tank.

Other activity packages include:

Introductory Scuba Course
    US$90 per person
Open Water Referral Course
    US$175 per person
Full Certification Course
    US$400 per person
Sailing
    Minifish – US$12 per hour
    Sunfish – US$14 per hour
    Catamaran – US$17 per hour
Windsurfing
    US$12 per hour
Glass-bottom Boat Trip
    (usually to an area just offshore from Playa del Amor) US$7 per person
Kayaking
    US$6 per hour (for two people)
Playa del Amor Trip
    US$16 per boat, includes landing on shore (maximum four people)

Cabo Acuadeportes' services include PADI and NAUI diving certification courses, advanced diving courses, night dives, guided snorkel tours from 10:30 am to 12:30 pm, whale-watching tours (January to March) and small-boat fishing trips. If you're diving or snorkeling in November and December, watch for sea lions in their mating season.

Some divers have complained of poor underwater visibility near Land's End and claim that tourist hotels have dumped raw sewage into the bay. Local residents report that this situation has been corrected, but ask dive shops about water conditions and sewage.

Boat Trips Most travel agencies can arrange trips to El Arco (the natural arch at Land's End), the local sea lion colony and Playa del Amor on the yacht *Trinidad* (☎ 3-14-17) and other boats for about US$15 to US$30 per hour. Dos Mares (☎ 3-32-66) sails its glass-bottom boats every 20 minutes from 9 am to 4 pm, and will drop off and pick up passengers on Playa del Amor.

From the dock at Plaza Las Glorias, the *Pez Gato I* and *Pez Gato II* (☎ 3-24-58) offer two-hour sunset sailings on catamarans, which, faithful to Cabo's schizophrenic ethos, segregate their clientele into 'booze cruises' and 'romantic cruises'. Both feature open bars and cost US$30 for adults, US$15 for children. The Amigos del Mar Dive Center (see above) offers similar cruises for US$25, plus snorkeling and whale-watching (in season).

The *Nautilus VII*, a semisubmersible craft, offers one-hour tours of the offshore marine sanctuary, with a chance to view whales, dolphins and sea turtles, for US$30 for adults, US$15 for children. Make reservations (☎ 3-30-33) at Blvd de la Marina 39-F, or at Baja Tourist & Travel Services (☎ 3-19-34).

The boating situation in Cabo San Lucas is rapidly changing with construction of the Marina Cabo San Lucas and other facilities. Yacht owners who want more information about the marina should phone ☎ (213) 541-3830 in Los Angeles, USA.

Fishing Most hotels can arrange fishing trips, but prearranged packages are the best bargain. For example, Hotel Solmar offers three nights accommodation and one day of fishing for US$190 per person, but nonguests pay at least US$235 per day, including fishing tackle and a two-person crew, for a 24-foot California-class boat for three passengers. Solmar has its own fishing fleet and will arrange special charters as well.

Another place to contact is the Twin Dolphin (☎ (800) 421-8925 toll free from outside California, (213) 386-3940) at Suite 1005, 1625 West Olympic Blvd, Los Angeles, California, USA 90015.

Minerva's Baja Tackle, at the corner of Madero and Blvd Marina, rents fishing gear.

Caliente Foreign Book
At the Plaza Náutica shopping center and at the Hotel Plaza Las Glorias, Caliente accepts bets for horse and greyhound race-

tracks, as well as football, basketball, baseball, boxing, and hockey in the USA. Several big-screen TVs are available for watching these events.

Festivals & Events

Cabo San Lucas is a popular staging ground for several annual events, most of which are fishing tournaments:

October 18
> *Día de San Lucas* – One of few legitimately local celebrations, this is the festival of the town's patron saint.

Late October
> *Cabo San Lucas Gold Cup* – This is a less serious event than other Cabo fishing tournaments.

October or November
> *Bisbee's Black & Blue Marlin Jackpot Tournament* – Proceeds from this marlin-fishing competition go to Cabo's Escuela El Camino, a local school. Entry fees are US$2000 per four-person team.

Early November
> *Pete Lopiccola Memorial Marlin Tournament*

Places to Stay

Except for camping and RV parks, budget and even mid-range accommodation are scarce in Cabo San Lucas. Visitors who are unsure about staying here might prefer San José del Cabo, where lodging is cheaper and it's still convenient to make day trips to Cabo San Lucas.

Places to Stay – bottom end

Camping In theory, local officials have banned free camping at sites like *Playa Arroyo Salto Seco*, just east of the exclusive Club Cascadas de Baja, on the pretense that campers have been robbed. Many suspect, however, that developers covet this area and others such as *Playa Barco Varado* (Shipwreck Beach), at Km 9 on the highway to San José del Cabo, near the Hotel Clarion Cabo San Lucas. People still camp at Arroyo Salto Seco, but the site has no services and is very dirty. Shipwreck is accessible via an unmarked dirt road – watch carefully for the turnoff.

The most congenial camping, with dependable services, is at Dutch-operated *Surf Camp Club Cabo* (☎ 3-33-48), about 1 mile (1.6 km) east of Cascadas de Baja by a narrow dirt road. Full hookups are available, but tent campers are equally welcome. Rates are US$5 per person; a cabaña and two apartments with kitchenettes are available for US$30/40 single/double.

Faro Viejo Trailer Park, inconspicuous and difficult to find on Calle Rosario Morales between Matamoros and Abasolo, about 1 mile (1.6 km) north of downtown, has RV sites with full hookups for US$12. Given its limited shade and messy bathrooms, the park is way overpriced and not recommended despite the attraction of what may be Cabo's best restaurant (see Places to Eat, below).

About 2 miles (3 km) east of Cabo San Lucas on the Transpeninsular are *San Vicente RV Park* (☎ 3-07-12) and *Vagabundos del Mar* (☎ 3-02-90) trailer park. The former caters mostly to long-term residents and rarely has vacancies; the latter has occasional openings for about US$15, but the heavy rains of November 1993 damaged some of its facilities, which include full hookups, a swimming pool, drinking water and an ice machine.

Just east of Vagabundos, *Cabo Cielo* (☎ 3-07-21) is a mostly barren, graded area but the sites along its eastern edge, however, are shady with full hookups, and the spotless bathrooms have excellent hot showers. Fees are US$10 per site.

El Arco Trailer Park, overlooking Cabo San Lucas from a mesa 3 miles (5 km) west of town, has 60 spaces with full hookups and hot showers for US$12 per vehicle site or US$7 for tents. Its restaurant serves standard antojitos and more elaborate dishes like steak and scampi.

Hotels For US$22/27 single/double, *Hotel Casablanca* (☎ 3-02-60), on Calle Revolución near Calle Morelos, is the cheapest place in town, offering clean but dark rooms with concrete floors, hot showers and ceiling fans. *Hotel Marina*, on Blvd Marina at Calle Madero, has modest motel-style, air-conditioned rooms around a small swimming pool. Singles/doubles cost US $25/40.

Next cheapest is the comparable *Hotel Dos Mares* (☎ 3-03-30), on Calle Zapata between Calle Hidalgo and Calle Guerrero, which charges US$26/30 single or double, plus US$7 for each additional person and a refundable towel deposit of US$8.

Places to Stay – middle

Hotel Mar de Cortez (☎ 3-14-32), at Calle Lázaro Cárdenas and Calle Guerrero, is a pseudo-colonial building with air-conditioned rooms and private bath; there's also a swimming pool and an outdoor bar/restaurant. Newer single/doubles cost US$38/42 in high season, but rooms in the older part of the hotel, for US$29/33, are good value. Low-season rates (June to mid-October) are about 25% less. Make reservations at the hotel's US representative (☎ (408) 375-4755 or (800) 347-8821) by writing PO Box 1827, Monterey, California 93942.

The sparkling new *Siesta Suites Hotel* (☎/fax 3-27-73), on Calle Zapata between Hidalgo and Guerrero, has one-bedroom apartments with fully equipped kitchenettes for US$35 to US$45 for two persons, plus US$5 for each additional person. The local mailing address is Apartado Postal 310, Cabo San Lucas; the US contact number is ☎/fax (909) 945-5940.

The *Medusa Suites* (☎ 3-08-80) at the corner of Calle Ocampo and Calle Alikán, advertises 'junior suites' with air-conditioning, color TV, telephones and complete kitchens for US$45.50 per night.

Places to Stay – top end

The *Giggling Marlin Inn* (☎ 3-06-06) on Calle Matamoros between Lázaro Cárdenas and Blvd Marina, is an afterthought to its boisterous namesake restaurant next door, with mid-range services at upscale prices. Rooms are dark and viewless, but all have full kitchens and air-conditioning for US$85/110 single/double. Its US representative (☎ (818) 907-7219) is at Suite

207, 13455 Ventura Blvd, Sherman Oaks, California 91423.

The *Hotel Meliá San Lucas* (☎ 3-10-00, fax 3-04-20) is a huge, quasi-Spanish, orange stucco edifice near the Hacienda Beach Resort, run by the Madrid-based Compañía Meliá. Spacious, well-decorated rooms all have air-conditioning, mini-refrigerators, safes and TV, and most also have a balcony or patio. This five-star complex has five-star rates – depending on the season, singles range from US$135 to US$194, doubles from US$145 to US$205 and suites US$305 to US$385 – plus 10% tax and 10% service.

The *Hacienda Beach Resort* (☎ 3-01-22 in Cabo San Lucas, (213) 205-0015 or (800) 421-0645 toll free in the USA) is a resplendent, five-star luxury hotel in a Spanish hacienda style, with fountains and tropical gardens. Cabo Acuadeportes operates a water-sports center on the beach in front of the hotel; other facilities include tennis and paddle-tennis courts, a swimming pool and a putting green. Garden patio rooms start around US$118, but rise rapidly for beach cabañas (US$146 to US$168), deluxe suites (US$170), and townhouses (US$175 to US$260 for one to four people).

Hotel Solmar (☎ 3-00-22 in Cabo San Lucas, (310) 459-9861 in the Los Angeles area or (800) 344-3349 toll free), on the Pacific side of Cabo San Lucas, is a secluded, stone-walled beachfront resort whose air-conditioned rooms all face the ocean. Amenities include tennis courts, horseback riding and swimming pool. Singles/doubles start at US$120 in low season (1 June to 1 October), plus 10% room tax and 10% service (for the room, meals and other gratuities). Various package deals include fishing trips and outside restaurant meals. For more information, write PO Box 383, Pacific Palisades, California 90272.

Hotel Finisterra (☎ 3-00-00, 3-01-00) is a luxury hotel on a bluff with both ocean and bay views, just off Blvd Marina. Singles/doubles are US$90/100, plus 20% for service charges and taxes. All rooms are air-conditioned, a few also have fireplaces; other facilities include a small swimming pool, tennis courts, a restaurant/bar and a travel desk. Its Whale-watcher Bar, on the Pacific side, is ideal for viewing sunsets and, from January to March, for spotting passing cetaceans. Rooms facing the bay rather than the ocean are US$10 cheaper. For reservations in the USA, ☎ (800) 347-2252 or (714) 476-5555; its US agent is Baja Hotel Reservations, 18552 MacArthur Blvd, Suite 205, Irvine, California 92715.

Places to Eat

Cabo's countless restaurants cater to vacationing tourists, with prices much higher than elsewhere in Baja. A modest lunch of three fish tacos, for example, costs well over US$5 in a restaurant and not much less from a corner taco stand. *Super Tacos de Baja California*, a hole-in-the-wall on Morelos between Revolución and 20 de Noviembre, specializes in inexpensive (US$1 and less) seafood tacos, including calamares (squid) and *pulpo* (octopus) with salsa picante. For freshly squeezed juices and chocolate milk shakes, try *Jugos Tuti Fruti*, next to the bus station.

One of few real budget choices in central Cabo, the *Broken Surfboard*, on the west side of Calle Hidalgo between Morelos and Zapata, prepares burritos, hamburgers, fish with rice, salad, tortillas and beans and a few other items. It has sidewalk seating.

Cabo Gourmet, on Lázaro Cárdenas between Matamoros and Ocampo, provides take-out meals of exceptional quality, including outstanding sandwiches, cold cuts and cheeses.

El Galeón, a rotunda-shaped building on Blvd Marina near Avenida Solmar, specializes in mesquite-grilled lobster and beef. *El Coral*, at the corner of Blvd Marina and Calle Hidalgo, proclaims 'authentic Mexican food', but its cheap double margaritas and similar drinks are a better value than its rather ordinary meals. Breakfast is available any time, day or night, but it adds a 6% surcharge to all credit card purchases.

The moderately priced *Giggling Marlin Restaurant & Bar*, on Calle Matamoros just south of Lázaro Cárdenas, is popular for partying, but the food is mediocre except for the appetizers. After imbibing enough alcohol, patrons appear to enjoy being hoisted like trophy marlins, and then photographed in the act! Happy hour is 2 to 6 pm.

Van Halen-owned *Cabo Wabo Cantina*, on Calle Guerrero between Niños Héroes and Lázaro Cárdenas, is better known for its sound system than its cuisine (tacos), but the food is at least palatable and, by some accounts, improving rapidly. *El Squid Roe Cabo Grill*, on Calle Lázaro Cárdenas between Calle Morelos and Calle Zaragoza, is one of countless Carlos 'n' Charlie's restaurants with casual decor, better known as a gringo watering hole than for its fairly ordinary food.

Cabo's only Japanese restaurant, *Señor Sushi's*, no longer serves sushi. On Blvd Marina near Guerrero, it tends to attract a drinking and dancing crowd rather than serious diners, but it's very good and moderately priced by current standards. The *Shrimp Factory*, just up the block, specializes in seafood. *Salsitas*, in the Plaza Bonita mall on Blvd Marina just south of Lázaro Cárdenas, is highly regarded for Mexican specialties. For a wide selection of spicy salsas, try *Chile Willie's* at the corner of Hidalgo and Zapata. *Manuel's*, at the corner of Blvd Marina and Calle Cabo San Lucas, earns raves for its carnitas.

La Golondrina, one of Cabo's prettiest restaurants, was one of the few buildings left standing after a flood devastated most of the town in 1906. Meals are expensive, but portions are large and management, which also runs highly regarded Faro Viejo (see below), does not object to shared portions. It's just south of Lázaro Cárdenas, across from the Pemex station near the eastern entrance to town.

El Rey Sol, two blocks south of the Golondrina, serves appealing Mexican food and seafood from breakfast (try *machaca* (bore) and eggs) to dinner (fish cooked to order and garlic shrimp); prices are moderate by Cabo standards. Other restaurants in the vicinity include *Pea-*

cock's, *El Delfín* (seafood), *The Office* (with tables right on the beach) and *Mama's*, known for seafood and salads. *Alfonso's*, at Playa El Médano, serves nouvelle cuisine from a usually set US$30 five-course menu.

Faro Viejo Trailer Park Restaurant, inside its namesake trailer park at Calle Matamoros and Calle Rosario Morales, lures rich and famous gringos from their beachfront hotels for barbecued ribs, steaks and seafood. Prices are upscale, but many visitors go out of their way to dine here. *Mi Casa*, on Calle Cabo San Lucas just across from Parque Amelia Wilkes, features a pleasant home-like environment and excellent Mexican and seafood specialties. *Romeo y Julieta*, just west of the point where Blvd Marina turns east towards Land's End, is a local institution for pizza and pasta.

Panadería San Angel at the corner of Calle Morelos and Calle 16 de Septiembre, offers typical Mexican pastries and biscuits. Cabo's best bakery, *Mobeso's* caters mainly to the best restaurants and groceries, but also sells pastries and single loaves of a wide variety of breads from an inconspicuous location just west of the traffic circle at the junction of Blvd Marina and Calle Cabo San Lucas.

The *Mercado Castro*, a supermarket at the corner of Calle Revolución and Calle Morelos, is a junk-food paradise with shelf upon shelf of sterile pretzels, potato chips and peanuts as well as produce, canned goods and pastas. Campers and boaters can stock up on staples here, but *Almacenes Aramburo* at the corner of Hidalgo and Lázaro Cárdenas has a larger selection.

Entertainment

Cabo Wabo Cantina, on Calle Guerrero north of Lázaro Cárdenas, features live music from late at night to early in the morning, and occasionally sponsors special events, like a blues festival with bands from the USA. *Lukas*, a dance club on Lázaro Cárdenas near the intersection with Gómez Farías, is a popular nightlife spot.

Barhoppers will reportedly find Mexi-

co's largest selection of tequilas at *Pancho's*, on Calle Hidalgo between Calle Zapata and Blvd Marina.

Things to Buy

Cabo's most comprehensive shopping area, at the corner of Madero and Hidalgo, is the sprawling Mercado Mexicano, which contains dozens of stalls with crafts from all around the country.

Casas Mexicanas, part of the highly regarded Mi Casa restaurant, is a crafts shop featuring wood and wrought iron furniture, talavera pottery, pewter accessories, bed and table linen, religious and secular art, and just plain knickknacks.

In town are a few interesting shops, particularly on and around Calle Lázaro Cárdenas. Galerías Zen-Mar, on Cárdenas near Hotel Mar de Cortez, offers Zapotec Indian weavings, bracelets and masks, as well as traditional crafts from other mainland Indian peoples. At the corner of Matamoros and Cárdenas, the Giggling Marlin Co Store offers souvenirs whose main purpose is to promote the overrated restaurant and bar.

Faces of Mexico, on Lázaro Cárdenas between Matamoros and Ocampo, also has a good selection of artisanal goods.

One local specialty is hand-crafted black-coral jewelry, available at a state-owned store at Cabo's cruise ship dock, but tourists should refrain from buying this product, which will be confiscated at US ports of entry without the appropriate export permit from Mexico City. For information on export permits, see the Things to Buy section in the Facts for the Visitor chapter.

Getting There & Away

Air The closest airport is north of San José del Cabo; see the San José del Cabo Getting There & Away section for detailed information.

Aero California's main office (☎ 3-08-27, 3-08-48) is in the Centro Comercial at the north end of Plaza Imelia Wilkes, at the corner of Cárdenas and Hidalgo. Hours are

8:30 am to 6:30 pm Monday to Saturday, 9 am to 3 pm Sunday.

Bus The main bus terminal is at the corner of Zaragoza and 16 de Septiembre. Buses leave from here for:

San José del Cabo
(US$2) 11 times daily between 7 am and 10:15 pm
La Paz via Todos Santos
(US$9) eight times daily between 6 am and 6 pm
La Paz via San José del Cabo
(US$9) six times daily between 7 am and 6:30 pm

Autotransportes de La Paz has a separate terminal at the corner of Calle Leona Vicario and 16 de Septiembre. These buses only go to La Paz.

Getting Around
To/From the Airport The front desk of any of major hotel will help arrange a taxi or minibus to the airport; fares are govern-ment-regulated. From the Hacienda Beach Resort, sample fares are US$35 for one to four people and US$8 for each extra person, up to a maximum of eight.

Taxi Taxis are plentiful but not cheap; fares for destinations within Cabo San Lucas should average about US$5.

Car Rental AMCA (☎ 3-25-15), on Blvd Marina at the corner of Ortiz de Domínguez, is probably the most reason-ably priced rental agency. Budget has offices on Plaza Aramburo (☎ 3-02-41) at the corner of Cárdenas and Zaragoza, and in the Hacienda Beach Resort (☎ 3-02-51). Both are open 7 am to 7 pm daily.

Thrifty (☎ 3-16-66) has offices at Lázaro Cárdenas and Morelos, in the lobby of the Hotel Hacienda (☎ 3-16-67), and in the lobby of the Hotel Cabo San Lucas, at Km 15 on the highway to San José del Cabo. Dollar (☎ 3-12-50) is at Lázaro Cárdenas and Mendoza.

Glossary

Note: also see the Language section in the Facts about Baja chapter and for a list of food and drink terms, see the Food section in the Facts for the Visitor chapter.

acequia – irrigation canal, often stone-lined, in the Baja California missions

albergue juvenil – youth hostel, a relatively inexpensive but uncommon form of accommodation in Baja

antojitos – traditional Mexican dishes such as burritos, enchiladas and tacos

asentamientos irregulares – shanty towns of Tijuana, Mexicali and other border towns

bajacaliforniano – a resident of Baja California

bolillo – typical Mexican bread

borrego – bighorn sheep, a rarely seen species in the sierras of Baja California which is frequently represented in the pre-Columbian rock art of the peninsula

cabecera – administrative seat of a municipio (see below)

caguama – any species of sea turtle, but most commonly the Pacific green turtle *Chelonia mydas*, also known as the *caguama negra* or *caguama prieta* (literally, black turtle)

cardón – either of two species of *Pachycereus* cactus, a common genus in Baja

casa de cambio – foreign exchange house

casa de huéspedes – guest house, a relatively inexpensive form of accommodation, but uncommon in Baja

charreada – a rodeo, frequent during fiestas and other special occasions, and particularly popular in northern Mexico

charro – Mexican cowboy or horseman; mariachi bands often dress in gaudy charro clothing

chilango – a native or resident of Mexico City; depending on context, the term can be very pejorative

cholismo – rebellious youth movement, akin to punk, which has had some influence on the visual arts in Baja California

choza – hut

chubasco – in the Cape region of southern Baja, a violent storm approaching hurricane force, associated with summer low pressure areas in the tropical Pacific

científicos – under Mexican dictator Porfirio Díaz, a group of largely Eurocentric advisers who controlled the direction of the country's economy

cirio – 'boojum' tree *(Idria columnaris)*, a slow growing species resembling an inverted carrot, common only within a limited range in north-central Baja in the Sierra La Asamblea

colonia – neighborhood in Tijuana or other large city; literally a 'colony'

comida corrida – cheap fixed-price meal at a restaurant

corrida de toros – bullfight

corrido – folk ballad of the US-Mexico border region; corridos often have strong but subtle political content

coyotes – in Mexican border towns, smugglers who charge up to US$500 or more to spirit illegal immigrants across the US border

delegación – administrative subdivision of the municipio (see below)

ejidatario – member of an ejido (see below)

ejido – cooperative enterprise, usually of peasant agriculturalists, created under the land reform program of President Lázaro Cárdenas (1934-1940). Ejidos also participate in economic activities such as mining, ranching and tourism.

escaramuza – female rider in a charreada (see above)

estocada – in bullfighting, the sword lunge with which the matador kills the bull

fideicomiso – 30-year bank trusts which have fostered the construction and acquisition of real estate by non-Mexicans in Baja

Fonatur – Mexican federal government tourist agency

fronterizo – an inhabitant of the US-Mexico border region

frontón – a venue for jai alai; a ball game, resembling squash, of Basque origin

glorieta – traffic circle in a city; most numerous in Mexicali and Tijuana

gringo – term, often but not always pejorative, describing any light-skinned person but most often a resident of the USA

güero – 'blond', a normally descriptive term often used to describe any fair-skinned person in Mexico

hipódromo – horse racing track

INAH – Instituto de Antropolog\'a y Historia (National Institute of Anthropology & History), which administers museums and archeological monuments such as the extensive cave paintings in the Desierto Central of Baja California

internado – rural boarding school

jai alai – Basque game, resembling squash, played for bettors in Tijuana

judiciales – Mexican state and federal police

La Frontera – in colonial times (from 1774) the area where the Dominican priests built their missions; it extends from immediately south of present-day San Diego, mainland California, as far as El Rosario, at about the 30th parallel

librería – bookshop

llantera – tire repair shop, common even in Baja's most out-of-the-way places

machismo – an exaggerated masculinity intended to impress other men more than women; it is usually innocuous if rather unpleasant

maguey – any of several species of a common Mexico fibre plant (*Agave* spp), also used for producing alcoholic drinks like tequila, mescal and pulque

malecón – waterfront promenade, as in La Paz

maquiladora – industrial plant in Tijuana, Mexicali and other border towns which take advantage of cheap Mexican labor to assemble US components for re-exportation to the north

mestizo – a person of mixed Indian and European heritage

mezcal – alcoholic drink made from agave, a common fibre plant on the Mexican mainland

moneda nacional – 'national money', the Mexican peso as distinguished from the US dollar, both of which use the same symbol ($); often abbreviated as 'm/n'

mono – a human figure, as represented in the pre-Columbian rock art of the Desierto Central

mordida – a bribe (literally, 'the bite')

muleta – in bullfighting, a small cape used in the final tercio to bait the bull

municipio – administrative subdivision of Mexican states, roughly akin to a US county; the states of Baja California and Baja California Sur each consist of four municipios

NAFTA – North American Free Trade Agreement, a pact among the USA, Canada and Mexico which reduces or eliminates customs duties and other trade barriers. While supported by all three governments, NAFTA still faces considerable internal opposition in each country, partly from sectors with protected internal markets, partly from nationalists who object to foreign interference in their economies, and partly from labor and environmental activists in the USA who object to Mexico's low wages and weak environmental safeguards.

nao – in colonial times, a Spanish galleon on the Acapulco-Manila trade route; such galleons frequently took shelter in Baja ports on their return voyages

nopal – any cactus of the genus *Opuntia* which produces edible fruit (*tuna*). Its succulent lobes are also edible, but less nourishing. Both were common in the diet of pre-Columbian Baja California and are still widely consumed today.

ofrenda – offering to a saint in exchange for a wish or wishes granted

palapa – palm-leaf shelter

PAN – Partido Acción Nacional, a free-market oriented populist party which is strong in Mexican states along the US border, including Baja California. Its acronym, more than coincidentally, reproduces the Spanish word for 'bread'.

pan dulce – sweetish Mexican pastry

panga – fiber-glass skiff, used for fishing or whale-watching

panguero – one who owns or pilots a skiff; in practice, the word is synonymous with fisherman

pelotari – participant in a game of jai alai

Pemex – Petróleos Mexicanos, the Mexican government oil monopoly

picador – in a bullfight, a horseman who jabs the bull with a lance called a *pica*, weakening the bull without killing him

picante – spicy hot (as applied to food)

piñata – a papier-mâché animal full of candy, broken open by children at celebrations like Christmas and birthdays

plaza de toros – bullring

pollero – synonymous with coyote, a smuggler of undocumented immigrants (pollos or 'chickens') into the USA

Porfiriato – the defacto dictatorship of Porfirio Díaz, who held Mexico's presidency from 1876 until the revolution of 1911. Under Diaz's rule, much of Baja California was granted to foreign companies for ambitious colonization projects, most of which soon failed.

posada – at Christmas, a parade of costumed children re-enacting the journey of Mary and Joseph to Bethlehem

PRI – Partido Revolucionario Institucional, the official party of government in Mexico since 1946, but a direct descendent of the Partido Nacional Revoluctionario of the late 1920s

PRONAF – Programa Nacional Fronterizo, a scheme to promote economic development and foster Mexican nationalism along the US-Mexico border

propina – a tip, at a restaurant or elsewhere

pulque – mildly alcoholic drink extracted directly from the sap of the maguey. Because this foamy, milky liquid spoils quickly, it cannot be bottled and easily shipped long distances.

ranchería – subsistence unit of hunter-gatherers in the contact period with Europeans; later applied to units associated with Jesuit and other missions. Strictly speaking, the term implies a group of people rather than a place.

rancho – tiny rural settlement, ranging from about 20 to 50 people

rebozo – shawl

SEDUE – Secretaría de Desarrollo Urbano y Ecología, a Mexican government agency which regulates foreign hunting activity in Baja California and elsewhere in Mexico

s/n (sin número) – street address without a specific number

tequila – popular alcoholic drink made from the maguey plant *(Agave tequilana)*, a Mexican domesticate

tercio – any one of three separate segments of a bullfight

tope – speed bump

tortillería – a tortilla factory or shop

trapiche – sugar mill

veda – prohibition on hunting or fishing of a given species, either seasonally or permanently

yodo – iodine, sold in pharmacies for water purification

zócalo – central plaza, a term more common in mainland Mexico than in Baja California

zona de tolerancia – in border cities like Tijuana and Mexicali, an area in which prostitution and related activities are concentrated

Index

MAPS

TEXT

PLANET TALK

Lonely Planet's FREE quarterly newsletter

We love hearing from you and think you'd like to hear from us.

When... is the right time to see reindeer in Finland?
Where... can you hear the best palm-wine music in Ghana?
How... do you get from Asunción to Areguá by steam train?
What... is the best way to see India?

Every issue is packed with up-to-date travel news and advice including:

• a letter from Lonely Planet founders Tony and Maureen Wheeler
• travel diary from a Lonely Planet author – find out what it's really like out on the road
• feature article on an important and topical travel issue
• a selection of recent letters from our readers
• the latest travel news from all over the world
• details on Lonely Planet's new and forthcoming releases

To join our mailing list contact any Lonely Planet office (addresses below).

LONELY PLANET PUBLICATIONS
Australia: PO Box 617, Hawthorn 3122, Victoria (☎ 03-819-1877, fax 03-819-6459)
USA: Embarcadero West, 155 Filbert Street, Suite 251, Oakland, CA 94607
    (☎ 510-893-8555, toll-free 800-275-8555, fax 510-893-8563)
UK: 10 Barley Mow Passage, Chiswick, London W4 4PH (☎ 081-742 3161)
France: 71 bis rue du Cardinal Lemoine, 75005 Paris (☎ 1-46 34 00 58)

Also available: Lonely Planet T-shirts. 100% heavyweight cotton (S, M, L, XL)

Guides to the Americas

Alaska – a travel survival kit
Jim DuFresne has traveled extensively through Alaska by foot, road, rail, barge and kayak, and tells how to make the most of one of the world's great wilderness areas.

Argentina, Uruguay & Paraguay – a travel survival kit
This guide gives independent travelers all the essential information on three of South America's lesser known countries. Discover some of South America's most spectacular natural attractions in Argentina; friendly people and beautiful handicrafts in Paraguay; and Uruguay's wonderful beaches.

Bolivia – a travel survival kit
From lonely villages in the Andes to ancient ruined cities and the spectacular city of La Paz, Bolivia is a magnificent blend of everything that inspires travelers. Discover safe and intriguing travel options in this comprehensive guide.

Brazil – a travel survival kit
From the mad passion of Carnival to the Amazon – home of the richest ecosystem on earth – Brazil is a country of mythical proportions. This guide has all the essential travel information.

Canada – a travel survival kit
This comprehensive guidebook has all the facts on the USA's huge neighbor – the Rocky Mountains, Niagara Falls, ultramodern Toronto, remote villages in Nova Scotia, and much more.

Central America on a shoestring
Practical information on travel in Belize, Guatemala, Costa Rica, Honduras, El Salvador, Nicaragua and Panama. A team of experienced Lonely Planet authors reveals the secrets of this culturally rich, geographically diverse and breathtakingly beautiful region.

Chile & Easter Island – a travel survival kit
Travel in Chile is easy and safe, with possibilities as varied as the countryside. This guide also gives detailed coverage of Chile's Pacific outpost, mysterious Easter Island.

Colombia – a travel survival kit
Colombia is a land of myths – from the ancient legends of El Dorado to the modern tales of Gabriel García Márquez. The reality is beauty and violence, wealth and poverty, tradition and change. This guide shows how to travel independently and safely in this exotic country.

Costa Rica – a travel survival kit
Winner of the Lowell Thomas Travel Journalism award, this best selling guidebook offers complete coverage of Costa Rica. Sun-drenched beaches, steamy jungles, smoking volcanoes, rugged mountains and dazzling birds and animals – it's all here!

Eastern Caribbean – a travel survival kit
Powdery white sands, clear turquoise waters, lush jungle rainforest, balmy weather and a laid back pace, make the islands of the Eastern Caribbean an ideal destination for divers, hikers and sun-lovers. This guide will help you to decide which islands to visit to suit your interests and includes details on inter-island travel.

Ecuador & the Galápagos Islands – a travel survival kit
Ecuador offers a wide variety of travel experiences, from the high cordilleras to the Amazon plains – and 600 miles west, the fascinating Galápagos Islands. Everything you need to know about traveling around this enchanting country.

Guatemala, Belize & Yucatán: La Ruta Maya – a travel survival kit
Climb a volcano, explore the colorful highland villages or laze your time away on coral islands and Caribbean beaches. The lands of the Maya offer a fascinating journey into the past which will enhance appreciation of their dynamic contemporary cultures. An award winning guide to this exotic region.

Hawaii – a travel survival kit
Share in the delights of this island paradise – and avoid its high prices – both on and off the beaten track. Full details on Hawaii's best known attractions, plus plenty of uncrowded sights and activities.

Mexico – a travel survival kit
A unique blend of Indian and Spanish culture, fascinating history, and hospitable people, make Mexico a travelers' paradise.

Peru – a travel survival kit
The lost city of Machu Picchu, the Andean altiplano and the magnificent Amazon rain-forests are just some of Peru's many attractions. All the travel facts you'll need can be found in this comprehensive guide.

South America on a shoestring
This practical guide provides concise information for budget travelers and covers South America from the Darien Gap to Tierra del Fuego.

Trekking in the Patagonian Andes
The first detailed guide to this region gives complete information on 28 walks, and lists a number of other possibilities extending from the Araucanía and Lake District regions of Argentina and Chile to the remote icy tip of South America in Tierra del Fuego.

Also available:
Brazilian phrasebook, **Latin American Spanish** phrasebook and **Quechua** phrasebook.

Lonely Planet Guidebooks

Lonely Planet guidebooks cover every accessible part of Asia as well as Australia, the Pacific, South America, Africa, the Middle East, Europe and parts of North America. There are five series: *travel survival kits*, covering a country for a range of budgets; *shoe-string guides* with compact information for low-budget travel in a major region; *walking guides;* city guides and *phrasebooks.*

Europe
Baltic States • Dublin
Eastern Europe • Eastern
Europe phrasebook • Finland
France • Greece • Hungary
Iceland, Greenland & the Faroes
Ireland• Italy • Mediterranean Europe
Mediterranean Europe phrasebook
Poland • Prague • Russian phrasebook
Scandinavian & Baltic Europe
Scandinavian Europe phrasebook
Switzerland • Trekking in Greece
Trekking in Spain • USSR
Western Europe
Western Europe phrasebook

North America
Alaska • Baja California
Canada • Hawaii • Mexico

Central America
Central America • Costa Rica
Guatemala, Yucatán & Belize
Eastern Caribbean • Latin American
phrasebook

Africa
Africa • Arabic (Moroccan) phrasebook
Central Africa • East Africa
Kenya • Morocco, Algeria & Tunisia
South Africa, Lesotho &
Swaziland • Swahili phrasebook
Trekking in East Africa • West Africa
Zimbabwe, Botswana & Namibia

South America
Argentina, Uruguay & Paraguay
Bolivia • Brazil • Brazilian phrasebook
Chile & Easter Is. • Colombia • Ecuador &
the Galápagos Is. • Peru • Quechua phrasebook
South America • Trekking in the
Patagonian Andes •Venezuela

Mail Order

Lonely Planet guidebooks are distributed worldwide. They are also available by mail order from Lonely Planet, so if you have difficulty finding a title please write to us. US and Canadian residents should write to Embarcadero West, 155 Filbert St, Suite 251, Oakland CA 94607, USA ; European residents should write to 10 Barley Mow Passage, Chiswick, London W4 4PH; and residents of other countries to PO Box 617, Hawthorn, Victoria 3122, Australia.

North-East Asia
Beijing • China • Chinese (Mandarin) phrasebook • Hong Kong, Macau & Canton • Japan • Japanese phrasebook Korea • Korean phrasebook • Mongolia North-East Asia • Seoul • Taiwan Tibet • Tokyo

The Middle East
Arab Gulf States
Arabic (Egyptian) phrasebook
Egypt & the Sudan
Iran • Israel • Jordan &
Syria • Middle East
Trekking in Turkey
Turkey • Turkish
phrasebook • Yemen

South-East Asia
Bangkok • Burmese phrasebook Cambodia • Indonesia Indonesian phrasebook Laos • Malaysia, Singapore & Brunei • Myanmar (Burma) Philippines • Pilipino phrasebook Singapore • South-East Asia Thailand • Thai phrasebook Thai Hill Tribes phrasebook Vietnam • Vietnamese phrasebook

Indian Subcontinent
Bangladesh • India
Trekking in the Indian
Himalaya • Hindi/Urdu
phrasebook • Karakoram
Highway • Kashmir,
Ladakh & Zanskar
Nepal • Nepali phrasebook
Trekking in the Nepal Himalaya
Tibet phrasebook
Pakistan • Sri Lanka
Sri Lanka phrasebook

Islands of the Indian Ocean
Madagascar & Comoros
Maldives & Is of the
East Indian Ocean
Mauritius, Réunion & Seychelles

Australia & the Pacific
Australia • Australian phrasebook Bushwalking in Australia • Bushwalking in Papua New Guinea • Fiji • Fijian phrasebook Is of Australia's Great Barrier Reef • Melbourne Micronesia • New Caledonia • New Zealand New South Wales • Outback Australia Papua New Guinea • Pidgin (Papua New Guinea) phrasebook • Rarotonga & the Cook Is Samoa • Solomon Is • Sydney • Tahiti & French Polynesia • Tonga • Tramping in New Zealand • Vanuatu • Victoria

The Lonely Planet Story

Lonely Planet published its first book in 1973 in response to the numerous 'How did you do it?' questions Maureen and Tony Wheeler were asked after driving, bussing, hitching, sailing and railing their way from England to Australia.

Written at a kitchen table and hand collated, trimmed and stapled, *Across Asia on the Cheap* became an instant local best seller, inspiring thoughts of another book.

Eighteen months in South-East Asia resulted in their second guide, *South-East Asia on a shoestring*, which they put together in a backstreet Chinese hotel in Singapore in 1975. The 'yellow bible' as it quickly became known to backpackers around the world, soon became *the* guide to the region. It has sold well over half a million copies and is now in its 8th edition, still retaining its familiar yellow cover.

Today there are over 140 Lonely Planet titles in print – books that have that same adventurous approach to travel as those early guides; books that 'assume you know how to get your luggage off the carousel' as one reviewer put it.

Although Lonely Planet initially specialized in guides to Asia, they now cover most regions of the world, including the Pacific, South America, Africa, the Middle East and Europe. The list of *walking guides* and *phrasebooks* (for 'unusual' languages such as Quechua, Swahili, Nepali and Egyptian Arabic) is also growing rapidly.

The emphasis continues to be on travel for independent travelers. Tony and Maureen still travel for several months of each year and play an active part in the writing, updating and quality control of Lonely Planet's guides.

They have been joined by over 50 authors, 60 staff – mainly editors, cartographers & designers – at our office in Melbourne, Australia, 15 at our US office in Oakland, California and four at our European office in Paris; another five at our office in London handle sales for Britain, Europe and Africa. Travelers themselves also make a valuable contribution to the guides through the feedback we receive in thousands of letters each year.

The people at Lonely Planet strongly believe that travelers can make a positive contribution to the countries they visit, both through their appreciation of the countries' culture, wildlife and natural features, and through the money they spend. In addition, the company makes a direct contribution to the countries and regions it covers. Since 1986 a percentage of the income from each book has been donated to ventures such as famine relief in Africa; aid projects in India; agricultural projects in Central America; Greenpeace's efforts to halt French nuclear testing in the Pacific and Amnesty International. In 1994 $100,000 was donated to such causes.

Lonely Planet's basic travel philosophy is summed up in Tony Wheeler's comment, 'Don't worry about whether your trip will work out. Just go!'.